JOURNAL FOR THE STUDY OF THE OLD TESTAMENT SUPPLEMENT SERIES
112

Editors
David J.A. Clines
Philip R. Davies

BIBLE AND LITERATURE SERIES
29

General Editor
David M. Gunn

Assistant General Editor
Danna Nolan Fewell

Consultant Editors
Elizabeth Struthers Malbon
James G. Williams

JSOT Press
Sheffield

WISDOM
in
REVOLT

Metaphorical Theology in the
Book of Job

Leo G. Perdue

The Almond  Press · 1991

Bible and Literature Series, 29
General Editor: David M. Gunn
(Columbia Theological Seminary, Decater, Georgia)
Assistant General Editor: Danna Nolan Fewell
(Perkins School of Theology, Dallas, Texas)
Consultant Editors: Elizabeth Struthers Malbon
(Virginia Polytechnic Institute & State University, Blacksburg, Virginia)
James G. Williams
(Syracuse University, Syracuse, New York)

Published by Almond Press
Editorial direction: David M. Gunn
Columbia Theological Seminary
P.O. Box 510, Decatur
GA 30031, USA
Almond Press is an imprint of
Sheffield Academic Press Ltd
The University of Sheffield
343 Fulwood Road
Sheffield S10 3BP
England

Typeset by Sheffield Academic Press
and
Printed on acid-free paper in Great Britain
by Billing & Sons Ltd
Worcester

British Library Cataloguing in Publication Data

Perdue, Leo G.
    Wisdom in revolt : metaphorical theology in the Book of
    Job.
    1. Christianity. Scriptures
    I. Title   II. Series
    223.1

    ISSN 0309-0787
    ISSN 0260-4493
    ISBN 1-85075-283-4

CONTENTS

ABBREVIATIONS

AB	Anchor Bible
Acta Or	*Acta Orientalia*
AJSLL	*American Journal of Semitic Languages and Literatures*
ANEP	*Ancient Near East in Pictures*
ANET	*Ancient Near Eastern Texts*
AThr	*Anglican Theological Review*
BASOR	*Bulletin of the American Schools of Oriental Research*
BDB	Brown, Driver, Briggs, *Hebrew and English Lexicon of the Old Tesdtament*
BHS	*Biblia Hebraica Stuttgartensia*
BHT	Beiträge zur historischen Theologie
Bib	*Biblica*
BJRL	*Bulletin of the John Rylands Library*
BKAT	Biblischer Kommentar zum Alten Testament
BO	*Bibliotheca Orientalis*
BWANT	Beiträge zur Wissenchaft vom Alten (und Neuen) Testament
BWL	*Babylonian Wisdom Literature*
BZAW	Beiheft zur Zeitschrift für die alttestamentliche Wissenschaft
CBQ	*Catholic Biblical Quarterly*
CJTH	*Canadian Journal of Theology*
CTA	A. Herdner, Corpus des tablettes en cunéiformes alphabétiques
EvTh	*Evangelische Theologie*
FOTL	Forms of Old Testament Literature
FRLANT	Forschungen zur Religion und Literatur des Alten und Neuen Testaments
GKC	Gesenius' Hebrew Grammar, ed. E. Kautzsch, trans. A.E. Cowley.
HAR	*Hebrew Annual Review*
HAT	Handbuch zum Alten Testament
HSM	Harvard Semitic Monographs
HSS	Harvard Semitic Studies
HUCA	*Hebrew Union College Annual*
IB	*The Interpreter's Bible*
IDB	*The Interpreter's Dictionary of the Bible*
Interp	*Interpretation*
JAAR	*Journal of the American Academy of Religion*

JBL	*Journal of Biblical Literature*
JEOL	*Jaarbericht. . . ex oriente lux*
JNES	*Journal of Near Eastern Studies*
KAT	*Kommentar zum Alten Testament*
KuD	*Kerygma und Dogma*
MIO	*Mitteilungen des Instituts für Orientforschung*
MVAG	*Mitteilungen der vorderasiatische-ägyptischen Gesellschaft*
NTT	*Nieuw theologisch Tijdschrift*
Or ns	*Orientalia*, new series
OTL	Old Testament Literature
OTS	*Oudtestamentische Studiën*
RB	*Revue Biblique*
REx	*Review and Expositor*
SAHG	*Sumerische und akkadische Hymnen und Gebete*
SBLDS	Society of Biblical Literature Dissertation Series
SBT	Studies in Biblical Theology
ISIAW	*Studies in Ancient Israelite Wisdom*
SPOA	*Les sagesses du Proche-Orient ancien*
SVT	Supplements to Vetus Testamentum
TDOT	*Theological Dictionary of the Old Testament*
ThLZ	*Theologische Literaturzeitung*
UT	C.H. Gordon, *Ugaritic Textbook*
VT	*Vetus Testamentum*
WMANT	Wissenschaftliche Monographien zum Alten und Neuen Testament
WO	Die Welt des Orients
ZAW	*Zeitschrift für die alttestamentliche Wissenschaft*
ZThK	*Zeitschrift für Theologie und Kirche*

PART I

METAPHORICAL THEOLOGY AND MYTHIC PARADIGMS

Chapter 1

The Theology of Wisdom Literature: Issues and Approaches

1. Introduction: Cosmology and Anthropology in Wisdom

The theological tradition in which wisdom is grounded is creation. For the sages, God is the maker of heaven and earth whose creativity both forms and sustains a living cosmos (Prov. 3.19-20). Wisdom was considered the first and best of God's creative acts. In her hymn of self-adoration, Woman Wisdom, wearing the apparel of the Queen of Heaven, sings from her heavenly throne (Prov. 8.22-23):

> The Lord gave birth to me at the beginning of his work,
> the first of his deeds of old.
> In distant time, I was established,
> at the first, before the beginning of the earth.

Thus wisdom drew from the power of that originating act which God repeats each morning and every New Year.

In the crafting of their tradition, the sages used language to construct a mythic world into which they entered and in which they lived. This world is created, sustained, and revitalized by the power of words, particularly metaphors of creation. Once again enthroned Wisdom, who rejoices in and oversees the inhabited world, makes a promise to those who heed her invitation:

> For the one who finds me discovers life,
> and receives beneficence from the Lord,
> But the one who misses me is self-afflicted,
> all who hate me love death (Prov. 8.35-36).

To partake of creation's bounty, to live in harmony with humanity and creature, to acquire understanding of God and the world, to discover one's place in society and cosmos, and to participate in the shaping of social orders that impinge on creation, these were the gifts Woman

Wisdom offered. Together they comprised what it was to become wise.

No one today would take issue with Zimmerli's claim that Wisdom 'thinks resolutely within a theology of creation',[1] though few have attempted a comprehensive description. And even these efforts have not produced a unified and inclusive depiction of the distinctive place creation holds in the wisdom tradition. Indeed most efforts have been limited to the task and objectives of a prolegomenon to wisdom theology. This is due in no small measure to the difficulty encountering any attempt to forge a paradigm that allows for both proper detailing of the diversity of wisdom's content and the constructive ordering of its components into a unified whole.[2]

2. *Approaches to the Theology of Wisdom*

Preliminary investigations have pursued four organizing principles for treating wisdom's creation tradition: anthropology, theodicy, world-order, and the dialectic of anthropology and cosmology.

Anthropology. While many scholars have understood wisdom to be the human quest to master life,[3] perhaps the best example is Walther Zimmerli. In his seminal article on Qoheleth, Zimmerli argued this sage's question, מה טוב לאדם בחיים (literally, 'What is good for humanity in living?'), is central to the entire wisdom corpus. For Zimmerli, not only Qoheleth, but all of 'wisdom is radically anthropocentric'.[4] Thirty years later Zimmerli continued to place

---

1. Walther Zimmerli, 'The Place and Limit of the Wisdom in the Framework of the Old Testament Theology', *SIAW*, 316.
2. On a larger scale this is the same problem besetting any effort towards either a comprehensive Old Testament or Biblical Theology. For a critical review of recent efforts at Old Testament and Biblical Theology and a proposal for new methodological directions, see my *The Collapse of History: Creation, Narrativity, and the Reconstruction of Theological Language* (Overtures to Biblical Theology; Minneapolis: Augsburg–Fortress, forthcoming).
3. These include Walter Brueggemann, *In Man We Trust* (Atlanta: John Knox, 1972); John Priest, 'Where is Wisdom to be Placed?', *SIAW*, 281-88; 'Humanism, Skepticism, and Pessimism', *JAAR* (1968), 311-26; O.S. Rankin, *Israel's Wisdom Literature* (Edinburgh: T. & T. Clark, 1936); and Walther Zimmerli, 'The Place and Limit of the Wisdom', 314-26.
4. Walther Zimmerli, 'Zur Struktur der alttestamentlichen Weisheit', *ZAW* 51 (1933), 177-204.

anthropology at the center of sapiential thought,[1] though he came to locate the quest for good under the more encompassing rubric of creation, especially *creatio continua* and humanity's role and place in the world. Because of this abiding interest in the human, the goal of the sage is 'to master life' through knowledge of the world that illuminates proper existence. In faithful response to the Great Commission issued in primeval times, humanity's task was to go forth actively into the world to apprehend, establish, and order reality (Gen. 1.26-28).

Theodicy. While recognizing that creation theology is the ground of wisdom, a second group of scholars has contended that the justice of God is the center of sapiential tradition.[2] In his seminal article in 1970, James L. Crenshaw traced the trajectory of theodicy in the Old Testament through to its eruption in full fury in Job and quiet skepticism in Qoheleth.[3] For Crenshaw this critical tradition of the Old Testament, often ignored by scholars, points to the dark side of covenant, a theme expanded and nuanced in later publications.[4]

According to Crenshaw, it is only the wisdom tradition that openly and cogently explores the full range of this most central of theological problems in the Old Testament. Crenshaw came to place theodicy within the major sphere of creation theology, and outlined the distinctive features as follows:

> (1) The threat of chaos in the cosmic, political, social realms evokes a response in terms of creation theology; (2) in wisdom thought, creation functions primarily as defense of divine justice; and (3) the centrality of the question of God's integrity in Israelite literature places creation theology at the center of the theological enterprise.[5]

1. 'The Place and Limit of the Wisdom'.
2. James L. Crenshaw, 'Popular Questioning of the Justice of God', *ZAW* 82 (1970), 380-95; 'Prolegomenon', *SIAW*, 1-45; 'In Search of Divine Presence', *REx* 74 (1977), 353-69; and Burton L. Mack, 'Wisdom Myth and Mytho-Logy', *Interp* 24 (1970), 46-60.
3. 'Popular Questioning of the Justice of God'.
4. 'Introduction: The Shift from Theodicy to Anthropodicy', *Theodicy in the Old Testament*, ed. James L. Crenshaw (London: SCM, 1983), 1-16; 'The Human Dilemma and Literature of Dissent', *Tradition and Theology in the Old Testament*, ed. Douglas A. Knight (Philadelphia: Fortress, 1974), 235-58; and *Whirlpool of Torment* (Overtures to Biblical Theology; Philadelphia: Fortress, 1985).
5. 'Prolegomenon', 27.

While acknowledging that the concept of order is central to wisdom thought, Crenshaw contended that it was the questioning of divine justice that precipitated the theological restructuring of the tradition's understanding of God and the world. In the midst of chaos the appeal to creation affirms the ongoing possibility of discovering meaning and wholeness. And it is ultimately in Ben Sirah that a reinvigorated rational defense of theodicy issues forth in praise of the one who created all things in pairs.[1] The duality of good and evil is at the basis of creation and operates under the impress of divine service to reward the good and punish the wicked. Once again in Ben Sirah 'the original creative act and *creatio continua* bear witness to the justice of God',[2] Nevertheless, in wisdom literature justice took precedence over creation theology. The appearance and purpose of creation theology was to articulate a defensible doctrine of theodicy.[3]

Cosmology. A third understanding of creation in wisdom focuses on the principle of world-order.[4] Hartmut Gese's analysis of wisdom in Egypt considered Maat (the principle of 'truth, justice, and order' at times personified as the divine daughter of the sun god Re) to be the organizing principle for this tradition. Gese recognized that Maat encompassed two entwined spheres: *cosmos* and *societas*. Through the

---

1. 'The Problem of Theodicy in Sirach', *JBL* 94 (1975), 47-64.
2. 'Prolegomenon', 34.
3. 'In search of Divine Presence', 364. Crenshaw later appears to give more emphasis to anthropology as the key to understanding wisdom. This is apparent in his description of wisdom's cosmology: 'that way of looking at things begins with humans as the fundamental point of orientation. It asks what is good for men and women. And it believes that all essential answers can be learned in experience, pregnant with signs about reality itself'. And, 'the human responsibility is to search for that insight and thus to learn to live in harmony with the cosmos'. He notes that what is distinctive is humanism: 'men and women possess the means of securing their well being. . . they do not need and cannot expect divine assistance' (*Old Testament Wisdom* [Atlanta: John Knox], 17-21).
4. Hartmut Gese, *Lehre und Wirklichkeit in der alten Weisheit* (Tübingen: Mohr, 1958); Hans-Jürgen Hermisson, 'Observations on the Creation Theology in Wisdom', *Israelite Wisdom*, ed. John G. Gammie *et al.* (Missoula: Scholars Press, 1978), 43-57; H.D. Preuss, 'Das Gottesbild der älteren Weisheit Israels', *SVT* 23 (1972), 117-45; 'Erwägungen zum theologischen Ort alttestamentlicher Weisheitsliteratur', *EvTh* 30 (1970), 393-417; H.H. Schmid, *Gerechtigkeit als Weltordnung* (BHT 40; Tübingen: Mohr, 1968); and 'Creation, Righteousness, and Salvation', *Creation in the Old Testament*, ed. B.W. Anderson (Philadelphia: Fortress, 1984), 102-17.

act of divine creation both cosmic and human order was established. Even so, the limits to human perception and the remoteness of the gods made it impossible for Maat to be perceived in its totality. And there were even elements of reality which lay outside its domain, since the creator was also responsible for the forming of that which was imperfect (e.g. the lame and the blind, *Amenemopet* 24.8-20). Furthermore, order even in Egypt was not entirely static, for it had to be actualized in the world by the incarnation of Horus in the ruling king.[1]

According to Gese, this prominence of Maat in Egyptian thought was assimilated and transformed by Israel's sages to affirm the existence of a cosmic order and its necessary incarnation in the social structure. The Israelite wise also recognized in often poignant ways the limitations of human thought to perceive order in its entirety. Consequently, they articulated an understanding of divine freedom which transcended any mechanistic causality. Yahweh was not bound by immutable laws, but was free to act even against the best laid of human plans. This radical freedom of God broke through the ancient Near Eastern causal nexus and brought human fate under the grace of God. Nevertheless, order was the authoritative basis for all sapiential teaching.

A final example of approaching wisdom theology through cosmology appears in the work of Hans-Jürgen Hermisson. In his important study of the wisdom saying, Hermisson detected what he considered to be constitutive for sapiential thought: the saying is a form connecting deed and result, thereby recognizing, transmitting, and creating an order of life.[2] In a later article, he extended his argument about the basic form of Israelite wisdom to a comprehensive statement about sapiential theology.[3] In Hermisson's view wisdom sought regularity in the multiplicity of phenomena, a regularity observable in both nature and human society. This regularity led to a unified construction of reality which established a correspondence between what was observed and its perception. The developing sapiential epistemology led to the articulation of a creation theology in which order in the world was consistent with the process of human perception and the knowledge it acquired. The regularity, purposiveness, and beauty of wisdom as

---

1. *Lehre und Wirklichkeit in der alten Weisheit*, 5-32.
2. Hans-Jürgen Hermisson, *Studien zur israelitischen Spruchweisheit* (WMANT 28; Neukirchen: Neukirchener Verlag, 1968).
3. 'Observations on the Creation Theology in Wisdom', 43-57.

human perception were part of the essential nature of creation itself. This insight provided human life its *raison d'être,* for it implied that existence had purpose: to live so as to actualize and experience the beneficent order of creation. Sapiential teachings provided guidance for the proper way of existing in the world.

Cosmology and Anthropology. A fourth approach to creation theology in wisdom literature has been articulated by Gerhard von Rad. His treatment of early wisdom saw the tradition as practical insight rooted in the experience of life and the world.[1] Essentially gnomic and experiential, this first stage of wisdom was driven by the human desire to master life. And in their efforts sages came to observe not a total disarray of unrelated phenomena, but rather a certain regularity, an order, underlying all reality. Yet this regularity was never shaped into an all-embracing order in the fashion, say, of Maat in Egypt or a Greek cosmos. There was ever the imponderable, the mysterious, and the immeasurable which could not be fashioned into a systematic order that unified all reality. The world was an event which was dynamic and moving, not a being which was well integrated and static. One made one's way in this world by being aware of both the patterns of consistency that related phenomena and actions and the contingencies which ever threatened individual life. Though this earlier wisdom probably functioned within a theological frame of reference, it was only in a later stage that serious theological reflection led to the view of the creator who fashioned a world that was revelatory (Prov. 9; Job 28; Sir. 24) to those who 'feared God' and answered Wisdom's call.[2] Von Rad based his developmental understanding of wisdom from human experience to cosmology and from anthropology to theology on the view that creation was a late developing tradition in Israel, which did not achieve normative status prior to the sixth century BCE.

In his more mature reflection, von Rad qualified this evolutionary depiction of wisdom's development by emphasizing that there was no significant tension between faith and reason: 'For Israel there was only one word of experience and. . . this was apperceived by means of a perceptive apparatus in which rational perceptions and religious per-

---

1. 'Die ältere Weisheit Israels', *KuD* 2 (1956), 54-72 (= *Old Testament Theology* 1 [New York: Harper & Row, 1962], 418-41).
   2. *Old Testament Theology* 1, 441-53.

ceptions were not differentiated'.[1] For von Rad, experience of the
world was in some measure also an experience of God, though he
denied any latent pantheism was present in the concept. God transcended the world and its elements, and continued to maintain an air of
secrecy and mystery. Indeed God encountered one in the event of
experience, thereby eliminating the possibility of any symbiosis of
world and deity. But von Rad continued to deny the sages constructed
any simplistic theory of retribution. Indeed there were orders to be
followed in social existence enabling the wise to make their way in the
world, but there was no immutable causal nexus that structured human
events. Instead von Rad preferred to talk about the 'good', not a philo-
sophically defined virtue, but rather a 'social phenomenon', a life-
enhancing power which positively affected human society and the
individual by producing a 'sphere of blessing'. 'Good' was both a
force and an order beneficial for character and action.[2]

According to von Rad, the mystery and freedom of God combined
with the limits to human knowledge meant that it was impossible for
the sages to guarantee success in human action. But this recognition
also led to a positive openness to new experiences and understandings.
Thus to speak of a static world order which allowed no room for
divine freedom or contingent events would have contradicted the
thrust of wisdom's intellectual tradition.[3] And while the tradition
depicts the revelation of God in creation through the medium of wisdom, and affirms that creation has something to say which humans
may hear, the mystery and contingency remain. Nonetheless, creation
was good, and in no way hostile to human life. Its orders and generally consistent patterns made it possible for the wise to experience the
beneficence of God's good creation. Thus the sages tended to express
trust in the graciousness of the creator and affirmed the goodness of
life. While trust comes under attack in Job, the experience of the
theophany teaches this sufferer God is for him. Thus Job confidently
places his own destiny and that of creation back into the hand of God.

Evaluation. Each of these approaches to creation theology focuses on
at least one important theme in the wisdom tradition. Certainly the
anthropocentric trajectory traced by Zimmerli, Rankin and Priest

1. *Wisdom in Israel*, 61.
2. *Wisdom in Israel*, 80.
3. *Wisdom in Israel*, 97-113.

uncovers a very important dimension of wisdom literature. Wisdom does offer to its adherents instruction for making their way in the world. However, the tendency of this approach, if taken to an extreme, is to ignore the strong theological orientation of that guidance, especially in its early stages.[1] And it misconstrues too easily the tradition by making it highly individualistic and utilitarian. For the sages, the world is created by God who oversees a life-enhancing order that may be known and experienced through the guidance of wisdom. But the beneficence offered by this order is not achieved merely by human effort. Rather, well-being derives in part from insight rooted in the 'fear of God', i.e. trust in the beneficence of God and the wonder and the goodness of creation.[2] And as Schmid and von Rad have demonstrated, Wisdom considers individual behavior to affect society in positive and negative ways.[3]

To consider theodicy as the unifying center of creation thought is to read the tradition primarily through the lenses of Job and Qoheleth. No doubt theodicy is an important topic, but is it the unifying center of sapiential theology? The affirmation of the justice of God is a major feature of the doctrine of creation for the sages, but so too are the equally significant elements of the freedom of God, revelation through creation, the compelling beauty of nature, the response of praise, and both the expanse of and the limits to human knowledge. It would seem appropriate to regard theodicy as an important component of creation thought in the literature, coming to question especially during periods of social upheaval.

---

1. The recognition of the theological basis of wisdom instructions, especially in terms of creation, has resulted in a rejection of the once prevalent but now questionable view of wisdom as eudaemonistic and utilitarian in tenor and purpose. For assessments of the theological basis of early wisdom, see Hellmut Brunner, 'Der freie Wille Gottes in der ägyptischen Weisheit', *SPOA*, 203; A. De Buck, 'Het Religieus Karakter der oudste egyptische Wijsheid', *NTT* 21 (1932), 322-49; Berend Gemser, 'The Spiritual Structure of Biblical Aphoristic Wisdom', *VTS* 7 (1960), 102-28.

2. Siegfried Plath, *Furcht Gottes* (Arbeiten zur Theologie 2; Stuttgart: Calwer, 1962). Berend Gemser has correctly argued that this theological undergirding is present in the tradition from the very beginning ('The Spiritual Structure of Biblical Aphoristic Wisdom', *Adhuc Loquitur* [Pretoria Oriental Series 7; Leiden: Brill, 1968], 138-49).

3. H.-H. Schmid, *Wesen und Geschichte der Weisheit* (BZAW 101; Berlin: de Gruyter), 156-57; Gerhard von Rad, *Wisdom in Israel*, 74-75.

Order as a unifying center for creation theology in wisdom literature is more comprehensive than either anthropology or theodicy and
is a major theme in the tradition. However, this approach may distort
wisdom thought in a number of ways. First, order as 'justice' may take
on a too legalistic definition and lead inevitably to a hardened doctrine
of retribution. The outcome often is an inflexible, mechanistic system
of reward and punishment which disallows or restricts divine freedom. And the sages imposed constraints on the conception of order: an
inevitable mystery which characterized both divine behavior and
creation, limits to human perception which made epistemological
certitude an illusion, and a strong emphasis on the divine freedom
which did not yield to the tyranny of an impersonal order. Retribution, a twisted perversion of sapiential thought, was supported
primarily by the wise friends of Job.

Second, the theme of 'order', as Murphy has rightly seen, tends to
be contradicted by the alluring, passionate image of Woman Wisdom
wooing youth to her embrace.[1] The pursuit of wisdom is a life-long
response by the sage to the enchantment of the world and the desire
for knowledge which opens up storehouses of insight, effectuates
harmony, and brings contentment.

Third, the term 'order' does not connote well the imagery of goodness and beauty which also conveys the sapiential understanding of
creation. The world is wondrous in its beauty and life-sustaining
powers, and the response of the creature is to praise the one who made
and continues to sustain all life. To live wisely and well is to rejoice in
the goodness of life and to drink deeply and fully from its abundant
springs.

Fourth, order conveys incorrectly the notion of a static, unchanging
reality not susceptible to change. While the sages avoided the pitfalls
of a naïve modern liberalism which considered progress as inevitable,
neither did they portray order as static and inflexible. Instead creation
was a dynamic, organic process which was recreated by God on a
daily basis and openly responsible to human participation. Order was
created and sustained by wise action, but it was subverted by the fool
who disregarded wisdom and its life-enhancing power.

The dialectic of anthropology and cosmology is far more inclusive
of the variety of expression that characterizes the complexity of creation thought in wisdom literature, and will be followed in the ensuing

1. Roland Murphy, 'Wisdom and Creation', *JBL* 104 (1985), 3-11.

analysis of Job. But there are serious limitations with earlier constructions which should be avoided. Von Rad's somewhat evolutionary understanding of wisdom thought saw reflective theology, and especially creation, as a later development from a more secular, largely anthropocentric early tradition. However, many studies have pointed to the significant role creation played, even in the formative beginnings of the wisdom tradition,[1] and to remove it from the early stages results in serious misunderstanding.

Any presentation of the theology of creation in wisdom literature must be inclusive enough to embrace the broad extent of the literature and to give proper place to its variety of expression and understanding. After all, we are dealing with a literature undoubtedly produced by different 'schools' of tradents over many centuries who impressed the tradition with their own distinctive interests and insights. The tradition of the wise was dynamic and growing, always yielding to and critically embracing the influences of creative insights forged by the distinctive *Geist* of each new age. To force the ideas of the literatures into restrictive categories robs them of vitality and transforms the tradition's inner dynamic into a system which is too rational. Wisdom literature is not constructed by systematic theologians, but rather by poets who recognized and utilized the power of words, written and spoken, which constructed new languages of faith and meaning. Even those approaches which trace thematic trajectories, while providing unifying factors emerging from the tradition itself, tend to become too constrictive and rationalistic.

The wise poets forged a synthesis between the Dionysian dance and the Apollonian vision. Indeed there was the rational ordering of experience, but equally important was the passionate and joyous response to the beauty, goodness, and elegance of creation and life. But how to capture this duality of understanding is the scholar's question. This study makes the attempt by focusing on the important metaphors of creation which resided within mythic texts and shaped theology in the wisdom tradition in general, and Job in particular. In so doing, the effort is made to examine the following: the variety of ways the sages, especially the Joban poet, spoke about creation, the distinctiveness of the two creation traditions (cosmology and anthropology) as they have

---

1. Hermisson, 'Observations on the Creation Theology in Wisdom'; Gese, *Lehre und Wirklichkeit;* Schmid, 'Gerechtigkeit als Weltordnung'; 'Creation, Righteousness and Salvation'; Zimmerli, 'The Place and Limit of the Wisdom'.

developed in the literature in general and Job in particular, and the important interaction between cosmology and anthropology in the development of the book of Job. This approach is metaphorical theology.

3. The Metaphorical Process

Introduction. Religious language is metaphorical.[1] It describes the numinous which in part transcends the limits of space and time, by using finite expressions derived from the experiences of human existence. By the selection and transmission of central metaphors, a culture conveys the important features of its religious understandings derived from experiences of and reflections on the Holy.[2] Yet regardless of how apt the metaphor and how insightful into the nature of ultimacy itself, it is and always remains a creature born of finitude and limitation.

Properly understood metaphor is not a mere rhetorical device which embellishes but does not encompass the substantive essence of language. Rather metaphor is 'as ultimate as speech itself, and speech as ultimate as thought', being 'the instinctive and necessary act of the

---

1. David Tracy emphasizes that 'all major religions are grounded in certain root metaphors. . . In a particular religion root metaphors form a cluster or network in which sustained metaphors both organize subsidiary metaphors and diffuse new ones. These networks describe the enigma and promise of the human situation and predescribe certain remedies for that situation' ('Metaphor and Religion: The Test Case of Christian Texts', *On Metaphor*, ed. Sheldon Sacks [Chicago: The University of Chicago Press, 1979], 80). Among the many important studies on metaphor, in addition to Tracy, see: Ian Barbour, *Myths, Models and Paradigms* (New York: Harper & Row, 1974); Max Black, *Models and Metaphors* (Ithaca: Cornell University Press, 1962); 'How Metaphors Work: A Reply to Donald Davidson', *On Metaphor*, 191-92; Wayne Booth, 'Metaphor as Rhetoric: The Problem of Evaluation', *On Metaphor*, 47-70; Frederick Ferré, 'Metaphors, Models, and Religion', *Soundings* 51 (1968), 327-45; Nelson Goodman, 'Metaphor as Moonlighting', *On Metaphor*, 175-80; Karsten Harries, 'Metaphor and Transcendence', *On Metaphor*, 71-88; Sallie McFague, *Metaphorical Theology* (Philadelphia: Fortress), 1982; I.A. Richards, *The Philosophy of Rhetoric* (New York: Oxford University Press, 1936); Paul Ricoeur, 'The Metaphorical Process', *Semeia* 4 (1975), 75-106; *Interpretation Theory: Discourse and the Surplus of Meaning* (Fort Worth, TX: TCU, 1976); *The Rule of Metaphor* (Toronto: The University of Toronto, 1977); 'The Metaphorical Process as Cognition, Imagination, and Feeling', *On Metaphor*, 141-57; and Phillip Wheelwright, *Metaphor and Reality* (Bloomington: Indiana University Press, 1962).
2. Thorkild Jacobsen, *The Treasures of Darkness* (New Haven: Yale University Press, 1976), 3-5.

mind exploring reality and ordering experience'.[1] Language participates in the very essence of human nature, for this is the distinctive and primary feature of humans in contradistinction to all other life forms.[2] With the ability to imagine and think and to capture images and thoughts in language, humans have the unique capacity to develop meaning systems which construct, define, and interpret their world in its cosmic, religious, and social proportions. And essential to this world-building task performed by language is metaphor itself.[3]

Metaphor interfaces two distinctly different things or ideas (tenor and vehicle) in a sentence.[4] The tenor is the principal subject which is conveyed by a vehicle, or secondary subject.[5] This syntactical structure contributes meaning to the two principles which both interact and derive meaning from the relationship. In other words tenors and vehicles are meaning-giving, but also meaning receiving. And in the relationship between tenor and vehicle meaning for the sentence is constructed. Thus metaphors are semantic building blocks which not only construct worlds, but are themselves constructed by the very worlds they build. When forced outside the context of the reality systems which they produce, they become estranged from their semantic world which in turn disintegrates and returns to chaos.

It is not enough to describe the major characteristics of metaphor. Rather it is necessary to explain how metaphor works as it moves an implied audience through a process which begins with the shattering of previous structures of linguistic reality to the reconstruction of a new and more compelling one. This process includes the following stages.

1. John Middleton Murry, *Countries of the Mind* (London: Oxford University Press, 1931), 1-2.

2. Wheelwright, *Metaphors and Reality*, 19.

3. Nelson Goodman notes: 'Metaphorical use of language differs in significant ways from literal use but is no less comprehensible, no more recondite, no less practical, and no more independent of truth and falsity than is literal use. Far from being a mere matter of ornament, it participates fully in the progress of knowledge: in replacing some state 'natural' kinds with novel and illuminating categories, in contriving facts, in revising theory, and in bringing us new worlds' ('Metaphor as Moonlighting', 175).

4. I.A. Richards calls metaphor a 'double unit', involving two ideas, or two halves (*The Philosophy of Rhetoric*, 96). This is the interactional model of metaphors, as opposed to the comparison model in which one subject is compared to another.

5. Wayne Booth, *A Rhetoric of Irony* (Chicago: University of Chicago Press, 1974), 22.

Absurdity and Destabilization. Essential to the character of metaphor is the element of the absurd. This means that a metaphor depicts its object in a manner that is false when taken literally, for the relationship constructed is not one based on exact, factual correspondence.[1] For example, to say that creation is a battle between Yahweh and a primeval monster is literally absurd, even though this was one of the key metaphors in ancient Near Eastern mythology and the Old Testament. But it is the inappropriate quality, and with some metaphors, the very shock of the absurd, that initially engages the attention and awakens the mind to the possibility of new and significant insight.[2] In theological terms, a potentially revelatory state is presented. The effect produced by the metaphor initially then is disorientation, for the hearer is loosed from the moorings of literal understanding and expectation and cast into a suddenly different and overwhelming world in which the ordinariness of common understanding disintegrates. And it is in this state of disturbance that the normal language of meaning providing orientation and direction destabilizes. Disoriented and left without language and disorientation, the initial response, at least for a moment, can only be silence or incoherent ramblings.

Mimesis. Pursued through its progressive stages, metaphor may lead then to mimesis. Once the tenor is examined through the lens of its vehicle, a new set of imposed, unusual features becomes attached. Through this extraordinary set of associations, new insight into the tenor may result, leading to the recognition that something in the relationship between tenor and vehicle is unquestionably true, confirmed by the experience of the one engaged.[3] There may be then a

---

1. Ferré, 'Metaphors, Models, and Religion', 330; Ricoeur, 'The Metaphorical Process', 78-79; and *The Rule of Metaphor*, 199. Goodman remarks: 'The oddity is that metaphorical truth is compatible with literal falsity; a sentence false when taken literally may be true when taken metaphorically, as in the case of "The joint is jumping" or "The lake is a sapphire" ('Metaphor as Moonlighting', 175).

2. Ricoeur, 'The Metaphorical Process', 77-78: 'The strategy of discourse by which the metaphorical statement obtains its meaning is absurdity.' According to Ricoeur, the literal interpretation of a statement is destroyed and then is transformed into a meaningful contradiction which gives new semantic insight.

3. Goodman emphasizes: '"Metaphorical truth" does not mean that the truth of the sentence is metaphorical but that the sentence taken metaphorically is true' ('Metaphor as Moonlighting', *On Metaphor*, 175).

second shock in the binding of vehicle to tenor, but it is what Wheel-wright calls the 'shock of recognition'.[1] In one respect, if not more, the tenor and its vehicle have fused, becoming one, but only for the creative moments of imagination and reflection.

Transformation and Restabilization. Metaphor may then lead to trans-formation, a feature endemic to the very etymology of the word itself, *metamorphosis*, 'change, alteration, transformation'. Metaphors serve not only to alter the perception and therefore the meaning of an object, but, if they are especially compelling ones, they may even become organizing images which recreate the world into something more compelling and true, including one's imagining and activating of values.[2] Metaphors are potentially dangerous constructions, for they possess the innate power to transform one's vision of the world and the values inherent in that vision. Metaphors are not simply raw building blocks for the construction *de nouveau* of reality, but more, they possess a transforming agency which reconstructs, reshapes, and refashions existing conceptual materials into new and powerful sym-bolic worlds which define and interpret reality and thereby evoke significant human response and commitment.[3] And when they become the shared heritage of a culture through the network of common social language, metaphors become symbols that give vitality and life to the community which creates and transmits them through story and rite. At this stage in the process, metaphors serve to restabilize the frag-ments of speech made incoherent by absurdity, allowing coherence and reorientation to a different perception of reality. What is created is a new and compelling world in which the individual and community move and have their being. In this way language becomes event, for the hearer enters into the metaphorical world and actively participates in its reality. The individual as social being is created. And for both individual and social group identity is formed.

However, some metaphors become common stock metaphors inca-pable of eliciting significant response and transformation. Losing their semantic power to reshape human perception and identity, they become impotent and eventually may even die.[4] They cannot sustain

---

1. Wheelwright, *Metaphor and Reality*, 45ff.
2. Ferré, 'Metaphors, Models, and Religion', 331.
3. Ricoeur, 'The Metaphorical Process', 75.
4. McFague, *Metaphorical Theology*, 41.

the reality they have created, with the result that this world destabilizes and disorientation is experienced, only this time in an even more
threatening manner. For the collapse is not occasioned by radically
new and different metaphors, but by their absence. It is this void of
meaninglessness out of which no ready escape is seen.

Tension. Throughout these stages, metaphors possess a tensive quality
that energizes their vitality and continues to give them life and sustenance.[1] Even after new vision is created, tension remains. Invariably
there is something in the relationship between the tenor and vehicle
that is patently false. This is what Harries refers to as both collusion
and collision.[2] It is this tensive character between tenor and vehicle
which provides the power for both vitality and transformative
potentiality. Correlation and difference serve to sustain the integrity
and strength of all metaphorical language. However, when the tenor
and vehicle are made one, when metaphor is denied its semantic
integrity and is misshaped into a literal referent, when similarity
becomes identity, metaphor loses its dynamic, tensive power and dies.
Or far worse, metaphor is reborn as chaos, distorting and even
destroying true meaning by attempting to imprison the images of
metaphor within the walls of literal identity. The tenor becomes the
vehicle and thereby loses the integrity of its differentiated meaning.
The metaphor either dies, or, in the case of God-language, 'a false god
limps toward Bethlehem, waiting to be born'.

Ambiguity. Finally, metaphor is akin to ambiguity in the fact that
'ambiguous terms likewise have two or more different applications'.[3]
Metaphor may evoke potentially different types of personal experience—emotional, rational and evaluational—and be capable of two or
more applications in the extension of its range of meaning. By their
very definition, metaphors cannot possess 'steno-meanings', that is,
meanings which are shared by a large number of people in exactly the
same way.[4] Even so this does not allow for unrestricted imagination

---

1. McFague, *Metaphorical Theology,* 37; Wheelwright, *Metaphor and Reality,* 45-
69.
2. 'Metaphor and Transcendence', 71ff.
3. Goodman, 'Metaphor as Moonlighting', 176. He notes however that 'metaphor
differs from ambiguity in that a literal application precedes and influences a correlative
metaphorical application' (176).
4. Wheelwright, *Metaphor and Reality,* 33.

or for free associations. Variety of associations, though limited by cultural experience, is inevitable. Thus metaphors by their very nature defy one precise definition. When this is denied or proscribed, something quite intrinsic to metaphor is eliminated. Consequently, it loses its semantic value and dies.

4. *Metaphor and Theology*

Introduction. Religious language constructs models which are extended metaphors.[1] To be true to their nature and function appropriately, these systems or models should maintain the dominant features of metaphor, including the tension between the object of faith and action, that is God (the tenor), and the vehicle which ascribes meaning to and yet avoids merging with the Holy. Otherwise, an idol is created.[2] In addition metaphorical models should, like individual metaphors, disorient hearers by disturbing, even shattering conventional theological traditions, provide new and revelatory insight into the nature of God and religious life, and set forth constructions of meaning that engage the faith and devotion of their hearers. These models order the evocative images of a religious tradition which provides comprehensible guides and patterns for being in the world.[3] They provide orientation for the life of faith and action. These models may find enactment in creeds, psalms, and narratives. In the Deuteronomic creed (Deut. 26.5-9) the combined metaphors of Divine Warrior and Redeemer (*gō'ēl*) shape the faith in a God who breaks the power of cruel tyrants, delivers oppressed people from slavery, protects them from disasters, and gives them the land of Canaan. Yet, this credal synthesis of the components of metaphorical models is a rare phenomenon in the Bible. More often they are enacted in other forms, particularly narrative and hymn.

---

1. Barbour, *Myths, Models, and Paradigms*.

2. I would argue that metaphorical models are the basic paradigm from which specific genres of language (myth, lament, epic, etc.) derive content, literary structure, and meaning. These broad paradigms provide the context for the meaning of specific, cultural forms (e.g. *YHWH Melek* hymns, a specific cultural form in Israel, draw on the more comprehensive metaphorical model of Yahweh as Divine Warrior).

3. McFague, *Metaphorical Theology*, 103; and Tracy, 'Metaphor and Religion', 89.

Metaphorical Models. For the writers and tradents of the Old Testament (poets, sages, prophets, priests), narrative in the forms of national epic (e.g. the Yahwist), epic poetry (e.g. Exod. 15; Pss. 78; 105; 106; 135; 136), and creation stories (e.g. Gen. 1.1–2.4a; Ps. 104) are the dominant genres constructed by metaphorical models of faith.[1] For prose narratives they constitute the theme, motifs, characterization, structure, and plot (action within a temporal sequence) involving tension and resolution.[2] And if properly constructed, narratives may become for the implied audience the dramatic enactment of the metaphorical process. Metaphorical models may do much the same thing in poetic genres. They provide the literary and thematic *mots crochets* weaving together the major parts of the poem, the fabric and instrument for the structuring of individual strophes, the organizing center for motifs and mood, and the thematic threads of the entire poem. Yet they too may enact the metaphorical process for the audience in moving them from absurdity and disorientation to new vision.

Old Testament theology must begin with the metaphors which are present in narrative and poetic texts. The theologian should not be content to describe elements of faith, but must explain how narrative and poetry actualize faith and understanding for the implied audience. The task is not simply confessional recital but rather explanation of process. Then one may move to systematic conceptualization. In my judgment this conceptualization would clarify and extend the implicit features of the ancient models. This is proper theological interpretation. Conceived in this fashion, a system is not imposed on the text, but rather grows out of the paradigmatic features inherent in the ancient traditions.

Metaphors and the Mythic Traditions. When Israel's sages speak of God as creator, they do not do so in conceptual terms. Nowhere do the sages affirm, 'I believe in God the Father Almighty, Creator of Heaven and Earth'. Even if one agrees with von Rad's contested contention that Israelite creeds integrated creation only at a very late period (Pss. 135; 136; Neh. 9), it is well known that the major elements of salvation history do not appear in the wisdom texts

1. Tracy notes that the parables of Jesus 'achieve their parabolic status as conjunctions of a narrative genre and a metaphorical process' ('Metaphor and Religion', 90). This conjunction of genre and metaphorical process is essential to understanding the way religious texts work.

2. Robert Alter, *The Art of Biblical Narrative* (New York: Basic Books, 1981).

themselves. Rather God-language in this tradition is and remains focused on creation. Israel's wise shared with other ancient Near Eastern cultures and other native tradents four major metaphors for speaking about creation: fertility, artistry, word, and struggle (*Chaoskampf*).[1] In addition two others connote the role and status of humanity in God's creation: slave and ruler. The primary literary context for each metaphor and its extension was not a systematic formulation, but rather the mythical corpus of the ancient Near East. Metaphors were the organizing features for the literary patterns of ancient myths. Myths represent the conjunction of metaphorical process and narrative genre. Stated in another way, myths are the enactment of metaphorical process leading to the actualization of religious meaning. From this meaning cultural and social systems are constructed and legitimated.

In regard to content and function, ancient Near Eastern myths fall into a bipartite classification: myths of origins and myths of maintenance.[2] Cosmological myths of origins speak of primordial beginnings, sometimes narrating the birth of gods, but always telling of the creation of the world and the establishment of orders for life. Anthropological myths of origins tell of the creation of human beings and their purpose and function in the world. Myths of maintenance address either the ways the cosmos and its life structures are continued by actions of the gods or the predestination of humans to act and function in certain roles within the cosmic and social order. Often cosmological and anthropological myths are incorporated into the same traditions, especially those which become the classic formulations of a culture. This happens, for example, in both the Priestly (Gen. 1.1–2.4a) and J (Gen. 2.4b-25) narratives.

Mythic metaphors often made their way into other literary genres (e.g. Ps. 74), providing them content, structure and actualization. Myth then was the primal expression for conceptions of reality not only in the ancient Near East, but in Israel as well. While Israel's henotheistic and eventually monotheistic faith limited creation and providence to God, their religious genres (including epics, psalms, oracles, and wisdom poems) were heavily indebted to mythic traditions of surrounding cultures. Past efforts to contrast rather

1. See Claus Westermann, *Creation* (Philadelphia: Fortress, 1974), 39-40.
2. Mircea Eliade, *Cosmos and History. The Myth of the Eternal Return* (New York: Harper, 1959).

radically Israel's historical thought with ancient Near Eastern myth have now largely been missed.

It was from the mythic traditions and their reworkings by the other tradents and authors of ancient Israel that the sages drew their metaphors for expressing their theology.[1] Each myth contained its own distinctive configuration of metaphors and patterns. However, the same major metaphors recur in the mythological traditions, and, as we shall argue, there are underlying patterns which structure the common story of each mythical tradition and its dramatic enactment. This recurrence of pattern allows for some categorization of myths, though the recognition that each individual text has its own unique character that allows for some variation should be respected. These metaphors and patterns of myth provided the essential features used by the sages in the construction of their theology of creation. Indeed, the poet of Job makes significant use of two major mythic traditions of cosmology and anthropology and their root metaphors in structuring the present book.

It is my contention that the book of Job moves on two mythic levels. The internal structure of the book of Job is a dramatic enactment of a major anthropological mythic tradition in the ancient Near East, best illustrated by *Athra-hasis*. This tradition, centering on the metaphor of humanity as slave to the gods, develops the pattern of creation and judgment (predestination to slavery), slavery and toil, revolt against the gods, fall and threatened destruction, and concluding judgment and redemption.

However, the external structure of the book of Job, which contextualizes the internal mythic struggle of the hero, is the cosmological mythic tradition of conflict between the creator and the monster of chaos. The two best examples of this tradition are the *Enuma elish*, primarily a myth of origins, and the Baal Cycle, a myth of maintenance. The literary pattern common to these two myths includes battle, victory over chaos, kingship, judgment, and creation. Not only is this mythic tradition presupposed by the Joban narrative, it also contributes tensive interaction with the anthropological tradition incorporated in Job's struggle with the creator. Indeed, the two

---

1. Burton Mack has clearly demonstrated this in his study of the 'Wisdom Poems' ('Wisdom Myth and Mythology'). However, we would go much further in contending that myth provokes the major metaphors and models for sapiential language and thought in general.

mythological traditions intersect at the point of conflict: the creator's conflict with the chaos monster is mythically transferred to the struggle with Job, resulting in all-out revolt.

As with any theological tradition, wisdom struggled with the problems of the domestication of its language and the potential idolatry of its theological formulations. Its metaphors did not die, but they suffered the threats of abuse by those less perceptive and occasionally dogmatic tradents whose efforts almost led to the extinction of the tradition. The threat to wisdom came not from the clash of metaphors which led to heated and invigorating theological exchanges, but from the destructive misuse of religious language. What was at stake was the vitality of sapiential language and therefore the existence of the tradition itself. It is in the book of Job that these difficulties most noticeably emerge, as sages struggle to articulate a language that engages faith, revitalizes tradition, and recreates the world.

Chapter 2

METAPHORS OF COSMOLOGY AND MYTHIC PARADIGMS

1. *Metaphors of Cosmology in Ancient Near Eastern
and Biblical Literatures*

The Metaphor of Fertility. Intercourse, fathering/giving birth, mid-wifery, and parenting were ancient metaphors which shaped many myths of origins and maintenance. Tablet 1 of the *Enuma elish* begins with a theogony in which Apsu and Mummu-Tiamat, the primordial waters, commingle and give birth to the divine pair, Lahmu and Lahamu (the silt of the primeval ocean). They in turn produce Anshar and Kishar (the circular rims of heaven and earth).[1] Anshar and Kishar then produce Anu, the sky god, who fathers Nudimmud (Ea=Enki), great in wisdom and mighty in strength, without equal among the gods. When these gods disturb the peaceful tranquility of Apsu and Tiamat, the myth changes to one of conflict, involving the war between the younger gods and their primordial parents.[2] A similar theogony was produced in Ugarit[3] in which El was the 'Father of the gods',[4] and in Heliopolis of Egypt which details the origins of the Ennead.[5]

Gods were also the parents of humans, including both humanity in general and kings. In Sumer Ninhursaga was the earth-mother goddess, 'the mother of all children', both humans and gods. Called

1. Jacobsen, *The Treasures of Darkness*, 168.

2. *ANET*, 60-61.

3. André Caquot and Maurice Sznycer, *Ugaritic Religion* (Iconography of Religions 15; Leiden: Brill, 1980), 8.

4. Among El's epithets are several which point to the probable existence of a theogonic myth in at least an early phase of Canaanite religion: El and Asherah are the parents of the gods; El is *qnyn* ('our father') and *ab adm* (the 'Father of Humanity'), and the *bny bnwt* ('creator of creatures').

5. 'The Creation by Atum', *ANET*, 3.

'The Lady of the womb' and the 'Lady of form-giving', she was the power of the womb, nurturing the fetus to maturity. And as the midwife, she assisted at the time of birth to bring new life into the world.[1] However, her most important task was the engendering, care, and birthing of kings, before eventually giving them their insignia for rule.

According to Jacobsen the second millennium witnessed the rise of personal religion in Mesopotamia, with the metaphor of parents coming into prominent display.[2] The personal god was the father who engendered the worshippers, and the goddess the mother who gave them birth. They were also the caring parents who protected their children from demonic powers, brought luck and success, interceded with the gods, and guided in the proper paths. Indeed, this conception of personal religion was at the center of the crisis in Mesopotamian wisdom, as seen in *Ludlul bel nemeqi*[3] and 'The Babylonian Theodicy'.[4] Personal misfortune was seen as the inexplicable abandonment of the personal god or goddess, with no other recourse for the afflicted than to continue the lament in the hopes of returning divine protection and favor.

The metaphor of fertility was especially important in world maintenance myths of nature religions centering on the rhythm of fertility and sterility in creation.[5] In Sumer, Dumuzi's marriage to the goddess Inanna resulted in the fecundity of flocks and land.[6] However, his early death and descent to the underworld led to the sterility of nature. Inanna's weeping and search for his body led, at least in one text, to his return as the power in tree sap and vegetation, and thus the seasonal cycle of rebirth continued.[7]

The maintenance of world order in Ugaritic mythology revolved around a similar myth of fertility, featuring Baal and his consort

1. Jacobsen, *The Treasures of Darkness*, 104-109.
2. Jacobsen, *The Treasures of Darkness*, 152-64.
3. *ANET*, 596.
4. *ANET*, 602.
5. Foster McCurley, *Ancient Myths and Biblical Faith* (Philadelphia: Fortress, 1983), 73-124. Also see Othmar Keel, *The Symbolism of the Biblical World* (New York: Seabury, 1978), 201-202, for iconographic depictions of God's participation in the process of generation and birth.
6. The fertility metaphor, of which the myths of Dumuzi and Inanna were the most important expression, was the dominant one in Sumer in the fourth millennium (*The Treasures of Darkness*, 20-21).
7. McCurley, *Ancient Myths and Biblical Faith*, 73-75.

Anat.[1] The first part of the myth narrates Baal's defeat of Yam (Lotan, Judge River), the ruler of the seas and the prince of chaos. This action finally gains for Baal the rank of kingship, symbolized by the construction of his palace. On a mythic-cosmic level, the defeat of Yam and the building of the palace bring stability to the earth and secure fertility. The second part of the myth describes the conflict between Mot, prince of the underworld, and Baal, lord of the rainstorm, for rulership of the earth. Mot kills Baal and drags him into the underworld, whereupon sterility afflicts people, lands, and flocks. Going in search of Baal, lamenting and making intercession to El, Anat finds his body, buries him on Mt Zaphon, and slaughters animals as sacrifices to him. Anat eventually engages Mot in mortal combat and annihilates her lord's enemy. After Baal's resurrection, he resumes kingship over the earth, and the pair unite in sacred marriage, securing fertility once again. Representing a seasonal myth of the rainy and dry seasons, Baal's and Mot's respective periods of ruling over the earth, the recitation and ritual enactment maintain the eternal cycle of fertility and sterility. In this myth the metaphor of fertility, combined with those of conflict and word (El's edict which controls the spheres and times of reign for Baal, Yam, and Mot), maintains the created order.

A major epithet for El in the pre-Israelite tradition in Jerusalem, 'El, Creator (קנה) of Heaven and Earth', entered the Davidic–Zion tradition sometime during the monarchial period and remained a significant feature of the cultic *theologoumena* of Yahweh (Gen. 14.19, 22; Pss. 89.12 and 95.5).[2] Like El, Yahweh fathers

1. *ANET*, 129-42.

2. See the article by Martin Metzger who argues that *qoneh* means both 'owner' and 'creator' in creation contexts, for God possesses (therefore directs and oversees) what he creates ('Eigentumsdeklaration und Schöpfungsaussage', *Wenn nicht jetzt wann dann?* [ed. Hans-Georg Geyer *et al.*; Neukirchen: Neukirchener Verlag, 1983], 37-51). A three-line inscription found on the western hill in Jerusalem by Avigad in 1971 contains in the third line *qn'rs*, usually read 'creator of the earth'. Avigad assumes the preceding word, which is broken, is *'l* (EL), an identity supported by Patrick D. Miller, Jr. ('El, The Creator of Earth', *BASOR* 239 [1980] 43-46). Habel has pointed to the connection between this inscription and the epithet in Gen. 14.19 ('Yahweh, Maker of Heaven and Earth': A Study in Tradition Criticism', *JBL* 91 [1972] 321-27). This widespread epithet also has been found in a Hittite myth borrowed from Canaan in the divine name *Ikunirša*, in an 8th-century Karatepe list of gods (*'l qn'rs'*, in an Aramaic inscription from Palmyra (*['l qn ['Jr'[']J*); in four tessarae from Palmyra (*'lqnr'*), in an inscription from Hatra (*b'šmyn qnh dy r''*), and in a Neo-Punic inscription from Leptis Magna (*'l qn 'rṣ*). While the Karetepe text

offspring, especially Israel (Exod. 4.22-23; Hos. 11.1; Jer. 3.1–4.2)
and the Davidic son (2 Sam. 7; Ps. 89). In the first, Yahweh is the
father who engenders and provides loving nurture, an inheritance, and
discipline for the guidance of his people. In the second, the father-son
metaphor describes the origins of the king (Ps. 2) and especially the
relation between king and God, an enduring one of providential love
and discipline which could be strained but not ended. As the privileged
first-born, the Davidic king is exalted above all other rulers in a position of prominence and honor. And on his day of coronation God
speaks to the son, presumably through the oracle of a priest, and
announces: 'You are my son, this day I have begotten (ילד) you'
(Ps. 2.7). The sages of Israel extend this metaphor to include individuals, as seen in the presentation of wisdom as Yahweh's loving discipline for 'the son in whom he delights' (Prov. 3.11-12). Yet the
metaphor not only attributes this social role to God, but also intimates
physical generation.[1] God is not literally the father of Israel or David,
but the metaphor does evoke a status and relationship which gives
character, meaning and vision to religious language.

God is also the divine mother, whose epithet, 'God of Mercies',
derives from womb imagery (רחם = 'womb' = 'mercy').[2] God's
compassion for Ephraim, her 'darling child', is depicted in images of a
mother's tender feelings (Jer. 31.20), insuring that divine grace will
lead to Israel's redemption. Second Isaiah uses the image of a woman's
loving care for her infant child to speak of God's tender mercy for
Zion who feels abandoned in Babylonian exile (49.15). The birth
imagery is rather graphically displayed in Deut. 32.18 which portrays

associates the epithet with cursing, the other evidence, including Gen. 14, uses it in
the context of blessing. Thus, these appear to be dedicatory inscriptions to procure
the blessing of El (= Yahweh in Jerusalem) as creator (Miller, 'El, The Creator of
Earth', 43-45).

1. The attempt of many scholars, illustrated by von Rad in his 'Royal Ritual in
Judah' (*The Problem of the Hexateuch and Other Essays* [New York: McGraw–Hill,
1966], 222-31), to argue that kingship ritual involved only the notion of God's
adoption of the king as son at the day of coronation, is a partially misguided effort to
differentiate Israelite royal ideology from that of some ancient Near Eastern cultures,
especially Egypt, which tended to use father–son language to speak of kings'
divinity. While Israel did tend to deny divine status to its kings (Ps. 45 is a probable
exception), the metaphor is abused when rationalized in this fashion, for the
rationalization is based on a lapse into a literal interpretation which, of course, issues
from a misunderstanding of the nature of metaphor.

2. See Phyllis Trible, *God and the Rhetoric of Sexuality* (Philadelphia: Fortress,
1977).

God as the one who 'bore' (ילד) and 'gave birth' (חלל) to Israel (cf. Num. 11.12).

Significant for the sages is the depiction of God as the parent of Woman Wisdom in Prov. 8.22-31. In this hymn of self-praise Wisdom speaks of Yahweh giving birth (קנה) to her before the origins of the world and twice uses the expression of being 'brought forth' (חול), a term used for giving birth through the pain of contractions (Deut. 32.18; Job 39.1; Isa. 51.2; Ps. 90.2). This is one of the clearest cases of the use of ancient Near Eastern theogonic mythology by any Old Testament writer. Wisdom is metaphorically portrayed as a goddess who is the first[1] of God's creation, given birth by Yahweh before the beginning of the earth, before the mountains were shaped. This mythopoeic, metaphorical presentation of Wisdom establishes the authority of the tradition and undergirds its creative power. Through wisdom one returns to primal origins, enters the life-producing power of primordial activity, and continues to be sustained by ongoing creation.

Another significant use of fertility imagery involves Yahweh as the Lord of the womb, who brings about conception, creates and shapes the fetus, and delivers the child at birth. In the call of Jeremiah (1.4-10), Yahweh announces the predestination of the youth to be a prophet from the time he was in the womb. Even more directly, God speaks of having formed (יצר) him in the womb (בטן) and consecrated him to be a prophet before his birth (literally, 'before he came forth from the womb', רחם; cf. Ps. 139).[2] By contrast, in their reflection on and conceptualization of this metaphor, the conventional sages spoke of common origins and the moral responsibility of the well-to-do to care for the needs of the poor (Prov. 14.31; 17.5; 22.2; Job 31.13-15).

Archaeological excavations and Old Testament texts have demonstrated Israel's participation in the fertility metaphor primarily in popular religion. Legal proscription and prophetic invective against fertility practices demonstrate how important the mythos and practice of this tradition were to ordinary Israelites. Yet even the normative, canonical traditions give evidence of acceptable theological adaptations of the fertility metaphor by Israelite writers and tradents. While

---

1. First (ראשית) in the sense of chronology and quality, i.e. 'best'.
2. Elsewhere God is a midwife who delivers the newborn and places it upon the mother's breasts, an image used to speak of divine nurturing of life from its very inception (Pss. 7.6, 22.9-11).

normative Yahwism does not give God a female consort, the fertility metaphor was used to speak of God's relation to Israel: Yahweh is her husband. This was an especially favorite metaphor of Hosea (cf. especially ch. 2) which later entered the Jeremiah tradition (3.1–4.2; cf. Ezek. 16; Isa. 54.5-8). The courtship of Israel culminates in a marriage resulting in fertility, prosperity, and well-being, though the relationship threatens to disintegrate because of the wife's unfaithfulness. These prophetic examples, especially the bold formulation by Hosea, demonstrate the important adaptation of this mythical metaphor.

Besides the prophets, the sages also appropriated this mythical metaphor to speak of Woman Wisdom as the consort of God (cf. Wis. 6–9). Wisdom is a fertility goddess whose charm and seductive powers attract young students to follow after her. Thus she is the hierodule who looks out of her latticed window at foolish youths too easily seduced by the wiles of Woman Folly (Prov. 7.6-23),[1] and the fertility goddess who has constructed her temple and initiates her cult with a sacred festival to which the simple are invited (Prov. 9.1-6). She is both the life-giving deity who, like her divine prototypes (Maat, Isis, and Ishtar), holds in her right hand longevity and in her left wealth and honor (Prov. 3.18), and the Queen of Heaven who dispenses kingship, prosperity, and esteem to those who love her (Prov. 8.14-21). Those who answer her invitation find life, while those who spurn her favors experience death (8.32-36).[2]

This way of presenting creation in Israel (God gives birth to/fathers Israel, the Davidic king, wisdom, and the individual, and has as his consort Woman Wisdom and Israel) functions as a metaphorical model which appropriates but also breaks with the conventions of fertility religion. The theologians of Israel did not simply borrow the features of ancient Near Eastern fertility religions, but destabilized them with disorienting constructions which defied conventional understanding. Yahweh fathers or gives birth, but without the participation of a sexual consort. His consort is Woman Wisdom and Israel, but only in the realm of religious imagination. Of course the metaphor is absurd, but metaphors may be used to destroy convention in order to awaken

1. W.F. Albright, 'Some Canaanite–Phoenician Sources of Hebrew Wisdom', *SVT* 3 (1955), 1-15; and Gustav Boström, *Proverbiastudien* (Lunds Universitets Arsskrift, N.F. Avd. 1, 30/3; Lund: Gleerup, 1935).

2. Bernhard Lang, *Frau Weisheit* (Düsseldorf: Patmos, 1975).

new insight into the nature of reality. Reality is redescribed, and in its redescription is transformed into a new creation. In this case the language of fertility myths is used to move Yahwism beyond the orbit of the divinization of fertility and human sexuality in the direction of a transcendent God in control of but not equated with the processes of reproduction. And yet the metaphor is not a rejection of fertility, for this non-sexual God is intimately involved in the medium of reproduction which leads to the rhythm of life and death. The strict dichotomy between Canaanite nature religion and Israelite salvation history is a misconstrual of the biblical witness. Certainly the prophet Hosea, for example, should make this distortion obvious.

Further, the model points to a personal God who carefully molds the fetus and providentially cares for offspring as a parent does for a child, an unusual though not unparalleled concept in ancient Near Eastern religions.[1] Yahweh is involved in the life of Israel, the dynasty of David, and even individuals to create, care for, and redeem. Grace for Israel, the king, and the individual is rooted in the image of the caring and forgiving parent.

The Metaphor of Artistry. A second metaphor of creation in the ancient Near East is artistry. The creator is an artisan who fashions an object into an elegant piece of work. In the *Enuma elish* Marduk 'squares Apsu's quarter', 'measures the dimensions of Apsu', builds the palace of the great gods (the Esharra), and 'constructs stations' for the gods to occupy.[2] In the Old Testament the world is depicted as a house erected on foundations (Pss. 18.7; 82.5) with cosmic pillars, usually the mountains (Job 9.6; Ps. 75.3), supporting the vaulted roof (firmament or sky: cf. Gen. 1.6-7; Job 37.18).[3] For the sages wisdom is the design and skill of the artisan God necessary for creating and maintaining the well-ordered world:

---

1. The idea of a personal god/goddess, the specific one depending on one's profession and social class, is an impotant feature of Akkadian religion (cf. A. Leo Oppenheim, *Ancient Mesopotamia* [Chicago: University of Chicago Press, 1964], 171-227; and W.G. Lambert, 'Morals in Ancient Mesopotamia', *JEOL* 15 [1957–58, 184-96). However, the idea of the creator of the cosmos as the personal deity of an individual was usually reserved for royalty.

2. *ANET* 67, Tab. IV, 11.140ff. and V, 11.1ff.

3. Other examples of God as skilled architect and builder include Isa. 40.12; 48.13.

The Lord by wisdom founded the earth; by understanding he established the
heavens;
by his knowledge the deeps broke forth, and the clouds drop down the dew
(Prov. 3.19-20).[1]

In the personification of divine wisdom, she becomes the *technitas*, the
'artificer', who constructs and orders the world (Wis. 7.22).[2]

The building of a human house imitates this mythical metaphor, for
humans reactualize divine creation in constructing a world for their
habitation.[3] Thus the activity of house-building is normally accompanied by rituals and celebrations designed to place the structure
within the durative order of the cosmos. Through ritual and
mythopoeic imagination, the architect and builders return to the
primal origins of creation and draw from its power in planning and
erecting the dwelling. The design and skill to accomplish the construction are due to the divine wisdom of which these artisans partake.[4]

In more sacred undertakings, gods and rulers erect and maintain
temples and sanctuaries, actions that also are considered to be world-
building and maintaining. The portrait statue of Gudea of Lagash
represents the king as an architect, sitting before Ningursu with the
plan for the god's temple. The inscription indicates the temple was
built at the good pleasure of the Lord of Lagash and according to his
command.[5] In a dream Gudea had seen the tablet of Ninsaba, the god
of grain and scribal wisdom, on which were inscribed the plans for the
temple.[6] In a similar text, Solomon is given divine wisdom in a dream
at Gideon (1 Kgs 3.1-15), which would have included the knowledge
and requisite skill to construct the temple in Jerusalem according to

1. See Ps. 104.24.
2. This image of wisdom as artificer is possibly suggested by Prov. 8.30 where
wisdom is the *'amon*, either 'young child' or less likely 'master artisan' (R.B.Y.
Scott, 'Wisdom in Creation: The *'Amon* of Proverbs VIII 30', *VT* 10 [1960], 213-
23).
3. Mircea Eliade, *Cosmos and History*, 6ff. While no myth of origins has
survived from Ugarit, epithets of El point to his role as creator, including one crafting
metaphor: *bny bnwt* (17. i 25), literally 'builder of things built'.
4. Thus the artisans of the tabernacle and temple and their contents (Exod. 28.3;
31.6; 35.10; 36.1, 2, 4, 8; 1 Chron. 22.15; 2 Chron. 2.6, 12, 13) are 'wise', i.e.
possess the skill and knowledge to carry out the divine plans for the construction of
sacred buildings.
5. *ANEP*, no. 749; discussed by Keel, *The Symbolism of the Biblical World*, 17.
6. See *SAHG*, 66: 'Ninsaba, unless you ordain it, man builds no house, he builds
no city, he builds no palace.' Compare this to Ps. 127.1a: 'Unless the Lord builds
the house, those who build it labor in vain.'

divine design (1 Kgs 5.22-27). The elaborate description of the temple
plans and their execution dominates the central portion of the
Solomonic narrative (1 Kgs 5–8). The ritual dedication followed by
the proclamation of Deuteronomic law anchor both temple and society
within the order of the cosmos.[1] And through temple ritual and the
rule of justice, the duration of world and society is secured.

In the appropriation of this metaphor the sages speak of the
necessity of Yahweh's construction of a house (physical dwelling or
perhaps family) for it to endure (Ps. 127.1). They also use the
metaphor of house-building in Prov. 9.1-6, the first of two strophes
comprising an elaborate dualistic depiction of creation and chaos, life
and death, and wisdom and folly. In the initial strophe Woman
Wisdom is the goddess of life who constructs her elaborate and
spacious house (or temple), supported by seven pillars, pointing to its
elegant quality, stability, and perfection of design. To dedicate her
new edifice, she sends out her priestesses to invite the unlearned to
partake of her festive banquet of wisdom and well-being.[2] By this
appropriation of the mythical, crafting metaphor, the sages incorporate their tradition within the generative origins of reality. By
accepting the invitation to learn, one takes the path to wisdom and
participates in the ongoing, beneficent order of creation. In this fashion the sages constructed a social reality which interpreted, defined
and legitimated their world.[3]

---

1. This is clearly expressed in the *Enuma elish* in which the building of the
Esagila—'The house of the foundation of heaven and earth', Marduk's temple in
Babylon—is positioned within the myth of the creation of the world (*ANET*, 68-69).
After the Esagila had been built by the Anunnaki along with their own shrines, a
festival and rites of dedication are held, and the norms for the ordering of heaven and
earth are fixed. Temple-raising and ritual establish and maintain world order. Baal's
gaining of kingship, coupled with the building and ritual dedication of his palace
following the defeat of Yam, also maintain the order of the cosmos in Ugaritic
mythology (*ANET*, 129-38). In the Canaanite myth, Kothar wa-Khasis is the divine
craftsman who fashions the magically empowered weapons of war (*ANET*, 131) for
Baal to use in his impending battle and constructs him a magnificent palace of silver
and gold (*ANET*, 133-35).
2. The same contrast between wisdom and folly coupled with the house-building
image is found in Prov. 14.1: 'Wisdom builds her house, but folly with her own
hands tears it down.'
3. A more elaborate image is the depiction of the world as a city with walls and
gates. The sages also use this form of the metaphor to tell of Teacher Wisdom's
search to find and invite humans to learn from her. Thus she takes the paths to the
city and issues her call, standing by its gates, ascending its walls, walking its streets,

The metaphor of artistry is also prominent in myths of creation of the human race. In Egypt Khnum is the potter who shapes humans on his wheel from clay, while Enki (= Akkadian Ea) is the craftsman who creates form and shape. In the *Enuma elish*, Marduk, deciding to 'fashion artful works', turns to Ea and says,

> Blood I will mass and cause bones to be. I will establish a savage, 'man' shall be his name.
> Verily, savage-man I will create. He shall be charged with the service of the gods
> That they might be at ease![1]

In Israel God is both the potter who shapes clay into a human being (Gen. 2.7) and the weaver who knits together bones and sinews (Ps. 139.13). Thus human beings are the 'work of God's hand', the artistically shaped creature in whom there is great delight. Indeed the 'image (צלם, דמות) of God' in Gen. 1.26-28 presents humans as an 'idol' or 'image' created by skilled priests. This crafting model is used to subvert the conventional ancient Near Eastern understanding of idol-making, and resides, for example, at the basis of the conceptual formation of the polemic against idol satire in the Wisdom of Solomon (chs. 13–15). God is the one who by means of Wisdom, the grand artificer, crafts all of creation, including human beings in the divine image. The life and beauty of humans is contrasted with the image-makers who abuse the function of created elements to shape idols which neither breathe nor move.

In these instances of the artistry metaphor, what is suggested is that the creation is an aesthetically pleasing, indeed beautiful artwork which is to be admired, enjoyed, and praised. In the priestly narrative (Gen. 1.1–2.4a), God's evaluation of each major feature of creation as 'good' (*ṭôb*) and summary description of the entire cosmos as 'very good' (*ṭôb me'ōd*) is not primarily a moral but more an aesthetic judgment issuing forth in joyous praise of creation. The proper human

---

and entering its markets (Prov. 1.20-22; 8.1-4). This image is used to speak of wisdom's presence in the world, especially in the one inhabited by human beings. According to Prov. 8.22-31, Woman Wisdom is the child of the creator before whom she dances in grace and beauty. Indeed it is the dancing goddess who metaphorically expresses the dynamic form of wisdom as aesthesis. It is her cosmic dance which creates and sustains the inhabited world in which she delights. This is another image of the artistry metaphor (see Othmar Keel, *Die Weisheit Spielt vor Gott* [Göttingen: Vandenhoeck & Ruprecht, 1974]).

1. *ANET*, 68.

response is twofold. First the wondrous beauty of creation elicits human praise and thankful joy, a response often encapsulated in Israel's hymns (Pss. 8; 19; 33; 104; 147; 148). Indeed, elegant praise is one means by which humans participate in securing the continuation of the world (Ps. 22.3—God is 'enthroned on the praises of Israel'). The other response is human craftsmanship. In the production of works of beauty, whether house or poem, humans participate in the power of creation and aid in its continuation. Each work of art is a minute world, an aesthesis, which establishes and becomes an ordered creation.

The Metaphor of Word. The third major metaphor of creation in the Old Testament is word.[1] The power of language is a common theme in ancient Near Eastern literature. This power was captured in a variety of religious genres: magical incantations, blessings and curses, prophetic speech, names, edicts, and myths, to mention some of the more significant expressions.[2] Creation and world maintenance resulting from the power of language takes four primary forms: word (including naming), wisdom, edict, and breath (spirit). The most striking example of creation by word in the ancient Near East is 'The Memphite Theology'. The god Ptah conceived in his heart (which is also Horus) what he wished to create and then spoke the mental image into being and named the newly created object.[3] Thoth, the god of wisdom, became Ptah's tongue which spoke the creative word giving existence to all things, including the gods. Here heart and tongue are the creative agency in what is a clearly expressed statement of creation *ex nihilo*.

In Mesopotamia, creation by word found expression in the creative and destructive power of the edict which maintained the order of the universe. The universe was structured as a state, operating according

1. See Lorenz Dürr, *Die Wertung des göttlichen Wortes im Alten Testament und im antiken Orient* (MVAG 42; Leipzig: Hinrichs, 1938).

2. According to Jacobsen (*Treasure of Darkness*, 15), 'The creative power of the word underlies all Mesopotamian religious literature.' Religious language evoked the presence of the gods and created reality through its verbal representations. Incantations drove away evil powers, hymns activated the power of the immanent numinous, and laments actualized divine presence momentarily lost.

3. *ANET*, 4-6. 'Indeed, all the divine order really came into being through what the heart thought and the tongue commanded' (*ANET*, 6). See Viktor Notter, *Biblischer Schöpfungsbericht und ägyptische Schöpfungsmythen* (Stuttgarter Bibelstudien 68; Stuttgart: KBW, 1974), 23-24.

to divinely established laws (*me*), with the gods taking institutional roles for governance.[1] Order was not an eternal state originating at creation, but rather something to be achieved through the integration of competing and at times conflicting divine wills. This ordering of wills was set forth as a political state, the supreme authority for which was the divine assembly.[2] The decisions of the assembly normally fell into two spheres: judgment and sentencing of wrongdoers and the election and deposing of human and divine officers, especially rulers. The decision of the divine assembly was sovereign and supreme. The fates it established, fair or not, remained unchallengeable.

In the First Babylonian period, Marduk became the young warrior who saved the gods from the wrath of Tiamat and created the world.[3] As a condition of his serving as the champion of the assembly in the battle against the dragon, Marduk demanded and received the creative and destructive power of the edict of the assembly. Thus in the *Enuma elish* the great gods in the Assembly chose Marduk as their king and gave him the power of supreme decree. In both the ordering of the cosmos and the decision to create humankind, Marduk's decrees became authoritative law.

Law in Mesopotamia was anchored to the foundations of creation. The best-known example is contained in the prologue of the 'Code of Hammurabi'.[4] In primordial beginnings, when Anu and Enlil ordained Marduk ruler over humankind and exalted Babylon to the position of supremacy in the world, the institution of kingship and Hammurabi were chosen to establish justice in the land. With this legitimation, Hammurabi issues a lawcode, anchored in the foundations of heaven and earth, in order to bring order and well-being to the people. The code embodies the cosmic power of creation to shape and sustain Babylonian society.

In Israel the word of God was a cosmic power which created and sustained all reality. The classic presentation of creation by word is the priestly creation narrative in Gen. 1.1–2.4a. Here in a repetitious and therefore more efficacious pattern eight actions of creation are

---

1. Thorkild Jacobsen, 'Mesopotamia', *The Intellectual Adventure of Ancient Man* (Chicago: University of Chicago Press, 1946), 125-222.

2. Jacobsen, *The Treasures of Darkness*, 86-91.

3. Marduk replaces An who earlier in Sumerian theology was the head of the divine assembly of the gods who were his children. Through An's command anarchy was stilled and reality was ordered.

4. *ANET*, 163-80.

structured into a six-day period.[1] Through speaking, all creation comes into existence, and through naming, all things are given their place and function within God's majestic order. The priestly word guarantees the stability of the cosmic order (cf. Ps. 33). As creator Yahweh's decree (חוק) established the positions and functions of the various elements of creation. Jeremiah 31.35-36 points to the 'fixed order' (חוק) of creation (cf. Jer. 33.25), while Job 28.26 and 38.33 speak of the ordinances of the heavenly bodies and meteorological phenomena (Job 28.26; 38.33) and mention the prescribed limits imposed upon Sea to keep his floods from overwhelming God's created order (cf. Prov. 8.29; Jer. 5.22).

While wisdom is the skill and artistry to shape an object of beauty when used as a part of the crafting metaphor, it is also intelligence, knowledge, and the ordering power of rational thought expressed through power-laden, elegantly formed language. In the *Enuma elish* it was Ea, the god of wisdom, who gave counsel to Marduk, created humankind, and imposed upon it the service of the gods, thus establishing their place and function.[2] For Israel, wisdom is the ordering capacity used by God in the creation of the world. In Sirach 24 Woman Wisdom proceeds out of the mouth of God and is the life-giving mist which watered the earth (cf. Gen. 2.4b-6). Thus the tradition of the sages was anchored in cosmic beginnings and became the means by which they learned the secrets of the universe, came to a knowledge of God, and obtained life in its abundance (Wis. 7.15-22). As the revelation of God, Wisdom orders the cosmos and human society and provides instruction in the knowledge of God. Present in all of God's works, she points the way to the creator (Wis. 1.7; 8.1-4; 9.17-18).

Drawing on this metaphor of creation, the sages attributed great significance to both the creative and destructive power of language. For the wise, language was not an inert tool merely describing proper behavior, but an order-creating, life-sustaining power when used correctly and well and a destructive force when formulated by the fool.

> The mouth of the righteous is a fountain of life, but the mouth of the wicked conceals violence (Prov. 10.1).

---

1. See Walter Brueggemann, 'The Kerygma of the Priestly Writers', *The Vitality of Old Testament Traditions* (ed. W. Brueggeman; Atlanta: John Knox, 1975).
2. *ANET*, 68.

The tongue of the righteous is choice silver; the mind of the wicked is of little worth (10.20).

The lips of the righteous feed many, but fools die for lack of sense (10.21).

The words of the wicked lie in wait for blood, but the mouth of the upright delivers people (12.6).

Death and life are in the power of the tongue, and those who love it will eat its fruits (18.21).

Indeed it was the recognition of the power inherent within language to create worlds or to destroy them that led to the designation of the sage as the 'silent one', that is one who used words prudently and with discretion. By contrast, the fool was the 'heated one' who spoke and acted presumptuously and without discretion (Prov. 17.27; cf. 14.17, 30; 15.1, 4, 18; and 16.23).

Related to the metaphor of creation by word is the image of God breathing life into creation. In a hymnic section of 'The instruction for King Meri-Ka-Re', the creation and providential care of humanity is extolled in a variety of interlinking metaphors, including that of the animating breath of the creator:

> Well directed are men, the cattle of the god. He made heaven and earth according to their desire, and he repelled the water-monster. He made the breath of life (for) their nostrils. They who have issued from his body are his images.[1]

The same metaphor is frequent in creation and wisdom texts in the Old Testament: the 'breath' (נשמה), or 'spirit' (רוח) of God gives life and sustenance to all that exists. In the J narrative, 'the Lord God formed man of dust from the ground, and breathed into his nostrils the breath of life'. Humanity's existence results from the infusion of Yahweh's animating breath (Isa. 42.5), an indication that life is totally dependent on God and possible only as divine gift. At death vital breath returns to God (Qoh. 12.7). In the introduction to the flood narrative, God limits the time allotted for the possession of the divine breath by humans to 120 years (Gen. 6.3). Likewise, God's breath gives life to all of creation (Ps. 104.30), and should God draw in his breath all of creation would wither and die (Ps. 104.29). The Wisdom of Solomon

---

1. *ANET*, 417. For other Egyptian examples, see Notter, *Biblischer Schöpfungsbericht*, 145-49.

identifies wisdom with this life-giving and ordering spirit of God which permeates all of creation (1.6-7).[1]

The metaphor of divine word, edict, and wisdom eventually came to signify in scribal wisdom the written Torah which was the creative and sustaining power in nature, social life and individual life, the medium of divine revelation, and the source of true wisdom. This transition from creation by word to the Torah as the incorporation of the divine commandment is expressed most elegantly in two texts: Psalm 19 and Sirach 24. In the first piece, the initial strophe (1-4a) describes in majestic terms the revelation of God in creation through the 'speech' of nature. However, in the second half of the poem (strophes 3 and 4), the psalmist praises the law's incomparable value in leading away from evil and breaking the dominion of presumptuous sin. Instead of an abrupt transition between two separate texts awkwardly pieced together, the psalm is actually an elegantly crafted piece which speaks of the embodiment of natural revelation in the words of the Torah. Sirach 24 is a hymn of self-praise by Woman Wisdom who originated from the mouth of God, took up residence among the nation of Israel and became identified with the temple service and Law of Moses. The identification of wisdom with Torah is a common theme in Sirach's collection.

The metaphorical model of creation by word rejects the view that the creator is a *deus absconditus*, but rather portrays a God who is revealed in the 'language' creation speaks, i.e. in the order and beauty of created works. Scribal wisdom conceptualized this feature in viewing the Torah as the embodiment of the creative, life-giving word (command and will) of the creator (cf. Sir. 24). Further, the word model invalidates any view of God as capricious. God establishes justice as the order of creation and acts righteously in administering cosmic rule. The model also eliminates the view that creation is incalculable, for the creator issues edicts and laws designed to order elements and to provide guidance for existence. There are consistencies or patterns of action and behavior characterizing creation to which the sages point as a result of their experience and observation of the world.[2]

---

1. The divine breath, especially in the idiom, 'the blast (of the breath) of thy nostrils', is also a destructive force against wickedness and chaos (Ps. 18.15; Exod. 15.8).

2. Von Rad, *Wisdom in Israel*, 74ff.

2. The Metaphor of Struggle and the Mythic Paradigm
of the Battle with Chaos

A fourth significant metaphor for creation is struggle.[1] Creation concludes a struggle between the creator and primeval chaos, usually depicted as a monstrous dragon or serpent residing in the cosmic ocean. Important for our concerns is the literary pattern for the mythic tradition in which this metaphor operates: battle, victory over chaos, kingship, creation, and judgment. As we shall see, this mythic tradition provides the external structure for contextualizing the dramatic enactment of the book of Job.

The Metaphor of Struggle. While the metaphor of battle is rare in Egyptian literature, there are several important examples. The most detailed use of this metaphor occurs in a collection of papyri which begins with the following general introduction:

THE BEGINNING OF THE BOOK OF OVERTHROWING APOPHIS, THE ENEMY OF RE AND THE ENEMY OF King Wen-nofer—life, prosperity, health!—the justified, performed in the course of the every day in the Temple of Amon-Re, Lord of the Thrones of the Two Lands, presiding over Karnak.[2]

This text refers to the journey of the sun god Re, accompanied by his retinue in the royal barque, across the skies above the earth during the day and beneath the horizon at night. As the barque enters the dark cosmic ocean in the west during the evening, it is set upon by Apophis (*3pp*), the monstrous dragon, seeking to devour the sun and thus destroy creation. It is the task of the god Seth, who is among Re's retinue, to repel the monster and thereby ensure the safe journey through the dark night, until at dawn the barque enters the safe haven of the sky once again. To ensure the defeat of Apophis, Egyptian temples sought to empower the sun god by ritual and word to defeat his archenemy, thereby securing the order of creation. Ritual and recitation empowered the earthly king to defeat the nation's enemies, considered embodiments of chaos.[3]

---

1. For a detailed discussion, see McCurley, *Ancient Myths and Biblical Faith*, 12-57.

2. *ANET*, 6-7. While the papyrus dates from approximately 310 BCE, the language and theology of the myth push it back some two millennia.

3. The identification of Apophis with the Hyksos was made in the Second Intermediate period. The connection of the chaos dragon with Egypt in the Old Testament is a further case of this historicizing of myth (Ps. 74.14; Ezek. 29.3-5).

The creation section of the manuscript begins with the origins of Re, followed by creation as word, spitting, masturbation, shedding of tears, and birth (the theogony of the Ennead). The Ennead, composed of nine ruling gods, plus Horus, are those 'rich in magic' who are directed to destroy Re's enemies, collectively embedded in Apophis.

This text was accompanied by the ritual of placing a drawn figure of Apophis into a box bearing his name. The box was then burned, wiped with the left foot, and spat on while saying four times: 'Re is triumphant over thee, O Apophis!' and 'Pharaoh—life, prosperity, health—is triumphant over his enemies!' Placed in another box are the names of Pharaoh's enemies, including those of their parents and children, following the name of Apophis. Ritual burning occurred at sunset and again at sunrise. By word and ritual, Apophis and his historical incarnations were defeated and the order of nature and kingdom preserved.

The myth of the repelling of the dragon also entered Egyptian mortuary religion.[1] Found on coffins in the Middle Kingdom and later in the Egyptian Book of the Dead, the myth provided magical words to enable the deceased to negotiate their way through the dark haunts of the netherworld inhabited by Apophis, before they enter the afterlife. This myth secured the continued existence of an individual, by unleashing the power of incantation to re-enact Re's defeat of Apophis. Each sunrise signalled the creator's defeat of Apophis, the recreation of the world, and the gift of eternal life.

While the above formulation describes the maintenance of social and cosmic stability, one wisdom text, 'The instruction for King Meri-Ka-Re', originating in the First Intermediate period and used in the king's installation, suggests the battle with Apophis may also have dealt with world origins.[2] A wisdom instruction in which the deceased father of Meri-Ka-Re admonishes his son on the proper course of rule, the teaching was set within the Sed festival, celebrating and ensuring the peaceful, orderly transition of power.[3] The appearance of the new king signaled, then, the strengthening of order threatened by the death of the previous ruler. The order of society and nature was ensured.

---

1. *ANET*, 11-12.
2. *ANET*, 414-18.
3. See Leo G. Perdue, 'The Testament of David and Royal Egyptian Instructions', *Scripture in Context II* (ed. William W. Hallo, James C. Moyer and Leo G. Perdue; Winona Lake, IN: Eisenbrauns, 1983), 79-96.

In this teaching world origins and maintenance are both described (*ANET*, 417), with the conflict metaphor figuring prominently in both. Kingship and therefore the social order of Egypt are grounded in and maintained by the eternal order (Maat) of creation. The ritual passage of crown prince to the throne *and* the proper rule by the king are equally necessary for the preservation of social and cosmic order. This demonstrates that for the sages of Egypt proper and wise behavior, especially by but not limited to the king, created and maintained cosmic and social order.[1] The mythic pattern includes Re's victory over Apophis, his re-emergence from the cosmic ocean as divine ruler of the cosmos, his journey across the heavens during the day to establish justice, and the recreation of the earth. And this same pattern is actualized in royal ideology, especially in texts referring to the New Year's enthronement of the king whose role inaugurates a new period of justice and recreation of the earth.

The mythology of Egyptian kingship included the struggle with and victory over chaos in the myths of Horus and Seth.[2] The mythic narrative begins with Seth's killing of Osiris, the father of Horus. When Horus comes to avenge his father and fight for the throne of Egypt, Seth takes the form of a red hippopotamus and in the battle that rages is finally harpooned by Horus. With the defeat of Seth and the ascent of Horus to the throne, well-being is obtained for Egypt. Normally the myth was enacted during the enthronement of a new king. The victory over Seth secured order during the reign of the king, protecting him and his kingdom from the threats of historical and mythical enemies.

The classic expression of the battle metaphor occurs in Akkadian mythology, especially in the *Enuma elish*.[3] The present text most probably represents an adaptation of an older Sumerian theogony clearly evidenced in the initial section of the poem. The present form of the myth describes the ascendancy of Marduk, the god of Babylon, to kingship over the divine council prior to the act of creation.[4] This

---

1. Wolfgang Helck, *Die Lehre für König Merikare* (Wiesbaden: Harrossowitz, 1977); Perdue, 'The Testament of David', 85-87.

2. See Henri Frankfort, *Kingship and the Gods* (Chicago: University of Chicago Press), 36-47, 101-39.

3. See Jacobsen, *The Treasures of Darkness*, 165ff.

4. The myth is usually interpreted as the empire theology of Hammurabi. As Hammurabi ascended to kingship over the Babylonian empire, so Marduk rose to the position of king over the gods (H.W.F. Saggs, *The Greatness that was Babylon*

royal status resulted from Marduk's defeat of Tiamat, the chaos monster. Following victory, Marduk created the world and assigned to the gods their places and roles in the cosmos. Then Marduk's temple is built by the grateful gods, his rule is initiated by a festive banquet, and he is given fifty names which encapsulate his roles as creator, sustainer, provider, and head of the divine assembly. The constitutive elements of the pattern or metaphorical model at work in this myth are battle, victory over chaos, kingship, judgment and creation.

In the first millennium this myth was recited on the fourth day of the New Year's festival (*akitu*) at the time of the spring equinox and was designed to secure the order of creation and society. The ever-present and threatening Tiamat comes forth each year to challenge and do battle with the divine hero of Babylon.[1] The enthronement of the king was grounded in this mythos of creation, leading to the maintenance of legal, historical, and natural order for Babylonian society.

Excavations at Ugarit have not yielded a myth of origins, though the evidence of epithets of El point to the probable existence of this type of myth in an earlier period. Nor is El directly involved in the wars of Baal and Anat with Mot and Yam. However, the narrative of Sanchuniaton describes the birth of the old gods and El's gaining of kingship by emasculating his father, Shamem (= Uranos). This plot is present in the Hittite Kumarbi myth[2] and the theogony of Hesiod. El is the Divine Warrior who fights for his place in the pantheon of the old gods.[3] Taking his sister as his consort, he wages war against his father

---

[New York: The New American Library, 1962], 387ff.). The political order of the empire reflects the moral and natural order of creation (Jacobsen, *The Treasures of Darkness*, 191).

1. The myth was enacted as a cultic drama. This sacred action during the Akitu festival held at New Year was seen as the means of ritually assuring Marduk's victory and the recreating of the order of the cosmos and society. Politically construed the myth and sacred drama maintain Babylon's military power.

2. For a translation, see *ANET*, 120-25.

3. See James Barr, 'Philo of Byblos and His "Phoenician History"', *BJRL* (1957), 17-68; Frank Cross, *Canaanite Myth and Hebrew Epic* (Cambridge, MA: Harvard University Press, 1973), 40-43; Jürgen Ebach, *Weltentstehung und Kulturentwicklung bei Philo von Byblos* (BWANT 108; Stuttgart: Kohlhammer, 1979); Otto Eissfeldt, *Ras Schamra und Sanchunjaton* (Beiträge zur Religionsgeschichte des Altertums 4; Halle: Max Niemeyer, 1939); and Conrad E. L'Heureux, *Rank among the Canaanite Gods* (HSM 21; Missoula: Scholars Press, 1979), 29-48. Ebach deals only with the first two sections of the myth, the origins of the world and the development of culture, and not the myth of succession involving the battle of the gods for rulership. In his *Praeparatio evangelica* (9.20–10.55),

Shamem ('heaven'), on behalf of his mother Ars ('earth'). After subduing his father, El emasculates him and takes his place as the head of the pantheon. This latter evidence points to the widespread mythical theme of younger gods emasculating their fathers in order to replace them as kings over creation. El then became the creator whose sexual potency populated heaven and earth.[1]

While the earlier generations of this theogony are not present in any of the Ugaritic texts, El is the king of the gods who possesses the power of decree. He removes and appoints kings, and the gods normally do obeisance before him. And as head of the divine council, El dwells on the Mount of Assembly (*hursanu*).[2] At the base of this sacred mountain was the source of the cosmic waters. The symbolism of cosmic waters, sacred mountain, and divine edict suggests they are the means by which the stability of the created order is maintained.

Marvin Pope has presented a controversial case for the existence of a similar theme of conflict in Ugaritic literature in which Baal castrates El. Pope argues that the conflict between El and Baal may result from El's emasculation and displacement by Baal as active ruler of the

---

Eusebius of Caesarea includes long excerpts and information from the 'Phoenician History' written by Philo of Byblos. Philo claims he has translated a much older work of a certain priest of Beirut, Sanchuniaton, who lived before the time of the Trojan War, i.e. the latter part of the Late Bronze Age. However, Hartmut Gese, among others, questions this early date and instead places the material in the late Assyrian period, i.e. the 7th century BCE (*Die Religionen Altsyriens, Altarabiens und der Mandäer* [Die Religionen der Menschheit 10; Stuttgart: Kohlhammer, 1970], 31-33). While the author knew the Theogony of Hesiod and uses euhemeristic explanation, there is little reason to regard Philo's attribution of the myth to a Phoenician priest as fictional, as for example, P. Nautin has argued ('Sanchuniathon chez Philon de Byblos et chez Porphyre', *RB* 56 (1949), 259-73). For a convenient collection of the fragments of the myth, see F. Jacob, *Die Fragmente der griechischen Historiker* (Leiden: Brill, 1958), 802-24. For related myths see M.W. West, *Hesiod: Theogony* (Oxford: Clarendon, 1966); H.G. Güterbock, *Kumarbi, Mythen vom churritischen Kronos* (Zürich: Europaverlag, 1946); and H. Otten, 'Ein kanaanäischer Mythus aus Bogazköy', *MIO* 1 (1953), 125-50.

1. However, Philo later mentions that kingship passes from El to Zeus (= Hadad), apparently a peaceful transition of power without conflict. If so, there is no evidence to argue for conflict between El and Hadad (= Baal) on the basis of this myth. Further, the two generations of gods preceding El are not mentioned in the Ugaritic texts (L'Heureux, *Rank among the Canaanite Gods*, 46ff.).

2. The term in Akkadian means both 'mountain' and 'place of the river ordeal' (cf. E. Theodore Mullen, *The Assembly of the Gods* [HSS 24; Missoula: Scholars Press, 1980], 130-31).

earth and head of the assembly.[1] In support of Pope's thesis, it is clear that El is old, physically weak, and even intimidated by the fearsome appearance of Yam's messengers and the threats of Anat the Warrior goddess.[2] Further, Anat's and Asherah's proclamation, 'Baal is our king', could reflect a rejection of El's rulership. The conflict between El and Baal is evidenced in El's decree granting kingship to Yam in III AB C,[3] the reference to both Yam and Mot as the 'beloved' (*mdd, ydd*) of El, Yam's and Mot's status as the 'sons of El' (while Baal is usually the 'Son of Dagan'), and El's decree making Baal the prisoner of Yam. One particular myth even presents the efforts of El to plan and direct the death of Baal (CTA 12).[4] On the other hand, El laments over the death of Baal and its tragic implications for people and land, and then rejoices and takes his ease at his resurrection. However, El's fluctuating support of and antipathy towards Baal may represent the necessary function of maintaining stability in the universe, and not necessarily a previous battle leading to the older god's emasculation and displacement as king of the gods.[5] The tempestuous Baal must be limited by El, if a fragile order in the universe is to be achieved. In any case the Baal cycle presents Baal, not El, as the conqueror of Yam in the struggle to attain kingship and maintain world order.[6]

In the Baal Myth, the storm god of fertility maintains the seasonal order of the cosmos by defeating Yam, ruler of the seas. With his region legitimated by the construction of his palace, the order of the creation continues. Mot challenges Baal, leading to an eventual divi-

---

1. Pope even contends Baal banishes El to the underworld, where he dwells at the source of the two rivers (*El in the Ugaritic Texts* [SVT 2; Leiden: Brill, 1955], 92-104). Accordingly, El is a *deus otiosus*, who retains his former titles but has lost his place as the head of the pantheon. He is supported by Umberto Cassuto, *The Goddess Anath* (Jerusalem: Magnes, 1971); Arvid Kapelrud, *Baal in the Ras Shamra Texts* (Copenhagen: G.E.C. Gad, 1952); and Ulf Oldenburg, *The Conflict between El and Ba'al in Canaanite Religion* (Leiden: Brill, 1969).

2. Pope argues El is impotent, though his fathering of Dawn and Dusk in 'The Birth of the Gracious Gods' would seem to stand at odds this contention. Pope counters with the unlikely contention that the ritual preceding intercourse was designed to give the old god sexual potency (*El in the Ugaritic Texts*, 35-36).

3. Yam is given the command to drive Baal from the throne (CTA 1.21-22).

4. See T.H. Gaster 'The harrowing of Baal', *Acta Or* 16 (1937), 41-48.

5. Those rejecting Pope's thesis include Frank Cross, *Canaanite Myth and Hebrew Epic*; and Conrad E. L'Heureux, *Rank among the Canaanite Gods*.

6. See John Gray, *The Legacy of Canaan* (SVT 5; Leiden: Brill), 27ff.; and J.C.L. Gibson, *Canaanite Myths and Legends* (Edinburgh: T. & T. Clark, 1977), 7ff.

sion of rule: Baal is king during the rainy season, while Mot rules the earth during the dry season. Thus to the cycle of annual cosmic war (Baal vs. Yam) is added the theme of seasonal change and alternating seven-year periods of rain and drought (Baal vs. Mot). El's role as head of the divine assembly gives him the authority to issue decrees which maintain a fragile order, determining the times and spheres of rule for the three younger gods: Baal the land for six months, Mot the netherworld and for six months the land, and Yam eternal master of the seas.[1] While the pattern of this world maintenance myth varies slightly in terms of order from the *Enuma elish*, the major components are the same: battle, victory over chaos, judgment, kingship, and recreation. However, in the present form of the Baal Cycle, the pattern is partially repeated in the second half: defeat, battle, victory over death, judgment, enthronement, and recreation (resurrection). The major new element is the defeat of Baal which is necessary to initiate the second part of the myth. The myth was probably the text for a sacred drama enacted during the Canaanite New Year's festival which ritually revitalized the generative powers of creation, and through the ritual of the king's enthronement secured the stability and well-being of Canaanite society.[2]

Yahweh's battle with the chaos monster is a significant metaphor for speaking of world origins and maintenance in the Old Testament, though the variety of names and multiple themes and motifs suggest more than one mythical tradition is at work.[3] Chaos appears as Rahab, Leviathan, Tannin, Yam, and occasionally Tehom, while Mot appears in a few places as the king of the underworld. Behemoth is a monster

1. The political implications of Baal's becoming king are not evidenced, as is the case with Marduk's kingship.
2. The association of myth with ritual in Canaan is demonstrated by the ritual instructions involving recitation and sacrifice given in 'The Birth of the Gracious Gods' (*CTA* 23), though several scholars, including Gese, have questioned the ritual interpretation of the Baal Cycle (*Die Religionen Altsyriens*, 50, 78).
3. For detailed studies, see B.W. Anderson, *Creation versus Chaos* (New York: Association, 1967); Cross, *Canaanite Myth and Hebrew Epic*, 112ff.; Otto Kaiser, *Die mythische Bedeutung des Meeres in Aegypten, Ugarit und Israel* (BZAW 78, Berlin: Töpelmann, 1959); and Mary K. Wakeman, *God's Battle with the Monster* (Leiden: Brill, 1973). Also see G.R. Driver, 'Mythical Monsters in the Old Testament', *Studi orientalistici in honore di Giorgio Levi della Vida* I (Rome: Universita Gregoriana, 1956) 243-49; C.H. Gordon, 'Leviathan. Symbol of Evil', *Biblical Motifs* (ed. A. Altmann; Cambridge, MA: Harvard University Press, 1966), 1-9.

of chaos in the Apocrypha and probably in Job as well. Unfortunately it is impossible to draw clear distinctions between the chaos figures:

Rahab	Isa. 30.7; 51.9-11; Ps. 89.1-11
Leviathan	Isa. 27.1; Ps. 74.12-17
Tannin	Isa. 27.1; 51.9, Ps. 74.13; Ezek. 29.1-16; 32.2-8
Yam	Exod. 15.1-18; Hab. 3.1-19; Ps. 74.13
Mot	Hos. 13.14; possibly Hab. 3.13b
Behemoth	*1 Enoch* 60.7-9; *4 Ezra* 6.49-52; Gen. 49.25; Deut. 33.13, Pss. 33.7; 77.17; 104.6-7; Hab. 3.10

A general analysis of these texts reveals the following observations:

1. Some texts refer to God's defeat of chaos during creation (Isa. 51.9-11).
2. Some point to God's victory in maintaining world order (Hab. 3.1-19).
3. Others anticipate God's overcoming chaos in the eschatological Day of the Lord, or time of judgment (Hab. 3.1-19; Isa. 27.1; Pss. 74; 89; cf. *1 Enoch* 60.7-9; *4 Ezra* 6.49-52; Rev. 20).
4. Still others describe God's subduing of historical enemies who embody chaos (Exod. 15.1-18; Isa. 30.7; Ezek. 29.1-16; 32.2-8 [all Egypt]; and Hab. 3 (Babylon?).

The metaphor of *Chaoskampf* occurs in three literary contexts: the lament, the theophanic hymn, and eschatological prophecy. All three have to do with God's coming in judgment to set things right, i.e. world maintenance. And each reflects the constitutive pattern at work in myths of origins and maintenance which feature the battle metaphor.

Psalm 74 is a community lament protesting the destruction of the temple during a time of mourning. Kraus locates the date between the destruction of Jerusalem (587 BCE) and the rebuilding of the temple (520 BCE).[1] Following the community's protest to an indifferent God who has not responded to the community's humiliation (vv. 1-11), a hymnic section intrudes to praise God as King 'from of old' (מקדם) who performed saving acts (ישועות).

The three acts of salvation to which the community makes reference are the primordial battle with the chaos monster before creation, the defeat of the waters of the Red Sea during the Exodus, and the

---

1. H.-J. Kraus, *Psalmen* 1 (2nd edn; Neukirchen: Neukirchener Verlag, 1961), 514-15.

ordering of creation, specifically the structuring of time. In this strophe, God defeated the chaos monster and gave the remnants of his carcass as food to the people in the wilderness, an allusion to divine sustenance of the people during the wilderness wandering.[1] The splitting open and drying up of springs echoes the action taken by God at the Red Sea in the deliverance of the trapped Israelites (Exod. 14–15; cf. Isa. 51.9-11). God then ordered reality by differentiating day from night, appointing the heavenly bodies to their proper place, establishing bounds for the earth, and setting up the calendar. Creation and the control of history are acts of order which produce and sustain life. The third section of the psalm (vv. 18-23) returns to the lament by calling on God to remember (זכר = actualize)[2] his salvific acts of old, to have regard for the covenant, and to rise up in judgment. This call for theophany is an important, often encountered feature of the metaphorical model of the battle with chaos.

Significant then is the presentation of God's ascent to kingship during primordial times by means of the defeat of the chaos monster and the later victory over chaos *redivivus* at the Red Sea. Myth and history are forged into a common metaphorical pattern. Now the community calls upon a strangely silent God whose temple lies in ruins, whose people are destitute, and whose name is disgraced. To reclaim the position of kingship, God must arise once again, defeat the new historical embodiment of chaos (the Babylonian empire?), rebuild the temple, and re-establish righteous judgment on the earth.

The Mythic Paradigm of the Battle with Chaos. There is then in the Old Testament a literary pattern drawn from world origin and maintenance myths in the ancient Near East which feature the combat metaphor. The pattern includes the battle between the god of order and the chaos monster leading to the latter's defeat, the construction of a temple and a festival of enthronement for the divine ruler, judgment which shapes the new order, and (re)creation of the cosmos and humanity. It is this narrative extension of the dominant combat metaphor in ancient Near Eastern myth which gives shape to the Old Testament texts just discussed. As we shall see, the external mythic

---

1. Cf. Anat's feeding of Mot's carcass to the birds and Marduk's using of Tiamat's corpse to create the cosmos.
2. H. Eising, 'זכר', *TDOT* 4 (Grand Rapids: Eerdmans, 1982), 82-87.

world of the book of Job is that of the battle of Yahweh with chaos, specifically the two monsters, Behemoth and Leviathan.[1]

3. *Metaphors of Cosmology in Wisdom Literature*

The three metaphors of fertility, word, and artistry are central to conventional wisdom literature's presentation and understanding of creation. Israel's sages used the fertility metaphor to portray especially the image of God fathering and giving birth. In the hymn of self-praise by Dame Wisdom in Prov. 8.22-31, Wisdom, clothed in the dress of a goddess, tells of her beginnings:

> Yahweh fathered me (קָנָה) as the first of his power,
> Before all things made in the distant past.
> From of old I was poured out,
> From the beginning, before the origins of the earth.
> When there were no depths I was begotten (חוֹלָלְתִּי),
> When there were no streams abounding with water;
> Before the mountains were sunk down (into the depths),
> Before the hills I was given birth (חוֹלָלְתִּי) (Prov. 8.22-25).

In four verses, Wisdom, speaking of both her origins and primacy in creation, thrice uses the language of birth. In the first instance, she announces Yahweh has fathered her, while in the latter two cases she is 'born' by means of the birth contractions. Since the two-fold occurrence of the verb חוֹלָלְתִּי is a passive without a clear identification of the mother, the possibilities are God, more likely in this case, or an intimation of the myth of the earth-mother goddess (cf. Job 1.21). Form-critically this introduction to the hymn is quite similar to the opening theogony of the *Enuma elish* quoted earlier (*ANET*, 60-61). Wisdom is a goddess in origin who in the preceding strophe (8.12-21) reigns over the cosmos as divine Queen dispensing the privilege of rule to kings and endowing them with wisdom and wealth (cf. Solomon in 1 Kgs 3–11). In the present hymn, this child of God is present at and participates in the ordering of the world. As graceful daughter she performs her dance of delight before God and rejoices in

---

1. Loren Fisher, 'Creation at Ugarit and in the Old Testament', *VT* 15 (1965), 313-24. It is quite possible that Israel also participated in a New Year festival celebrating the victory over chaos and the recreation of the earth. Enthronement of the Israelite monarch and the securing of well-being of the nation would have been a constitutive part of this proposed festival.

both the creation and its inhabitants, actions which order the world and link its inhabitants to the creator.

The second metaphor of creation is word. Sirach's hymn in Sir. 39.12-35, for example, affirms the beneficence of all aspects of God's creation by means of a duality in which 'goodness' is defined functionally. Thus even seemingly 'evil' things (e.g. snakes and scorpions) are good in terms of their function, that is to punish the wicked, while 'good' things function to reward the righteous. In this hymn, the sage describes God's ordering and maintaining creation in terms of language:

> By his word he ordered the water,
> And by the utterance of his mouth its reservoir (Sir. 39.17).

Later, in writing of the function of fearful and vile creatures to punish the wicked, Sirach uses the metaphor of God's edict which determines their behavior:

> They will leap forth when he commands them,
> And in accordance with their decree they will not rebel against his mouth
>   (39.31)

It is the power of Yahweh's language which forms and maintains creation.[1]

---

1. The metaphor of word also provides the basic theological model for Qoheleth, though with different implications than for Sirach. For Qoheleth God is the royal despot whose decree has established the unwavering pattern of creation and the fate of humans (Qoh. 1.3-11). What happens on earth has been 'named', that is called into existence and determined, including the destiny of humans, yet humans are not informed by God. In Kafkaesque fashion, God determines the destiny of each person, yet the decree as well as the creator remain hidden in mystery that 'one may find out' one's own fate or that of others (Qoh. 8.16-17). The only aspect of destiny one may know with certainty is that death awaits for both the good and evil, religious and secular, wise and foolish. One is under divine power ('in the hand of God'); whether for good or for evil, one cannot know. God has given each one divine breath (a related word image) that empowers human life, yet at death the breath returns to God, while the body returns to dust (Qoh. 3.19-21; 8.8; 12.7). The form of the text, an autobiographical instruction, is based on Egyptian royal prototypes. This coupled with the Solomonic fiction maintained for the early part of the narrative ('son of David', 'king in Jerusalem') indicates that the major metaphor for human existence in traditional wisdom, kingship, is used aphoristically by Qoheleth to indicate that human existence is slavery, with the destiny of each irrevocably and unknowably fixed by 'the God' (Qoh. 3; 8.16-17). The one boon in life, 'joy' primarily derived from labor, is itself a 'gift' of God, that is, not within human control.

The third metaphor, artistry, is also taken up by the sages in the articulation of their theology. Prov. 3.13-20 is a hymnic description of Dame Wisdom who, like the Egyptian goddess Maat, offers to her devotees life in one hand and honor and riches in the other. The fourth and concluding strophe of this poem, vv. 19-20, speaks of God's use of wisdom in creating the world:

> The Lord founded the earth by Wisdom,
> He established the heavens by insight;
> By his knowledge the deeps were split,
> And the clouds dripped with dew.

In this strophe wisdom is both a blueprint and the requisite skill of the divine artisan in constructing the cosmos like a well-planned, well-built house.[1] In Prov. 3.19 the foundations of the earth are laid and become the base for pillars supporting the heavens. The cosmic pillars, usually the mountains on the horizon (Ps. 18.7; Job 26.11), are equated with columns supporting the roof of a house. In v. 20 there is faint echo of the cleaving in half (בקע) of the chaos monster (בהמות), though like the P narrative in Genesis 1, the language appears to be stripped of all conflict imagery. There seems instead to be simply the separation of the primeval deeps (plural) into the upper and lower waters, followed by moisture dripping from the clouds and fertilizing the earth, the first act of creation in J. Order is established with only the faintest hint of a cosmic struggle with primeval chaos.

What unites these three metaphors in conventional Wisdom is their view of reality as an aesthesis, a harmonious and beautiful order in which the various components of creation have their place, function, time, and norms for existence. Creation is a well-constructed, elegant house, its arrangement and appearance one of beauty and delight, and its laws those of a harmonious society regulated by authoritative decrees. The task of the sage was to shape aesthesis through language and act, perceive and delight in its coherence and elegance, and contribute to its maintenance through righteous existence, proper and elegant language, the construction of law codes and moral instructions, and acts imitative of divine creativity. This is the meaning of the 'fear of God' which for the traditional sages is the basis for all wisdom. These metaphors express the sage's confidence that the world is

---

1. Cf. Prov. 9.1-6; 24.3; Job 38.4-7.

orderly, intelligible, beautiful, and just. And while there were limits to knowledge and troubling instances of the chaotic, the sage trusted in a beneficent creator who provided for the needs of creatures and maintained the ongoing order of creation. Even more, reality (cosmic and social) was moving, pliable, dynamic, and open, not closed to human participation in either shaping and structuring or distorting and destroying. Thus the theological basis for social ethics in wisdom was provided. The chief means for participating in the process of creation were the constructing of beauty and order in language and art, the dedication of lively passion to the pursuit of Dame Wisdom (the study of wisdom within school and family settings), the procreation of offspring within marriage, and the careful articulation of elegant language which shaped the social order. In these ways creation was maintained, life was regenerated, and the path towards sagehood was taken.

The fourth metaphor, battle, is found primarily in Job, though it makes an occasional appearance in more conventional wisdom texts, for example, in the Wisdom of Solomon. The mythological struggle with primeval chaos points to a world which is not static and well ordered, but rather a dynamic reality where justice must prevail for life to continue. Otherwise, reality, both nature and society, returns to oblivion. The battle metaphor could and at times did degenerate into a limiting nationalism in which Yahweh was Israel's deity fighting on her behalf. But a proper extension and conceptual formulation of the metaphor raises Yahweh beyond the national boundaries of Israel's self-interest to a universal God who is in mortal combat with mythical chaos and its historical incarnations. Indeed, the prophets (cf. Amos) were perhaps the most disorienting in their use of this metaphor to speak of a universal God active in history whose coming in the Day of the Lord, i.e. the time of judgment, spelled disaster and not salvation for Israel. And more, the metaphor gave significant place to chaos, even evil, as a real and potent force. While the metaphor did not imply the denial of the sovereignty of God, chaos was nevertheless a powerful force with which God must contend. And there is ever the frightening possibility that one day chaos might prevail. Thus reality is not tranquil and orderly, but rather is in a process of struggle, created and maintained only by the continual striving for justice. Consequently, humanity's being in the world involved struggle, not sabbath rest. Conflict, while potentially destructive, could also become a creative power leading to an order of justice and well-being in the cosmos and society.

Chapter 3

METAPHORS OF ANTHROPOLOGY AND MYTHIC PARADIGMS

1. *Metaphors of Anthropology in Ancient Near Eastern and Biblical Literatures*

The Metaphor of Ruler. To speak of humanity's role and function in terms of ruler is an important metaphor in Israel and the ancient Near East. Indeed, this metaphor became the dominant one for priestly theology and conventional wisdom in the exilic and post-exilic periods. And as I shall argue below, it is this metaphorical tradition that comes under critical attack in the book of Job.

In Egypt of the Old Kingdom, divinity, descent from the gods, responsibility for establishing and maintaining social and natural order through law, ritual, and wisdom, and transition to the afterlife through mortuary religion were attributes and privileges limited to rulers. Ordinary mortals were created to serve the gods, especially the one incarnate on the Egyptian throne. This is evidenced in the major social myth of Egypt, the Horus–Osiris complex in which the dead king came to rule the Underworld as Osiris, and his son, Horus, sat upon the throne of the Two Lands.[1] The pyramids of the Old Kingdom symbolized the center of Egyptian civilization and its undergirding social myth: human community was structured around the divine kings who alone were granted the possibility of eternal life, though they occasionally granted immortality to those few select nobles who served them well. For the sages of the Old Kingdom, wisdom was limited to the aristocracy, and the hope for eternal life was based on service to the divine king. Otherwise, humans were created to serve the gods,

---

1. See Frankfort, *Kingship and the Gods*, 15-212; and John Wilson, *The Culture of Ancient Egypt* (Chicago: University of Chicago Press, 1951), 69-103. The mythic pattern of kingship included the defeat of Seth, the birth (creation) of Horus, the installation of the king as Horus incarnate on the throne, and the gaining of life and well being for nature and Egyptian society.

especially the ruling kings. Early Egyptian myths of origins did include the rebellion of humanity against the gods, especially the rule of Re (whose son sat upon the throne of Egypt), but with catastrophic results. The social order revolving around the king was mythically legitimated—rebellion meant devastation by the gods.

However, with the collapse of the Old Kingdom and the chaos of the First Intermediate period, the demand for justice from king and gods began to be loudly heard. Even attacks on Re began.[1] Now the king was subject to the requirements of justice (Amen-em-het).[2] By the New Kingdom features of kingship began to be applied metaphorically even to lowly-placed Egyptians. The Book of the Dead from the New Kingdom demonstrates that Egyptian mortuary religion became democratized, and lower elements of society could hope to become Osiris and live in the afterlife. Even petty officials like Amen-em-Opet were thought to participate in activities which brought about social order—to act creatively as only the king and nobles once did in establishing and maintaining Ma'at.[3] In the latest examples of Egyptian wisdom (Ochsheshonq and the Papyrus Insinger), peasants could expect to participate in wisdom's tasks and goals for this life and experience the world beyond.[4]

In Israel a similar process occurred. One major stream of early wisdom was associated with the ruler, close advisors who were often chosen on the principle of kinship, and other members of the royal court. Wisdom was a characteristic of the ruler which enabled him to establish order in the kingdom and to rule in righteousness (Isa. 11.1-9).[5] The Davidic king was the 'son of God' and mediator between heaven and earth whose legal word, aesthetic crafting, actions of sacrifice and New Year's ritual created and maintained justice.[6] The

---

1. R. Otto, *Der Vorwurf an Gott* (Hildesheim: Gerstenberg, 1951).

2. Wolfgang Helck, *Der Text der Lehre Amenemhet* (Wiesbaden: Harrassowitz, 1969).

3. Irene Grumach, *Untersuchungen zur Lebenslehre des Amenemope* (München: Deutscher Kunstverlag, 1972).

4. B. Gemser, 'The Instructions of 'Onchsheshonqy and Biblical Wisdom Literature', *SVT* 7 (1960), 102-45.

5. See Leonidas Kalugila, *The Wise King* (Coniectanea Biblica, OT 15; Lund: Gleerup, 1980).

6. See Ivan Engnell, *Studies in Divine Kingship in the Ancient Near East* (Oxford: Blackwell, 1967); A.R. Johnson, *Sacral Kingship in Ancient Israel* (Cardiff: University of Wales Press, 1967); Sigmund Mowinckel, *He That Cometh* (New

covenant of kingship in Judah was rooted in the order of creation itself (Ps. 89). However, a metaphorical model of human existence was constructed at least by the time of the Babylonian exile. Now all humans bore the divine image and were exalted to rule over God's creation. In Wisdom literature, the traditions of royal wisdom were democratized and applied to all who sought wisdom's path. Regardless of social standing the sage was one who responded to wisdom's call and engaged in wise actions creating social order. Order was not simply created through the *hieros gamos* of ruler and royal consort, but also through marriage to Woman Wisdom. The ruler metaphor emphasized the goodness of human nature and the freedom to go forth into the world to master life and to rule responsibly as the vice-regents of God. As ruler, humanity actively participated in the beneficent ordering and sustaining of nature and society.

Several biblical texts illustrate this late development by using king-ship to speak metaphorically of human existence. The classic example is the Priestly narrative of creation in Gen. 1.1–2.4a (cf. Ps. 8). The P narrative, following the temporal order of the seven-day week, presents God's forming of humanity, male and female, as the last and climactic act of creation.[1] This positioning underscores humanity's supreme position in the world. In addition to the literary-theological placement in the narrative, two other features point to the emphasis placed on humanity. The first is the decision of the divine council to create humanity, both male and female, in the image of God (Gen. 1.26-27):

> Then God said, 'Let us make humanity in our image, after our likeness; and let them have dominion over the fish of the sea, and over the birds of the air, and over the cattle, and over all the earth, and over every creeping thing that creeps upon the earth'. So God created humanity in the divine image, in the image of God he created them; male and female he created them.

For the priestly writers, the divine image signifies, first of all, human-ity's participation in divine creativity. As creation in its entirety is declared by God to be 'good', that is beautiful, life-sustaining, and orderly, so humans by virtue of the divine image may participate in that beneficent ordering and aesthetic shaping of world and society as

York: Abingdon, 1954); Karl-Heinz Bernhardt, *Das Problem der altorientalischen Königs-Ideologie im Alten Testament* (SVT 14; Leiden: Brill, 1965).

1. For a discussion of creation theology in the P document, see Gerhard von Rad, *Genesis* (rev. edn; Philadelphia: Westminster, 1972), 22ff.

God's vice-regents. This is to exist in the image of God, to be like
(דמות) the creator. Secondly, the divine image (צלם) also underlines
human freedom and responsibility to be active in the world, to
function as God's surrogate in establishing and maintaining this
beneficent aesthesis. As ancient Near Eastern kings erected statues of
themselves in the different parts of their kingdoms to signify their
presence, authority, and rule, so the priests conceived of humans as the
royal deputies of God who signified and actualized divine presence,
authority, and rule.[1] Through good and righteous actions of humans,
divine dominion (רדה) extends over creation.

The second feature to note is the divine imperative directed to
human beings:

> And God blessed them, and God said to them, 'Be fruitful and multiply, and
> fill the earth and subdue it; and have dominion over the fish of the sea and
> over the birds of the air and over every living thing that moves upon the earth'
> (Gen. 1.28).

Two observations are important. First of all, P understands that procreation is a major way in which humans participate in divine
creativity. Indeed the blessing of God is issued to humans, enabling
human life and the divine image to continue.[2] And in this creative act,
which extends the dominion of God, both sexes participate, emphasizing that the world is ordered through the exchange of love, not
through militant conquest, a concept that most certainly challenged the
empire theology of Babylon and the temptation to acquiesce to its
vision during the exile (cf. Isa. 40–55). For P humans may fulfill this
divine imperative to rule only by turning to one another, in comple-
menting each other in the male-female relationship. By contrast,
'violence' (חמס), understood in the P section of the primeval history to
be the shedding of blood (Gen. 6.11, 13), destroys creation and
returns the world to chaos.

The second observation is that the imperatives 'to rule' (רדה) and 'to
subdue' (כבס) direct humans to reign as kings over the earth and its
creatures, not each other. These imperatives extend God's trust to
human creatures to rule responsibly and well, and not as destructive

---

1. Gerhard von Rad, *Old Testament Theology* 1, 144ff.
2. Earlier God's blessing is bestowed upon sea creatures, including the sea
monsters, and birds (Gen. 1.22), an action that presumably extended to all living
things. For a discussion of blessing as life-enhancing, see Claus Westermann,
Blessing (Philadelphia: Fortress, 1978).

tyrants and exploiters of creation. This is to rule as God rules. When humans oppress other humans, when divinely granted freedom is denied to any race, sex or nation, when the earth and its creatures are exploited and corrupted, the image of God is perverted and the structures of life are undermined. The world returns to chaos.

Traditional wisdom used this royal metaphor to describe human existence in the world. True, in its earlier stages, wisdom was associated with the ruler and aristocracy in Israel and the ancient Near East. However, the theme of kingship was eventually democratized to include all of humanity. Wisdom was not limited to the king, but became a gift of God to all who accepted the invitation to study. The fiction of royal status by Qoheleth is one solid example of this. Another is the poem about Woman Wisdom in Proverbs 8, especially the second (vv. 12-21) and fourth (vv. 32-36) strophes.

> I, wisdom, dwell in prudence, and I find knowledge and discretion.
> The fear of the Lord is the hatred of evil, pride, self-exaltation, and a perverse mouth I despise.
> I have counsel and sound wisdom, I possess insight and might.
> By me kings reign, and rulers decree what is right.
> By me princes govern, and nobles, all righteous judges.
> I love those who love me, and those who seek me shall find me.
> Riches and honor are with me, enduring wealth and righteousness.
> My fruit is better than gold, even refined gold, and my increase than choice silver.
> I walk in the path of righteousness, in the midst of the paths of justice.
> Giving existence as an inheritance to my lovers, and their storehouses I fill (vv. 12-21).

What is most significant about this part of Woman Wisdom's self-praise is her presentation as an ancient Near Eastern goddess of fertility and wisdom who selects and then sustains kings in their rule.[1] She possesses the gifts of rule, power, wealth, honor, and wisdom, which she imparts to her royal consorts and lovers. And yet Wisdom offers her gifts, not simply to a ruling class, but to all 'who seek her'.

This democratization of ruler as a metaphor for all those who seek wisdom's invitation is even more clear in the final and concluding strophe:

> And now, O sons, hear me, happy are those who keep my ways.
> Listen to my instruction and become wise, and do not let it go.

1. See Lang, *Frau Weisheit*.

Happy is the one who listens to me, watching daily at my doors, guarding the
    door posts of my gates.
Because the one who finds me finds life, and obtains favor from Yahweh.
But the one who misses me, harms himself.
All who hate me love death (vv. 32-36).

Now Wisdom, who had taken to the streets and pathways of human life
and entered the cities where mortals live, offers her invitation of life
to all who would come and learn of her.[1]

The Metaphor of Slave

The other metaphor for human nature in the ancient Near East was
slavery. As we shall see, the Joban poet sets this metaphor in tension
with the sapiential metaphor of king. This tension provides much of
the dramatic energy for the movement of the plot and participates
significantly in the formulation of the meaning of the book.

The slave metaphor was rooted in the religious foundations of
Mesopotamian society. The major culture myth of Babylon, the
Enuma elish, fashioned a theological anthropology which tended to
direct Babylonian and Assyrian understanding well into the late Iron
Age. This metaphorical depiction fended off the relatively few
attempts to claim a divine status for the king and made the quest for
immortality one of vanity.[2] Even the king was the slave of god,

---

1. See the general invitation to feast at Wisdom's table to all who are unlearned
(Prov. 9.1-6). The mythic pattern of kingship appropriated by the sages included the
struggle with Dame Folly, the acceptance of Wisdom's invitation, and the gifts of
crown, wealth and life.
2. The words of Siduri, the ale-wife, to Gilgamesh as he engaged in his quest for
eternal life, are typical of Mesopotamian anthropology (*ANET*, 90):

Gilgamesh, whither rovest thou?
The life which thou pursuest thou shalt not find.
When the gods created mankind,
Death for mankind they set aside,
Life in their own hands retaining.
Thou, Gilgamesh, let full be thy belly,
Make thou merry by day and by night.
Of each day make thou a feast of rejoicing,
Day and night dance thou and play!
Let thy garments be sparkling fresh,
Thy head be washed; bathe thou in water.
Pay heed to the little one that holds on to thy hand,
Let thy spouse delight in thy bosom!
For this is the task of [mankind]!

responsible only for carrying out divine instructions for the building and maintenance of temples. True the *hieros gamos* was a significant activity of the king, but even here his inferior position to the gods was maintained by the Dumuzi myth. The king was still the mortal whose marriage to Ishtar, the goddess of fertility, was obviously one of inequality. And the ritual of degradation during the New Year festival when the insignia of kingship were removed and the king was humiliated by the high priest served to underscore the king's position of slave to the gods. Service to the gods through the commands of the king and the social and religious ordinances of temple and state provided the direction for human existence. Humanity was created for no other purpose. 'Personal' religion, which was separate and apart from the state cultus, allowed for a relationship to exist between an individual and his/her god or goddess.

However, even here the relationship was still one of master and slave, though the slave could expect proper treatment, including care and protection from the deity. As Lambert has observed, Babylonian religion, especially through the avenue of wisdom literature, developed a view of the gods as just. Thus during the periods of social crisis, for example the Cassite Dark Ages, the issue of theodicy threatened the bulwark of Babylonian religion. Yet only one classical wisdom text rejected service to the gods and personal religion, 'The Dialogue of Pessimism'. Even so this text negates all meaning and despairs of life itself, suggesting that suicide is the proper response to senseless existence.

The theme of revolt is an obvious extension of the metaphor of slave in Mesopotamian literature. First the lower gods and then humanity rebel against the dreary existence of life lived in service to the gods. Creation is experienced, not as beneficent and good, but as abject and debilitating drudgery. Nevertheless, for such actions humanity is almost exterminated, save for the compassionate intervention of Ea. The boon from revolution was the decision of Enlil to establish civilization. Even so the theological anthropology of slavery remains. The slave metaphor eradicates significant human freedom, places severe restrictions on the human capacity to create and shape cosmos and society, and constructs an unbridgeable chasm between the divine sovereign and the human creature.

The classic culture myth of Babylonian was the *Enuma elish*. Tablet VI describes Marduk's decision to create humans after the defeat of Tiamat and the creation and ordering of the heavens and the calendar.

After listening to the gods and perhaps the complaints of captive lower deities who had feared execution or lives of enslavement for their part in supporting Tiamat, Marduk takes council with Ea and speaks of his plan:

> Blood I will mass and cause bones to be.
> I will establish a savage, 'man' shall be his name.
>> Verily, savage-man I will create.
> He shall be charged with the service of the gods
> That they might be at ease!

Ea, the wise counselor, advises Marduk to punish only the leader of the rebel gods, the one who urged Tiamat to join battle. Only he should perish for the insurrection. Marduk gives his royal consent, and Kingu is tried and condemned to death as the rebel general. Ea has Kingu executed, and uses his blood to fashion humankind. Carrying out the will of Marduk, Ea then imposes upon the human race the task of service to the gods. The relationship between gods and humans is that of master and slave.[1]

Even the role of the king in Mesopotamian society was chiefly to perform service to the gods. In one Babylonian text Ea's creation of humanity is described:

> He created the king to be custodian of the temple, he created mankind to discharge service to the gods.[2]

---

1. A similar myth is found in Egypt. In a text dating from the New Kingdom (14th–12th centuries BCE), 'Deliverance of Mankind from Destruction', the theme of revolution against the rule of Re and the near annihilation of humanity is central. The myth begins by speaking of the self-creation of Re, the king of the gods and humans. 'Then mankind plotted something in the (very) presence of Re.' Re learns of the plot against him and secretly summons the high gods into council. Then Re addresses Nun his father and the eldest gods, indicating that humanity, whom he created through his divine tears, has contrived revolution against him, asking for their counsel before he decides to slay them. Re receives the approval of Nun to destroy the rebels. The gods then advise Re to send his Eye to find the rebels who have fled into the desert to escape his wrath, and then to send Hathor (who becomes Sekhmet, the goddess of violence) against them. Yet Hathor's bloodlust is so insatiable that after the slaughter begins it appears the entire human race will be exterminated. Re decides to intervene on humankind's behalf to save them from total destruction. Mixing red ochre with beer, he puts 7,000 jars of the liquid in the place where Sehkmet was to come at dawn to finish her grisly task. Drinking what she thinks is human blood, she becomes intoxicated and humanity is saved from extinction.

2. See P. Garelli and M. Leibovici, *Schöpfungsmythen*, 148 (cited in Keel, 269).

The king was in charge of what Oppenheim describes as 'the care and feeding of the gods'.[1] The king was responsible for the building and maintenance of temples for the gods and for providing for their everyday needs—food, drink and clothing—through offerings and sacrifices.[2]

In Israel the metaphor of slave was used on occasion to describe the relationship of the ruler to God. The ruler was responsible for building and maintaining the temple and was to live a life of service to Yahweh in supporting social and cosmic order. However, as a metaphor for human existence, it was Job, followed by Qoheleth, who took the metaphor of slave and presented it as the proper way of understanding human existence. And if the usual dating of the poem of Job in the exilic or early post-exilic period is on target, it may well be that this metaphor was a serious challenge to the emerging anthropological metaphor of king in P, Psalm 8, and the wisdom tradition. The poet of Job challenges the royal metaphor with the view that humans experience creation as a life of slavery, for they are in bondage to an oppressive and corrupt tyrant who savages his own human creatures. It is this clash of anthropological metaphors for understanding human existence and divine providence that provides the tensive quality and therefore the theological drama for the book of Job. When human existence is experienced as slavery due to divine decree, revolt against the orders of the cosmos and the creator occurs. Indeed oppressive slavery leads to the revolt of Job against God, a revolution that eventuates in Job's application of the royal metaphor to himself in order to repudiate divine rule. Job is the slave who would be king. But to become king Job must depose God as the Lord of Heaven and Earth.

---

1. A. Leo Oppenheim, *Ancient Mesopotamia*, 171-227.

2. A rather striking example of the dependency of the gods on human slaves is presented in the Akkadian myth of the flood. After Enlil had destroyed all of humanity by means of the flood, with the exception of Utnapishtim, the gods became famished due to the lack of sacrifices to feed them. When Utnapishtim finally pours out a libation and offers a sacrifice on Mt Nisir after seven days of flood and seven additional days of the receding of the waters, the text describes the somewhat less than fastidious reaction of the gods:

> The gods smelled the savor,
> The gods smelled the sweet savor,
> The gods crowded like flies about the sacrificer.

2. The Mythic Paradigm of Revolt against the Gods

Revolt against the Gods. Related to the metaphor of slave is the subsidiary theme of the revolt of humanity against divine rule. The most significant example of this theme is found in the Babylonian myth, *Atra-hasis*.[1] The opening lines provide the theme: 'When the gods like men bore the work and suffered the toil.' The story opens with the cosmos inhabited only by the gods. The three high gods shared rulership among themselves: Anu heaven, Enlil the earth, and Enki-Ea Apsu, the water beneath the earth. Enlil, lord of the earth, assigns to the lower gods (Igigi) the backbreaking task of digging and constructing the dyke and river irrigation system which was the foundation of the Babylonian economy. After forty years of drudgery, these lower gods rebel, burn their tools, and lay siege to Enlil's palace. Terrified, Enlil convenes the divine assembly and the decision eventually is made to create humankind in order to relieve the lower gods of work. After Mami and Enki join efforts to produce the first humans from clay mixed with the blood of a slaughtered god, Mami addresses the gods.

The second major section of the myth then describes the growth of the human population and the problem of 'noise' which disturbs Enlil's sleep. Consequently, he decrees that the human population will be reduced by a series of disasters, each of which is thwarted by the instructions given by the beneficent Enki. Finally, Enlil sends the flood to destroy humanity and binds Enki by oath not to interfere. But by a ruse Enki gives Atra-hasis instructions to build a boat, allowing him with his family to escape the ravages of the deluge. Though Enlil is angry that some have escaped, the gods have recognized the consequence of losing their slaves: they would have to work! While the end of the myth is fragmentary, it appears that Enlil comes to accept the existence of humanity, but requires that these barbarians be organized into social classes, so as to reduce the 'noise'. Thus social ordering shapes the cosmos and keeps humanity from destruction by the gods. Civilization is a divine action that humans must imitate, or face the wrath of the gods.

The mythic pattern which arranges both major divisions of this text involves the following: judgment (predestination), slavery and toil, revolt, fall, and redemption. While lower gods rebel successfully to

1. W.G. Lambert and Alan R. Millard, *Atra-hasis: The Babylonian Story of the Flood* (Oxford: Clarendon, 1969).

gain freedom from oppressive service, humans revolt and fail. Redemption depends on the intercession of a humanitarian god. And civilization, including especially the institution of kingship which orders and structures human society, is the gift of the gods to humanity. While the entire society is geared to service to the gods, at least order in creation and society makes life possible. Rebellion is not successful in throwing off the yoke imposed by the gods, but the order of civilization leading to the maintenance of life is gained.

Hubris, Revolt and Fall. A variant of the mythic pattern of revolt against the rule of the divine king and head of the gods also occurs in ancient Near Eastern mythical literature. In this case, revolt is occasioned not by the experience of creation as slavery but rather by the hubris of the human creature who desires to sit on the throne of the ruler of heaven and earth.

Ezek. 28.1-19 historicizes the myth of rebellion against the ruler of the divine council. This text contains two parts: vv. 1-10 which comprise a judgment oracle against the King of Tyre, enlarged by the motif of royal wisdom, and vv. 11-19, a probable lament which is also expanded by the wisdom motif. The first section incorporates the myth of the Primal Man, a primordial king who dwelt at first among the gods, but then sought to replace the king of the divine council. Wisdom is the charismatic endowment of the ruler which enables him to rule justly as God's vice-regent and act as a faithful steward of creation's resources. Instead this king has abused his wisdom by using it to obtain personal wealth, a greed that eventuates in full-scale revolt. Considering himself divine, this king sought to replace the judge of creation. Instead the divine judge condemned this folly with a decree which resulted in the eradication of the king's royal splendor and expulsion from the place of the gods. He was cast down into the 'Pit'. This myth was used to describe the arrogance of the King of Tyre who was to be destroyed along with his city.

The second section, the lament, is a dirge over the deceased King of Tyre. Once more the images of the Primal King are used to speak of one who was 'full of wisdom and perfect in beauty' and lived in the primeval garden with God. Yet filled with pride, the king was expelled from the mountain of God and cast down to earth where he was exposed before other kings and consumed by divine fire. In both cases, hubris, the desire of the creature to take the place of the creator, is the original sin leading to revolt. The result is expulsion and death.

Wisdom, given to the king to enable him to establish justice and social order, is corrupted by personal ambition, and the result is alienation from God and eventual destruction (cf. Isa. 14.4b-21).

Part II

Wisdom in Revolt

Chapter 4

INTERPRETING THE BOOK OF JOB: PRELIMINARY ISSUES

1. *Cosmology and Anthropology in Job*

The Battle with Chaos. More than any other Wisdom text from Israel, the book of Job makes significant use of ancient Near Eastern creation mythology. And the variety of metaphors and myths of creation in Israel's cultural environment plays an important role in the articulation of the book's meaning. It is my thesis that the world of meaning constructed by the book of Job is shaped by two mythic patterns of creation. The cosmological pattern, represented by the *Enuma elish* and the Baal Cycle, follows the sequence of battle, victory, kingship, judgment, and (re)creation. It is this mythic pattern which constructs the external reality in which the drama of Job is situated. Indeed, it is this world of meaning which the character Job seeks to subvert and to replace with a new and compelling reality: one in which human kings rule over nature and direct the course of history without the intrusions of the gods.

The Revolt against the Gods. The internal discourse of Job is shaped by a second mythic structure. This anthropological pattern is best represented by *Atra-hasis*, which consists of two parts, each with the following sequence: judgment (slavery), slavery and toil, revolt, fall, and judgment culminating in redemption. In his experience of creation as slavery, Job rebels against divine rule and seeks to ascend to the throne of heaven and earth. Challenged by this mortal upstart, God, who has come to contest the dragon for rulership over the cosmos, must first contend with Job.

Central to two mythic patterns are root metaphors, respectively battle and slavery. These are the dominant images for speaking of the origins and sustaining of creation and for understanding humanity's place and function in the world. The point at which these two patterns intersect is struggle. While the cosmos is ordered and maintained by God's recurring battle with the dragon, humans, who experience creation as slavery, rebel against the creator and attempt to overthrow divine rule. The battle with chaos and the struggle for justice are the intersecting poles of mythic reality shaping the meaning of the book of Job. In Job's own struggle for justice, he comes face to face with the Divine Warrior who has come to battle Leviathan for rule over the cosmos.

2. *The Metaphorical Process*

The mode of narrative enactment in Job combines the deconstruction of conventional understandings of cosmology and anthropology with the metaphorical process in which both characters within the drama and the implied audience go through the stages of absurdity and destabilization, mimesis, and transformation and restabilization, leading to the reconstruction of a new hermeneutic. As is true of any metaphor, tensiveness and ambiguity continue through each stage and even characterize the incipient nature of the new reality created by the metaphor of struggle. By means of this dramatic enactment, the book of Job leads to the beginnings of a new metaphorical model of faith. And to use the concluding words of the divine judge, the book aims at *speaking correctly* about God, as Job, his servant, has done. The entire movement of the book is theological, that is, the articulation of language about and to God.

3. *Preliminary Considerations*

The critical issues common to the interpretation of Job continue to be the questions of date, form and literary integrity.

Date. The one clue to the time-frame of the book occurs in Ezek. 14.14-20, where Noah, Daniel, and Job are mentioned as the three heroes of righteousness. Assuming Ezekiel's comments come shortly before the Babylonian destruction of Jerusalem in 587 BCE, the legend of a virtuous Job was well known by at least the early 6th century. Of course Ezekiel's reference may refer only to the narrative tale (Job 1–2; 42.7-17) and not to the poetic dialogues which may have been written a considerable time later. The two popular dates for at least the major section of the poetry are the Babylonian exile[1] and the Persian period.[2] Proponents of the exilic date point to the Ezekiel reference to the hero Job, the presumed dependency of Jer. 20.14-18 on Job 3, the conception of 'the satan (accuser)' as an office but not as a personal name (contrast 1 Chron. 21.1), the worship of heavenly bodies which became a problem during the Assyro-Babylonian period, the significant number of Aramaisms, a style comparable to II Isaiah, and the crisis of the fall of Jerusalem and the deportation to Babylon. Advocates of the post-exilic date mention the reference to 'kings, counselors, and princes' as reflective of the Persian hierarchy (Ezra 7.28, 8.25, and Esth. 1.3ff.), argue the exaltation of an Edomite would have countered the exclusivism of the reform by Ezra, and consider the absence of polygamy to be later than the Deuteronomic code which allows the practice as late as the late 7th century BCE. My own preference is to allow for stages in the development of the present book. I suggest the following trajectory: the prose narrative during the monarchy, the poetic dialogues during the exile, and Job 28 and the Elihu speeches after the exile.

Form.[3] The literary form of Job has been compared to genres originating in three separate social contexts: cult, law, and wisdom. Moving into the cultic sphere, Claus Westermann has argued that Job is a dramatized lament in which Job complains and his friends argue. Structurally the dialogues of the friends are a consolation speech, though in content they are disputations. The same is said to be true of the Yahweh speeches in Job 38–42.[4] Harmut Gese's 'paradigm of the answered lament' is similar to Westermann's position. Gese appropriates the literary genre and structure of the lament, offering the following sequence for Job: distress, complaint, divine response and restoration.[5] In a different direction, Heinz Richter argues that the book reflects the process of Hebrew jurisprudence. Thus the majority

---

1. Samuel Terrien, 'Job', *Interpreter's Bible* 3 (New York: Abingdon, 1954).

2. Georg Fohrer, *Introduction to the Old Testament* (New York: Abingdon, 1968), 330; A. de Wilde, *Das Buch Hiob* (OTS 22; Leiden: Brill, 1981), 52.

3. Murphy's volume on the forms of Wisdom literature provides a convenient summary of the different assessments of the literary form of Job (*Wisdom Literature* [FOTL 13; Grand Rapids: Eerdmans, 1981]).

4. Claus Westermann, *The Structure of the Book of Job* (Philadelphia: Fortress, 1981).

5. *Lehre und Wirklichkeit in der alten Weisheit*.

of the individual genres present in the book come from the legal sphere. Richter sees 4–14 as the attempt at a preliminary settlement, and 15–31 as involving a formal effort to obtain a legal settlement. Chapters 32–37 contain Elihu's appeal of the case, while 38–41 present God's judgment and Job's withdrawal of the accusation.[1] Staying within the arena of wisdom, George Fohrer sees Job as a disputation (*Streitrede*) between sages seeking to prove their own positions and to dismiss the counter-arguments of their opponents.[2]

A different tack has been taken by a number of scholars who look at Job as a unique literary composition, not confined to a single form or life setting. This is the approach of 'New Criticism'. For example, J.W. Whedbee has argued that Job is a comedy composed of two elements: 'a vision of incongruity that involves the ironic, the ludicrous, and the ridiculous' and a story with a happy ending where the hero is restored to human society and his relationship with God. The friends of Job, including Elihu, are classic examples of the *Alazon*, the pompous fool who unsuccessfully attempts to appear wise.[3]

A similar position to the literary reading is the one represented by Marvin Pope. He has concluded there is no single classification into which the book may be placed.[4] Instead of a single genre with one life setting, many forms are brought into the literary structure, including those from law, wisdom and psalms. Thus the book is a literary text, not a specific genre. Pope characterizes Job as unique in literary form.

Much of the disagreement over the form of the book results in part from a failure to recognize the evolving morphology of the Joban tradition which culminates in the coalescence of three separate genres: didactic narrative, lament, and disputation. This is not to deny, of course, the literary skill and shaping of the book by the poet who provided the major structure. The poet, combining the techniques of historian and story-teller, draws together traditional forms and creates

1. Heinz Richter, *Studien zu Hiob* (Theologische Arbeiten II; Berlin Evangelische Verlagsanstat, 1955), 131. Similarly see G. Ernest Wright, 'The Lawsuit of God: A Form Critical Study of Deuteronomy 32', *Israel's Prophetic Heritage*, ed. B.W. Anderson and Walter Harrelson (New York: Harper and Row, 1962), 22-68; B. Gemser, 'The *rîb*—or Controversy Pattern—in Hebrew Mentality', *SVT* 3 (1960), 120-37.

2. Georg Fohrer, *Das Buch Hiob* (KAT 16; Gütersloh: Gerd Mohn, 1963).

3. J.W. Whedbee, 'The Comedy of Job', *Semeia* 7 (1970), 182-200; also see Norman Habel, *The Book of Job* (OTL; Philadelphia: Westminster, 1985); and J. Gerald Janzen, *Job* (Interpretation; Atlanta: John Knox, 1985).

4. Marvin Pope, *Job* (AB 15; Garden City: Doubleday, 1965), xxxi.

a compelling literary composition. The major forms and the coalescence of their trajectories in the book of Job may be traced as follows.

Hans-Peter Müller has identified a genre he calls the 'sapiential, didactic narrative', represented by the Joban narrative, the Joseph Story, and the Tale of Ahikar.[1] To these I would add the Egyptian 'Protests of the Eloquent Peasant', the Akkadian 'Poor Man of Nippur', and the Hittite 'Tale of Appu'. In these stories the hero is introduced and characterized by a particular virtue or ability. He then engages in an action confirming the virtue or talent. Then follows the introduction of the anti-hero or antagonist(s) whose deceitful action results in the hero's serious misfortune. The action proceeds by means of conflict in which the hero demonstrates virtue or special ability. The climax is a judgment scene which confirms the hero's integrity and restores or exalts him to a place of honor, while announcing punishment for the antagonist. The functions of the sapiential narrative are twofold: the hero personifies a virtue, complex of virtues, or special ability valued in the wisdom tradition, and the narrative postulates an order of reality in which the described virtue or ability is meaningful for human existence. The narrative of Job in chs. 1–2 and 42.7-17 continues this literary trajectory in the Hebrew wisdom tradition along with later expansions found in the Septuagint, Targums, and the pseudepigraphic Testament of Job.

The second literary trajectory in the Joban tradition is the lament. This includes the Sumerian 'A Man and His God', the Akkadian *Ludlul bel nemeqi*, two Akkadian texts from Ugarit (R.S. 25.460 and Louvre AO 4462), a Middle Kingdom Egyptian text ('the Lamentation of Khakheperre-sonbe') and with certain modifications Job's two soliloquies in 3 and 29–31.[2] In addition to the common theme of the righteous sufferer, these texts include many of the significant features of the individual lament: invocation, complaint(s) or description of suffering, reproachful questions, petition for help, condemnation of enemies or imprecation against wrongdoers, affirmation of confidence, confession of sins or assertion of innocence, acknowledgement of divine response, vow or pledge, and hymnic praise and blessings. Of significance also is the mode of first person narration. The book of Job

---

1. 'Die weisheitliche Lehrerzählung im Alten Testament und seiner Umwelt', *WO* 9 (1977), 77-98.
2. See Eberhard Gerstenberger, 'The Psalms', *Old Testament Form Criticism* (ed. John Hayes; San Antonio: Trinity University Press, 1977), 179-223.

incorporates this trajectory in many places in the poetry, but especially in the two soliloquies that introduce and conclude the dialogues (3; 29–31).

The third, and eventually dominating, trajectory of the Joban tradition is the disputation, a form represented by the following texts: 'The Babylonian Theodicy'[1] and the Egyptian 'Dialogue Between a Man and His Ba'.[2] Formal examples of the disputation which lack the Joban theme of the righteous sufferer include: the sarcastic letter of Hori to Amenemope (*ANET* 475, 479), several of Gordon's Edubba essays,[3] many fables (the Sumerian 'Emesh and Enten', the Sumerian 'Disputation between Summer and Winter', the bilingual 'Disputation between the Fox, the Wolf, and the Lion; and the Akkadian 'Disputation between the Ox and the Horse'),[4] and the judicial *rîb* (Deut. 32, Jer. 12, and frequently in Second Isaiah).[5] In regard to formal structure the disputation typically contains four parts: the address of the opponent, the accusation (indictment), the argument, and either the concluding summary statement or counsel given to the opponent.

Several Joban texts of the ancient Near East point to the convergence of two of these literary trajectories: the Sumerian 'A Man and His God' combines elements of the narrative with the lament, while the 'Protests of the Eloquent Peasant' is an example of the convergence of the narrative and disputation. The 'Dialogue between a Man and his Soul' combines the disputation and the lament. However, for the first time in the morphology of the Joban tradition, the biblical book of Job brings together all three trajectories: didactic narrative in 1–2, 42.7-17; lament in 3 and 29–31; and disputation in 4–27 and 38.1–42.6. Two later insertions occur in a second and third edition: the Elihu intrusion in chs. 32–37 which continues the disputation, and the poem on the inaccessibility of wisdom in 28. However, the first major edition and the final canonical shape of Job are dominated by the disputation. Not only do we have three lengthy cycles of debate between Job and the three friends, with no apparent resolution, but also further

---

1. *ANET*, 601-604 (see Leo G. Perdue, *Wisdom and Cult* [SBLDS 30; Missoula, MT: Scholars, 1977], 105ff.).

2. *ANET*, 405-407 (see Perdue, *Wisdom and Cult*, 31ff.).

3. E. Gordon, 'A New Look at the Wisdom of Sumer and Akkad', *BO* 17 (1960), 122-52.

4. *BWL*.

5. B. Gemser, 'The *rîb*—or Controversy—Pattern in Hebrew Mentality', 120-37.

dissputation in the climax (Job 38.1–42.6), with Yahweh coming not
only to pronounce judgment but also to debate. Even the four Elihu
speeches are disputations, though they are not well integrated into the
structure of the work.[1] The book is not created *de nouveau*, but
follows a traditional trajectory of typical forms. The traditional
features do not eliminate the creativity and freedom of the poet in
shaping the story. Yet they do give structure to the story, and allow
for a formal content in which meaning is shaped.

The argument for form has two important implications. First, the
book of Job must be interpreted within the tradition of wisdom literature, and not another setting. The three forms—didactic narrative,
disputation, and the lament of the righteous man—are specifically
nuanced by wisdom features. Second, literary form has important
implications for understanding the metaphorical theology of the book.
If correct in arguing that the battle and slave metaphors, which
intersect especially at the point of revolt, shape the book, the conflict
inherent in disputation would provide an appropriate literary form.
The book encompasses, then, a war of words between a famous hero
of the wisdom tradition and the Creator of heaven and earth.

Literary Integrity. The question of literary integrity has been the most
contested issue in the modern study of Job. The major questions center
on the following texts: the Elihu speeches in 32–37, the relation of the
prose narrative (1–2, 42.7-17) to the dialogues, the Yahweh speeches
and Job's responses (38.1–42.6), the Wisdom Hymn (28), and the
arrangement of the third cycle of dialogue (24–27).

The conclusion that the Elihu speeches appeared sometime after the
composition of the poetic dialogues is based on the following observations: Yahweh's speeches in 38–42 begin with a rebuke of the person
who last spoke, which fits Job but not Elihu; Elihu is absent in the
Prologue and not mentioned in the Epilogue when the three opponents
are named; some of the content of Elihu's final speech anticipates
Yahweh's answer and borrows from the Yahweh speeches (e.g. 37.14-
20); the arguments of Elihu, in spite of his statements to the contrary,

---

1. Canonization arbitrarily arrested the current shape of the Joban tradition in the
biblical book of Job. That the morphology continued to evolve is evidenced by the
expansions in the LXX and the Targum at Qumran (11Qtg Job; J.P.M. van der Ploeg
and A.S. van der Woude, *Le Targum de Job de la grotte XI de Qumran* [Leiden:
Brill, 1971]). And the Testament of Job retells the narrative of the patient Job and
inserts its own expansion—a testament of the dying Job to his gathered children.

simply restate those of the three opponents; his responses are artificial efforts to take Job's speeches and respond to them point by point, as though they were already present in final form; and Job does not respond to these speeches; indeed there is no indication that Job is even aware they have been made.

Efforts to include the Elihu speeches as original to the poetic dialogues have recently resurfaced.[1] Drawing from the method of 'close reading', Habel and Janzen have included them as integral to the book. For example Habel argues that Elihu is presented as the arbiter whom Job has summoned to adjudicate his legal case against God. Instead Elihu renders the decision that a mortal cannot engage El in litigation. Further, the Elihu episode is 'a deliberate anticlimax, which retards the plot and leads the audience to expect a plot development which is the opposite of what happens'.[2] The audience concludes Job will not get his day in court, and then is shocked by the theophany. While Habel's argument is ingenious, it fails to convince not only because it does not successfully answer the above doubts, but also because it raises its own problems as well: Elihu is nowhere presented as the arbiter; indeed he even mentions the 'mediator' as the heavenly intercessor in 33.19-28; further Job abandons the hope for an arbiter by recognizing that he will have to deal with God; the challenge in 31.35 is directed explicitly towards the throne of heaven, not a human intermediary; and the form of the Elihu speeches are disputations, not the judicial (even if not binding) pronouncement of an arbiter.

Janzen argues the speeches are integral to the book because they are presented as divinely inspired revelation posed as the alternative to the Yahweh speeches in 38.1–42.6. Thus Job is called upon to decide which is the true revelation. And by contrasting the two sets of speeches (Elihu's and God's) there is a rejection of Elihu's retributive justice as a proper understanding of exile. Janzen's arguments also fail to convince. First, as early as 4.12-17 Eliphaz claims direct witness to a specific dream revelation, while Elihu attributes inspiration to the spirit which is present in *all* people. Second, Janzen himself admits that the content of Elihu's speeches merely repeats the three opponents. Third, is it believable that Job is really being asked to decide between the authenticity of Elihu's revelation and Yahweh's? To whom does Job respond? Fourth, how could it be a choice for Job to make

1. Habel, *Job*; Janzen, *Job*.
2. Habel, *Job*, 33.

between the two revelations, when Yahweh's speeches comprise a direct repudiation of Elihu's retributive justice as a proper response to suffering? If it is obvious to an audience that Yahweh's revelation negates that of Elihu, why would it not be to the character Job? The Elihu speeches do retard the action, but so much so that they produce tedium, not the necessary respite needed by the audience. The speeches are best explained as a later addition to a literary trajectory that is centuries old. They are written by a scribe who wished to espouse traditional retributive justice and personal piety in attempting to answer the blasphemous Job.[1]

The relationship between the prose narrative and the poetic dialogues has also been strongly debated in Joban research. In sum, the positions have formed along three major fronts. The first position dates the narrative either in the monarchial or the premonarchial period, perhaps originating as an adaptation of a Canaanite hero epic.[2] In this case, the story is taken by a later poet and used as a foil for introducing a new text that repudiates the narrative's theology of suffering as divine discipline. A second position argues the narrative and dialogues were separate pieces brought together by a later editor either to be read as a continuous story or to juxtapose two very different texts. And a third position contends the narrative and dialogues were both written by the same author and were intended to be read together.[3]

There are difficulties in easily associating the narrative with the dialogues. The narrative introduces 'the satan' as an antagonist who strangely disappears after the end of ch. 1; Job, the pious and patient sufferer of the Prologue, becomes the impious, impatient rebel in the dialogues; Job is rebuked by God in 38.2 and 40.2, but is praised for speaking correctly about God in the Epilogue; the theme of suffering as divine testing and the truthfulness of the theory of retribution in the narrative are negated completely by the dialogues; and the name Yahweh in the narrative is replaced with El and El derivatives and epithets in the dialogues, with the exception of the prose introductions to the speeches from the whirlwind in 38.1; 40.1; 40.6, and a disputed occurrence in 12.9. On the other hand, the prose introduction provides

1. A. de Wilde, *Das Buch Hiob* (*OTS* 22; Leiden: Brill, 1981), 2-5.
2. Foher, 'Überlieferung und Wandlung der Hioblegende', *Studien zum Buche Hiob* (2nd edn; Gütersloh: Gerd Mohn, 1982); Nahum Sarna, 'Epic Substratum in the Prose of Job', *JBL* 76 (1957), 13-25.
3. Janzen, *Job*, 22-24; Habel, *Job*, 35-39.

the necessary preparation for the dialogues. Finally, the judgment scene in 42.7-17 does appear to be a necessary refutation of the friends and a legal decision by the divine judge that Job is 'correct' in what he said about God earlier. It appears the poet has taken a popular wisdom tale and given it a new reading by connecting it to the poetic dialogues. The result is a refutation of the narrative's theory of the unquestioned sovereignty of God and the retributive discipline undergirding ethical response. The new reading not only demonstrates that suffering as discipline is sheer nonsense in the world of Babylonian holocaust, but also that righteous existence in the world demands contending with God.

A compelling case against the authenticity of the speeches of God and the responses of Job has not been successfully mounted. However, many efforts to compact the two speeches and two responses into a single God speech followed by one response of Job have been under-taken.[1] According to some, the second speech on Behemoth and Leviathan is not in the same interrogative form as the first speech, and appears to add nothing to the original argumentation. Further, the Leviathan section is unduly long in comparison to those dealing with Behemoth and the other beasts in 38.39–39.30 and 40.15-24. And the second speech of Job repeats some of the first God speech: 42.31 = 38.2, and 42.4 = 38.3b and 40.7b. My own position is to accept the present arrangement. While interrogatives dominate the first speech and descriptive praise the second, it is clear that both Yahweh speeches alternate questions with descriptions. Further, the lengthy Leviathan speech does provide an inclusio for the dialogues (cf. 3.8). To remove it would not only violate the text's literary integrity, but would also eliminate the climactic and most important occurrence of the combat metaphor in the entire book. Likewise the two responses of Job are maintained in their present form, for they are a necessary and crucial indication of Job's movement from indictment, to silence, to praise.

The 'Poem on the Inaccessibility of Wisdom' (28) has often been regarded as late. In the present arrangement of the book, the poem is placed in the mouth of Job, at the crucial point where he concludes his dialogues with the friends and begins the lament-like soliloquy in 29–31. Indeed it is the position of the poem that has led some scholars to argue it belongs in its present place. Part of the difficulty with 28 is the present disruption of the latter part of the third cycle, a point

---

1. Fohrer, *Introduction to the Old Testament*, 327-29.

which will be addressed below. Yet the thesis of the poem—the inability of humans to find and understand divine wisdom—simply does not fit the consistently constructed arguments of Job and the friends to this point. Both Job and the friends claim access to and some understanding of wisdom, though the friends have argued that the wisdom of God transcends human comprehension. However, it is the radical negation of human ability to discover wisdom that makes this poem so different. Indeed the poem would better fit the speeches of God than those of the human antagonists, for in the theophany the direct assault on Job's and human wisdom is undertaken. Yet in its current place, Job 28 anticipates and therefore undercuts the shocking nature of God's negation of human wisdom. It would seem best to regard the poem as a later insertion, written and placed into the dialogues to represent the views of a pious sage who objects to the quest to discover wisdom. Understood in this way, the hymn condemns at least implicitly both Job and his friends for attempting the impossible, that is, to come to a knowledge of the wisdom of God.

Some have seen the poem as an 'interlude' between the end of the dialogues and the beginning of the theophanic speeches. In a variation of this effort, Habel attempts to retain the poem as integral to the original composition of the book by regarding it as an authorial judgment on the futility of the search for wisdom in the dialogues between Job and the friends. God's design and governance of the earth cannot be discovered. Yet, were this the case, a significant part of the answer of the Yahweh speeches would have been anticipated and therefore upstaged. Besides, the present structure of the poetic book gives no indication here or elsewhere of authorial intrusion. One finds a third person point of view, which might be equated with authorial intrusion, only in the narrative Prologue and Epilogue. Indeed, in the present arrangement of the book the hymn is attributed to Job.

Perhaps the knottiest literary problem to unravel in the book of Job is the obvious disarray of the third cycle.[1] Following the consistent pattern of the first two cycles of debate, one anticipates that this last cycle would have three speeches of Job alternating with three from the friends. However, in the present arrangement Zophar has no final speech at all, while Bildad is given a truncated speech in 25.1-6. Further, the lengthy Job speeches appear to include material quite uncharacteristic of his earlier arguments, but more than appropriate

1. Fohrer, *Introduction to the Old Testament*, 326-27.

for the position consistently argued by the friends (especially 27.13-23; and probably 26.5-14). The simplest rearrangement to achieve a proper and understandable order is

21	Job
22	Eliphaz
23	Job
24	Zophar (?)
25.1-6; 26.5-14	Bildad
26.1-4; 27.1-12	Job
27.13-23	Zophar.[1]

While the book of Job is a compilation of several redactional stages, the effort by later tradents and redactors is made to integrate constructively their material into the earlier levels. And each addition or redaction reconstitutes the meaning of the text. While careful *literary* analysis does uncover the seams of redactional work, it should not be concluded that the book is therefore a jumble of confusing editorial parts which are not integrated into the structure of the book. It is true that the Wisdom Hymn (28) and the Elihu Speeches (32–37) disrupt the flow of the earlier poetic book. But when seen in their proper role, i.e. later articulations of faith language, then a proper understanding of the components of the entire book may be derived. But what I am primarily after is the meaning of the book prior to the addition of the hymn and the Elihu speeches; that is, the literary composition put together by the artist usually known as the Joban poet.

---

1. Habel, *Job*, 37.

Chapter 5

DIVINE JUDGMENT AND HUMAN DESTINY:
THE NARRATIVE TALE AND THE OPENING SOLILOQUY

1. *The Narrative Tale: Divine Judgment (Job 1–2)*

Introduction. In following the mythic tradition exemplified by *Atrahasis*, the prologue (chs. 1–2) centers on judgment in which the destiny of Job is determined by the head of the divine council, Yahweh. Job, already characterized as the 'slave' (עבד) of God, is sentenced to two torturous fates: the loss of wealth, children and status, and the affliction of unspeakable physical agony. In these two decrees, Job's existence is reduced to utter wretchedness. However, the initial reactions by Job appear to be pious acceptance of Yahweh's decrees.

The prologue was originally a didactic tale in which the hero embodies a virtue or complex of virtues valued by the wisdom tradition.[1] In this case the twin virtues of traditional wisdom, 'fear of God and turning away from evil', are personified in the character Job.[2] The type of religiosity represented by Job in the first scene (1.1-5) is the sapiential ideal: wise behavior rooted in faith leads to divine protection and the rewards of large family and wealth. The illustration and

---

1. H.-P. Müller, 'Die weisheitliche Lehrerzählung im Alten Testament und seiner Umwelt', *WO* 9 (1977–78), 77-98. For the narrative as a Canaanite legend similar to the Danel story, see Shalom Spiegel, 'Noah, Danel, and Job', *Louis Ginzberg Jubilee Volume* (New York: The American Academy for Jewish Research, 1945), 305-56.

2. Siegfried Plath (*Furcht Gottes* [Arbeiten zur Theologie 2; Stuttgart: Calwer, 1962], 54-55) argues that in the sapiential usage of 'fear of the Lord', there are three distinctive features. The 'fear of the Lord' leads to the gift of wisdom (Prov. 9.10), modesty (Prov. 8.13) and good fortune (Prov. 10.27). In general 'fear of God' means subjection to the will and authority of the creator and ruler of the world who has established meaningful orders for the course of the world and the life of the individual. Fear of God is expressed in humble and trusting submission to this divine rule which leads then to well-being and the turning away of evil (68).

confirmation on the character's virtue is normally a feature of the initial scenes. In the Prologue, Job is so scrupulous in his religious devotion that he continues to offer 'burnt sacrifices' for his children, just in case they have sinned by cursing God in their hearts. Further, the close relation with a personal deity is an important feature of Akkadian religion and appears central to the Joban literature of the righteous sufferer. In Akkadian wisdom, the wise person carefully fulfills cultic responsibilities to the personal god in return for protection and reward.

The next development in the didactic tale is the appearance of an antagonist who seeks to undo the hero and his virtue by plot, temptation, or subterfuge. In Job's case, it is at first 'the satan' who questions the basis for Job's integrity, arguing before the council it is only divine protection (a 'hedge') that Job seeks for his services. Were disaster allowed to strike, Job would curse God to his face. The didactic tale then proceeds with one or more episodes of conflict between the hero and antagonist, with the hero emerging unscathed with virtue intact. Job survives two devastating series of catastrophes and responds to each with praise and affirmation, not curse and denial. He even chastises his wife, who becomes the second antagonist by tempting him to curse God and end his misery.

The visit of the three friends who come to console Job may well have led in the older version of the didactic narrative to a dialogue in which they eventually concluded Job was being unjustly treated by his personal deity and therefore should renounce him. Presumably Job's response would have been similar to those of other righteous sufferers: he maintains his integrity and appeals to God to redeem him. In so doing he would have expressed admirably in word and deed the virtue of patient suffering and faith in the unlimited sovereignty of Yahweh whose freedom knows no limits.

The Metaphor of Word. The metaphor which shapes and structures the prologue is the edict of the judge of the divine assembly, drawn from the mythical traditions of Mesopotamia and Canaan. Important for creation theology and the metaphorical model governing the didactic narrative are the two scenes in heaven involving the divine assembly. In the first scene in heaven (1.6-12), the divine assembly convenes presumably during New Year when, in Babylonian mythology, the fates of humans are determined for the coming year. In Babylonia the divine assembly was comprised of 'the great gods', some fifty in number, and the seven 'gods of the fates'. In the *Enuma elish*, the council of the gods convenes in response to crisis, and has the authority to select a god to deal with the crisis. He makes Marduk king, and he issues edicts to which even gods are subject. Marduk receives the absolute power of the edict in exchange for his defeat of Tiamat. As ruler of the assembly, Marduk issues the decision to create humanity and to order and structure the places and functions of both gods and creatures. The divine edict both shapes and maintains the order of reality. In the *akitu* festival, the gods met to determine the destinies of nations and people for the coming year, a practice reflected in later rabbinic understanding of Rosh ha-Shana.

The divine council in Ugaritic mythology[1] was known as 'the assembly of the (sons of) gods', or 'the assembly of El'. It was presided over by El who held the power of decree. The meeting place was *hursanu*, El's mountain, which was the center of the cosmos and the place of judgment.[2] El's decrees maintained order in a universe placed at threat by contentious gods vying for kingship over the earth.

The divine council in Israelite religion was designated by the following: 'the council of El' (Ps. 82.1), the 'assembly' (Amos 8.14), 'the mount of meeting' (Isa. 14.13) and 'the council' (Ps. 89.8). The members of the assembly are the gods, usually called 'the sons of the gods/God' (Ps. 82.6), and the 'holy ones' (Deut. 33.2-3; Job 5.1). Located on Mt Zion which was the center of creation (Pss. 46; 48; 76), the place of Yahweh's dwelling ('tent of meeting' and later the Solomonic temple) and the location for the waters of paradise, the assembly, headed by Yahweh, had the responsibility for governance of the world. As judge, Yahweh's edict ordered and maintained creation (Job 38.11, 33), condemned the wicked to destruction (including the gods [Psalm 82]), and determined the destiny of nations and people (Deut. 32.8; Ps. 82; Isa. 40; 1 Kgs 22.19-23). It was here that know-

---

1. Mullen, *The Assembly of the Gods*; and Frank M. Cross, 'The Council of Yahweh in Second Isaiah', *JNES* 12 (1953), 274-77.

2. Mullen, *The Assembly of the Gods*, 130-32. He further argues that the cosmic mountain has located at its base the life-giving source of waters and the entrance to heaven as well as the underworld. This case is the 'place of interrogation' where entrance to the underworld occurs (132, n. 37). El's tent is located at the source of waters, at the entrance to the underworld, and it is here that he gives his decrees. At the center of the earth, the region of paradise, El dwells and issues his decrees which maintain the order of creation.

ledge of divine rulership and the design of God's governance could be obtained (Jer. 23.18; Job 15.7-9).

The two most significant types of decrees generally issued by the head of the council had to do with rule (kingship) and life and death. And it is important to note that both Marduk and Yahweh were storm deities and warriors whose defeat of chaos led to their kingship over the divine assembly and whose power maintained their positions (Ps. 89.5-13).[1]

In the abbreviated scene in Job 1.6-12, the gods have convened in divine council (בני האלהים) and do homage to Yahweh, thus recognizing him as ruler of the assembly. They convene presumably on the mountain of God at the time of the New Year ('the day'), since no impending crisis or special request appears to have necessitated a special meeting.[2] This was the day of new creation, when the world is reconstituted by divine decree, following the defeat of chaos. Among the council members is 'the satan' ('accuser'),[3] the god responsible for discovering evil on the earth, for reporting it to the assembly for judgment, and for carrying out the edict on the earth. Yahweh's own suspicion leads to the query about the integrity of his slave Job. In response, the satan insinuates that Job's righteousness is based solely on his desire for divine protection. If removed, he would curse the Lord. The decision of Yahweh, contained in the authoritative edict that determines Job's destiny for the year, is to deliver him into the power of the satan for testing, with the limitation imposed that no personal

1. It is important to note that Ps. 82 refers to God's judgment against the gods for injustice which shakes the foundations of the earth, that is, destroys the created order. He warns them that continued misrule of the earth will result in their dying 'like Adam' (v. 7), perhaps alluding to the judgment of Yahweh in council against Adam for his revolt against divine decree prohibiting the fruit of the tree of knowledge of good and evil. See Gen. 6.1-4 which speaks of the marriage of the gods with human women—perhaps an attempt to overturn the decree of death for humanity by enabling humans to become divine. This revolt of the council and humans led to God's decree limiting humans to a life span of 120 years, and finally to the flood itself. The rebellious nature of the council of gods is underscored by Eliphaz in Job 4.17-18.

2. According to the Targum and later Jewish tradition, the fates for the coming year were established on Yom Kippur (H.H. Rowley, *Job* [Don Mills, Ontario: Nelson, 1970], 36).

3. The use of the definite article before 'satan' indicates an office, not a personal name. 'Satan' is used as a personal name in 1 Chron. 21.1 and Zech. 3.1. The term *satan* seems to be a legal title for the 'accuser' in the lawcourts (Ps. 109.6). For a detailed discussion, see Rivkah S. Kluger, *Satan in the Old Testament* (Evanston: Northwestern University Press, 1967).

harm should come upon God's slave. The decree is directly responsible for Job's catastrophic loss of all that he has.

In 2.1-6 another meeting of the divine assembly takes place during the following New Year ('the day'), when Yahweh admits to the satan responsibility for Job's losses. Even so the divine judge consents to test the satan's contention that personal harm to Job would result in cursing. The only limitation to the edict empowering the satan to harm Job is the proscription against death. Armed with the authority of the edict, the satan proceeds to afflict Job with loathsome sores covering his entire body.

The metaphor of creation in the Prologue, which continues in the Epilogue when Yahweh renders judgment, is that of word. In this case it is the legal rule or edict which determines order and destiny following the defeat of chaos in the battle preceding enthronement and judgment. As sovereign ruler, Yahweh's unalterable decree appears to remain unquestioned by Job, even when it results in highly unfair and grossly unjust catastrophes, including the death of his ten children.

The Metaphor of Slave. The place and function of humanity in the world of the prologue is that of slave (עבד, 1.8; 2.3) to the gods. Drawing on Mesopotamian religious precedent in which individual religion is encapsulated in obedient worship of the personal god and goddess, Job is presented as a perfect man who 'fears God and turns from evil'.[1] His scrupulous attention to cultic devotion is underlined in the very opening scene. Indeed, this 'fear of God' becomes the issue of contention as the satan argues it is only divine protection and reward, not selfless piety, that motivates Job's religious behavior. But the satan appears to be proven wrong, as Job responds according to the highest ideals of cultic loyalty to his personal god. To the first test in which he loses all that he has, including his ten children, Job responds in praise: 'I came forth naked from the womb of my mother, and I shall return there naked; Yahweh has given, and Yahweh has taken away; blessed be the name of Yahweh.' Using the birth metaphor of the anthropological tradition, Job praises his personal god as the one who had given him all that he has had and has providentially watched over him from his birth. Indeed Job submits that it was divine decree that made him wealthy and a father of ten children, and it is now that same destiny-establishing edict that has made him destitute (cf. Ps. 139.17). Instead

---

1. See especially 'The Babylonian Theodicy', *ANET*, 601-604.

of uttering a curse against his personal god, Job blesses Yahweh's name, language designed to support divine sovereignty and to praise the creator who determines the fates. The 'fear of God' is exemplified by the righteous Job's humble acceptance of God as creator and determiner of individual destinies.

The response to the second testing appears at first glance to be similar. After affliction with loathsome sores, Job disputes the wife's contention that should he 'curse' God and die: 'You speak as one of the followers of Dame Folly. Shall we receive good from the hand (power) of God, and not also evil?' And the narrator emphasizes that Job did not sin with his lips, though there is no reference this time to not cursing God in his heart. External language of blessing continues, though the narrator may be intimating that internal doubts are beginning to be raised by the character. And certainly the implied audience, well versed in conventional wisdom and granted privileged access to the sacred council denied to the character Job, has been disoriented by the new metaphors—Yahweh as corrupt judge, and humanity, even righteous sages, as slaves.

2. *The Opening Soliloquy: The Assault on Creation (Job 3)*

Introduction. The anthropological mythic pattern continues with the dialogues in 3–27 as Job begins to depict human nature and function in the images of slavery and toil. In contrast to conventional wisdom's portrait of creation as good and of humanity as kings divinely commissioned to go forth into the world and master life, Job experiences creation as oppressive slavery, sealed by an unalterable fate.

The Destabilization of Creation Language.[1] The opening chapter of the poetic dialogues (3.1-26) provides an abrupt change from the 'god-fearing' Job of the prologue to the initially despairing and finally angry rebel attacking the justice of God. Indeed the poet has used the old hero legend of Job to raise questions about the integrity of Job, the moral nature of the universe, and most importantly the power and justice of God. But now that the setting is given, Job joins his wife and the satan in an assault on the justice of God. After *seven* days and nights of silence, a period immediately evoking the imagery of

---

1. See my article, 'Job's Assault on Creation', *HAR* 10 (1987), 295-315.

creation (Gen. 1.1–2.4a), the opening words of Job are a curse, exactly as the satan had predicted and the wife had prompted.

Introduction (vv. 1-2)

1. Afterwards, Job opened his mouth and cursed his Day.[1]
2. And Job responded and said:

Strophe I (vv. 3-10)

3. 'Let the Day perish on which I was born,
   And the Night which said, 'A Mighty Man[2] is conceived'.

4. Let that Day be darkness,
   Let not Eloah above divine for it,
   Let not light break forth upon it.

5. Let primordial darkness and deep blackness defile[3] it,
   Let a thick cloud settle upon it,
   Let the priests[4] of Yam[5] fill it with terror.

6. Let the darkness of the underworld seize that Night,
   Let it not be joined[6] to the days of the year,
   Let it not enter the number (of days)[7] of the months.

7. Behold, let that Night be barren,
   Let no ecstatic cry occur in it,

8. Let the cursers of Yam[8] damn it,

---

1. Written in prose, 3.1 could belong to the prose narrative. However, it is more likely a transition to the new work written by the poet.

2. Interpreting גבר ('man') as 'mighty man, warrior, hero', on occasion one of royal stature (Exod. 12.37; Judg. 5.30), a meaning more often associated with גבור (Judg. 6.12; 11.1; 1 Sam. 9.1; Hab. 2.5; Zech. 13.7). The parallel text in Jer. 20.15 speaks of the birth of a 'male' (זכר).

3. Reading גאל as 'defile', not 'redeem'. The ritual of cursing would include desecration (cf. Mal. 1.7; Ezra 2.62 = Neh. 7.64).

4. Reading כמרי for כמרירי, a case of dittography. The כמר is the pagan priest (2 Kgs 23.5; Hos. 10.5; Zeph. 1.4), not the legitimate כהן priest of Israelite religion. The MT reading would translate: 'like bitterness (or perhaps 'darkness') of the day'.

5. Reading ים for יום ('day').

6. Reading יחד (qal imperfect jussive, 'to be joined') in place of the MT חדה ('to rejoice over'). See Gen. 49.6 which parallels the same two verbs, 'be joined' and 'come, enter' (בא). The parallel passage, Jer. 20.14-18, does have the motif of 'joy' (v. 15).

7. LXX adds εἰς ἡμέρας ('into days'), probaby an explanatory addition.

8. Reading ים for יום. Compare the Aramaic incantation: 'I will cast spells upon you with the spell of the sea and the spell of the dragon Leviathan' (G.R. Driver,

The skilled ones who awaken Leviathan,

9. Let the stars of its dawn become dark,
 Let it wait in hope for light but find only nothingness,
 Let it not look upon the eyelids of Dawn,

10. Because it did not close the doors of my womb[1]
 And conceal sorrow from my eyes.'

Strophe II (vv. 11-19)

11. 'Why did I not die at birth,[2]
 Expire at the time I came forth from the womb?

12. Why did the knees receive me,
 Or the breasts that I should suck?

13. For now I would be at rest and silent,
 I would sleep, then I would have rest,

14. With kings and counsellors of the earth,
 Those who rebuild ruins for themselves;

15. Or with princes who have gold,
 Who fill their houses with silver.

16. Or why was I not like an aborted fetus,
 Like infants who did not see light?

17. There the wicked cease their raging,[3]
 And there those whose strength has expired are at rest.

18. There the prisoners together are in repose,
 They do not hear the voice of the taskmaster.

19. The small and the great are there,
 The slave is free from his lord.'

SVT 3 [1955], 72). Also regard the 'cursers of Yam' as an attributive genitive with the meaning of Yam's cursers, that is, priests of Yam skilled to arouse Leviathan from the depths of chaos and to destroy Night, Job's primordial enemy.

1. LXX reads γαστρὸς μητρός μου ('my mother's womb'), probably an explanatory addition.

2. Literally 'die from the womb (מרחם)', i.e. at the time of birth.

3. רגז refers to God's wrath 'shaking' creation in Ps. 18.8 and Job 9.6. In Job 3, the allusion may be to the 'shaking' or 'noise' (rebellion) that led to the near annihilation of humanity by the gods in Akkadian mythology (cf. Lambert and Millard, *Atra-hasis*; cf. Isa. 14.16). If so, Job is indicating that the chaos wrought by the wicked that destroys creation is ended in death. This would be the first echo of the rebellion motif of the mythical model eventually used by the poet to describe Job's own assault against heaven.

Strophe III (vv. 20-26)

20. 'Why is light given to the weary,
    And life to the bitter in soul?

21. Those who wait for death (Mot), but he does not come,
    And dig for him like hidden treasures.

22. Those who rejoice greatly,
    And exult when they find the tomb.

23. Why to a man whose way is hidden,
    Whom Eloah has hedged in?

24. For my sighing comes before my bread,
    And my groanings are poured out like water.

25. For what I exceedingly fear comes upon me,
    And what I abhor approaches me.

26. I am not at ease, and I am not quiet.
    I do not rest for wrath comes.'

Verse 1 makes the transition ('afterwards') from the prose narrative to the opening chapter of the poetic dialogues, while v. 2 is the standard introduction to the individual speeches (4.1; 6.1, etc.). Beginning with v. 3, the remainder of the chapter is an elegantly crafted poem of three strophes appropriating major elements of the form and content of the individual lament: vv. 3-10—the curses against Day and Night; vv. 11-19—the wish to have died and entered Sheol immediately; and vv. 20-26—the desire to know why one is born to suffer.[1] The three temporal movements are the movement back to birth (past), the transition to death (future), and the return to present misery—shifts easily negotiated by the mythic language of religious poetry. Job moves from curses directed at negating his own birth, to the desire for death and the painless nonexistence of the underworld, to the awakening of the passion to understand why suffering is the common lot of humankind.

The dominant image is the contrasting pair of light and darkness (day/night),[2] a creation image descriptive of the fundamental duality

---

1. See David Noel Freedman, 'The Structure of Job 3', *Bib* 49 (1968), 503-508.

2. Light was the first of God's creation (Gen. 1.3-5), spoken into existence even before the making of the luminaries. Light is more than a natural element: it is a fundamental power which brings life, the manifestation of the presence and power of

of reality: day/night, life/death, birth/ death (the darkness of womb and grave), order/chaos, and knowledge/mystery. 'Darkness' (חשֶׁךְ) is the key word in the initial strophe (v. 4), while 'light' (אור) is the important term in the final strophe (v. 20). The mood of dark despair is set by the rich variety of words for darkness: חשֶׁךְ ('darkness'), צלמות ('death's shadow'), ענה ('thick cloud'), and אפל ('heavy darkness of the underworld').[1] Mythic darkness is to engulf all forms of light: נהרה ('daylight'), כוכבי נשׁף ('stars of twilight'), אור ('light'), and שׁחר ('dawn'), leading to total darkness. Also significant as a creation image is the feature of 'rest' (נוח), found in vv. 13, 17, and 26. In Genesis 1, God's resting (שׁבת) on the seventh day following six days of creation and the blessing of the seventh day combine to form a sanctifying action that enhances life and maintains the order of creation. What Job longs for, though it will not come, is the cessation of existence, the quiet repose of total oblivion, achieved by the negation of divine blessing.[2] In a direct attack on the entire cosmos, Job demands a complete inversion of creation that would move life back into the regions of chaos and nonexistence where all pain and suffering would cease. Toil and the drudgery of life would end. Failing this, he begins to demand an answer to the 'why' of pain in human existence, a query that eventually leads to disputation and an all-out assault on heaven itself.[3]

One of the more striking features of the lament-like soliloquy in ch. 3 is the disorienting reversal of creation language. The destabilization of metaphors which had shaped the mythological wisdom texts of origins and maintenance is attempted through the language of negation. Once the meaning systems of the models which had shaped and interpreted reality have disintegrated, the language and

---

God, and the illumination of insight; it is the force which overcomes darkness and keeps it at bay. Darkness is one of the features of chaos existing before the creation; it is associated with sheol and death, the absence of divine presence, the blindness of ignorance and folly, and the opponent of life and well-being (cf. O. Piper, 'Light, Light and Darkness', *IDB* 3 [1962], 130-31).

1. כמרירי יום ('like the bitterness of day' = 'eclipse') is the MT reading which we have chosen to alter (cf. our notes on 3.5 above).

2. The 'rest' (נוח) for which Job longs (v. 17) is an ironic use of the *terminus technicas* for the promised land in the salvation history tradition (מנוחה; Deut. 26.5-9). נוח is a synonym of שׁבת in Exod. 20.11; 23.12; and Deut. 5.14.

3. Dermont Cox, 'The Desire for Oblivion in Job 3', *Studi Biblici Franciscani* 23 (1973), 37-49; *The Triumph of Impotence* (Analecta Gregoriana 212; Rome: Gregorion University Press, 1978).

therefore the plausibility structures of society and religion deconstruct. The world returns to chaos.

The Metaphor of Word. The first metaphor that Job deconstructs is creation by word. The concluding verse of the prose story tells of the seven days and nights of silence which passed between Job and the three opponents when no word was spoken. The friends, devastated by the disconfirming experience of Job, have no language to speak. As regards mood, however, the void of silence is soon filled with the protest of angry curse.

The form of ch. 3 is similar to a lament, though without the standard invocation and petition for divine aid. In their place one finds a lengthy curse, consisting of seven incantations directed against the Day of Job's birth and the Night of his conception. Curses are normally uttered by skilled priests and magicians whose dark powers may be harnessed in proper formulae to destroy one's enemies.[1] As power-laden language, incantations are well known to the cultures of the ancient Near East.[2] In the Egyptian Book of the Dead, they provide the deceased with power against the monster Apophis during the journey to the afterlife,[3] while in creation myths they constrain the power of Apophis and enable Re to sail successfully through the dark subterranean ocean to recreate the earth with another dawn. Since Apophis was also identified with the king's historical enemies who threatened his rule, curses against this monster were designed to protect the Egyptian state, founded on the eternal order of creation (Maat).[4] Akkadian incantations were often initiated by references to creation in order that the curse may participate in the power of creation. For example, in the cursing of the worm thought to be

---

1. The best example is Balaam, hired by the King of Moab to destroy the invading Hebrews with curses (Num. 22–24). The irony is that God makes him utter life-enhancing blessings, instead of death-bringing curses. For a detailed study of the curse, see Willy Schottroff, *Der altisraelitische Fluchspruch* (WMANT 30; Neukirchen Neukirchener Verlag, 1969). Also see Sidney Blank, 'The Curse, the Blasphemy, the Spell, and the Oath', *HUCA* 23 (1950), 73-95.

2. In the Old Testament, the curse of God or prince is punished by death (Exod. 22.27), though it was commonly used in the curse of one's enemy (Judg. 9.27; 2 Sam. 16.5-13). Curse is the opposite of blessing, for instead of enhancing the structures of life it destroys them.

3. *ANET*, 11-12.

4. *ANET*, 6-7.

responsible for toothaches, one incantation begins with a cosmogony speaking of the origins of heaven and earth.[1]

By contrast, Job's use of sacred language in curse and lament is designed to awaken chaos to destroy. With seven incantations Job attempts to destroy his arch-enemies, Day and Night, not merely the times associated with his own birth, though they are certainly included, but the very temporal structure which separates and maintains the created order.[2] And Job calls on the powers of darkness, including the arousing of Yam and Leviathan from the Deep, to engulf Night, destroying the daily cycle that orders the cosmos. By the language of curse encapsulating the powers of primordial chaos opposing the cosmos since the beginning, Job engages in a frontal assault on creation.[3]

The number of incantations, some seven directed against Day and Night, echoes the temporal frame of the creation narrative in Gen. 1.1–2.4a. Indeed Fishbane has argued that the sequence of Job's incantations approximates that of the priestly creation:

Job 3		*Genesis 1*	
4a	That Day, Let there be darkness	5	The first day Let there be light
4b	Let Eloah *above* not seek it	7	And the waters *above* the firmament
5a	Let darkness defile it	2	and darkness was upon the face of the deep
		4	And God separated between the light and the darkness
6	That Night. . . days of the year	14	lights in heaven to separate day and night, and signs for days and years
8	Leviathan	21	Great sea monsters
9	hope for light	15	lights to give light upon the earth

1. Michael Fishbane, 'Jeremiah IV 23-26 and Job III 3-13: A Recovered Use of the Creation Pattern', *VT* 21 (1971), 151-62. The best example is 'A Cosmological Incantation: The Worm and the Toothache', *ANET*, 100-101.

2. Day and night comprise a frequent word pair in creation contexts: Gen. 1.5ff.; 8.22; Pss. 74.16; 136.7-9; Jer. 31.35.

3. The 'sea-cursers' and 'skilled ones' of v. 8 are incantation priests who possess the power to curse or bless, to destroy or heal. They are capable of 'charming' Leviathan, thereby subduing his power, or of 'arousing' him to action to destroy.

11	die from the mother's womb	26	Let us make man
13	rest in the tomb	2.2-3	Sabbath rest.[1]

Just as important for Job's word of negation is the formulation of
the initial incantation, which reverses the language event of creation in
Gen. 1.1–2.4a. In the Priestly document, God speaks creation into
existence using eight major commands (altogether 15 jussives and
imperatives). Job uses 16 jussives and prohibitions in his formulation
of the incantations, attempting to overpower the creative structure of
divine language. This is especially apparent in the shaping of the
incantation in Job 1.4 ('let there be darkness', יהי חשך), where Job tries
to negate the first act of divine creation, the commanding of light into
existence ('let there be light', יהי אור). In P the act of separating light
from darkness, naming day and night, and giving them their function
of ordering the temporal structure of reality, is the first and primary
act of creation. Consequently, the appearance of each new day
responding to God's command is a recreation of the temporal order.
Priestly ritual and calendar are designed to maintain the separation of
light and darkness and the recurring cycle of day and night. By contrast Job's curse destroys this separation, hurling Day and Night back
into the oblivion of undifferentiated chaos, thereby deconstructing
order and meaning.[2] With this series of curses, Job seeks to reverse
creation, thereby negating all life, including his own.[3]

The Metaphor of Fertility. The metaphor of birth enters the poem at
the beginning, in strophe one, and continues into the second where Job
wishes he had experienced a blissful transition from the repose of the
womb to the tranquility of the underworld. Even the image of the gift

1. Fishbane, 'Jeremiah IV 23-26 and Job III 3-13'. As Fishbane notes, Jer. 4.23-
26 is also a reversal of creation, echoing Gen. 1. God's resting on the Sabbath day at
the end of creation resulted in the stability of order and the maintenance of life, an
action imitated by humans who also rested on the Sabbath. By contrast Job's desired
rest was the repose of death, the negation of life.

2. This attack on P's formulation of creation would suggest that the Zadokites
along with their allies, the conventional sages (cf. Ben Sirach), are the two social
groups who come under the attack of the Joban poet. By destroying their social
construction of reality in which wisdom and cult establish the order of creation, the
political and social power wielded by these post-exilic groups would be neutralized.

3. The turning of day into night is brought about or threatened by the Divine
Warrior in theophanic hymns (cf. Amos 5.8; Job 12.22). This underscores the hubris
of Job the 'hero' who assumes divine power in this role of attempting to negate the
power of God in sustaining the order of creation.

of life in strophe three reflects the primal experience of the newborn leaving the mother's womb.

Strophe I consists of two parts. The introductory bicola (v. 3), bearing the mark of curse (קלל), contain the two related thematic movements of the strophe: Day of birth and Night of conception. Three curses are directed at Day in the first section of the strophe (vv. 4-5), while four additional incantations are directed against Night (vv. 6-9). Altogether, some sixteen jussives and prohibitions are uttered against these two personified enemies of Job. Verse 10 brings the strophe to closure by returning to the imagery of birth in v. 3. This metaphor focuses initially on the creation of the individual, in this case Job. One of the major traditions of creation in the ancient Near East presents the creator as the one who fathers or gives birth to descendants (human and divine), or as the one who shapes the fetus in the womb and like a midwife delivers the infant at the time of birth. Thereafter the personal deity assumes protective care over the individual's life (see Jer. 1.4-10; Job 10.8-13; Ps. 139.13-18). Each conception and birth is a new creation, the cause for celebration and rejoicing (1 Sam. 1–2; Lk. 1.46-55), and its time is marked and remembered. It is a primal time of passage from nothingness to being, from darkness to light, from unformed chaos to ordered life. Through memory and celebration the individual is ritually transported back to that time of origin to re-experience the freshness and vitality of new beginning. And renewed by festive occasion one moves boldly into the future to engage and embrace the fullness of life. Yet in Job's language of negation, memory has awakened tragic consciousness and the dark urge for the annihilation of all life.

Further, in P God's 'blessing' of humans, as opposed to curse, is the enhancement of procreative power to perpetuate the human race. And the command, 'Be fruitful and multiply', is the primal responsibility of humans who seek to actualize the divine image. Procreation, under divine blessing, is the means by which humans participate in the ordering and rule of God's creation. Priestly language in the form of ritual blesing incorporates and unleashes the powers of vitality for human existence. For example, in Num. 6.24-27 the ritual blessing includes the creation image of the light of the face of God. By contrast, instead of the language of blessing seeking to empower the vital forces of human creation, Job utters the curse which negates reproduction and brings about sterility. This is another instance of Job's attack on Priestly theology and language.

Like Dawn and Dusk in Canaanite mythology who embody and guard the temporal order of reality, Day and Night appear in the guise of two deities of fertility who engender life in the womb and bring it forth into the dawn of new creation.[1] Yet they are also the essential order of time, separated into two parts which contain the structure of cosmos and chaos, light and darkness, life and death. Against these two gods, Job utters incantations of sterility, designed to end their power to produce life and to return them to the realm of non-being where all life and light cease.[2] Day is to be engulfed by the darkness of death, the blackness of chaos, and the impenetrable cloud concealing the mystery of God.[3] Day will remain in darkness, afraid to appear, and God will not 'seek it out'.[4]

Now identified with feminine reproduction which this nocturnal deity controls, Night—guardian of the womb, who brings about conception, possesses the divine knowledge that the first stirrings of life have occurred, and even pronounces and therefore determines the sex of the child—is to become barren, incapable of conceiving, nourishing, and giving birth to new life.[5] Night will neither cry out in ecstatic climax during sexual embrace, nor respond to God's call to appear. Seized (לקח)[6] by darkness, Night will no longer couple (יחד) with the days of the year. Denying the embrace of Day and Night, the structure of time will collapse. The priests of Yam, speakers of ritual incantations whose words are infused with the dark powers of chaos, are to curse Night with sterility (Gen. 3), negating her reproductive powers. They are to arouse sleeping Leviathan, monster of the Deep,

1. See the myth of the birth of the two gods, Dawn and Dusk (*CTA* 23). The personification of Day and Night also occurs in Ps. 19.3-5.

2. Incantations of sterility were common in the ancient Near East. The קלל curse is used in Gen. 3.17 as a curse of infertility directed against the arable soil. Here the curse is issued against the fertility of Day and Night.

3. Eclipses were mythically conceived as the sun being swallowed by a cosmic serpent or dragon.

4. See the magical power sometimes associated with the verb דרש (Judg. 6.29; 2 Kgs 8.8; 1 Sam. 9.9) especially in regard to seeking a divine oracle (Fishbane, 'Jer. IV 23-26 and Job III 3-13', 154). Thus the incantation uses magical power to restrain God by negating the power-laden word of the oracle to find what is lost.

5. The image of Night has shifted to the feminine, as the deity responsible for the fertility of the womb now becomes mythically identified with feminine reproduction. 'Barren' (גלמוד) is used to speak of Zion in exile as a widowed and sterile woman (Isa. 49.2).

6. לקח is used here in the sense of sexual assault (cf. 2 Sam. 11.4).

to devour her, like Apophis who threatens to swallow the sun during its nocturnal journey across the foreboding cosmic ocean. Swallowed by Leviathan and lost without the guiding light of the stars of her morning twilight (נשׁף),[1] Night will yearn for the appearance of consort Day and seek out his embrace, but will clutch only at emptiness. Night will not escape the grasp of chaos to gaze on the enchanting eyelids of Dawn which slowly open to emit the red light signaling the stirrings of Day from slumber. Rather she is doomed to barrenness and darkness, because she did not close the womb which gave Job life,[2] leading to his travail (עמל).[3] The power of curse has transformed the metaphor of fertility into one of barrenness.[4]

The destabilization of the metaphor of fertility continues into the second and third strophes. The second strophe (vv. 11-19) is also composed in two parts, both of which are initiated by 'why'—the double questions of vv. 11-12 which parallel the single question of v. 16. In the move from direct curse to the indictment of accusatory lament, Job questions why he did not die at birth, why his mother brought him forth and gave him nourishment and why he was not stillborn (cf. Qoh. 6.4-5). Implicit is Job's indictment of God as creator and sustainer of the individual from the time of formation in the womb and birth. God—as the Lord of the womb (רחם), a theological belief residing behind the epithet 'God of Mercies' (רחמים)—was called upon in laments to continue the care and protection given to the psalmist from the time of conception, nourishment, and birth (Pss. 22.9-11; 139.13-16). Job's wish to have died at birth is a repudiation of the tradition of divine conception and providential care for the individual.

---

1. 'Twilight' may refer to evening (2 Kgs 7.5, 7; Isa. 5.11; Prov. 7.9) or morning (Ps. 119.147, Job 7.4), though here it is the former due to parallelism.

2. The opening and closing of the womb is a divine power (see Gen. 17.16-19; 25.21-26; 29.31; 30.22-24; Judg. 13.2-5; 1 Sam. 1.1-28).

3. עמל refers to the toil and pain of life in laments (Ps. 90.10; Jer. 20.18), and in Qoheleth, to meaningless labor having no lasting significance (1.3; 2.10).

4. The sixth and concluding lament of Jeremiah (20.14-18) shortens and adapts this first strophe involving the cursing of birth. In Jeremiah the power of the curse is also rooted in the primal power of salvation history (the obliteration of Sodom and Gomorrah). This destabilization of the birth metaphor is equally shocking, since the call narrative of the prophet (1.4-10) is rooted in the theology of God's shaping Jeremiah in the womb and predestining him to be a 'prophet to the nations'. For Jeremiah as well as Job, the curse against birth is at least indirectly a cursing of the creator.

Images of repose ('lying down', 'quiet', 'sleep', 'rest', 'without
care', 'at ease') are used by Job to describe nonexistence in Sheol.
Although the underworld is normally abhorred as the place of
calamity, restraint, impotence and darkness, Job longs for its peaceful
bliss.[1] With a rapid transition from womb to tomb, Job would have
escaped the trouble that now has seized him. Sheol, uncreated by God
and associated with the Deep in Hebrew cosmology, is the belly
(Jon. 2.3) or womb (Prov. 30.16) with which Job seeks to replace
that of his mother.[2] It is the 'land of no return', a place of deep darkness, the primeval blackness of chaos, devoid of all order and light
(Job 10.21-22). As the place where all memory ceases, Job would not
be plagued with remembering and reactualizing his own beginning (cf.
Pss. 6.6; 88.5; Qoh. 9.5). And the concluding verse of the strophe
also echoes one sapiential conceptualization of the fertility metaphor,
but reverses it in a stunning fashion. For the traditional sages, creation
by God in the womb meant common origins for all, both rich and
poor, and therefore the incumbent responsibility of the well-to-do to
care for the underprivileged needy (Prov. 22.2; Job 31.13-15). By
contrast Job implies that life is one of unbearable oppression for slaves
and the poor. For Job the birth metaphor is not used to substantiate the
theology of justice as both social responsibility and the right to goods
necessary for existence, but rather death is the great equalizer where
great and small, rich and poor, free and slave find peace. Even the
transformation of the lament is disorienting, for the goal is not the
customary expectation of redemption leading to life, but the inviting
silence of death.

The last reference to the metaphor of birth is found in the third and
concluding strophe. Life is described in terms of the gift of light,
which in the context of birth imagery points to the first experience of
the newborn child. The image is also conceptualized as intellectual
understanding of the problem of human suffering and why death,
though it is eagerly sought, does not come. The obliteration to which

1. See the 'Dialogue of a Man with His Soul', *ANET*, 405-407.
2. Normally Sheol was understood as outside God's domain (Pss. 6.5; 30.10;
88.11-13; 115.16-17), though divine power could deliver from death (Ps. 30.4;
Prov. 23.14; Hos. 13.14). Thus Job seeks the one domain where God's oppressive
power does not normally extend (though see Prov. 15.11; Job 11.7-9; 20.5-6). For
a detailed study of Sheol and death, see Nicholas J. Tromp, *Primitive Conceptions of
Death and the Nether World in the Old Testament* (Biblica et Orientalia 21; Rome:
Pontifical Biblical Institute, 1969).

Job attempts to consign all of reality is withheld him. Yet it is here that the first clearly expressed, not merely inferred, indictment against God is made, and it is done so with the birth metaphor. Job indicates that God has not only given life to humans, but also has 'shut them in' (סוך), providing no explanation of why they are in torment. The same verb is used one other time: Job 38.8, which describes the birth of Yam, whose destructive waters are 'shut in', that is kept from flooding the cosmos and negating all life.[1] Only in ch. 3, God keeps humans in darkness, providing no explanation as to the reason for their suffering. This is the first of many times that images applied to chaos will be used to describe Job's own situation.

The Metaphor of Artistry. The metaphor of artistry is echoed in the second strophe. In his description of the bliss of the underworld,[2] Job sounds very much like Qoheleth (cf. 9.1-2) in indicating that death greets one and all, regardless of social standing. In this description of the mighty who will enter Sheol, Job speaks of 'kings and counselors of the earth who rebuild ruins for themselves'. 'Ruins' (חרבות) usually refers to desolate cities (Lev. 26.31, 33; Isa. 44.26), including Jerusalem (Isa. 52.9), and on occasion to the destroyed temple (Ezra 9.9). As noted earlier, kings were commissioned by the gods to erect, maintain, and rebuild sacred cities and temples for divine dwelling.[3] These actions were ritual ones which constructed and ordered creation as well as human society. For Job, even the mighty kings, engaged in

---

1. Cf. Marduk's restraints imposed on the flood waters of chaos after the slaughter of Tiamat (*ANET*, 67).

2. A similar depiction of death is found in 'The Dialogue of a Man with his Ba', though the man, despairing of life in the present, looks forward to the joy and serenity of afterlife with the gods where Maat will truly prevail. Job of course looks forward only to the nothingness of the grave.

3. See Mircea Eliade (*Cosmos and History*, 6ff.). The construction of temples as a cosmogonic act is clearly expressed in the *Enuma elish* where the narrative of the building of the Esagila, Marduk's temple, is positioned within the myth of the creation of the world (*ANET*, 68-69). After the Esagila had been built by the gods, a festival with rites of dedication are held, and the norms for heaven and earth are established. One of the best examples of a king engaged in rebuilding ruined temples and reinstituting their cultic orders is Nabonidus. Temple-raising and reconstruction (accompanied by ritual) order and maintain the cosmos.

the sacred task of world-building, meet the same end as the lowliest of slaves who in life were driven by the shouts of the taskmaster.[1]

The Metaphor of Battle. The final metaphor destabilized in Job's initial soliloquy is the battle with the dragon. As previously described, this metaphor was central to many myths of origins and maintenance in depicting reality as an ongoing struggle between the creator and the dragon, life and death, and order and chaos. It is the defeat of the dragon that precedes primordial creation (cf. the *Enuma elish*), and it is the annual victory over Sea that enables the cycle of life to continue (cf. the Baal Cycle). However, the primordial defeat of the dragon prior to the creation of the world does not lead to the eternal vanquishing of this enemy of existence. Thus Marduk, having divided Tiamat into halves with a great gulf in between, sets up crossbars and guards to keep the waters in her veins from coursing into the expanse and destroying creation.[2] Even so the power of the dragon resurges at the end of the year, before finally being subdued by Marduk in combat once again. Thus chaos is a real and present danger, ever challenging the power and cosmic rule of the creator and requiring defeat each year for life and order to continue.[3]

Job's incantation in v. 8 calls upon the 'Yam-cursers',[4] priests skilled in the power of curse, 'to awaken, stir up (עור) Leviathan',[5] the dragon who slumbers in the depth of the cosmic ocean, to devour Night and thereby collapse the temporal order of creation. The 'Yam-

1. 'The Dialogue of Pessimism' also reflects on the same end that awaits the great and small, the righteous and the wicked. In section IX the servant says to his lord: 'Go up to the ancient ruin heaps and walk around; look at the skulls of the lowly and the great. Which belongs to someone who did evil and which to someone who did good?' (*ANET*, 600-601).

2. *ANET*, 67. (Cf. Job 7.12; 38.10-11; Ps. 1.6-9; Prov. 8.29.)

3. See Gen. 49.25 (= Deut. 33.13) which speaks of the 'Deep lying in wait below', echoing the myth of chaos awaiting, in threatening posture, the opportunity to devour creation.

4. Yam in Canaanite mythology was a son of El and Asherah and the ruler of the primeval ocean who sought suzerainty over the earth, but was repelled by Baal and Anat. Yam often appears as the nemesis of Yahweh who takes the place of Baal in the mythic struggle in Israelite texts (Exod. 15; Job 7.12; 38.8-11; Ps. 46; Hab. 3.15).

5. See Isa. 27.1; Ps. 74.12-17; Job 40.25–41.26; Ps. 104.25-26; and *UT* 67.i.1-3. In Job the references to Leviathan in chs. 3 and 40.25–41.26 form the inclusio for the poetic book. Any attempt to excise the Leviathan section from the Yahweh speeches, or to reduce Leviathan to an ordinary creature (i.e. crocodile), does violence to the poetic structure of the book.

cursers' are those priests who, on the one hand, use the power of ritual language to charm Yam and lull the dragon to sleep, say in the fashion of the priests of Re,[1] or in imitation of Ea who charmed to sleep Apsu, making him easy prey for the sword.[2] On the other hand, these 'skilled ones' are also the incantation experts who employ magic for destructive ends by arousing the powers of darkness and using them to destroy.[3] In pre-battle ritual, enemies are cursed so as to divest them of power, and make them defenseless. An illustrative Aramaic incantation incorporates magical power involving Sea and Leviathan:

> I have. . . confronted the evil foes [and] said to them if you have in any way sinned against Abuma son of Gribta etc.]. . . I am enchanting you with the spell of the Sea and the spell of Leviathan the dragon. . . I am bringing down upon you the ban and excommunication which were set upon Mount Hermon and upon Leviathan the dragon and upon Sodom and Gomorrah.[4]

Anshar instructs Marduk prior to battle, 'calm [Tiamat] with thy holy spell'.[5]

With the devouring of Night resulting in the darkening of the stars of its twilight, the dragon would succeed in obliterating the cycle of night and day, thus ending the temporal order. The stars are not simply natural elements, but become in theopoetic imagination the armies of God, the heavenly hosts, the most significant of whom were gods with cosmic responsibilities. Indeed they respond in praise to God's magnificent construction of the world (Job 38.4-7). To devour the stars is to vanquish the cosmic army of the creator.[6] Like Apophis

---

1. *ANET*, 6-7.

2. Also see the incantations used by Tiamat and Marduk prior to their engaging in combat.

3. This reverses Isa. 51.9-11, which is a lament of the community designed to arouse (עור) Yahweh from sleep to come forth to do battle against Rahab. Also see Job 41.2 where Leviathan is so fearsome that no mortal dare 'stir him up' (עור) in order to do battle against him. Only the Divine Warrior has the might to subdue this terrible dragon.

4. Text 2 of J.A. Montgomery, *Aramaic Incantation Texts from Nippur* (Philadelphia: University Museum, 1913). See C.H. Gordon, 'Leviathan. Symbol of Evil', *Biblical Motifs* (ed. A. Altmann; Cambridge, MA: Harvard University Press, 1966), 1-9.

5. *ANET*, 64.

6. See Judg. 5.20-21 which speaks of the 'stars from the heavens' fighting against Sisera.

seeking to swallow the barge of Re in the dark cosmic ocean,[1] Leviathan's engulfing of the stars of twilight, imprisoning Night in an eternal void of darkness forever yearning for the appearance of the light of Day, would not only negate Job's conception but all pregnancies and all life. These forbidden priests (2 Kgs 23.5; Zeph. 1.4) are brought into Job's service to destroy creation. His efforts to awaken Leviathan should not be seen as merely the rhetorical embellishment of poetic language. The language attempts to destabilize all mythical formations of reality, leading not only then to the collapse of meaning but also the universe itself. And as is clear from the grand hymn to Leviathan which is sung by the Divine Warrior (Job 40.24–41.26), shortly before the battle ensues, it is the language of Job, the disputation he has constructed, that has aroused the beast threatening all creation.[2]

In this lament-like soliloquy, transformed by the language of incantation, Job's own metaphors of meaning have collapsed. With the darkening of vision, orientation to existence is lost, and the easy escape offered by death beckons. And from the fragments of collapsed meaning, the outcry of anguished torment and broken faith seeks to destabilize all metaphorical models. All hermeneutics of religious belief must fail. For in that collapse God will be forced from the throne of heaven and earth.

The Metaphor of Ruler. As noted in Chapter 3, the dominant metaphor for humanity in conventional wisdom is ruler. Like Solomon, wisdom's greatest hero and patron, humanity is made to rule over God's creation in a reign which supports and extends beneficent order in nature and society. Yet, in similar fashion to the metaphors of creation, Job destabilizes the language of the anthropological tradition with its pattern of divine conception, providential care, rulership over God's creation, and active participation in ordering cosmos and society.

In the first strophe (vv. 3-10), Job utters his incantations of sterility against Day and Night, personified as the gods of conception and birth. Cursed is Night who pronounced the oracle: 'A Mighty Man (גבר) is

---

1. *ANET*, 6-7, 11-12. Cf. *CTA* 6. In Mesopotamian mythology Shamash descends into the underworld to bring judgment (*BWL*, 121-38).

2. One other allusion to combat is the 'terrifying' (בעת) of one's enemies before engagement (Job 15.24; Isa. 21.4).

conceived.' If *geber* is repointed to *gibbôr*, the oracle is not simply announcing the birth of a male, but a 'hero' or 'warrior', a title for a king (cf. Isa. 9.7). Oracles announcing the births of crown princes are common in the ancient Near East[1] and Israel (Isa. 9.2-7; 11.1-11), and in the royal ritual of Judah the king was 'begotten' by God on the day of enthronement. The imagery associated with royal birth emphasized providential care for the ruler, legitimated his rule, and suggested divine status if not nature. This imagery was appropriated at times for the births of non-royal figures. For example, the prophet Jeremiah is predestined from birth to his calling, promised divine presence and deliverance, and 'set this day over nations and over kingdoms'. In the democratization of the metaphor (cf. Ps. 112.2, a wisdom psalm), individuals praise God for their conception, birth, and care (Ps. 22; 139) and for exaltation to rule the earth and its creatures (Ps. 8). It is not necessary to understand Job as holding the social position of ruler as Albertz has argued, but the language in the opening soliloquy and later does point to the importance of the royal metaphor in expressing the poet's anthropology. Yet this anthropological tradition, shaped by the royal metaphor and its pattern, is destabilized by Job. Instead of praising God for life and royal status, Job curses the personified gods responsible for his birth. Instead of using the birth tradition to call on Yahweh to rise up and protest his 'royal' son, Job attempts to negate his life by returning to the dark regions. Instead of praising God for giving him the position of ruler over creation and speaking of the responsibility of caring for the earth and its creatures, Job attempts to return the world to the oblivion of night.

Royal imagery reappears in the second strophe (vv. 11-19), when Job wistfully yearns for the silence of the tomb. In Sheol Job would join the mighty ones, 'kings and counselors of the earth who built ruins for themselves' and wealthy princes who had filled their 'houses' (palaces or temples) with treasure. As suggested earlier, the erecting of 'houses', especially palaces and temples, was a primary task of kings whose building actions ordered the world and brought well-being to the nation. Palaces signified and legitimated royal rule, while temples were a microcosm of the world where rites renewed the vital forces of creation. Yet Job would take his place with these mighty ones who enter into the depths of Sheol and find their final rest. Even kings

1. See 'The Legend of King Keret' and 'The Tale of Aqhat' (*ANET*, 142-55).

cannot escape the destiny of all humans, both great and small. In the grave, king and slave sleep together, no longer separated by power and status.

Here Job is no royal figure, socially or metaphorically, who goes forth into the world to master life and order creation. He is a tortured creature longing for the repose of death. And for the first time Job refers to 'prisoners', probably royal 'slaves' taken captive in war,[1] who in death cannot hear the voice of their taskmasters (Exod. 3.7; 5.6, 10, 13, 14) and the 'slave' (עבד) who finally gains release from his lord. Those whose lot is onerous in life experience the same ultimate fate as kings and rulers of the earth, and even discover in the depths of Sheol the 'rest' denied them in life. As is clear from chs. 7 and 14, Job begins to compare his own life, and eventually human existence in general, to the dreaded lot of slaves whose only hope of freedom resides in the liberation of death. Like the foreign slave who must serve the master for a lifetime, Job and humankind find no escape from the dreaded lot of human existence. And the one master from whom the slave Job most desperately seeks escape is God.[2] The metaphor of slave makes its first appearance in the poetry and begins the deconstruction of anthropological language centered in the metaphor of king. And it is the experience of creation as oppression that provides the generative energy for the continuation of the narrative structure.

3. *The Metaphorical Process: Absurdity and Destabilization*

The myth of the battle with chaos provides the overarching external structure that contextualizes the drama of Job, while the slave metaphor and its mythic tradition shapes the internal literary pattern. As may be concluded from the Akkadian and Old Testament texts reflecting the cosmological tradition, the exaltation of the mighty storm god to the position of ruler of the gods results from the defeat of chaos. The Canaanite myths present a variation in that El is too old to continue to fight and has lost direct rule of the cosmos. What remains is his power of decree establishing who shall rule over the earth, a power that continues at least because of his craftiness

1. R. de Vaux, *Ancient Israel* 1 (New York: McGraw-Hill, 1961), 80ff.
2. The master–slave relationship is a common religious metaphor in Mesopotamia (Lambert and Millard, *Atra-hasis*, 1969).

('wisdom').[1] Yet El is susceptible to judicial corruption, occasioned by either seduction or intimidation. Even the challenging of his decrees is not unprecedented. Subsequently, what is at stake in the prologue and indeed the entire book is not only Job's humble and trusting submission to the will of the creator and ruler of the cosmos, i.e. acceptance of his destiny as Yahweh's slave, but also the nature of divine rule itself. Certainly the satan, appearing all the more in this story as the real power on the earth, has either undermined the justice of God's governance or simply uncovered its moral bankruptcy and weakness in inciting the unoccasioned attack on Job. Job's wife,[2] and presumably the friends in the earlier version, also repudiate the morality of divine rule. Indeed, it is the satan who appears to have power to rule over the earth, though limited by the divine edicts, as he goes forth in search of evil and effectuates, much like Enlil, the will of the council.

In the prologue the audience is given a direct look at the operation of the divine assembly and especially the nature of the God who issues edicts determining the governance of the world, specified in the decrees concerning Job's fate. A deity, either poisoned by suspicion or too much like the aged and failing Canaanite El, rules over the divine assembly. The narrative does not simply deal with the integrity of a virtuous hero, but more importantly raises the very question of Yahweh's power, justice and moral governance of the world. Questions are raised, and doubts begin to emerge, as the conventional wisdom metaphor of the just God loses its evocative power, and is replaced with one of a corrupt judge and failing ruler whose suspicions lead to the devastating of the faithful slave. The absurdity of this metaphor disorients both the character Job and the implied wisdom audience.

The anthropological metaphor of slave is equally devastating. Conventional wisdom's view of human nature and function was expressed by the metaphor of king, and in the period of exile and post-exile received support from priestly theology. Now the famous sage of hoary tradition, the pious Job, is the 'slave' of God, ravaged by divine cruelty. The moral order of the wages was rooted in the justice of God

1. El's authoritative decree is certainly challenged by Baal's bold rejection of the decision to make him slave to Yam (*ANET*, 130). Seduction (Asherah's, *ANET*, 133) as well as intimidation (Anat's, *ANET*, 137) are also evidenced.

2. The LXX's expansion of the speech of the wife to Job further underscores both her rejection of the 'fear of God' as the proper response to suffering, and the implication that God is unfaithful and immoral.

who permeated creation with righteousness and maintained the structures of life. Now Job is the humiliated slave, subjected to unwarranted abuse. The absurdity of the metaphor of God as a corrupt and weak judge intersects with that of the metaphor of slave to disorient the audience, and to fragment their conventional, sapiential mythos.

By the conclusion of ch. 3, it is clear that the former faith of the legendary sage has completely fragmented. Now in the pathos of despair, Job characterizes his life as the drudgery of a slave who has no hope for liberation, save for that provided by death. While Job has not yet come to conclude that all human life is slavery, he is only one step removed from that stunning realization. Furthermore, the cosmological pattern of the God who has created humanity to experience such inexplicable agony begins to take shape. The 'why' of Job's question begins to attract the external mythic tradition represented by the *Enuma elish* in which the God of creation is the judge predestining humanity to the existence of slavery. And the calling upon those skilled in the black arts to arouse Leviathan, the eternal enemy of God, prepares for the appearance of the image of the Divine Warrior. Job's own pathos begins to take shape within the intersection of the mythic patterns of creation by conflict and human existence as slavery. The basis for revolt against the creator has been laid. But the implied audience, also disoriented, begins to look for a less risky venture. For this, they turn, at least initially, to the words of the friends.

Chapter 6

DIVINE JUSTICE AND HUMAN SLAVERY: THE FIRST CYCLE

1. *Eliphaz: The Defense of Divine Justice (Job 4–5)*

Introduction. Eliphaz makes his response (ענה) to Job's opening soliloquy in a disputation consisting of six strophes: introduction and initial rebuke (4.1-6); arguments for retribution based on experience and the analogy with nature (4.7-11), and revelation (4.12-21); the power of curse by the righteous (5.1-7); doxology praising the God of power and justice (5.18-16); and blessing assuring pardon and redemption (5.17-27). In this disputation Eliphaz seeks to counter the disassembling curse-lament of Job with words of affirmation and praise of God whose power, wisdom, and justice maintain the equilibrium of the created order. Central to the argument of Eliphaz is the rule of God, understood by the Deuteronomic doctrine of retribution which affirms God punishes the wicked, but rewards the righteous. Indeed God may chasten even faithful servants, but they should wait in confidence, sure of divine redemption. Eliphaz bases his argument not only on the epistemological canons of wisdom (experience, analogy from nature, and the assessment of human nature),[1] but also on prophetic revelation (4.12-17), and the faith of praise expressed in the language of doxology (5.8-16). Yet what is non-sapiential about the confident faith of Eliphaz is the disallowance of question and disputation.[2] The 'fear of God' in the faith of Eliphaz has become cocksure fundamentalism, unyielding in its claims to absolute truth and intolerance of critical questioning and contrary expressions. It is this rigidity of attitude that is incapable of engaging existence in torment, whether that of the righteous Job or the nation decimated by holocaust. The sacred canopy of Eliphaz' construction strains under the enormity of

---

1. Later he appeals to the authority of tradition (Job 15.18-19; cf. Bildad in Job 8.8-10).
2. Von Rad, *Wisdom in Israel*, 97ff.

evil present in Job's and the human experience, the weight of theological expression which gives rightful place to questioning of divine
action, and unyielding rigidity which disallowed openness to change
and new insight.

The Abuse of Metaphor. The language which Eliphaz uses to erect and
support the sacred canopy legitimating his social reality is metaphorical. Yet the metaphors of creation called into play by this staunch
defender of the faith have not become dead, incapable of evoking
responsive commitment. Rather they have been abused by a rigid
literalism which does not allow for the imaginative play characteristic
of the authentic metaphorical process. Indeed tensiveness and most
certainly ambiguity have passed from view. The line of differentiation
separating metaphor from referent is crossed, leading to a fusion
which misconstrues and destroys. Metaphor has been reshaped into
hardened, idolatrous dogma which distorts the power of language to
build new worlds of faith. Uncontested, Eliphaz' fundamentalism
misdirects faith's search for understanding towards a blind avowal of
its own simplistic propositions.

Strophe II (4.7-11) argues for the authenticity of divine retribution
on the twin pillars of experience and analogy from nature. Both pillars
are braced by motifs drawn from the metaphorical models of creation.
In vv. 7-9, Eliphaz asks and answers his own question about retribution, not really a serious question for it allows for no reflection, much
less measured response:

7. Please remember—who is the innocent who has perished, or where are
    the upright who were cut off?
8. As I have seen the powers of iniquity and the sowers of travail are they
    who reap the same.
9. By the breath of Eloah they perish, by the wind of his nostrils they meet
    their end.

The abuse of creation language by Eliphaz is noticed on two occasions
in these verses. First, he uses the term 'memory' (זכר), common to
laments where the community appropriates redemptive tradition to
engage the crisis of suffering and apparent abandonment by God.
Unless memory is improperly selective, the tradition contains features
of crisis and wrongful breach until God acts to deliver. Indeed the
suffering of the righteous individual and community is the stimulus
which awakens complaint and leads to the engagement of creation
faith. The image of the Divine Warrior is evoked to exhort God to use

the power that subdued the chaos monster at creation and again at the Red Sea for the community's or individual's redemption (cf. Ps. 77.11-20). Yet Eliphaz abuses the tradition by affirming that the righteous neither perish nor are cut off. Sacred tradition and experience, the authentic basis for lament, are distorted.

In his second misuse of creation language, Job's opponent takes up the life-giving breath (נשמה and רוח) of God which in the creation of humanity tradition animates human beings (Gen. 2.7) and at death returns to the creator (Qoh. 12.7). In the cosmological tradition God's exhaling renews and sustains all creation, whereas inhaling leads to nature's withering and decay (Ps. 104.27-30). In Eliphaz's speech this metaphor for creation (a specific form of the metaphor of word) is bent and misshaped to fit a retributive system which makes it a destructive agent of God's wrath against the wicked (cf. 2 Sam. 22.16 = Ps. 18.16). Ironically in his attempt to defend the righteous rule of God, Eliphaz has destabilized the very linguistic tradition expressing that sovereignty.

Eliphaz uses the argument of analogy from nature to support the dogma of retributive justice, asserting that nature is created to destroy the fiercest of animals.

> The roar of the lion and the voice of the hunted lion, the teeth of young lions are broken.
> The fierce lion perishes from lack of prey, and the whelps of the lionness are scattered (4.10-11).

By contrast the cosmological tradition speaks of God as the 'Lord of the Creatures', who not only creates but also providentially nourishes and sustains non-human life (Ps. 104). Even 'young lions' seek their prey from God who provides it for their existence (Ps. 104.20-22). And along with the beasts of the field they have their own places for habitation and time (nightfall) for hunting. With humans they share the bounty of the earth and God's protective care. Even the anthropological tradition which speaks of humanity's sovereignty over the creatures still imposes human responsibility for their care (Gen. 2.4b-25). Senseless slaughter and the eating of blood, symbolic of the potency and therefore sacredness of life, is prohibited by covenant in the P document (Gen. 9.1-17). In making the center of reality a relatively small number of humans who meet a rather narrowly defined code of morality, Eliphaz transformed creation and the creator who sustains life into destructive forces annihilating wild beasts. The hunger and death of wild beasts, to whom Eliphaz imputed evil, by analogy supports the dogma of retribution for humans. Or at least Eliphaz so argues.

Eliphaz moves toward exhortation in the fifth and sixth strophes as he counsels Job to seek God and ask for deliverance (5.8-16). Enfolded within the fifth strophe is a doxology, a word of praise sung either by the falsely accused who seek (דרש) redress from God and confidently await a declaration of innocence or by the guilty who acknowledge the fairness of their verdict and extol the God of justice. For the guilty it is tantamount to confession. Whether mercy is extended or not, the guilty confess in the language of praise the righteousness of God who oversees the judicial process.[1] Once again word theology, specifically the decree of the divine judge who intercedes and saves the humble, becomes the paradigm for speaking of God's rule.

Exhortation

8. But[2] I would inquire of El, and before Elohim I would place my cause.

Doxology

9. The one who creates great things[3] beyond comprehension, wonderful things without limit.
10. The one who gives rain upon the face of the land, and sends water upon the countryside.

---

1. F. Horst, *Hiob* (BKAT 16; Neukirchen: Neukirchener Verlag, 1969), 64. Note Joshua's exhortation to the guilty Achan to 'praise God' as witness to the justness of the lot casting's identification of him as the one breaking the ban (Josh. 7.19; cf. Amos 4.13; 5.8; 8.8; 9.5ff.; Jer. 13.5ff.; 1 Sam. 6.5; Ps. 118.17-21; 2 Chron. 30.8). For detailed discussions see James L. Crenshaw, *Hymnic Affirmation of Divine Justice* [SBLDS 24; Missoula, MT: Scholars Press, 1975]); and 'The Doxologies of Amos and Job 5.9-16 and 9.5-10', *ZAW* 79 (1967), 42-51. Crenshaw argues that the doxologies of Amos derive from the same sapiential tradition reflected by Job 5.9-16 and 9.5-10.

2. אולם ('but'), found more often in Job than any other OT text, is a strong adversative used to contrast what follows with what has preceded (2.5; 11.5; 12.7; 13.3-4). Thus, in spite of the trouble that afflicts all humanity, and the calamity that befalls the wicked, Eliphaz exhorts Job to turn to the God of justice for mercy and deliverance.

3. עשה גדלות ('creates great things') is used in Job to speak of acts of creation (Job 9.10; 37.5), while referring in other contexts to salvation history (Pss. 71.19; 106.21). This points to the wisdom shaping of this doxology, since salvation history is not a part of wisdom theology prior to Ben Sira in the 2nd century BCE.

11. Exalting the lowly to a high place, and raising to safety those who mourn.
12. The one who frustrates the machinations of the calculating, allowing their hands no abiding success.
13. The one who captures the wise in their own deceit, and the counsel of the shrewd becomes hastily contrived.
14. They shall confront darkness by day, and grope for their way at noontime as at night.
15. But the desolated[1] shall be saved from their mouth, and from the hand of the strong.
16. And the poor shall have hope, for injustice has shut her mouth (5.8-16).

Interestingly it is Eliphaz who counsels Job to take his case (דברה) to God, 'seeking' (דרש) him in the sanctuary in order to present a petition for divine redress. What follows is the citation of a cultic–legal doxology with its typical hymnic participles ('creates', 'gives', 'sends', 'frustrate', 'captures') praising divine actions in three thematic movements: creation (v. 9), nature (v. 10), and society (vv. 11-16).

In the book of Job the 'making/doing of great things' and 'wonders' refers to God's actions in repulsing the chaos monster, creating the world, and directing the forces of nature: Job 9.9-10; 37.5; 14; 42.3 (cf. Pss. 96.3; 98.1). The initial line of the fifth strophe affirms that God's power of decree as the head of the divine council is anchored in the position of being the conqueror of chaos and the creator of the world. And the doxology demonstrates that the legal process is anchored in both the moral rule of God and just order permeating creation. However, world-order is not a self-perpetuating system which operates outside the sphere of divine activity. Rather it is the moral and just character of God which originated and continues to maintain its integrity.

The second movement centers on the primary act of God in maintaining the natural order of creation: the sending of the 'gift' of rain to refresh a thirsty earth, enabling life to continue. For the J narrative, the first act of divine creation was the raising of a mist over the face of the dry wilderness, transforming barren desert into arable soil (Gen. 2.4b-6; cf. Deut. 11.14, 17; 28.12; 1 Kgs 8.35-36; Job 36.27; Ps. 147.8; Isa. 41.18-19; 43.19; 44.3-4; 55.10; Jer. 14.22; Mt. 5.45). According to Deuteronomic theology, God's giving or withholding

---

1. Reading *mohorabh* ('desolated') for *meherebh* ('from the sword'). See E. Dhorme, *A Commentary on the Book of Job* (London: Nelson, 1967) 67; and Rowley, *Job*, 55.

rain depended on Israel's obedience to covenantal law. However, in this doxology rain is a 'gift' which God may bestow as an act of mercy transcending covenantal privilege and standards of moral rectitude not met by sinners. While God is just, divine freedom is uninhibited by all national and moral limitations.

The third and longest movement (vv. 11-16) speaks of divine participation in human history where the God of justice humbles the wise and mighty who believe they are in the control of their own destiny, and that their own counsel will lead them to success (Pss. 7.15; 9.16, 35.8; 57.7; Prov. 26.27; 28.10). This doxology repudiates the arrogant self-sufficiency of political advisors and kings who wrongly think that hard-headed realism and statecraft rooted in proven experience and sage counsel is sure to reap benefits for themselves and their nations.[1] They are the ones who are engulfed by chaos, who wander blindly even at the height of the noonday sun (Gen. 19.11; Deut. 28.29, Isa. 59.10). It is this corrupting of wisdom (cf. Ezek. 28.17) that leads to a subverting of creation. What is fundamentally wrong with this type of wisdom is its hubris, i.e. its incorporation of the primordial quest of humans to become gods in control of their own lives and destiny by the obtaining of divine wisdom, a theme explored in several biblical texts (cf. the J Narrative in Gen. 2-3, 11).[2] This theme and its tragic results are captured in the language of exaltation of the humble and humiliation of the wise and mighty (cf. Ezek. 28). Hence the doxology contains the image of the return of chaos, specifically contained in the language of 'darkness by day' and eclipse or 'night at noonday'. By contrast God exalts the needy and poor, rescuing them from the hands of their oppressors, and shutting the mouth of injustice. In the lawcourt, justice and mercy will be extended to the poor by their righteous redeemer who is creator and ruler of heaven and earth. Thus, the way is clear for Job: he should bring his petition to God and sing this doxology before the divine magistrate who is just and merciful, sure to redeem the lowly from their distress.

Eliphaz's advice at this point is consonant with mainline Israelite theology, especially in understanding God as the one who rules earth

---

1. See McKane's exposition of this type of political sagacity opposed by the prophets (*Prophets and Wise Men* [SBT 44; Naperville, IL: Allenson, 1965]).

2. Artur Weiser, *Hiob* (7th edn; ATD 14; Göttingen: Vandenhoeck & Ruprecht, 1980), 52.

and nation in justice tempered with mercy. And the counsel is in agreement with the process of legal redress in the judicial sphere. By approaching God for a legal decision, Job would show that he submits to the sovereignty of God and the rule of divine justice. With the decision from God, whether a verdict of guilty or innocent, the possibility for restitution would await.[1] Yet what perverts the theology of the doxology which Eliphaz cites is the narrow confines of the doctrine of retribution. As noted earlier, for Eliphaz the wicked receive no justice in the gate (5.4), they are crushed by their oppressors with no one to redeem them. By contrast God hears the petition of the poor who, for Eliphaz, must be the righteous, momentary victims of unjust oppressors. Eliphaz has taken a doxology which speaks of God's universal reign, a reign which freely provides sustenance for all creatures and exerts itself even in the unmerited exaltation of the poor, and perverted it into a cold system of retributive justice.

Metaphors of Human Nature. The third strophe (4.12-21) presents another argument for retribution, this time in the form of special revelation contained in a dream. A spirit appeared to Eliphaz and said:

> 17. Can humanity be righteous before God?
>   Can a man be pure before his creator?

This revelatory word is construed by Eliphaz into a doctrine of a corrupt human nature:

> 18. He does not even trust his servants,
>   And he imputes error in his messengers.
> 19. How much more the inhabitants of houses of clay, whose foundation is
>   in the dust, they are crushed before the moth.
> 20. From morning until evening they are destroyed, they perish forever
>   without name.[2]
> 21. Is not their tent-cord plucked up within them?
>   They die, and without wisdom.

Eliphaz fashions his version of theological anthropology to include the universal depravity of human nature, a feature characteristic of the slave metaphor. The parallel questions of the dream spirit are taken by Eliphaz to point to human depravity which negates the possibility of

---

1. Horst, *Hiob*, 64.
2. MT's םישׁ ('placing') makes little sense. BHS suggests reading םשׁ ('name') in its place.

being judged righteous or standing morally pure before the creator. Eliphaz implies that in God's crafting of humans, they were made wicked, and therefore incapable of trust. Eliphaz constructs no high anthropology making humans the bearers of the divine image and the surrogates of God's sovereignty over the earth (cf. Gen. 1.26-28; Ps. 8). Rather he draws from the Mesopotamian creation tradition which speaks of the perversion of humans from the very beginning. For example, the friend in 'The Babylonian Theodicy' blames the gods for creating humans evil by nature:

> Narru, king of the gods, who created mankind,
> And majestic Zulummar, who pinched off the clay for them,
>   And goddess Mami, the queen who fashioned them,
> Gave twisted speech to the human race.
> With lies, and not truth, they endowed them forever (*ANET*, 604).

In a similar fashion, Eliphaz uses the crafting metaphor to speak of God as a divine builder who constructs 'houses of clay', with 'foundations in the dust', that is, bodies which are made of fragile substances which quickly disintegrate. Those who 'dwell in houses made of clay' are impure, weak mortals who die quickly like the moth and 'without name'. Naming not only brought creatures into existence, but also gave them character and rules for life. In many texts, including those of wisdom, the gaining of a name meant respect, a noble goal for this life, and a continuance of honor beyond death in the memory of the community (Gen. 12.2; 2 Sam. 7.9; Qoh. 7.1). In a sense a 'good name' meant survival beyond the grave by acquiring a place of honor in the memory and tradition of family and community. Yet Eliphaz seems to be referring to something more specific than universal human depravity. For if his comments about the quick destruction of humans who die 'without name' and 'without wisdom' are universal in application, then his earlier and later arguments in support of retribution based on a moral order and a just God are contradictory. Rather Eliphaz may be speaking of the fate of humans who engage in revolt against the rule of God. The revolt motif appears in his statement that humans are unworthy of divine trust, even less so than members of the divine council.[1] This may allude to the mythic theme of the rebellion of lower gods and humans, doomed to be slaves, against the sovereign reign of God, a Joban theme to be treated later. Suffice it to say that Eliphaz implicitly warns Job of the grisly

---

1. See the comments earlier about the third movement of the doxology (5.11-16).

fate of rebels in primordial times who revolted against God in quest for immortality (cf. 'name') and divine wisdom (Ezek. 28; Gen. 3; 6; 11). They were exterminated or scattered, and died 'without name and wisdom', the very things for which they strove.

In the fourth strophe (5.1-7)[1] Eliphaz speaks of the power of the curse (קבב) uttered by the righteous against the wicked, resulting in their devastation (Prov. 24.24-25). Drawing on the cursing motif of Genesis 3 in which the cursed soil (אדמה) produces thorns and thistles along with a meager yield extracted only by great effort,[2] Eliphaz speaks of the evil his curse inflicts on the wicked (5.3-7). His malediction is rooted in this primeval tradition of origins and draws on the power of the curse of God against the soil in order to afflict the wicked with calamity wrought through language:

3. I saw an evil man taking root, and suddenly cursed his land.[3]
4. 'Let his sons be far from salvation, and let them be crushed in the gate with no one to deliver.
5. As for his harvest let the hungry devour it, let him take it from thorns.[4] and the thirsty[5] trample upon[6] their (the sons') produce.'[7]

---

1. See D. Clines, 'Job 5.1-8: A New Exegesis', *Bib* 62 (1981), 185-94.
2. The cursing of Gen. 3 also involves descendants and the land. However, the most important text for understanding Eliphaz' curse is Gen. 3.17-19:

> And to Adam he said, 'Because you have listened to the voice of your wife and you ate from the tree which I commanded you saying, 'You shall not eat from it',
> Cursed is the land (אדמה) on account of you, in pain you shall eat from it all the days of your life.
> Thorns and thistles shall sprout forth (צמח) to you, and you shall eat the produce of the field.
> In the sweat of your brow you shall eat bread, until you return to the land, because you were taken from it.
> Because you are dust (עפר) and to dust you shall return.

3. נוה is a poetic word for habitation, country, or domain in the country (Job 8.6; 18.15; Prov. 21.20). Yet it may also refer to family in the same manner as 'house' means both dwelling and family (cf. Prov. 3.33).
4. צנים apparently means 'thorns' (Prov. 22.5). The line continues the curse against the harvest. Not only are the hungry to devour it, but also it is to be filled with thorns.
5. Reading צמים ('snare'?) as צמאים ('thirsty ones').
6. Taking שאף as the second root in *BDB*, 983 (Pss. 56.2; 57.4; Amos 8.4). The first root would also fit the context: 'pant after' (Jer. 2.24; 14.6).
7. חיל ('wealth, strength') does have the meaning of 'produce' of the vine and fig-tree (Joel 2.22).

6. For surely[1] evil comes forth from the dust (עפר), and trouble sprouts up
   (צמח) from the soil (אדמה);
7. For humanity is born to trouble.
   and the Sons of Reshef fly upward (5.3-7).

Eliphaz attempts to match Job's cursing of existence with his own
incantation against a wicked man. Using the form of personal
experience,[2] Eliphaz observed a wicked man who had achieved well-
being ('taken root') and uttered a destructive curse against his
'habitation' (נוה), that is his land and his offspring, both of which provide support and continuing life. The sons are to be victims of
injustice in the courts, with no 'redeemer' to save them from oppression when it comes. The harvest meant to sustain the man and his
family is to be devoured by the hungry and thirsty, and filled with
thorns. The last two lines (vv. 6-7) provide rationalization for the
affliction of the wicked man. The first line (v. 6) explains that the
cursed soil is to be the course of evil for the wicked. And the last line
points to the general condition of humanity: people are born to
experience travail in life, just as assuredly as the Sons of Reshef, the
god of pestilence and death,[3] bring forth disease and death from the
underworld. These last two rationalizations are closely associated.
Eliphaz contends that dust (עפר), the material from which humans are
made (Gen. 2.7; 3.19), and the arable soil (אדמה) from which they are
taken (Gen. 2.7), are the very source of evil that both characterizes
human nature and plagues their existence. Reflecting chthonic images,
the soil not only grows crops necessary for existence, but also
produces thorns, weeds, disease, and even famine when it denies its
yield. Dust is often associated with death and weakness in the Bible,[4]
and has this connotation in Eliphaz' speech. He is drawing on a
tradition of cursed soil similar to that found in the Yahwist narrative,
yet without God's redemptive removal of curse following the flood
(Gen. 3.17-19; 8.21).

---

1. Habel (*The Book of Job*, 117) in vocalizing MT's *lo'* ('no') as *lu'* ('surely').
2. James L. Crenshaw, 'Wisdom', *Old Testament Form Criticism* (ed. John Hayes; San Antonio, TX: Trinity University Press, 1974), 256-88.
3. See D. Conrad, 'Der Gott Reschef', *ZAW* 83 (1971), 157-83; and W.J. Fulco, *The Canaanite God Resep* (New Haven: American Oriental Society, 1976). Cf. Deut. 32.24 and Hab. 3.5. The sufferer in *Ludlul bel nemeqi* also speaks of demonic attack from the regions of the soil and underworld.
4. Job 7.21; 10.9; Gen. 3.19; Ps. 104.29; Qoh. 3.20.

2. *Job: The Destiny of Slavery (Job 6–7)*

Introduction. The elements of Job's cosmology of a Divine Warrior who comes not to defeat the dragon and preserve life, but to destroy his own creature, come together for the first time with his presentation of humanity as predestined slaves. The intersection of the cosmological tradition and the anthropological metaphor of slave provides the key for Job's speeches throughout the remainder of the dialogue with the friends.

Job's response to Eliphaz is a disputation composed of two 'alphabetizing poems' (6.2-23 = 22 lines; 6.28–7.21 = 23 lines) separated by two transitions (24-27, 28-30).[1] In the first poem Job takes up Eliphaz' proposal to present his case before God for adjudication by denouncing the justice of God and accusing the comforters of being fair-weather friends who have denied him the loyalty of friendship and sacrificed their own integrity. In a trial before the Almighty they would become treacherous witnesses afraid to utter words of truth. In the second poem, Job poignantly depicts human existence in terms of a mistreated, miserable slave and as breath that quickly vanishes. And in a parody of Psalm 8 which extols God's exaltation of humanity to the position of king over creation, Job, the suffering and embittered slave, accuses God of singling him out for malicious attack.

Destabilizing the Metaphors of Creation: The Metaphor of Battle. Two creation metaphors form the basic structure of language for these two poems comprising the major elements of Job's disputation: the battle with chaos and word (specifically the divine decree that would rescue Job from his dreadful plight and the breath which invigorates creation and human existence).

Poem I (6.2-23)

Strophe I (vv. 2-7)

2. If only my vexation were weighed, and my misfortune were placed upon a scale.
3. They would then be heavier than the sands of the sea.
   Is this why my words have been wild talk?
4. Because the arrows of Shaddai are with me,

---

1. R. Murphy, *Introduction to the Wisdom Literature of the Old Testament* (Collegeville, MN: Liturgical Press, 1965), 25.

My breath drinks their wrath.

5. Does the wild ass bray when he has fodder, or does the ox low over his feed?
6. Can something tasteless be eaten without salt, is there taste to the slime of purslain?
7. My appetite refuses even to touch them; my life loathes my bread.[1]

Strophe II (vv. 8-13)

8. Oh that my petition might be granted, and God would concede to permit my hope.
9. And God would be pleased to crush me, he would release his hand and sever me in two.
10. Yet I would be consoled, I would spring forth in joy.
     Although I have not denied the words of the Holy One, he has not mercy.
11. What strength do I have that I should wait,
     And what is my end that I should make myself patient?
12. Is my strength the strength of stones, or is my flesh bronze?
13. Indeed no help remains in me, and insight is driven from me.

In the first poem (6.2-23), Job characterizes God as the Divine Warrior whose arrows (חץ) have pierced his body and 'terrors' (בעותים) stand in military formation (ערך) against him (cf. Ps. 88.13-18). Subdued, helpless and in pain, Job begs God to dispatch him (literally 'crush' = דכא) with a final blow, severing (בצע) him in two.[2] The arrows of God are a common image of divine justice (Deut. 32.23, 42; Pss. 7.14; 38.3; 58.8; 64.8; 120.4) and are a part of the panoply of the Divine Warrior coming to do battle with chaos to re-establish justice on the earth (Ps. 18.15 = 2 Sam. 22.15; Hab. 3.11; Zech. 9.14; Pss. 77.18; 144.6). In theophanic hymns the Lord's weapons, including spears and shafts, pierce the enemy, while his mace crushes their head (cf. Hab. 3).[3] The 'terrors' most likely refer to the entourage of awesome warriors who accompany the Divine Warrior to battle. In Habakkuk 3 'pestilence' and 'plague' march in battle array as Yahweh leaves Sinai and marches towards Edom.

---

1. Reading זהמה בדי for MT המה בדוי (cf. Job 33.20).
2. Cf. 'crushing' (דכא) Rahab in Ps. 89.11 and 'the crooked serpent' in *ANET*, 137. 'Severing' reflects the splitting open of the chaos monster (Ps. 74.13; cf. *ANET*, 67).
3. See J. Jeremias, *Theophanie* (WMANT 10; Neukirchen: Neukirchener Verlag, 1965).

The imagery of theophanic hymns drawn from military actions praised in victory songs has its metaphorical base in creation myths describing the battle with chaos by gods of creation and order. Marduk's weaponry for use in the war with Tiamat and her forces included a specially constructed bow and arrow, along with mace, lightning, a net, a variety of winds, including the *Imhullu* ('Evil Wind'), the flood-storm, and the storm-chariot drawn by fearsome horses. And in the description of the battle, Marduk drove the Evil Wind into Tiamat's mouth to keep it open, and shot his arrow through the cavity into her belly, penetrating the heart. When he began to create the world, Marduk split Tiamat's carcass in half 'like a shellfish' using the halves for the upper and lower waters.[1] He finally crushed her skull with his mace and severed her arteries. Baal's weaponry wielded against Prince Yam were two specially constructed maces, cast and endowed with magical force by the craftsman god Kothar-wa-Hasis. With these two maces, Baal drove Sea from his throne and struck him between the eyes. And it is only due to the intervention of Queen Asherah that Baal does not crush the helpless Yam with a final blow.[2] What is striking about Job's use of this mythical imagery is his portrayal of himself as the object of God's military might. Without cause or explanation the Divine Warrior has assaulted him with full fury, seeking to destroy him as though he were the chaos monster rivaling divine rule and threatening to destroy creation. And unlike Yam, he has no divine intermediary.

Another use of the metaphor of battle occurs in the second poem as Job sets form his legal complaint against God:

Am I Yam or the Dragon,[3] that you have set up a guard against me? (7.12).

The establishing of a 'guard' (משמר)[4] echoes the precautionary action taken by Marduk following his dividing of Tiamat into two parts. The

---

1. *ANET*, 66-67. The splitting of the chaos monster is reflected in Hebrew poetry: Ps. 74.12-17 and Isa. 51.9-11. The dividing (בדל) of the waters in Gen. 1.6-7 is a faint echo of this mythical image (cf. Prov. 3.20 = בקע).

2. Cf. Ps. 74.13-14 which speaks of God 'breaking (שבר) the heads of the dragons' and 'crushing (רצץ) the heads of Leviathan'.

3. 'Dragon' (תנין) is a common term for the chaos monster in the Hebrew Bible (Pss. 74.13; 148.7; Isa. 27.1; 51.9; Ezek. 28.3; 32.2). Ps. 74.13 also parallels Yam and dragon.

4. This is the term for a military guard or watch (Jer. 51.12; Neh. 4.3, 16, 17) or guardpost (Neh. 7.3). In 7.20, God is bitterly accused of being the 'watcher (נצר) of humans', an expression transformed from the usual notion of providential care

upper part is sealed as the sky, and to keep the raging waters in place Marduk inserts a bar much in the fashion of a gatepost and sets up a watch, giving them the command not to allow Tiamat's waters to escape. Though killed by Marduk, Tiamat still poses a threat against the order of creation.

The Metaphor of Word. This metaphor figures prominently in this response of Job, first in the legal process designed to obtain a just and redemptive verdict from the divine judge, and second in the divine breath that animates creation. In the first poem, Job wishes he could accept Eliphaz' counsel to petition God for a trial that would result in exoneration and redemption:

> O that my vexation would be weighed, and my calamity[1] would be lifted onto scales.
> They would be heavier than the sands of the sea; it is for this reason my words were full of rage (6.2-3).

If Job's great misfortune could be weighed on just scales, the enormity of the outrage he has been made to suffer could be accurately measured. However, it is not Reshef, or the human condition, or even his own sin that is responsible for his plight. Rather, it is God who is behind this savage attack. Dare he appeal to his merciless enemy for justice? But even worse, Job's friends who know his character have betrayed the bonds of intimacy, afraid to witness on his behalf, terrified the same calamity would befall them. Job has not asked them to bribe the judge, nor has he requested they serve as his 'redeemer', to enable him to 'flee' (מלע) his adversary (צר) or to 'ransom' (פדה) him from his oppressors. The 'savior' or 'redeemer' was normally the next-of-kin whose intercession saved the unjustly accused or whose legal assumption of responsibility, say for the guilty's debt, rescued life and property.[2] By contrast the comforters are characterized as traffickers in human lives, casting lots for destitute orphans, and haggling over the debtor's price paid out for a friend. Choosing not to stand alone before a cruel judge, at least for the moment, Job decides to set forth his accusatory lament (7.11-21), bitterly questioning why God does not see the justness of his complaint and pardon (נשא פשע)

(Deut. 32.10) to one in which God, like the guards posted by Marduk, stands at his watch to observe the misdeeds of humanity, now seen as his chaotic opponent.

1. Reading היחי (K) as והוחי (Q).
2. See de Vaux, *Ancient Israel* 1, 21-22.

any transgression he may have committed. At the least, Job hopes for a cessation of God's furious attack which would allow the divine slave to die in peace.

Once again Job subverts the theological systems formed by the language of creation, in this case the combined metaphors of combat and word (breath). God is the Divine Warrior who has engaged in malicious and unwarranted attack on the servant Job. Instead of the subduing of chaos as a prelude to the ordering of creation, the assault on Job is debilitating and destructive. While wishing he could take up the counsel of Eliphaz to petition God for a just and righteous edict that would rectify the injustice against him and lead to his restoration, Job for the time being refuses this recourse due to the fear of his friends to testify and to the corrupt nature of the divine judge. Finally, the metaphor of divine breath is used to speak, not of God's gracious gift of life and providential sustaining of the creature Job, but of the brevity and vanity of existence in torment.

The Metaphor of Slave. Job's anthropology is constructed linguistically in the second poem (7.1-21) by radically contrasting his own view of human nature with that of conventional wisdom. These are captured in the metaphors of slave and king.

Strophe I (vv. 1-6)

1. Is it not humanity's lot to endure hard service on earth? Are not their days like those of the hireling?
2. Like a slave who gasps for the shade, and like a hireling waiting expectantly for his wage?
3. Thus, I am allotted empty months, and nights of weariness are apportioned to me.
4. If I lie down then I say, 'When shall I arise?' But the evening continues on and I am surfeited with restless tossings until the dawn.
5. My flesh is clothed with worms and clods of dust, my skin hardens and then oozes once again.
6. My days pass more swiftly than a weaver's loom, and they come to an end without hope.

Strophe II (vv. 7-16)

7. Remember that my life is but a breath, my eyes will never again see good.
8. The eyes of the one who sees me will not behold me, your eyes are upon me, but I am no more.

9. As a cloud fades and disappears, thus the one who descends into Sheol shall not come up.
10. He will not return again to his house, and his dwelling place shall recognize him no more
11. Therefore I will not restrain my mouth, I will speak in the distress of my spirit, I will complain in the bitterness of my being.
12. Am I Yam or Tannin, that you should place a guard against me?
13. If I say, 'My couch will comfort me, my bed will ease my complaint',
14. You frighten me with dreams, and you terrify me with visions.
15. So that I would choose strangling, death rather than my bones.
16. I protest! I shall not live forever. Leave me be, for my days are but a breath.

Strophe III (vv. 17-21)

17. What is man, that you make him great, or that you consider him?
18. That you examine him each morning. That you test him every moment?
19. How long will you not look away from me? How long will you not leave me alone, until I swallow my spittle?
20. I have sinned. What do I do to you, O watcher of humanity? Why have you made me your target? Why am I a burden to you?[1]
21. Why do you not pardon my trangression, and pass over my iniquity? For now I shall lie down in the dust, and you shall seek me but I shall not be.

The second poem likens the human condition to that of harsh, debilitating, slave labor from which there is no respite until the body degenerates and life swiftly passes away (7.1-6). The metaphor of slave is drawn from the anthropological tradition in Mesopotamia. In the *Enuma elish*, Marduk decides to create humanity in order to serve the gods and to relieve them from harsh toil.[2] This decision by the head of the divine council establishes the eternal destiny of humanity. The same view of human destiny is a major theme in *Atra-hasis*.[3] In the opening lines, the lower gods are given the onerous task of having to work on the dyke and river irrigation system. After a successful revolution, Enki and Mami produce the first humans to relieve the gods of their heavy toil.

---

1. The MT has 'to me' (עלי, a Tiq Soph), while the LXX has 'to you'.
2. Tab. VI, 11.1-2, *ANET*, 68.
3. Lambert and Millard, *Atra-Hasis*.

Job uses three terms to describe the human condition: עבד ('slave'), צבא ('harsh labor'), and שׂכיר ('hired laborer'). In Israel slaves[1] were of two origins. Foreign captives, normally taken in war, and their descendants (Lev. 25.44-46; Exod. 12.44) were slaves for life and served the palace and temple as property of the state, while Hebrew slaves could serve another Hebrew for only six years. At the end of that period, the Hebrew slave had the option of going free or becoming a slave for life (Exod. 21.2-11; Deut. 15.12-18). Female Hebrew slaves were not given that option and remained as concubines for their male owners. Impoverished Israelites without a next of kin to redeem them and thieves who could not repay their debt normally entered slavery, though once the debt was paid or forgiven they could be released (Lev. 25.48). Freedom for Hebrew slaves could also be obtained by the voluntary action of the master, the redemption price being paid by a next of kin, wrongfully inflicted bodily injury (Exod. 21.26-27), the year of Jubilee (Lev. 25), and, for women, becoming the wife of the owner. Being chattel, slaves were bought and sold at the discretion of their owners who could assign them to work at any task. Very few laws protected slaves. Personal injury at the hands of the master could result in freedom (Exod. 21.26-27), and owners who beat their slaves so that they immediately died were punished (Exod. 21.20). If the slave survived the beating for a day or two, the owner suffered no sanctions. Slaves were to rest on the Sabbath (Exod. 20.10; 23.12) and were allowed to participate in the cultic activities of the family (Deut. 12.12, 18), including festivals (Exod. 12.44, Deut. 16.11, 14). Treatment largely depended on the goodness of the owner, which in certain instances could be rather gracious.

The second descriptive term for the human condition is צבא. While the term may be used to refer to military service (Num. 1.3, 20; 1 Chron. 5.18; 7.11) or cultic action performed by the Levites in the sanctuaries (Num. 4.3, 23, 30, 39, 43), it also means harsh, degrading and compulsory service that is imposed on a slave by a lord. Second Isaiah uses the term to speak of the exiles languishing in degrading slavery in Babylonian captivity before Yahweh's redemption in the New Exodus (Isa. 40.2; cf. Job 14.14). It is in this last sense that Job describes not merely his own life, but that of life in general.

---

1. See de Vaux, *Ancient Israel* 1, 80-90; Walter Zimmerli and Joachim Jeremias, *The Servant of God* (SBT 20; Naperville, IL: Allenson, 1965).

שכיר means 'hired laborer', one who hires his services for a certain task, a set period of time, and an agreed upon wage (Exod. 12.45; Deut. 15.18; 24.24; Lev. 19.13; 22.10; 25.6, 40, 50). These workers are either foreigners or Israelites who, having lost their land and all other means of support, are forced by necessity to work for wages. Usually they were agricultural laborers who were very poor, barely survived with the cheap wages paid, and were often cheated of their meager pay (Jer. 22.3; Sir. 34.22). The law protected them by requiring they be paid in the evening, at the end of each work day (Lev. 19.13; Deut. 24.14-15), and prophetic judgments were uttered against those who oppressed the 'hirelings', indicating that the law often was violated (Mal. 3.5).

These three terms are used metaphorically in Job to describe the human condition as one of onerous, debilitating labor. Humans are foreign slaves who languish without any hope of freedom under the oppression (צבא) of cruel masters. Humanity is a slave who works in the scorching heat, longing only for the 'shade' or 'shadow' of evening to gain relief, or a 'hireling' who has only one hope—that the owner will not cheat him of the promised, meager wage at day's end. Pointing to the approach of night (7.4) when relief is gained or wages are given may suggest the imagery of death which is the one and only means of release from the degradation of human existence. This would fit the language of the second strophe of the opening soliloquy (3.11-19) where in Sheol the 'slave is free from his master'. As is the case in Mesopotamian mythology, humans have one eternal destiny—to serve the gods, an everlasting decree from which there is no escape save death.

Then in a lament-like appeal (7.7-10), Job asks God to remember (זכר) that his life is 'breath' (רוח), the vital force which enters humans at birth and returns to its divine source at death (Job 10.12; 12.10; 27.3; cf. Gen. 2.7; Qoh. 12.7). He will never again 'see the good', i.e. experience the well-being and fullness of life that is wisdom's goal (cf. Ps. 34.12). He will soon descend into Sheol, the 'land of no return' which has no exit. In drawing on the tradition of the creation of humanity, Job reminds God of the weakness of human creatures and the brevity of their existence (cf. Pss. 78.39; 103.14-18; 144.3-4). What is so different in Job's lament, however, is that the typical plea for deliverance is transformed into reproach. Divine memory will not recall redemptive acts of old or participation in the creation of the individual (Pss. 20.4; 25.6, 79.8).[1] This sufferer simply wants God to allow him to die in peace.

When Job turns to active protest and accusation (7.11-21), he once again speaks of life as 'breath'. Only this time the words are those of rejection and bitterness: 'Leave me alone, for my days are breath (הבל)'. The term for 'breath' (הבל), the *leitmotif* of Qoheleth, portrays life as evanescent, worthless and vain (Pss. 39.6, 12; 62.10; 94.11; 144.4; Qoh. 2.1, 14, 15). Job would choose strangling over his torturous existence where he has become the target of divine attack. And unlike the bold and defiant Gilgamesh who goes on his quest for immortality, and hence desires to become a god, Job despairingly declares that he 'would not live forever'.[2] Job does not threaten to grasp divine status for himself. No ale-wife need remind him of the limited life-span that is allotted to all human creatures, nor would he wish to continue the pain and meaninglessness of his own bitter existence. If the quest for immortality is the basis for divine attack, then God has misjudged the creature's motives, for Job chooses death over life. Here Job strips the tradition of human creation of all positive theological import. There is no divine care in the shaping of the fetus, or in the breathing of life into the body, or providential oversight of the new and developing life. God's breath is no vital force animating Job's existence. Rather life is a vapor which quickly vanishes, devoid of any and all significance.

---

1. Clements, 'Zakhar'; and Brevard Childs, *Memory and Tradition in Israel* (SBT 37; Naperville: Allenson, 1962). זכר is especially used in the petition of the lament to remind God of his promises (Exod. 32.13; Deut. 9.27) and of his salvific deeds on behalf of his people in the past. And through memory, salvation is actualized for the present generation (cf. Horst, *Hiob*, 116).

2. 'The Epic of Gilgamesh', *ANET*, 73-99. The exception is Utnapishtim, who, because he survived the flood, was granted along with his wife the gift of immortality. Cf. Adapa's quest for immortality which also ends in failure (*ANET*, 101-103). Aqhat's rejection of Anath's seductive offer of immortality typifies the standard Canaanite understanding:

'Fib not to me, O Maiden,
        For to a Youth thy fibbing is *loathsome*.
Further life—how can mortal attain it?
        How can mortal attain life enduring?
Glaze will be poured [on] my head,
        Plaster upon my pate;
And I'll die as everyone dies,
        I too shall assuredly die' (*ANET*, 151).

What subverts the royal anthropology of some Israelite traditions is the third strophe (vv. 17-21) of this second poem, which parodies Ps. 8.5-6 in the fashion of the lament in Ps. 144.3-4. As noted earlier, Psalm 8 extols God for exalting lowly humanity to the status of king over creation. The key verses of this psalm read:

What is man that you remember him,	מה אנוש כי תזכרנו
and the Son of Man that you visit him?	ובן אדם כי פקדנו
You have made him a little less than the gods,	ותחסרהו מעם אלהים
with honor and glory you have crowned him.	וכבוד והדר תעטרהו

The lament in Ps. 144.3-4 begins in the same way; but in the second bicolon, a disconcerting shift is made to describe the frailty of the human creature.

O Lord, what is man that you regard him,	יהוה מה אדם ותדעהו
or the Son of Man that you think of him?	בן אנוש תחשבהו
Man is like a breath,	אדם להבל דמה
his days are like a passing shadow,	ימיו כצל עובר

The psalmist, portrayed as a king, uses the tradition of the exaltation of undeserving humanity to remind God of the frailty of the human condition and therefore his own, and to move the Divine Warrior to come in judgment to destroy his enemies and deliver him from the distress of chaos.

Job also begins with a quotation of Ps. 8.5, and likewise makes an unexpected transition in the second bicolon (7.17):

What is man that you make him great,	מה אנוש כי הגדלנו
or that you consider him?	כי תשית אליו לבך
That you examine him every morning,	ותפקדנו לבקרים
that you test him every moment?	לרגעים תבחננו

However, unlike Psalm 144, Job does not use the tradition to call upon divine deliverance from suffering. Rather, his parody deconstructs royal anthropology in speaking of a God who exalts humans, not for glory or protective care, but for merciless judgment and destruction. פקד ('visit, examine') is used in the Exodus tradition to speak of God's gracious and protective care which redeems Israel and destroys her enemies (Exod. 3.16; 4.31; Ps. 80.15). Yet it is also to speak of God's searching out and punishing of the wicked (Ps. 17.3 and Jer. 6.15). In Job God's surveillance is unrelenting scrutiny leading to merciless destruction both of his servant and humanity in general. Humanity, including Job, is no royal figure or exalted creature, chosen to rule over God's creation and confident in a gracious providence. Rather humans are slaves, victimized by the destiny allotted them and the terrors wrought by a cruel and suspicious sovereign.

3. *Job: The Plea for Justice and Mercy (Job 9–10)*

Introduction. Bildad's response to Job (ch. 8) echoes the arguments and standards of knowledge earlier used by Eliphaz, though the polite insinuations that Job has sinned have become more directly and callously stated. Particularly the reference to the death of Job's children as due to God's punishment for their sins is the cruelest example. Nevertheless, Bildad restates Eliphaz' counsel that a legal decision from God should be sought, if indeed Job is innocent and righteous. In that case God would arise, an image pointing to a decision by the divine judge, and deliver Job from his distress. Job's disputation (9–10) directed against Bildad announces his intention to cease lamenting and to plead his case before the divine council. However, Job examines the perils in such an undertaking, recognizing how great the odds are against his obtaining a fair and just verdict from God who would not only hear his case as judge, but also would bring charges against him as his antagonist. For God, 'might makes right'. Indeed Job's *Angst* is expressed in an internal struggle between the continuance of accusatory lament, the pursuit of lawsuit, and the cessation of all effort in the hopes of gaining some relief from the drudgery of toil before entering the realm of eternal night.

The Metaphor of Battle. Actualizing the mythic structure of the battle model, the theophanic tradition of the Divine Warrior coming to defeat chaos and order life through the power of the divine edict is depicted in the form of the doxology encased in the first strophe. But the manner in which the doxology is misshaped indicates that Job's intent is to destabilize the language of praise and faith, not to affirm and unleash its faith-creating power.

Strophe I (9.2-12)

2. Truly I know that this is so, but how may a person be righteous before God?
3. If one desires to file suit against him, he could not answer him once in a thousand times.

4. He (God) is wise of heart and mighty in strength, who can harden
   himself against him and prevail?
5. Who moves mountains and they do not know, when he overturns them
   in his anger.
6. Who shakes the earth from its place, and its columns tremble.
7. Who commands the sun not to rise, and seals up the stars.
8. Who alone stretches out the heavens, and treads upon the back of Sea.[1]
9. Who makes Aldebaran and Orion, Pleiades and the Chambers of the
   South (Wind).
10. Who makes great, inscrutable things, marvelous things without number.
11. Behold he passes by me, but I see him not.
    He moves on, but I perceive him not.
    Before he seizes,[2] who can restrain him.
    Who dares to ask him, 'What are you doing?'

Job's hesitancy to follow the friends' counsel to seek out God for
legal redress[3] is expressed in this first strophe (9.2-12) which envelops
a doxology. While Job utters a doxology (9.5-10) very much like the
one offered by Eliphaz in 5.9-16—indeed the tenth verse quotes,
though with ironic intent, the opening verse of Eliphaz' psalm—it is
the meaning that radically differs.[4] The function of the doxology,
drawing from the theophanic imagery of prophetic announcements of
judgment (Amos 1.2; Mic. 1.3-4) and the hymn's description of the
Divine Warrior coming to defeat chaos and set the world in order
once again (Pss. 76.9; 99.1; 104.32), is to praise the righteous judge
either for an anticipated verdict of acquittal of the unjustly accused or
for the fairness of the decision to condemn the wrongdoer. The latter
case is tantamount to a confession of guilt. However, Job's use of the
doxology is significantly different. He utters the doxology, not as

---

1. Two Hebrew MSS have עב ('cloud') in place of L's ים (Sea). במתי is translated
'back' on the basis of Ugaritic *bmt* (Pope, *Job*, 70; cf. Marduk's trampling the back
of Tiamat [*ANET*, 67]). For a discussion, see F. Cross and D. Freedman, 'The
Blessing of Moses', *JBL* 67 (1948), 191-210. Also cf. Deut. 33.29.

2. L's חתף is a variant of חסף which occurs in several Hebrew MSS. חתף refers to
the oppressor's seizing of the poor (Ps. 10.9) and to the abduction of the young
women of Shiloh by the men of Benjamin for wives (Judg. 21.21).

3. ריב, which refers in this context to initiating a legal case (Isa. 3.13; 51.22;
57.16, Amos 7.4; Prov. 25.8), is a frequent term in Job (as a verb in Job 9.3; 10.2;
13.8, 19; 23.61; 33.13; 40.2; as a noun in Job 13.6; 29.16; 31.13, 35). It also has
the more general meaning of 'disputation' (Gen. 31.36; Exod. 17.29; Hos. 2.4) of
which a legal dispute is part.

4. K. Budde, *Das Buch Hiob* (2nd edn; GHAT 2; Göttingen: Vandenhoeck &
Ruprecht, 1913), 42; and R. Gordis, *The Book of Job* (New York: 1978), 522.

confident praise in the creator's just rule, but rather as an indictment of one whose brutal use of power and exploitation of wisdom have led to violent acts against creation.

The doxology has two thematic movements: the approach of the Divine Warrior to do battle with Prince Yam (vv. 5-8), and the shaping of the constellations of all creation with a wisdom beyond understanding (vv. 9-10). To these customary themes Job adds a third—oppressive use of power by the *deus absconditus* against humans (9.11-12). The description of the tumult of nature (cf. Judg. 5.4-5; Pss. 68.8-9; 114.3-7; and Hag. 2.6, 21) contains the common Ancient Near Eastern theme of the moving and shaking of heaven, earth and mountains before the awesome and powerful gods.[1] The image of a catastrophic earthquake associated with the coming of God is found in Judg. 5.5; Ps. 77.19; Isa. 41.15; Jer. 4.24; Ezek. 28.20; Joel 2.10; Amos 8.8; Nah. 1.5, and Hab. 3.5. So powerful is the earthquake that the pillars on which the earth is set tremble (cf. 1 Sam. 2.8; Ps. 75.4; Job 26.11; 38.4-6), threatening to collapse the created order. And the divine command, instead of calling forth the rising of the sun, keeps it submerged within the watery depths of the cosmic ocean so that its rays are blotted out by the darkness of the underworld (cf. Isa. 13.10; Amos 5.8; 8.9). Even the stars are sealed in their chambers and are not called forth to give their shining light that limits the dark power of chaos at night, heralds the appearance of the sun at the beginning of the radiant dawn, and rules over the seasons of farming and travel.[2] Such actions normally demonstrate

---

1. Jeremias, *Theophanie*, 151. In Sumer it was Enlil who, as the 'Lord of the Storm', was responsible for maintaining order on the earth (cf. A. Falkenstein, *Sumerische Hymnen und Gebete*, 77). In Babylonia, Adad, the storm god, was connected with theophany in nature. See S. Langdon's translation of IV R 28 No. 2 (*Babylonian Penitential Psalms* [Oxford Editions of Cuneiform Texts 6; Paris: Librairie Orientaliste Paul Geuthner, 1927], 31-32):

    10. Ramman, when he rages the earth quakes before him;
    12. The great mountains are shattered before him.
    14. At his raging, at his wrath,
    16. At his roaring, at his thunder,
    18. The gods of heaven ascend unto heaven,
    20. The gods of earth enter into the earth,
    22. Shamash on the eastern horizon of heaven is shrouded in darkness.
    24. Nannar passes into obscurity on the western horizon.

God's power over the astral deities. And God once again subdues Sea as in primordial times, trampling as a victorious king upon the back of the defeated dragon,[1] thus signaling his right to continued dominion over the earth (cf. Pss. 18.8-16; 77.17-20). This return of creation to chaos, as the mighty warrior comes forth and does battle with either the dragon or the raging Sea, is in character with mythical depictions from the ancient Near East and with the dependent Israelite theophanic tradition. Thus in Habakkuk 3 the mountains tremble and quake before the threatening approach of God from Sinai, and the great lights of heaven, the sun and the moon, stand still. What is central to the theophanic tradition is the idea of God's invincible power as he approaches to 'set things right', to redeem oppressed Israel from the hands of the wicked nation portrayed in the role of primordial chaos.[2] The key concern in these hymnic descriptions is the coming of the mighty warrior to save, an act of ordering which restores the world to the rule of justice. No power in heaven or on earth can resist the righteous indignation of God. However, what is unique and therefore disorienting about Job's theophanic description is that the typical quaking of the earth is not in response to God's deeds (coming to chaos and order creation), but rather is the deed itself. And the wrath of God, normally directed against chaos, including Israel's enemies,[3] is now channeled towards the cosmic order.[4] In other words, God's fury is unleashed to destroy creation, including Job. Destruction, not redemption and the ordering of creation by justice, is the goal of divine action. The metaphors of the battle with chaos and the ordering power of word which commands the stars and establishes justice through decree are now used to speak of God's destruction of creation.

---

2. Gen. 1.14 establishes the order of the lights in the firmament to designate sacred times, seasons, and the calendrical passage of time, while Amos (5.8) speaks of Kima and Kesil which mark the seasons of seedtime and harvest.

1. Hab. 3.15 speaks of Yahweh trampling sea with his horses (דרכת סוסיך בים), while Mic. 1.3 and Amos 4.13 describe him as 'treading upon the heights of the earth' (על במותי ארץ). All are theophanic texts.

2. Jeremias, *Theophanie*, 10. See Isa. 30.27-33; 59.19; Jer. 25.30-31 for descriptions of God coming to defeat his human enemies.

3. See Nah. 1.2-11. In Job the 'wrath' of God is a motif with two different nuances: the friends speak of God's righteous indignation against the wicked (4.9; 20.23, 28; 35.15), while Job describes the anger of God as an irrational force directed against him and all of creation (14.13; 16.9; and 19.11).

4. Cf. Jer. 10.10; Jeremias, *Theophanie*, 24.

Job again attempts to destabilize the metaphors of creation and their power to construct a language of faith.

This chaotic power of God is then contrasted with the second thematic movement which describes the creative ordering of reality in primordial times: the 'stretching out of heavens', the making of the constellations, and the creating of 'great, inscrutable things, marvelous things without number'. The last image refers to creation in general, while the first two specify the creation and ordering of the heavens. 'The stretching out of heaven' refers to the unfurling, spreading out, and securing of a tent (Gen. 12.8; 26.25; 35.21), and is a common image for the creation of sky and clouds (Job 37.18; Ps. 104.2; Isa. 44.24;[1] 45.12; 51.13; Jer. 10.12). The making of the constellations is the action of God in establishing temporal order by marking the sacred and agricultural seasons, times for travel, and calendrical units of days, weeks, months and years (cf. Gen. 1.14). The exact identity of the four constellations is debated. עשׁ[2] has been identified as the seven stars (LXX), the evening star (LXX, V Job 38.32), the Great Bear (Ursa Major with the three stars of the tail as the 'sons' or 'daughters' of the bear), Capella (with the two Kids Zeta and Eta), Alpha Tauri (with either the Hyades or the Rain Stars as sons), Leo (with Beta, Eta, Gamma, Delta and Epsilon), or Aldebaran (with the sons being the Hyades).[3] כסיל ('fool'), usually identified with Orion, is portrayed in the legend of a giant who rebelled against the gods and was punished by being chained to the heavens (cf. Job 38.31; Isa. 3.10; Amos 5.8). In Greek Mythology the giant Orion was a mighty hunter whose head rose above the clouds and whose feet walked upon the floor of the sea. Killed by the goddess Artemis or Gaea, Orion was placed with his weapons in the heavens, where according to Hesiod he hunted the Pleiades.[4] His rising and settings also marked the times of sowing, storms, and quiet.[5] כימה is the

---

1. This text, like Job 9.8, also emphasizes that God 'alone' creates the heavens.

2. See Job 38.32 which has the variant spelling עישׁ.

3. De Wilde, *Hiob*, 142-44. De Wilde explains that around 500 BCE Aldebaran's late setting was April 18, late rising October 28, early rising May 28, and early setting November 7. Its late rising and early setting designated the time of early rains and plowing, while its early rising coincides with the period of hot climate (*Hiob*, 144).

4. See Pope, *Job*, 70. Orion was associated with the mighty heroes of various cultures, including Nimrod, Gilgamesh, and Hercules. Tur-Sinai thinks this reference (cf. Job 38.32) reflects a myth of rebellion of Titans against the rule of God. Thus God defeats and transforms them into stars (*Job*, 157-58).

5. De Wilde, *Hiob*, 145.

Pleiades, a constellation of seven stars, whose early setting proclaimed
the coming of winter and early rise pointed to the beginning of harvest
(cf. Job 38.31; Amos 5.8).[1] In Greek mythology they were sisters of
the Hyades pursued by Orion. The fourth constellation, the 'Chambers
of the South (Wind)', is the most enigmatic, but possibly refers to the
southern part of the Milky Way with its dazzling bright lights (cf. Job
39.26). Also out of the South came the powerful winds of winter
storms.[2] God's establishing of the dominion and times for these constellations gave order to the seasons, making agriculture and safe
travel possible, differentiating between 'good and evil' times. In
primeval days the ordering of time marked the natural cycle and the
order of fertility and sterility. God's wrath against creation contrasts
with primordial rage against chaos which led to the defeat of the giants
(constellations) opposing divine rule. Now God obliterates the signs of
the heavens governing the seasons of life and recreation. Temporal
order dissolves (cf. Gen. 8.22).

Job adds a third thematic movement to the doxology which points to
God's participation in human history and concentrates on two features
of that activity: inscrutable divine presence and power which takes
what it will without challenge. The first feature is that of divine
presence in human affairs, which, however, remains undetected by
humans. The hiddenness of God is one of the great difficulties for Job,
who, though he wishes to confront his adversary and speak face to
face, finds it impossible to locate the divine presence (cf. Qoheleth).[3]
The other feature uses two common expressions for unlimited,
sovereign power: 'who will restrain him' (מי ישיבנו) and 'who will say
to him "What are you doing" (מי יאמר אליו מה תעשה)?' The first
expression is used by Zophar to refer to God's uncontested might and
the power of the edict to judge and put in prison (11.10), while Job
uses it to speak of God's unchallenged determination to carry out the
divine plans (23.13). The second is a question which no ordinary
mortal dares put to the king (human and divine), whose position and

1. De Wilde, *Hiob*, 144-45.
2. De Wilde, *Hiob*, 145-47.
3. Cf. the friend who explains to the sufferer that 'the plan of the gods is remote'
(Section VI, 'The Babylonian Theodicy', *ANET*, 602), and the lament of the sufferer
in *Ludlul bel nemeqi*:

> Who can know the will of the gods in heaven?
> Who can understand the plans of the underworld gods?
> Where have humans learned the way of a God? (*ANET*, 597).

edict are supreme (Qoh. 8.4; Dan. 4.35). Thus God is a mighty oppressor who 'seizes' according to divine caprice (Judg. 21.21; Ps. 10.9), for there is no one, god or mortal, who dares oppose the heavenly Warrior.

The second strophe of ch. 9 (vv. 13-24) continues to feature the internal struggles with Job, as integrity confronts terror and the passion to demonstrate personal innocence and God's malicious caprice confronts the fear of the intimidating power of God. And in this confrontation integrity prevails. Consumed by the conviction of his own righteousness and the unavoidable conclusion of the malevolent wickedness of God, Job decides to bring charges against the creator of heaven and earth. Now Job sets forth his own anticipated struggle with the dragon slayer.

Strophe II (9.13-24)

13. A god could not restrain his (El's) anger; even the helpers of Rahab bowed beneath him.
14. How much less could I possibly answer him, or even choose my words with him?
15. Although I am innocent, I could not answer him; I must implore my judge for mercy.
16. If I called and he answered me, I would not believe that he was hearing my voice.
17. For he crushes me with a whirlwind, and he multiplies my wounds without cause.
18. He does not allow my breath to return, but rather fills me with bitterness.
19. If it is a matter of strength, behold he is mightier.
    But if it is a matter of justice, who will arraign me?
20. Though I am righteous, my own mouth would condemn me.
    I am pure, but he would hold me perverse.
21. I am innocent, I do not care for myself, I despise my life.
22. It is all the same, therefore I say: he brings both pure and wicked to their end.
23. If a lash kills suddenly, he laughs at the calamity of the innocent.
24. The earth is given over to the wicked; he covers the face of its judges.
    If it is not he, then who is it?[1]

The strophe begins (v. 13) with an example of the frightful power of God drawn from the *Chaoskampf* tradition. Even a god could stand

---

1. The initial letter of each line is א (aleph), save for v. 18 which has א (aleph) as the second letter (לֹא) and v. 21 which has א (aleph) as the third letter (וְתָּאמַר).

no chance of 'turning back the anger' of El, that is, opposing him successfully in combat and at least battling him to a standstill until he withdrew. One example of such a battle between gods leading to a standoff occurs in the Baal cycle during Mot's second challenge to Baal's earthly rule.

Job's example of the invincible might of God is the humbling of the 'helpers' of Rahab' (עזרי רהב).[1] This most likely refers to a primordial battle between El and the chaos monster Rahab similar to the one between Marduk and Tiamat in Babylonian mythology, leading to the victory over chaos and the creation of the earth. In Ugaritic mythology, not only Baal but also his consort engages chaos in battle. Anat boasts of having crushed Yam and a host of monsters.[2]

Since even the mighty chaos monster and his army of gods were defeated and made to bow the knee (שחח) of submission,[3] Job ponders how he, a mere mortal, could hope to confront God in court and answer his charges. God's intimidating presence would elicit a confession of guilt, even though Job is certain of his own innocence. And in v. 17, Job returns to the image of himself as the chaos monster against whom the full destructive wrath of God has been unleashed:

> For he crushes me with a whirlwind,
> And he multiplies my wounds without cause.

Taking on the character and appearance of the storm god, Marduk brought into battle against Tiamat a full array of powerful winds, including the 'Evil Wind' which he released into her gaping jaws to keep them forced open, until he could send his arrow through her mouth into the heart.[4] Baal too is the storm god who rides his chariot on the clouds with mighty wind, thunder and lightning his weapons. And in the theophanic descriptions of God, he is accompanied by a mighty whirlwind (Nah. 1.3) as he comes to destroy the wicked and

---

1. As a name for the chaos monster Rahab is unique to Hebrew mythology (Isa. 51.9; Ps. 89.10-11; Job 26.12-13). Used in parallel lines with Yam and the 'dragon', the mythological references indicate he was 'crushed', 'smitten', and 'cut in pieces' by God in a primordial battle, prior to creation. In the historicizing of the myth, Egypt is identified with Rahab in Ps. 87.4 and Isa. 30.7 (see Mary Wakeman, *God's Battle with the Monster* [Leiden: Brill, 1973], 56-61).

2. *ANET*, 137.

3. שחח is used to refer to humbling of the proud and mighty, especially on the 'Day of the Lord' when God comes to sit in judgment (Isa. 2.11, 17; Ps. 107.39).

4. *ANET*, 67.

establish justice on the earth (cf. Isa. 28.2).[1] Now God unleashes his whirlwind and crushes (שׁוּף)[2] Job, 'multiplying his wounds without cause'. God's attack is lethal, and its brutality is much the same as Anat's slaughter of Mot or as Marduk's dismemberment of Tiamat.[3]

Not only has the Divine Warrior brutally assaulted Job as though he were chaos, but he does not allow the divine, life-giving breath (רוח) to return. The 'gift' of God's breath animates all creation (Ps. 104.30), while its withdrawal leads to withering and decay (Ps. 104.29). Instead of the divine breath, God fills Job with 'bitterness' (מרר; cf. Lam. 3.15). Attacking him with a 'whirlwind' and withholding his 'breath' are complementary images pointing to God's destruction of Job. This assault is 'without cause' (חנם), an expression echoing the words of the divine judge in the Prologue who admitted the edict issued to destroy Job was groundless (חנם, Job 2.3). While the character Job is unaware of God's own admission of guilt in the second scene in heaven, the audience has witnessed this stunning confession and is once again reminded of it just as the decision is made to indict the creator.

The Metaphor of Word. Verse 19 signals the beginning of Job's determination to pursue litigation. He intends to appear before the divine council and to bring charges against its judge. If the case were to be settled on the basis of strength alone, God would obviously emerge the victor through intimidation and the threat of violence. But if the rules governing jurisprudence (משׁפט) are maintained, Job believes he will win. With the hopeful anticipation that this condition will be met and willing to risk a life that has lost all value, Job boldly asserts his own innocence and sets forth his indictment of God's misrule. The head of the divine council has become like one of his corrupt judges who derives sadistic pleasure from sentencing the righteous and

---

1. Three related terms for 'whirlwind' are שׂערה (Job 9.17; Nah. 1.3), שׂער (Isa. 28.2), and סערה (Ezek. 1.4; Job 38.1; 40.6). The image is also figurative of the wrath of God in Isa. 29.6; 40.24; 41.16; Jer. 23.19; and 30.23.
2. Ironically the only other occurrence of this verb is Gen. 3.15 where the enmity between the woman's seed and that of the serpent is described. Addressing the serpent, Yahweh says: 'he shall *crush* your head, and you shall *crush* his heel'. That same enmity exists between God and Job, leading God to destroy his adversary.
3. *ANET*, 140, 167.

guilty to execution, or laughs when the whip inadvertently kills.[1]
Indeed the legal system, which is supposed to be rooted in cosmic
justice, established at creation and maintained by divine enforcement,
has been perverted by God. God is the one who has made justice blind,
enabling the wicked to inherit and rule the earth.[2]

Although the decision to file suit against God has been made, Job is
reluctant in the third strophe (9.25-35) to continue. Convinced that a
corrupt God will hold him guilty in a legal decision, Job would prefer
to have recourse to a legal procedure in which he could be assured of
justice from the heavenly court. In the context of this internal
struggle, Job hits on the idea of an arbiter (מוכיח) who might reconcile
the two opponents with just arbitration (cf. 16.18-21; and 19.23-27):
'Would that there were an arbiter between us,[3] who might lay his hand
upon us both.'[4] This arbiter would not only be fair but also would
have the authority and integrity not to be persuaded by God's brute
strength.

The Metaphor of Artistry. The fourth strophe (10.1-17) is a lament-
like complaint which draws on God's creation of the individual.[5]
Metaphors of God as craftsman and Lord of the womb responsible for
conception and birth are brought together in this model. Normally the
reference to the tradition of the creation of the individual in a lament
is designed to move God to redeem the one he has crafted and providentially guided (cf. Ps. 139.13-18). However, Job destabilizes the
metaphors of artistry and birth by depicting God as the potter who
skillfully fashioned him in the womb, not for the purpose of

1. Contrast the stringent rules for judges set forth in Exod. 18.13-26; Deut. 1.9-
17; 16.18-26 (see de Vaux, *Ancient Israel* 1, 152-55). To 'cover the face of judges'
is to bribe them to pervert justice (cf. Exod. 23.8).

2. I.e. against Wisdom's assertion that only the righteous inherit the land, while
the wicked and their descendants 'are cut off' (Ps. 37.9, 11, 34; Prov. 2.21;
10.30). A complaint similar to Job's description of the perversion of justice and the
rule of the wicked is made by the man weary of life in 'The Dialogue between a Man
and his Ba' (*ANET*, 406-407).

3. Reading לא (*lu'*, = 'would'), a conditional particle introducing a case which
has not been or is not likely to be realized, for MT's לא (lo' = 'not').

4. See William Irwin, 'Job's Redeemer', *JBL* 81 (1962), 217-29. M.B. Dick
('The Legal Metaphor in Job 31', *CBQ* 41 [1979], 37-50) and Habel (*Job*, 196-97)
refer to Near Eastern legal documents pointing to the existence of a legal arbiter
who could issue a non-binding decision to settle a dispute before an actual trial was
convened. Both sides had to agree to the settlement for it to be binding.

5. Or as Hesse notes, *Klage* returns, but now in the form of *Anklage* (*Hiob*, 85).

providentially caring for his welfare, but to destroy him. Toward the conclusion of the strophe, this metaphor clashes with the portrait of God as the divine hunter who seeks Job out like a lion to slay him.

1. I loathe my life; I will vent my complaint; I will speak out in my bitterness.
2. I shall say to God, 'Do not condemn me; make known to me why you are contending with me.
3. Is it good for you to oppress, to despise the labor of your hands, while you shine your light upon the plan of the wicked?
4. Do you have eyes of flesh, or do you see as a human sees?
5. Are your days as the days of a human, or are your years as the days of a man?
6. That you seek out my iniquity, and search for my sin?
7. Although you know I am not guilty. There is none to save from your hand.
8. Your hands have fashioned and made me, but afterwards you turn around[1] to swallow me up.
9. Remember that you shaped me like clay, but now you are returning me to dust.
10. Did you not pour me out like milk, and curdle me like cheese?
11. You clothed me with skin and flesh, you knitted me with bones and sinews.
12. You created for me life and love, and your providence guarded my spirit.
13. But these things you hid in your heart; I know this was your intent.
14. If I sin then you watch me, you do not acquit me of my iniquity.
15. If I am guilty woe unto me; if I am righteous I could not lift up my head. Have your fill of dishonor and look upon my affliction.
16. If it (my head) rises up, you hunt me like the lion; once more you work your wonders against me.
17. You renew your witnesses against me, and you increase your vexation against me.
   Fresh troops are arrayed against me' (10.1-17).

Showing no concern for a life of painful slavery which has lost all appeal, Job utters an accusatory complaint against a silent God whose edict has condemned him to a horrible fate. At the center of this invective is the tradition of the creation of the individual, which presents God as the artist who creates Job, even as a potter molds and fashions a piece of clay into a pleasing vessel (Gen. 2.7, 21-22; Ps. 139.13-16; Jer. 18.1-11), and the 'Lord of the womb' responsible for conception, nurturing in the womb, birth and providential care. In

---

1. Reading אחר סבות ('afterwards you turn around') for MT's יחד סביב ('together round about') on the basis of LXX's μετὰ ταῦτα μεταβαλών.

Gen. 2.7-8 God is the potter (יוצר) who makes Adam from the dust
(עפר) of the ground (אדמה), while Second Isaiah often speaks of God
as the potter who formed Israel (Isa. 43.1, 21; 45.9, 11)[1] even from
the womb (Isa. 44.2, 24). Likewise the Servant of the Lord in
Isa. 49.5, the prophet Jeremiah (Jer. 1.5), and the individual
(Isa. 43.7; Ps. 119.73) are fashioned by God in the womb. These
metaphors for divine activity evoke the images of necessary skill in the
fashioning of humans, the opening (or closing) of the womb, the
providential oversight that begins at conception and continues through
life, and the intimate knowledge of both human nature and the specific
character of the individual. Thus the psalmist praises the wondrous
quality of divine works and knowledge used when he 'was being made
in secret, intricately wrought in the depths of the earth' (Ps. 139.15).[2]
Indeed, when the fertility and artistry metaphor are combined,
providence takes on the character of predestination: Israel is destined
to be God's people and Jeremiah is to serve as the 'prophet to the
nations' (cf. Isa. 49.1-3). For humans the metaphors evoke the images
of election in being 'the work of God's hands',[3] the special gift of
God's care, divine shaping of human nature, and predestination. The
destiny God has set for the human creature cannot be lightly taken or
dismissed (cf. Isa. 45.9; Jer. 20.9).[4] Second Isaiah uses this feature of
the tradition in a 'woe-oracle' (45.9) to depict the ludicrous nature of
attempting to challenge the sovereignty of God. And since the creator
has shaped the individual in the womb and continued to watch over his
creation, only God knows in intimate detail the 'work of his hand'
(Ps. 139.14-15).

   With a consistency well marked to this point, Job once again
subverts metaphor in order to divest language of its world-making
capacity. In this case Job accuses God of being the artist who now has
turned against the 'work of his hands' (יגיע כפים),[5] to oppress and hold
in contempt the object of labor. And in a ghastly depiction, God is the

----

1. Cf. Isa. 64.8; Job. 4.19; 33.6.
2. For the Old Testament the craftsmanship and skill of the artist and artisan were
identified with 'wisdom' (Exod. 28.3; 31.3, 6).
3. Cf. Job. 14.15; 34.19; Ps. 138.8.
4. The verb יצר often means to 'preordain' (Isa. 22.11; 37.26; 46.11).
5. See Gen. 31.42; Ps. 128.2. These other two instances of the expression refer
to the result or product produced by labor. A more common expression for the
artistry metaphor is מעשה ידים ('work of [his, your] hands'): Job 14.15; 34.19;
Pss. 8.7; 19.2; 102.26.

cannibalistic parent who now like Sheol devours his own offspring. Inexplicably the creator despises and seeks to destroy what he has produced. Further, God has forgotten the limitations of the human creature he has fashioned and therefore is unable to understand the pathos of Job's situation. With two rhetorical questions which challenge the motive of God's persecution, Job reminds God of human weakness and the brevity of life:

> Do you have eyes of flesh, or do you see as a human sees?
> Are your days as the days of a human, or are your years as the days of a man?
> That you seek out my iniquity, and search for my sin? (10.4-6).

'Flesh' (בשׂר) is a term which especially underscores the infirmity of human existence dependent on God to give vitality through divine breath (cf. Job 34.14-15; Ps. 78.38-39). 'Eyes of flesh' and 'seeing as a human sees' are parallel images of human knowledge, which Job consistently acknowledges is limited. The shortness of human life is often underscored in Job, being compared to a breath, cloud, flower, or shadow which quickly appears and then vanishes (Job 6.7; 14.2). With a strong measure of satire, Job asks if God has creaturely limitations that might explain the ruthless efforts to destroy an innocent man.[1] Yet Job quickly asserts the tradition's emphasis on divine knowledge of the creature when he charges that God is well aware that Job is free of any guilt. And since Job has no *go'el* to deliver him with informed testimony, he stands in the unenviable position of having to appeal for mercy from a knowing God turned cruel.

In vv. 8-11 a series of contrasts are drawn which completely subvert the tradition of the creation of the individual. The first negation is found in v. 8:

> Your hands have fashioned and made me, but afterwards you turn around to swallow me up.

The first bicolon has the metaphor of the divine potter forming in the womb the one lamenting. The normal, expected movement for a lament would then develop the theme of God's loving, providential care for the creature. Instead Job negates the tradition by accusing God of now turning to destroy (literally 'swallow up', בלע), not sustain, what has been created. Like the insatiable Mot whose gullet

---

1. See Fohrer, *Hiob*, 214.

swallows Baal,[1] an image also descriptive of the voracious appetite of Sheol (Prov. 1.12), God has turned to devour the creature of his own making.

The second negation is constructed by v. 9:

> Remember that you shaped me like clay, but now you are returning me to dust.

Once again the first bicolon begins with a metaphor from the creation tradition. Using the image of the potter working with the moist clay to create a vessel, Job begins as though he were asking God to actualize (literally 'to remember' [זכר]) the salvific power of creation to deliver him from distress. As God gave him existence by breathing into the shaped clay the breath of life (Gen. 2.7), so now God should act to revitalize the threatened life of the creature. Or so one would expect Job to say. By contrast in the second bicolon Job picks up the motif of the edict of death issued in Genesis 3 ('to dust you shall return', חשוב אל עפר), echoed later by Qoheleth (Qoh. 12.7: 'dust returns to the earth' (וישב עפר על הארץ)), to complain that God is 'returning [him] to dust' (אל עפר תשיבני).[2] Only Job has defined no known divine commandment leading to the sentence of death.

The third contrast, much more extensive than the first two, is developed in vv. 10-17. The section begins with what appears to be a credal affirmation of the creation tradition common to laments:

> Did you not pour me out like milk, and curdle me like cheese?
> You clothed me with skin and flesh, you knitted me with bones and sinews.
> You created for me life and love, and your providence guarded my spirit
> (10.10-12).

In the first part, the conception of Job is described as the process of cheesemaking, while in the second God is the weaver who clothes Job with skin and flesh and knits together bones and sinews (cf. Ezek. 37.5-8). The third line moves to the typical theme of God's providential care (פקדה)[3] for the life which was created, care that was

---

1. *ANET*, 138, 140. See Jon. 2.1 where the fish swallows Jonah and takes him down into Sheol.

2. Cf. Pss. 104.29; 146.4; and 90.3 which states: 'You return (שוב) the human creature back to the dust (דכא), and you say, "Return (שוב), O sons of humanity"'.

3. The verbal form of this word often points to God's gracious visitation that brings salvation and well-being: Gen. 21.1; 50.24, 25; Isa. 23.17; Jer. 15.15; 27.22; 29.10; Pss. 8.5; 65.10. Ps. 65.10 praises God's 'visitation' of the earth that leads to its abundant fertility. The providence of God involves both the vital actions

the extension of 'steadfast love' (חסד)[1] granted to Job from the time of the imparting of the divine breath (רוח). It is this gracious visitation of God, his protective oversight, that guards (שמר) or sustains the vital force (divine breath) that animates Job's being.[2] God's gift of life, granting of steadfast love, and providential care are central to the creation tradition and provide the basis for an appeal for divine salvation.

Continuing to deconstruct the theology of this tradition, Job turns to assail the divine motive for creation:

> But these things you hid in your heart; I know this was your intent.
> If I sin then you watch me, you do not acquit me of my iniquity.
> If I am guilty woe unto me; if I am righteous I could not lift up my head; Have
>   your fill of dishonor and look upon my affliction.
> If it (my head) rises up, you hunt me like the lion; once more you work your
>   wonders against me, and you increase your vexations against me; fresh
>   troops are arrayed against me (Job 10.13-17).

God's intention in the creation of Job does not conform to the general affirmations of the tradition. God's true motive in creating Job was to engage in a constant surveillance of his actions, to 'watch'[3] for every fault and to use any real or imagined iniquity as the basis for punishment. Job affirms that he is basically innocent of any significant wrongdoing, though he admits he has at times committed minor wrongs, especially during his youth, and possibly unwitting sins. Were he intentionally sinful, he would quite readily suffer punishment. Although he is convinced of his 'innocence' (צדקתי),[4] he knows he will

---

that create and promote life and peace and the punishments that bring an end to the wicked (Num. 16.9; Isa. 10.3; Mic. 7.4).

1. Katherine Doob-Sakenfeld, *The Meaning of hesed in the Hebrew Bible* (HSM 17; Cambridge, MA: Harvard, 1977).

2. Psalm 104 is the most laudative description of God's providential care for all of creation. Cf. the hymnic section found towards the end of 'The instruction for Meri-Ka-Re' which describes the creator's provisions for the life and well-being of humans (*ANET*, 417). Qoheleth bemoans the fact that no one has the 'power to retain the spirit' and override divine destiny which determines the day of birth and the day of death (Qoh. 8.8).

3. The satirical force of this expression, 'watch' (שמר), should not be missed. Normally when used of God the term refers to providential care and protection (Gen. 28.15, 20; Exod. 23.20; Job 29.2; and Ps. 91.11). Yet Job's God watches him, not to protect him from harm and to sustain his life, but to maintain a constant vigil to discover real or imagined evil and then to punish him for these 'crimes'.

4. In this context the term refers to one who is pronounced legally innocent by a judge (Ps. 143.2; Isa. 43.26).

not be restored to a place of honor. Indeed were he to attempt to be restored to honor, God would 'hunt him like a lion' and 'once more work his wonders against him'.

In their use by Job, these latter two expressions continue to subvert normal conceptualizations of metaphor. As a ritual act lion hunting is more than simply the sport of kings undertaken for royal pleasure. The royal hunting of lions and certain other dangerous animals was an act of ordering and sustaining the kingdom. Ritually conceived, wild beasts were embodiments of chaos threatening the cosmic and social order.[1] The hunt was a sacred act held at auspicious times of festival which imitated the creator's slaughter of the chaos monster. Instead of issuing a just edict which would restore Job to his place of honor, God becomes the divine hunter seeking to kill the human servant. Also subverting language through hyperbole and parody, Job decries God's efforts to keep him from being restored to a place of honor by 'working his wonders against him'. פלא ('work wonders') refers to divine acts of creation, sustaining the order of the cosmos (cf. Gen. 37.14), and redemption (cf. Judg. 6.13).

Finally, in this text, which continues to subvert the language of creation and justice, Job laments God's perversion of legal process by 'renewing' (חדש)[2] the witnesses (presumably the comforters) who testify against him and by supplying 'fresh troops' (צבא) to oppose him in battle. These troops, normally the heavenly hosts who fight on God's behalf, are now arrayed to do battle with Job. In his dual role as head of the divine council and the slayer of the dragon, God has targeted Job for cruel and unjustified destruction.

The Metaphor of Fertility. The last strophe (10.18-22) in this speech of Job reverts to the third chapter's imagery of God as Lord of the womb and Job's own wish that he had died at or before birth:

> 18. Why did you bring me forth from the womb? Would that I had expired and no eye had beheld me.
> 19. It would be as though I had never lived; I would have been carried from the womb to the grave.

---

1. Othmar Keel, *Jahwes Entgegnung an Hiob* (FRLANT 121; Göttingen: Vandenhoeck & Ruprecht, 1978), 62-63.
2. The verb normally means the creative act of renewing life (cf. Ps. 104.30). Job uses the verb ironically to speak of the revitalization of Job's opponents, who not only are afraid to testify on his behalf, but actually turn to witness falsely against him.

20. Are now my days few? Let him ease. Let him withdraw from me so that I
    may be cheerful.
21. Before I go where I shall not return, To the land of darkness and deep
    darkness.
22. A land where light is like the darkness, deep darkness and chaos, where
    light is like darkness.

The metaphor of fertility includes the image of God as the one who grants or withholds conception, blesses the breast and womb (רחם), shapes the fetus, and like a midwife brings forth the newborn.[1] The epithet 'Lord of Mercies' (רחמים) expresses feminine compassion associated with the womb. Here, as in the second strophe of ch. 3, Job regrets that God has brought him forth out of the womb like a midwife assisting the mother at birth.[2] Had God not acted, Job would have died in the womb, never to have been seen by any human eye. Job repudiates the tradition of the creation of the individual, not by denying God's involvement, but rather by disavowing the intention to sustain, protect and care. Instead, God brings forth human creatures to torment, until they perish in agony.[3]

4. *The Metaphorical Process: From Destabilization to Mimesis*

In the first cycle Eliphaz has attempted to construct a cosmology of Deuteronomic retribution in which God is the maker and righteous overseer of a moral order permeating creation. However, Eliphaz radically shifts the conventional sapiential portrayal of humanity from rulers to slaves. Indeed, humans are corrupt by nature and sure to sin. Their only hope for salvation is to confess their guilt, praise the creator of all, and beg for mercy from the righteous Lord. Eliphaz seeks to combine a cosmology of retributive justice with an anthropology of humanity as slave, corrupt by nature, in his effort to contest Job's argument.

In his pathos, Job cries out for support from his friends, yet discovers that they have become not compassionate comforters, but rather arch-conservative defenders of the faith. This means they will defend any and all actions of God as wise and just, and condemn all human efforts as so many filthy rags. Job's response to them is to con-

---

1. Gen. 49.25; Job 31.25; 38.8; Ps. 22.10-12; Isa. 46.3; Jer. 1.5.
2. Cf. Jer. 20.18 and Job 3.11.
3. Job often ends his speech with a vision of death (Job 7.21; 14.20-22; 17.13-16; 21.32-33).

tinue to take the offensive, destabilizing through the outrage of his own experience all root metaphors of creation. Now God is the divine sadist who has engaged in combat against creation and one of its noblest human creatures. And the human creature no longer is the exalted king, ruling in *noblesse oblige* both nature and society. While not accepting the friends' dark view of human nature, Job opts instead for a description of human function as that of abused slavery to the gods.

In the first cycle, Job deconstructs the root metaphors of the two traditions of creation: cosmos and humanity. Battle, word, artistry and fertility are turned upside down. Not only is God the Divine Warrior who has attacked creation, but also the wicked and corrupt judge who laughs at the destructive force of his own evil decisions. As artist God has created not a human object of beauty and delight, but rather one for sadistic torture. And as divine parent, God conceives, forms, and nurtures Job in the womb, not out of love, but out of the desire to bring suffering and pain.

At this point in the drama, a new and terrifying vision of reality has begun to emerge in the speeches of Job. Frightening images of the metaphors of *cosmos* and *anthropos* have been shaped, turning the world upside down. It is a world in which God as Divine Warrior runs amok, wreaking wanton havoc. And it is a nightmare world of terror and misery, as humans are mistreated slaves who serve a sadistic master. Job and his implied audience have experienced a second shock, but it is what Wheelwright describes as the 'shock of recognition'.

Chapter 7

PROTEST AND REVOLT:
THE SECOND AND THIRD CYCLES AND THE OATH OF INNOCENCE

1. *Job: The Illusion of Redemptive History (Job 12–14)*

Introduction. In the first cycle of debate, Job has deconstructed the
cosmological tradition of the combat myth by depicting God as the
Divine Warrior who has come to destroy creation. In addition, Job's
own experience of creation as burdensome toil and endless suffering,
shaped by the tradition of humanity as slave to the gods, has led him to
the point of desperation. If he cannot prevail upon God to deliver him
from death, his only recourse is revolt. Yet, while he hopes to indict
and remove the creator from the throne, what gives Job pause for
thought is his own mortal weakness and insignificance. If he has no
arbiter, i.e. no divine intercessor, to present his case before the divine
assembly or to enter into Sheol, following his death, to rescue him
from the darkness of the tomb, what hope remains? In chs. 12–14,
Job's despair deepens as he continues to gather unavoidable evidence
that God is a malicious tyrant who seeks to destroy his own creation.

The Destabilization of the Metaphor of Word. Job's speech in chs. 12–
14 is a disputation which incorporates features of the hymn (12.13-25)
and lament (14). Chapter 12 consists of 3 strophes, the last two of
which (vv. 7-11, 12-25) make significant use of creation theology.

Strophe II (12.7-12)

7. But ask the beasts and they will instruct you, and the birds of the heavens
    and they will tell you.
8. Or speak[1] to the earth and it will teach you, and the fish of the sea will
    inform you.

1. שׂיח, 'to speak, talk' (Judg. 5.10; Pss. 60.13; 105.2; Prov. 6.22).

9. Which among all these does not know that the hand of Yahweh has done
   this.
10. He who has the life of every living thing in his hand, and the breath of all
    human flesh.
11. Does not the ear test words, or the palate taste its food
12. Among the aged is wisdom, and insight in the length of days.

In his disputation with the three friends, Job uses a common source of
knowledge in Wisdom, i.e. nature, to underscore his argument. Sapiential epistemology centered on the revelation of God in the orders
that undergirded all life. The patterns that guide the phenomena of
nature and human society pointed to relationality, consistency and
repetition. Drawing on cosmic mythology, the wise believed that God
through wisdom established a beneficent, life-giving order (צדקה,
'justice, righteousness, harmony') which permeated the world, giving
it coherence, regularity, harmony and beauty.

While the sages tended to avoid a dogmatic theory of retribution,
they did affirm that righteous human behavior helped to create and
sustain structures for life, while wicked behavior undermined them.
To exist in conformity with order, to live in harmony with nature and
society, to experience and express beauty, and to create aesthesis
through word and deed was to be 'righteous' (צדיק). Mythically conceived, human society was to imitate and be governed by cosmic
order. For society to be 'righteous' (צדק) and to experience the
beneficence of God's good creation, it must develop institutions and
laws which reflected this order. Nature, society and the individual
were not separate, unrelated categories, but rather were intercon-
nected spheres, each impacting significantly upon the others. The key
to life and well-being, both for society and the individual, was
wisdom. Through close observation, the evaluation of experience,
critical reflection, and elegant crafting of language, powers of knowledge granted by God to the wise, sages conceptualized the features
and dictates of cosmic and societal order in their instructions which
they imparted to their students.

Knowledge of the world also led to an understanding of God who is
revealed through this creative order. Normally disdaining the ecstatic
knowledge of prophets and the cultic revelation of the priests, the
sages argued that rational inquiry and critical reflection on their
experience of the world led to the knowledge of God. To experience
the world was to experience God. Metaphorically articulated, creation
speaks a language which the wise can hear, understand, and formulate

into their own instructions for life. Indeed the consistency of life-sustaining order made possible human trust in the creator. Of course the sages recognized limits to their knowledge and readily affirmed the mystery and freedom of God which allowed divine action to transcend all patterns of constancy and sameness. And the elements of creation, including human beings, did not always act consistently and in an orderly way. Divine participation in history, human evil, and inexplicable actions of nature were not always consistent with expectations derived from observable patterns of behavior. Nevertheless, the sages had confidence in the general regularity and justice of order, and they trusted in the goodness and life-sustaining providence of God.

Job draws on this cosmological tradition of the sages, articulated in the theology of creation by word, when he disputes the friends' contention that retributive justice and the moral nature of God are doctrines beyond contestation. Not only is God just, say they, but as Zophar has affirmed (11.1-12), divine wisdom transcends all human understanding. Indeed Zophar wishes that God would speak directly to Job and reveal the secrets of wisdom (11.5-6). The revelation to which Zophar appeals is direct and supernatural, not the traditional wisdom of the sages based on observation and rational inquiry. Zophar's interpretation of theology is not faith seeking understanding, but rather human credulity bowing the knee to unassailable dogma. Yet ironically he asserts that Job's claim to wisdom is patently false. In contesting Zophar's (and the other friends') argument, Job appeals to nature as the one recognized source for the knowledge of God. Speaking with mythopoeic imagination, common to the metaphorical process, Job demands that his opponents 'ask' the non-human creatures who can 'instruct' (ירה) and 'reveal' (נגד) to them the true nature of God. This is the basic formulation of Wisdom's understanding of divine revelation: God is revealed through the order of creation. Nature teaches humans a language they can learn, a hermeneutic of who and what God is.[1]

---

1. Revelation through creation was not unknown in other cultures. See the message of Baal to the goddess Anat delivered through his messengers:

I've a work I fain would tell thee,
  A speech I would utter to thee,
Speech of tree and whisper of stone,
    Converse of heaven with earth,
    E'en of the deeps with the stars (*ANET*, 136).

The categories of creation mentioned are drawn from the classical traditions of creation in Genesis 1–2: 'beasts' (בהמות), 'birds of the heavens' (עוֹף הַשָּׁמַיִם), 'fish of the sea' (דְּגֵי הים), and the 'earth' (אָרֶץ).[1] And like the heavens, firmament, and cycle of day and night which speak a language that is silent and yet understood (Ps. 8), so the earth and its creatures instruct the wise in the proper understanding of God.[2] What is so different is the content of what the earth and its non-human creatures reveal: the 'hand (power) of God', responsible for devastating a blameless Job, 'has done this', that is made him a laughingstock, the object of contempt, while 'the tents of despoilers are at peace, and those who provoke God take their ease'. The creation and its creatures who continually suffer at the hand of God can truly testify to divine cruelty. However, far worse than a morally bankrupt cosmos and human community is a perverse God whose merciless power destroys the innocent and sustains the wicked. The earth and its creatures reveal the perversity of God. Placed in this context, the confessional statement of v. 10 has a hollow but ominous ring:

> He who has the life of every living thing in his hand ('power'),
>   And the breath of all human flesh.

Normally the first line of this confession is found in the praise of thanksgiving for divine protection which secures God's people from all threat (Isa. 49.2). However, for one who has suffered heavily at the hand of God, the image is not one of providential care but of terror.[3] The second line is also the language of confessional praise: the divine breath freely imparted gives life, even as its withdrawal leads to

1. See Gen. 1.26. The categories and order here are 'fish of the sea', 'birds of the air', 'the beasts', 'all the earth', and 'every creeping thing'. The final category is not found in Job 12, though BHS suggests amending שׂיח ('speak') to חיה ('beast'). Pope understands ארץ to mean 'underworld' (cf. Job 10.21-22), so that the four spheres of the universe would be represented: earth, sky, underworld and sea (*Job*, 91). However, for the sages the underworld was not a source of knowledge, since no one could return to tell the experience. ארץ should be maintained in the normal meaning of 'earth', since Job is speaking of creation as the source of sapiential knowledge of God.

2. See A. de Guglielmo, 'Job 12.7-9 and the Knowability of God', *CBQ* 6 (1944), 476-82.

3. See Job 1.11; 2.5; 6.6; 10.3, 7, 8; 13.21; and 19.21. Qoheleth captures the ambiguity of divine behavior in his statement that the righteous and wise are in the 'hand of God', though they cannot know if it is because God loves them or hates them (9.1).

the withering and death of all nature (Ps. 104.29-30). For Job the confession is no longer one evoking trust in a deity who gives and sustains life, but rather a dire warning about the God who readily delights in destroying what has been created. Fragile humanity stands on the edge of oblivion, subject to the whim and caprice of a malevolent power. Thus Job warns the friends to assay the silent words that all creation utters against the creator and thereby to take their heed (v. 11). The traditional affirmation in v. 12 that wisdom belongs to those advanced in years forms an inclusion returning to Job's personal attestation to his own wisdom in vv. 2-3.

A Doxology of Terror. The third strophe in this lengthy speech is Job's special rendition of a doxology which incorporates his view of the nature and activity of God in human history. As noted earlier, doxologies are uttered by the accused who either are seeking legal redress in the sanctuary or are the confession of those who have been found guilty of their crimes. Now the falsely accused Job, unjustly found guilty and sentenced to agonizing torment and degrading death, parodies the doxology of confession.

A second instance of destabilization of word theology, in this case hymnic praise, is found in Job 12.13-25, a doxology to the destructive power of divine providence.

Strophe III (12.13-25)

13. With him (God) is wisdom and might, he has counsel and insight.
14. Behold he tears down, and there is no rebuilding; he imprisons a person, and there is no release.
15. Behold he withholds the waters, and the lands dry up; when he sends waters forth, they engulf the land.
16. With him are strength and sound wisdom, the deceived and the deceiver belong to him.
17. He makes counselors walk naked, and makes fools of judges.
18. He loosens the instruction[1] of kings, and ties a waistcloth on their loins.
19. He makes priests walk about barefoot, and ruins wise officials.
20. He takes away the speech of those who are trusted, and deprives the aged of discernment.
21. He pours contempt upon princes, and loosens the girdle of the strong.

---

1. Maintaining MT's מוסר ('instruction, discipline') over against the proposed change in BHS to אסר ('bond'): 'loosens the bond'. The figurative expression of binding an instruction to the heart or neck is found in Prov. 6.21-22.

22. He reveals deep mysteries from darkness, and brings to light deep darkness.
23. He exalts nations and destroys them, he expands them and then leaves them forsaken.[1]
24. He removes reason from the leaders of the people of the earth, and makes them wander in a pathless waste.
25. They grope about in the darkness with no light, causing them to stagger like one who is drunk.

The dual *leitmotif* of the doxology is struck in the initial bicolon (v. 13): with God are 'wisdom' and 'might'. And what is not only glaringly absent, but resoundingly repudiated, is the justice of God. The initial verse contains three related terms for wisdom: חכמה ('wisdom'), עצה ('counsel'), and תבונה ('insight'). For the sages God's wisdom represented the knowledge and skill to make and sustain the structures of creation, and the eloquence of speech creating the world. And through the gift of divine wisdom, humans were able to shape and maintain social systems which reproduced and reflected cosmic order. 'Counsel' is both sagacious advice leading to success and a well-conceived plan resulting in well-being. As divine counselor Ea is the one who advised Marduk in the plan to create humanity to serve the gods. As divine counselor God is the one who conceives the blueprint for the regimen of all categories of creation, for sustaining the structures of life (Isa. 28.23-29), and for determining the destiny of individuals and nations (Prov. 19.21 and Isa. 14.24-27). A frequent synonym for wisdom, 'insight', is both the faculty of perception and the act of understanding (Prov. 2.6, 11; Job 26.12). These faculties dispel chaos and folly and enable correct and life-giving decisions to be made and carried out. What is central to all three terms is the metaphorical power of word and speech used in creating and sustaining the world (Prov. 3.19-20; Ps. 33.10-11).

'Strength' (גבורה) refers especially to the power of human warriors (Judg. 8.21; Prov. 8.14; Isa. 3.25). As a characteristic of the Divine Warrior it is the power used to subdue the dragon (Job 26.14), to establish the mountains and still the roaring of the seas of chaos (Ps. 65.7-8), to maintain divine rule over the nations and the earth (Pss. 66.7; 89.14), and to save from the threat of destruction (Ps. 106.8).

---

1. Following Gordis' repointing of ויזחם to mean 'leave, forsake' (*Job*, 140-41).

But the two themes of v. 13 are summarized in vv. 14 and 15 where the confessional nature of the poem shifts to parody: God uses wisdom and might, not to create and sustain life and nations, but to destroy them. The first theme contrasts a major *leitmotif* in Jeremiah (1.10): God does not tear down the structures of life and society in order to rebuild them, but to prohibit their being restored. And instead of allowing humans to participate in divine wisdom and power to create social spheres in which justice and life flourish, God limits, constrains, and even denies them to human leaders. God encloses humanity in a building which has no exit. The second theme resumes the depiction of God's destructive edicts governing nature which either withhold the rain to cause wilderness, drought, and famine (cf. Amos 4.6-8) or inundates the earth with floodwaters destroying life (cf. Gen. 6-8).[1]

The *leitmotif* is repeated in v. 16: 'with him are strength (עֹז) and wisdom (חוּשִׁיה)', and the remainder of the poem develops God's actions in history which oppose societal constructions of reality. Ideally, God imparts charismata, including especially wisdom, to leaders of human communities to enable them to lead righteously and well (cf. 1 Kgs 3—'Solomon's Wisdom'). In a sweeping indictment falsely clothed as words of confession and praise, Job argues that these very leaders responsible for creating and maintaining order in society are singled out for the abuse of divine caprice. God denies to leaders the wisdom and strength which enable them to govern (Job 12.21a and 24b = Ps. 107.40).

The major reference to God's returning of chaos occurs in v. 22: God unleashes the waters of the primeval ocean to inundate the created order, and causes deep darkness to engulf the light. The raging waters and darkness were the two primary features of primordial chaos (Gen. 1.2). In addition, this reversal of creation is paralleled by God's capricious direction of history: nations are enlarged and made great only to be destroyed and abandoned. Wisdom literature is silent about the traditions of salvation history and covenant before Sirach and the Wisdom of Solomon, choosing to orient its teaching to creation theology. However, in traditional Wisdom God does participate in human history by nurturing the righteous and bringing destruction to the

---

1. Unlike J and P, Job posits no human guilt that is the cause of the primordial flood. Job's reference may include both common flooding and the cosmic flood of Genesis.

wicked (Prov. 10.3, 29; 15.3, 29) and by requiring standards of
justice be maintained in all human communities (Prov. 11.; 17.5;
20.10; 22.22-23). The sages affirm that God gives wisdom to
counselors and kings, who must make both legal and military decisions
which strongly affect the well-being of the nation (Prov. 24.3-6; 31.2-
9). In one metaphorical use of this tradition, Woman Wisdom praises
herself as the one who enables kings to rule wisely and well
(Prov. 8.15-16). But before Sirach there is no particular sapiential
doctrine that God guides human history toward a well defined, climactic goal, or that Israel is the elect through whom God works to
establish justice among the nations. This was the theology of the
prophets and their successors, the apocalyptic seers.

Job, however, denies that God has any plan for the nations or any
goal towards which he guides history. By contrast the very gift of
wisdom by which rulers successfully direct nations to experience life
and well-being is withheld. And without the light of understanding,
leaders wander lost in the chaos (תהו, v. 24)[1] which God has
uncovered. It is through mere whim or wicked caprice that God
directs the rise and fall of empires. Thus the chaos wrought in creation
is paralleled by that brought upon human communities. Indeed wisdom
and might are with God alone, but he uses them not to sustain, but to
destroy.

The Metaphor of Slave and the Death of the King. After the resumption of disputation, first against the friends (13.1-12) and then against
God (13.13-28), Job issues another lament-like complaint descriptive
of the hopeless condition of human existence and the inescapable conclusion in death.

Strophe I (14.1-6)

1. A human being, born of woman, is of few days, and sated only with
   drudgery.
2. One sprouts like a flower which then withers, and one passes like a
   shadow which cannot remain.[2]

---

1. תהו is used of primordial chaos in Gen. 1.2 and Jer. 4.23, while Deut. 32.10
uses the term to refer to the desert. Both sea and wilderness were seen as symbols of
lifeless, alien chaos.
2. 'Flower' is a common figure for the brevity of life (Pss. 37.2; 90.6; 103.5; and
Isa. 28.1-4; 40.6-8), as is 'shadow' (Job 8.9; Ps. 144.4; and Qoh. 6.12). In the
passage from Second Isaiah, a comparison is also made between the short duration of

3. Upon such a one you fix your stare, and bring him[1] into judgment before you.
4. Who can produce something clean from what is unclean?[2] No one.
5. Indeed one's days are numbered, the number of one's months are fixed by you, one cannot surpass the prescribed limit you have ordained.
6. Turn your gaze from this one and desist, until like the hireling one should finish[3] one's day.

The metaphor of word, specifically referring to the edict of the divine judge, evokes for Job a decision that is final and unchangeable. Sentenced to a life of slave-like 'drudgery', the exact number of days (cf. 21.21) are set (חרוץ)[4] by divine decree (חוק)[5] which cannot be abrogated (לא יעבור).[6] There is no hope that one might ascend to the heavens like the wise Adapa and at least attempt to gain from the divine assembly the decree of immortality.[7] Rather the one plea

human existence and the eternal word of God. Normally the image of brevity of human life is contrasted with the eternity of God (cf. Ps. 103.14ff.). However, Job deconstructs the positive theological import of the image and transforms it into one of indictment (Fohrer, *Hiob*, 255).

1. Reading 'him' with the LXX for MT's 'me'.
2. Job echoes the earlier words of Eliphaz that God has created human nature to be evil (4.12-21; cf. Job 15.14; 25.4-6; Ps. 51; Sir. 10.18, and 'The Babylonian Theodicy', II.275ff.; *ANET*, 604). How then can the creator expect perfection from a tainted creature? The image of 'clean/unclean' may reflect the language of P's assessment of female impurity for seven days following giving birth due to the discharge of blood (Lev. 12). However, the idea of being born in sin is foreign to P. Instead, for Job and the friends, the 'uncleanness' associated with birth becomes an image for the corruption of human nature.
3. רצה means 'to count, complete' (Lev. 26.34, cf. Dhorme, *Job*, 198), not 'desire'.
4. The term is used in Dan. 9.27 to refer to a fixed, legal division by God.
5. חק means 'legal statute' or 'decree' (Exod. 18.16 and Jer. 31.6), though it is specifically used to mean 'prescribed limit' or 'boundary' in regard to the cosmological sphere of the heavens (Ps. 148.6) and sea (Jer. 5.22).
6. Predestination is also affirmed by Qoheleth and the friends. However, while the friends faithfully accept it as a dimension of divine sovereignty, and Qoheleth acquiesces to its inevitability, Job protests against its unfairness. Indeed Job argues against God on the basis of a moral order to which even God must be subject. The image of setting a divine decree (חק) which cannot be transgressed (עבר) is a favorite one in creation and wisdom texts in speaking of limiting the realm of Sea (Job 38.10-11; Ps. 104.9; Prov. 8.29; and Jer. 5.22) at the time of creation so that the cosmos cannot be inundated by his proud waves. But here it is used to speak of the individual's destiny set by God.
7. *ANET*, 101-103. Adapa was deceived by Ea, his creator and the god of wisdom, into rejecting the bread and water of life offered by the gods.

issuing in the anguished cry of Job and all humanity is that God should cease 'watching' them, turn away, and at least allow them to die in peace when the hopeless drudgery of existence is finally past.

Most important in this lament-like poem is the second strophe (14.7-12) which contrasts the finality of human death with the hope that a tree may sprout again and live even after being cut down.

Strophe II (14.7-12)

7. For there is hope for a tree; if it is cut down it could sprout again, and its shoots might not fail.
8. If its root grows old in the soil, and its stump dies in the dust.
9. At the scent of water it will sprout up, and put forth branches like a young plant.
10. But a man dies and is brought low,[1] he expires and then where is he?[2]
11. Waters fail from a lake, a river parches and dries up.
12. So a human lies down and does not rise up, until the heavens are no more he will not awaken, he will not be roused from his sleep.

The contrasting imagery of fertility and sterility dominates this strophe. Water and trees are common fertility symbols in the Bible and the ancient Near East. The mythological origins of the tree symbol are found in ancient Near Eastern myths which present the tree's lifespan and powers of rejuvenation as emblematic of longevity, death and rebirth, and immortality.[3] In Sumer, the myth of Dumuzi and Inanna (who became Tammuz and Ishtar in Akkadian mythology) spoke of the marriage of a young god, representing the reproductive power of the date palm, to Inanna, the goddess of fertility.[4] After Dumuzi's death at a young age,[5] Inanna goes weeping in search of her dead lover, finds and resurrects him, and together they consummate

---

1. חלש occurs in only two other places: Exod. 17.13, where it refers to the defeat of Amalek, and Isa. 14.12, where Day Star, attempting to ascend to the heights, is 'brought low' to the Pit. The term echoes this myth of the fall of Day Star's prideful attempt to replace El as the head of the divine assembly. However, to this point, Job has denied he has any ambition of replacing God as ruler of the cosmos. He changes his mind by the time of the concluding soliloquy (29–31).

2. The LXX, S, and one Heb. MS have אין ('he is not') for L's איו ('where is he').

3. For iconographic examples, see Keel, *The Symbolism of the Biblical World*, figs. 46, 47, 48, 479 and 480.

4. See Jacobsen, *The Treasures of Darkness*, 22-74; and McCurley, *Ancient Myths and Biblical Faith*, 75-78.

5. In one ominous development of the myth, Inanna turns over Dumuzi to the underworld in order to escape death herself.

their sacred marriage, leading to the same cycle once again. This myth was celebrated as a date harvest ritual, in which the king played the role of Dumuzi and the queen (or high priestess) that of Inanna. Other versions of the story presented Dumuzi as a shepherd or hunter who embodied the reproductive power of animals necessary for human survival. Dumuzi's return is described only in one text. Here he returns as *damu*, the power of fertility in tree sap and vegetation. The ritual of lamentation was performed at a sacred cedar in the temple compound of Uruk. The tree represented his mother and was the site of his birth. The festival was designed to lead to the regeneration of tree sap at the end of the dry season. The myth passed into Babylonia where Ishtar, the goddess of love and war, became a more violent and savage Inanna. Hence when she offers to Gilgamesh wealth and glory as her partner, the bold hero spurns her advances, noting the wretchedness of Tammuz and other partners whom she consigns to the foul stench of death when her love grows cold.[1] A similar myth involves Baal as a dying and rising god who is freed from the under-world by his consort Anat, the slayer of Mot, the god of death. However, it is Asherah, the earth-mother goddess, who is represented by a sacred tree at the Canaanite high places. Occasionally the tree was carved in the shape of the goddess, but its continued sprouting signaled her generative powers (cf. Hos. 4.11-14).

As a symbol of immortality in the paradise myth (Gen. 2–3), the tree of life, planted in the garden which is watered by the four rivers of the earth, represents a divine gift offered to the first pair in their innocence, though denied them after their eyes are opened and they obtain the knowledge of good and evil. Here the Yahwist draws on the Mesopotamian tradition of the king as the Primal Man who tends the garden and guards the tree of life. And in one addition to Isaiah, the rejuvenation of the defunct dynasty of David is described in terms of shoots and branches growing from the stump (גֶּזַע) and roots of a cut tree (Isa. 11.1),[2] while Ezekiel's allegory portrays the dynasty as a cedar of Lebanon, and the exiled Jehoiachin as a young twig removed from its branches. The association of tree, including 'tree of life', with

1. See the Myth of Osiris and Isis, where Osiris represents the generative power of the grain.

2. See Isa. 40.24 where גֶּזַע is also used to describe princes and rulers whose stem barely takes root in the soil before Yahweh withers it with his searing breath. The mythical associations of kingship and tree (illustrated by the Dumuzi tradition) reside in the background.

kingship continued with the appropriation of the myth by the sages. The ideal sage was the king, though royal attributes were often referred to sages in general. Thus the tree of life refers to the gift of longevity and blessing offered by goddess Wisdom to the sage (Prov. 3.18 = 1 Kgs 3.3-14; cf. Prov. 11.30; 13.12; and 15.4 where the deeds and virtues of the wise are a 'tree of life'). In the first psalm, the righteous sage who avoids the company of wicked people and reflects on Torah is likened to a fruitful tree planted by an everflowing stream,[1] while Job describes his former life in the image of a well-watered tree (29.19).[2] However in both Mesopotamia and Israel, resurrection from the dead was not for mortals, even those who were kings. The underworld was 'the land of no return', a dreadful place where a weak and shadowy existence might continue for a time until the finality of complete extinction.

Hence Job's use of the image of a tree reminds all mortals of the ominous fate which awaits them, from which there is no last-minute reprieve or ultimate release. Dumuzi and Baal may await expectantly for deliverance and rise from the dead, but they are dying and rising fertility gods, not humans incapacitated by mortal weakness. Unlike incantation priests who can awaken Leviathan from slumber, no power in heaven or on earth can 'arouse' (עור, v. 12; cf. Job 3.8) humans from the dead.[3]

The third strophe portrays Job's momentary desire to enter Sheol and hide there until the destructive wrath of God might pass. Since Sheol normally resides outside the dominion and knowledge of God, Job hopes that he would have respite from persecution there until a divine reprieve and final deliverance would come.

Strophe III (14.13-17)

13. O that you would place me in Sheol to conceal me, that you would hide me till your anger is past. That you would issue me a decree and remember me.
14. If a man dies, will he live again?

---

1. Cf. Ps. 92.12-15 which likens the righteous to the palm tree and cedar in Lebanon which are planted in the sacred groves of the temple, evoking images of paradise, creation, and life. In addition, see Isa. 6.13; 40.24; and 53.2.

2. By contrast the wicked is one whose 'root' and 'branches' wither (Job 18.16).

3. The language of resurrection (קום, קיץ) from the dead, found in Isa. 26.19 and Dan. 12.2 (late eschatological texts), is explicitly used and negated by Job.

All my days of harsh service I would expectantly wait, until my
release should come.

15. You would call out, and I would answer, you would long for the work
of your hands.

16. For then you would number my steps, and would not keep vigil over my
sin.

17. My transgressions would be sealed in a bag, and you would plaster over
my iniquity.

Job compares his future stay in Sheol to harsh, oppressive slavery
(צבא), a term used for the exiles' stay in Babylonia (Isa. 40.2).[1]

For Job these days of slavish drudgery and imprisonment in the
underworld could be endured, if only he could hope that eventually
God would either personally enter the underworld or send an emissary
to obtain his 'release' (הליפה). Longing for the 'work of his hands'
(10.3, 8-12), God would secure his redemption from death, providentially caring for his well-being, and forgiving his iniquities.

The release of dying and rising fertility gods (e.g. Baal and
Inanna = Ishtar) from the underworld or at least their revitalization
(Dumuzi = Tammuz and Osiris) was a common theme in ancient
Near Eastern mythology. The use of the imagery of the tree
(= vegetation) in the preceding strophe suggests that the mythological
imagery continues to be exploited in this present section. Inanna
(= Ishtar), languishing in the underworld, gained release through the
intercession of a deity before the high court and the decision of Enki
(= Ea) to intervene and obtain her release. Baal, slave to Mot, gained
freedom through the violent intervention of the goddess Anat. Dumuzi
was also brought back to life to unite once again with the fertile
goddess Inanna, as was Osiris (to couple with Isis, producing Horus).
As a result, nature, which had withered, was revitalized and then
flourished with abundance. Yet Job is a mortal (גבר) who could only
wistfully dream of God's intercession and redemption.

In several other contexts, Job seems to hope that a 'redeemer' (גואל)
might appear who would rescue him from the sentence of death and
from imprisonment in Sheol. In 9.33 this figure is an 'intercessor'
(מליץ) who serves the legal function of arbitrating a just reconciliation
between God and Job, and in 16.18-22 this 'intercessor', located in
heaven, would establish Job's innocence. In 19.23-27, a notoriously

---

1. Job earlier used the term to refer to the harshness of human life in general (7.1).
He also characterized his residence in Sheol as a time of release, when 'prisoners do
not hear the voice of the taskmaster' (3.11-19).

corrupt text, the figure appears to be a 'redeemer' (גּוֹאֵל) who will stand on Job's grave and intercede for him, obtaining, if not Job's release from death, at least his vindication. Even Elihu uses the image of a heavenly 'intercessor' (מֵלִיץ) and 'messenger' (מַלְאָךְ) who petitions God on behalf of righteous sufferers and obtains their release from the Pit (33.22-28).[1] However, though Job may continue to hope for this mediator who would intercede for him before the high court, he finally realizes it is the divine judge who must issue the edict of release. And it is this unavoidable reality that rudely awakens Job from his dream.

This obsession with the dark side of death coupled with the earlier tree imagery may reflect the 'hero' tradition traced by Jacobsen in ancient Mesopotamia. According to Jacobsen, the 'Gilgamesh Epic' brings together two independent traditions, one in which the power of fertility in the earth—associated with Dumuzi released from the Netherworld—could be magically appropriated by the royal hero who became the divine consort of Inanna in the *hieros gamos*.[2] In this tradition fear of death becomes an obsession, leading to fruitless efforts to obtain immortality. The conclusion is that death is the final evil from which no one escapes.[3] The other trajectory is the military power of the historical king.[4] In this case death is not feared. Gods are flouted, even opposed, and the hero engages in the quest for immortality through the glory of great deeds. At first Job explores the possibility of resurrection by use of the language of the tree (= Dumuzi) which may come back to life, but quickly dismisses the hope for release from the underworld. While obsessed by the fear of death,

---

1. See William A. Irwin, 'Job's Redeemer', *JBL* 81 (1962), 217-29.
2. This is reflected in 'The Death of Gilgamesh' and 'Gilgamesh, Enkidu, and the Netherworld' (Jacobsen, *Treasures of Darkness*, 193ff.). In 'The Epic of Gilgamesh' Ishtar offered to Gilgamesh the role of consort, which he rudely rejected, incurring the wrath of the goddess (Tablet VI; *ANET*, 84).
3. Thus the words of Siduri to Gilgamesh:

> 'Gilgamesh, whither rovest thou?
> The life thou pursuest thou shalt not find.
> When the gods created mankind,
> Death for mankind they set aside,
> Life in their own hands retaining'.
> (Tablet 10, iii, 1ff.; *ANET*, 90).

4. This is represented by 'Gilgamesh, Inanna, and the Bull of Heaven' and 'Gilgamesh, Enkidu, and the Netherworld' (Jacobsen, *Treasures of Darkness*, 193ff.).

the dream of resurrection is quickly dispelled as only an empty illusion. At this point, though Job rails against the creator, there is yet no outright rebellion against God. But as the dialogue continues, defiance of God and the flouting of death take on an increasing role, until Job eventually challenges God for the rule of the universe. On a mythic level Job attempts to become the hero whose design is the overthrow of the rule of God.

The hollowness of Job's wish for rebirth is underscored by the final strophe's complete negation of human hope for deliverance from suffering and the ultimate fate of death.

Strophe IV (14.18-22)

18. However, as the mountain falls and crumbles, and the rock moves from its place,
19. As water wears away stones, and torrents wash away the soil of the land, thus you destroy the hope of a man.
20. You overpower him forever, and he passes away, changing his countenance, you dispatch him.
21. His sons come to honor, but he does not know it; they are brought low and he does not realize it.
22. He is pained only by his own flesh, and he weeps only for himself.

Images of Job's hopelessness (cf. 9.5-10) reappear in the description of the crumbling of mountains and the coming of floods to wash away the dust (עפר) of the earth.[1] As the creation slowly wears away, so does human hope. Death brings with it excruciating pain and eliminates any perception of the fortune even of valued descendants, who, in traditional Israelite and wisdom thought, allowed one to transcend the limitations of individual finitude through corporate existence into the future. In death Job sees only agony and the settling of dark shadows blinding human awareness of the living.

2. *Eliphaz: The Fall of the Primal King (Job 15)*

Introduction. Eliphaz continues to defend his own construction of retributive cosmology and slave anthropology. However, he adds a significant element which will provide an important new dimension: the myth of the Primal Man. Eliphaz senses that Job is on the verge of

---

1. 'Dust of the earth' is not only the substance from which humans are made, but also refers in P to the land destroyed by the flood (Gen. 8.13).

rebellion against God and that in such face would invite destruction. The only royal metaphor for humanity which Eliphaz presents is that of hubris-filled humans whose attempt to overthrow the ruler of heaven and earth is met with the swift and terrible wrath of God.

Eliphaz no longer continues his earlier pretence of comforter and understanding counselor. Casting sympathy and tact to the wind, he enters into a direct, full-scale indictment of Job designed to contest, even to belittle the authority of his self-professed wisdom. By contrast Eliphaz legitimates his own teaching by an appeal to the authority of the ancients confirmed by his own experience.

The Disassembling Power of Language. Images of words and speaking dominate the first strophe: 'answer' (ענה), 'speech' (דבר), 'words' (מלים), 'teach' (אלף) 'mouth' (פה), 'tongue (לשון), 'pronounce guilty' (ירשיע), 'lips' (שפתים) and 'condemn' (ענה).

Strophe I (vv. 2-6).

Shall a sage answer with knowledge of wind, and fill his belly with the east wind?
Shall he argue with speech which does not profit, with words which do not benefit?
But you are destroying piety, and restrain meditation before God.
For evil teaches your mouth, and you choose the tongue of the crafty.[1]
Your own mouth has pronounced you guilty, not I, and your lips have condemned you.

Attributing to language the power to destroy as well as create, Eliphaz characterizes Job's speeches as 'wind' (רוח) and 'east wind' (קדים). רוח most probably alludes to the mighty wind of chaos mentioned in Gen. 1.2 as 'moving back and forth over the waters of the Deep', while קדים is often the dessicating, violent wind blowing from the desert across the land and scorching all which lies in its path (Gen. 41.6, 23, and 27). Far from suggesting that Job is a windbag whose words have no effect, the image describes the devastating power of his language which destroys (פרר) piety and prohibits meditation. 'Destroys' (פרר) is a verb used to describe God's conquest of the chaos monster in Ps. 74.13. As a sage, Eliphaz affirms the world-creating

---

1. ערום is the same word used to describe the serpent whose seductive language led to the fall (Gen. 3.1). The term has negative connotations only in Gen. 3.1; Job 5.12, and here. In Proverbs it is used in a positive fashion (e.g. 12.23; 14.15).

power of proper language and its ability to construct an interpretative system in which religious piety can make sense.

For Eliphaz Job is not the sage, but rather the fool whose language destroys, not creates. Like the calculating, destructive wisdom (ערום) of the serpent in Genesis 3 and Woman Folly in Proverbs 1–9, Job's language is deceitful and seductive. And what Job destroys is the theological tradition that shapes faith and produces well-being for society and creation. Or to use the words of Eliphaz, Job is destroying 'piety' and restraining 'meditation'. 'Piety' (יראה) is a key theological term for the sages. 'Fear of God' succinctly expresses the affirmation of the sovereignty of God as creator and just ruler of the world. It is not only the beginning but also the primal confession of Wisdom. 'Meditation' (שׂיחה) refers to the contemplation of God's 'torah' (Ps. 119.97), 'testimony' (Ps. 119.99), 'precepts' (Ps. 119.15, 78), 'statutes' (Ps. 119.23, 48), 'word' (Ps. 119.148), 'wonders' (Ps. 77.13) and 'marvelous deeds' (Ps. 119.27). For exilic and post-exilic sapiential piety, meditation focuses on two objects which reveal the nature of God and provide insight into pious and righteous existence: creation and Torah. Psalm 19 illustrates very clearly what Eliphaz sees as central to wisdom: meditation and reflection on the life-giving, world-ordering torah and the 'wonders' and 'marvels' of creation's origins and rule lead to righteous existence and sagacious language producing well-being for the individual, community, and all creation. But Job's speech is a chaotic wind threatening to topple the very pillars of social and cosmic order.

Royal Wisdom and the Primal Man. The second strophe continues the metaphor of word and creation by focusing specifically on two features: first, the imagery of the divine council where the decrees of God are formulated and issued, and second, the myth of the Primal Man who was present at creation and privy to the pristine decisions of God that ordered all creation:

Strophe II (vv. 7-16)

7. Are you the Primal Man, and were you brought forth before the hills?
8. Did you listen in the council of God, and did you take wisdom for yourself?
9. What do you know that we do not, what do you perceive that is beyond us?

10. Both the hoary and venerable are among us, more advanced in age than your father.
11. Are God's consolations too slight for you, or the word that he gently spoke to you?
12. Why does your mind carry you away, and why do your eyes flash?[1]
13. Because you turn your anger against God, and you bring forth words from your mouth?
14. What are humans that they should be clean, or those born of woman, that they should be innocent?
15. Behold he places no trust in his holy ones, even the heavens are not clean in his sight.
16. How much less one who is abominable and corrupt, humanity who drinks iniquity like water!

The motif of the Primal Man is common to many ancient Near Eastern myths and was appropriated by several biblical texts. Normally a king, the first human created by the gods, lived in paradise, possessed divine wisdom, and guarded the tree of life. Royal traditions made use of the metaphor to speak of the origins of kingship and the participation of each subsequent king in the role of this primordial ruler. However in several biblical texts the tradition took on a negative feature, as the Primal Man rebels against the authority of God and the divine council. The Yahwist (Gen. 3–11) and Ezekiel 28 both argue that it is hubris, the desire of the creature to assume the divine status of the creator, which is at the root of rebellion. For the Yahwist wisdom (= the 'tree of knowledge of good and evil') was limited only to God who created the world and ruled the divine council. Presumably wisdom was the characteristic of God that ordered the world and all life. The man and woman desired to become 'like gods', that is, to possess the primary element of the divine character that differentiated between deity and human. With divine wisdom the human pair thought they could assume the role of king and sustainer of creation and determine their own destinies. This is the hubris leading to the violation of the divine edict that denied wisdom to the couple and resulted in their expulsion from the garden. The intent of the edict was not to restrict or even proscribe human well-being, but rather to make possible human life and the ongoingness of creation. Divine law created and sustained life. Its violation led to disruption of the created order and ultimately to death. Ezekiel 28

---

1. The LXX has ἐπήνεγκαν ('lifted' = ירמן) for MT's ירזמון ('flash'), a *hapax legomenon*. The image of the LXX's translation is that of haughtiness, self-exaltation.

portrays the First Man as the possessor of divine wisdom. His sin was the desire to sit on El's throne and therefore replace him as the head of the divine pantheon. In this position, the First Man would have possessed the ultimate power of the universe, the divine decree that created or destroyed. Hubris corrupted his wisdom and resulted in his being cast down from the sacred mountain of El into the Pit. This alternative mythic structure, which involves hubris, revolt and fall, is the one to which Eliphaz appeals in substantiating his accusations against Job and his defense of divine justice. It is not merely sarcasm that shapes the voice of Eliphaz, but an articulation of a mythic structure, a world of pride, rebellion and death, into which Job is dangerously attempting to enter.

This is the tradition on which Eliphaz draws as he asks Job if he 'were born (ילד) the Primal Man (ראשׁון אדם)', 'if he were brought forth (חול) before the hills'. This first of human creatures was not made, but rather was born, presumably to divine parents,[1] a typical characteristic of rulers who claimed to be the offspring of various gods by mythically tracing their royal origins to the Primal Man. The metaphor of birth for the origins of the First Man purposefully echoes the language used of the beginnings of Woman Wisdom in Prov. 8.22-31. Using the images of birth, Wisdom sings: 'I was brought forth before the hills' (לפני גבעות חוללתי), a line quoted by Eliphaz in 15.7.[2] In this hymn of self-praise Wisdom stood as the first of God's creations, served as the instrument used in ordering and structuring the world, and mediated between the 'world of humans' and the creator. Eliphaz rejects Job's claim to know the nature of God and the workings of divine rule in creation and history (ch. 12). Is Job the First Man? Was he like Wisdom, the first-born of creation, the guiding principle in shaping the cosmos and directing the world? Further, asks Eliphaz, has Job stood in the divine council (סוד אלוה) where the decrees directing the operation of creation and the destinies of nations and individuals are formulated? Few have been privy to the knowledge of the inner workings of that assembly, save for an occasional prophet (1 Kgs 22; Isa. 6; and Jer. 23.9-22) or a legendary figure in epic

---

1. While ילד is used to mean 'to father' or 'to give birth', חול means to produce with birth pains (Isa. 51.2; Job 39.1; Ps. 90.2; Deut. 32.18). The last two texts point to God's giving birth (to the earth and to Israel respectively).

2. In the same context, Wisdom says she was the 'first' (ראשׁית) of God's 'ways', first in origins and rank, a similar claim being made for the Primal Man in a variant of the mythical tradition.

traditions (Utnapishtim, Adapa, Enoch). Thus Eliphaz, in vv. 7-8, echoing a dreaded mythic tradition to warn Job against entering its world, rejects the authority and truthfulness of Job's knowledge by asking him if he possesses that divine wisdom which originated before all creations. By contrast Eliphaz claims that the wisdom of the ancients, living and dead, is the authoritative and valid source from which he and the other friends draw.

The high value placed on ancient wisdom is a significant theme in the ancient Near East. In Egypt Paypyrus Chester Beatty IV, verso ii 5–iii 11, contains a Late Bronze Age wisdom text, 'In Praise of Learned Scribes', a panegyric to primordial sages 'who lived after the gods, who could foretell what was to come', and who achieved ever-lasting names because of the wisdom incorporated in their teachings.[1] The roll call of great scribes included Hor-dedef, Ii-em-hotep, Neferti, Ptah-em-Djedhuti, Khety, Khakheper-(Re)-seneb, Ptah-hotep, and Ka-iris. Most of these are known and date from the period of the Old Kingdom. Included among their gifts of wisdom was the ability to foretell accurately what was to come, perhaps the most telling proof of the truthfulness of their teaching. In Mesopotamian mythical and sapiential sources, there are scattered references to the seven *apkallu's*, ancient sages from hoary antiquity who were paired with seven legendary kings. Apparently famous counselors, they ordered society with their instructions,[2] transmitted to humankind technology and art (thus they were also called the *ummanu*, 'master craftsman'), and angered the gods by some form of now largely forgotten rebellion. Thus the tradition was suppressed, with only the 'Myth of Adapa' continuing to be well known.[3] Since even Job's father is younger than the ancients, it is clear Job can appeal to no special, primeval wisdom. Rather Eliphaz claims this hoary tradition for himself.

1. *ANET*, 432-34.
2. Lambert and Millard, *Atra-Hasis*, 15-21.
3. Erica Reiner, 'The Etiological Myth of the "Seven Sages"', *Orientalia* 30 (1961), 1-11; Benjamin Foster, 'Wisdom and the Gods in Ancient Mesopotamia', *Orientalia* 13 (1974), 344-54; and W.H. Shea, 'Adam in ancient Mesopotamian Tradition', *Andrews University Semitic Studies* 15 (1977), 27-41. Adapa of course was the model sage and follower of the god of Wisdom, Ea, who gave him divine wisdom, but not immortality. In defiance of the gods, he broke the wing of the south wind, was tried by Anu and the council, and—due to Ea's deceit—refused the bread and water of eternal life offered him.

In the latter part of the second strophe (vv. 11-16), Eliphaz characterizes Job's words as rebellion against God, and with the earlier
allusions to the Primal Man tradition and the theme of revolt against
the gods, he warns Job of the ultimate fate of rebels. Eliphaz then
returns to the metaphor of the edict in v. 11, when he characterizes
the decision (דבר) of the head of the assembly as 'consolations' and a
word that 'deals gently' with Job. Whatever Job's fate, he should rest
assured that his destiny is tempered with mercy, for surely he deserves
far worse than he now receives. And mentioning once again his rather
dark view of the corruption of human nature, Eliphaz reminds Job
that even the members of the divine assembly are not trusted because
of their evil (cf. Gen. 6.1-4). How much less could God trust wicked
humanity, whose nature is thoroughly evil. Once again Eliphaz echoes
the revolt of gods and people, a common theme in ancient Near
Eastern myth, in order to warn Job of the impending disaster that
awaits his futile rebellion against God.[1]

The final strophe (15.17-35) is a grisly description of the terrible
destiny of the wicked. What is striking about this section is the battle
imagery used in vv. 24-28 to describe the futile attack of the wicked
against God:

24. His adversary terrifies him, and distress overpowers him, like a king
    skilled in battle.
25. For he has stretched out his hand against God, and he made himself a
    warrior against Shaddai.
26. He charged him in arrogance, with his thick-bossed shields.
27. For he smeared his face with his fat, and he placed grease upon his thigh.
28. Yet he will inhabit desolated cities, houses without inhabitants, destined
    to become ruins.

The wicked are portrayed as a pompous and silly king who arrogantly
dares to assault God, greasing his body in preparation for battle (2
Sam. 1.22) and charging with warriors' shields. Yet the only empire
he will win is one that lies in ruins, without inhabitants. Normally in
mythical traditions, gods fight against gods (e.g. the *Enuma elish*, and
the Baal cycle). Mighty Gilgamesh, who was part god, fought along-
side his heroic though mortal companion Enkidu against the 'Bull of
Heaven' and Humbaba, the monster guarding the forest of the gods.
The punishment for this outrage was the decree of death for Enkidu.
However, there are accounts of gods fighting humans in war, one of

---

1. Pope, *Job*, 116. See the earlier comments on Job 4.17-21.

the most striking depicting Lady Anat's savage slaughter of humans with carnage so great that 'she plunges knee-deep in knights' blood, hip-deep in the gore of heroes' (*ANET*, 136). Fools and Titans may dare to take on the gods, but they do so at their peril.

3. *Job: The Appeal to a Redeemer (Job 16–17; 19)*

The Battle with Chaos. Job's response to Eliphaz continues with features of disputation and lament providing the major elements of the poem. Images of word theology appear in the appeal to the earth and the heavenly witness to plead with the divine judge (16.18–17.1), while the fertility metaphor briefly occurs in the familial image in the conclusion (17.14). However, the dominating metaphor is the *Chaoskampf* graphically depicted in the second strophe:

Strophe II (16.6-17)

6. If I should speak, my pain would not be assuaged; if I should forebear, what would go away?
7. Surely now he has wearied me, you have devastated my community.
8. You have seized me, that is my witness. My pain arises against me, it testifies against me.
9. His anger has torn and raged against me; he has ground his teeth against me; my enemy has sharpened his eyes against me.
10. They have opened wide their mouth against me; they have struck my jaw; together they have massed themselves against me.
11. God has delivered me up to the evil one;[1]
12. I was at ease, and he cut me asunder; he seized the back of my neck, and he dashed me to pieces; he raised me up to be his target.
13. His archers surround me; he cleaves open my kidneys showing no quarter; he pours out my gall upon the earth.
14. He opens in me breach upon breach, and he charges against me like a warrior.[2]
15. I have sewn sackcloth upon my skin, and I have cast my strength into the dust.
16. My face is reddened from weeping, and the shadow of death is upon my eyes.
17. Although there is no violence in my hand, and my prayer is pure.

---

1. Reading with one Heb. MS עַוָּל ('unjust, evil one'; cf. Job 8.21; 27.7; 29.17; 31.3) for עֲוִיל ('evil wickedness').
2. See Ps. 24.8 for the divine epithet, El Gibbor ('Divine Warrior').

In this strophe Job responds to Eliphaz's description of the wicked man foolishly arming himself and recklessly attacking God (15.24-27). Yet Job reverses the metaphor, making it the Divine Warrior who assaults him, a weak and defenseless mortal, with fury and wild abandon. The rage of an enemy (צר)[1] who attacks like a wild beast his opponent is depicted in shocking images: in terrible wrath God 'tears' (טרף)[2] Job and 'grinds' (חרק)[3] his teeth in fury against him. As a merciless warrior fighting a fierce and gruelling battle against an enemy, God has 'exhausted' (לאה) Job, destroyed (שמם)[4] his band of supporters (עדה),[5] cut him asunder (פרר),[6] seized the back of his neck (ערף),[7] 'dashed him to pieces' (פצץ), 'cleaved open (פלח) his kidneys', and poured out his gall upon the earth. Like a defeated warrior, Job is taken prisoner and placed into the hands of God's troops, the wicked, who torment him with taunts (cf. 1 Sam. 17.26) and strike his jaw.[8] Then Job becomes a city under attack, with God's archers surrounding him and engineers opening countless breaches[9] in his city wall, allowing for the final charge of the Divine Warrior. Without strength or defenses, Job's only recourse is that of any defeated warrior or city.[10] He engages in mourning rites, hoping for mercy from the victor.[11]

Depictions of God as the raging warrior destroying divine foes are common in the Old Testament (Exod. 15; Ps. 68; Hab. 3; and Wis.

1. צר refers to an enemy seeking to destroy a city or nation in Amos 3.11; Num. 10.9; and 24.8.
2. The verb refers to a wild beast (lion or wolf) mauling its victims (Gen. 37.33), though it is most often used as a metaphor for the savageness of slaughter in battle (Deut. 33.20; Gen. 49.27; and Ps. 22.14).
3. The verb expresses deep feelings of intense anger against an enemy, resulting in the gnashing or grinding of teeth (Pss. 12.10; 35.16; 37.12; Lam. 2.16).
4. The verb is used of the almost complete destruction that results from war (Jer. 10.25).
5. This 'congregation' mentioned by Job could refer to his family, though more likely it refers to any who would or should defend Job against this attack by God. They have been devastated, leaving Job defenseless and alone to face the brutal attack of God.
6. Tracing the verb (יפרפר) to פרר, which is used of Yahweh's splitting in two Prince Sea (Ps. 74.13; cf. Marduk's splitting open of Tiamat, *ANET*, 67).
7. The image suggests the fleeing enemy (Gen. 49.8; Exod. 23.27; and Ps. 18.41 = 2 Sam. 22.41).
8. See Ps. 3.8; Mic. 4.14.
9. See Amos 4.3; 1 Kgs 11.27; Neh. 6.1; and Ps. 144.14.
10. Job 19.11-12 also depicts God's attack on Job as an invading army laying seige to a city.
11. See 1 Kgs 20.30-34.

5.17-23) though the opponents are chaos (Ps. 74.12-17), the evil nations (Ps. 79.6-7), the wicked (Ps. 22.13) and a sinful Israel (Ps. 78.21-31). Indeed in laments, the psalmist will call upon the Divine Warrior to arise and destroy the enemy (Ps. 7.7; 31.1-3). On occasion, the psalmist complains God is the warrior who has attacked him (Ps. 38.1-2; 44.24-27; 88.16-19), with Lamentations 3 perhaps the most graphic and detailed depiction. The metaphor is drawn not only from military songs depicting victory, but also from myths narrating the warrior's slaughter of chaos (*ANET*, 67, 140-41). Now it is El Gibbor who falls upon Job to destroy him. It is no longer a matter of a just God seeking to defeat the wicked and establish justice upon the earth. Nor is Job the psalmist who experiences the attack of God, but then can call upon him to show compassion and rescue from disaster (Lam. 3.22-27). Instead Job inexplicably has become the enemy whom God seeks to annihilate without 'mercy' (חמל). Thus Job must turn to two mediators to help him obtain justice. Echoing the primeval tradition of Abel's spilt blood crying out for vengeance against Cain (Gen. 4.10), Job asks the Earth to support him as a witness in his accusations against God.[1] Creation itself will join with Job in the trial of God. And Job once again refers to his heavenly intercessor (מליץ), say in the form of a humanitarian god like Ea, who he hopes will establish his innocence before the divine assembly. Job seeks powerful allies in his assault on heaven, including an insider in the divine council who will speak out for justice.

The Deconstruction of the Metaphor of King. Of particular import for 19.2-12 is the continuation of the battle metaphor and its combination with the royal metaphor describing Job's existence. Taken together, the deconstruction of the hermeneutical model of these two metaphors is central to Job's assault on creation theology.

Strophe I (19.2-12)

2. How long will you cause me distress, and crush me with words ?

---

1. The earth is often personified as a witness in lawsuits (Deut. 32.1; Isa. 1.2; Jer. 6.19; 22.29; Mic. 1.2).

3. Some ten times you have cast reproach upon me; are you not ashamed to treat me ill?[1]
4. Even if it is true that I have gone astray, my error abides with me.
5. If it is true you exalt yourselves against me, and make my reproach a reproof against me,
6. Know that God has subverted me, he has laid siegeworks[2] against me.
7. Behold I cry out, 'Violence!', but I am not answered. I shout aloud, but there is no justice.
8. He has walled up my way so that I may not pass by, he has placed darkness upon my paths.
9. He has stripped my glory from me, and taken the crown from my head.
10. He has torn me down from every side as I go forth, he has removed my hope like a tree.
11. He has kindled his anger against me, he considers me as his enemy.
12. His troops come together against me, they have besieged me with their power, they encamp around my tent.

Once again God is the Divine Warrior who assaults Job, now portrayed as a humiliated king and a besieged city. This combination of king and city occurs in the David–Zion complex and other royal traditions in equating the king or ruling dynasty with the capital city (e.g. 1 Kgs 8; Jer. 21.11–23.8; Amos 1.3–2.5). In this world constructed by metaphor, Job's besieged 'tent' refers to both his royal dwelling and his capital city (v. 12; cf. Isa. 16.5; Amos 9.11; Lam. 2.4). Like a king who sees the ravaging of his country and the siege of a sinister army set to attack the capital, Job cries out 'violence' (חמס), a term often designating the bloody slaughter of populations by a ruthless army (Judg. 9.24; 2 Sam. 22.3; Hab. 2.8, 17; and Obad. 10). But it is also the same term used by P to describe the 'violation' of the earth (Gen. 6.11-12). This 'violation' led to the return of chaos in the Flood. Like a king who attempts to intercede to God on behalf of his people and city, Job enters into mourning rituals and appeals for divine aid, but there is no answer. Indeed there is no 'justice' (משפט), which may refer either to the decree of the divine judge or to the action of the righteous God in delivering the king and his city from the attacking army (Ps. 9.5). Now God has laid siege to Job's city (v. 6) and has blocked all exits and roads, making escape

---

1. חבר occurs only here in the Old Testament; thus the meaning is uncertain. Based on parallelism with 'cast reproach' (בוש) and an Arabic cognate, BHS suggests reading חבר ('to ill-treat').

2. Reading מצור to mean 'siegeworks' (Qoh. 9.14) not 'net' (Prov. 12.12 and Qoh 7.26).

impossible (v. 8). This may also reflect the practice of building a fence or wall around a city to protect the besieging army against sorties from the city and to prevent all means of escape, even at night.

The royal metaphor appears most significantly in v. 9 which deploys the image of the ritual humiliation of a king. In Mesopotamian coronation ritual, the king was divested and stripped of all royal symbols in a ceremony of degradation.[1] The return of royal insignia, which belonged to the gods and were dispensed at their pleasure, demonstrated the king ruled at divine discretion, and not by means of his own power. Even after enthronement, the king remained a mere mortal who did not join the ranks of the gods. The ritual involves, then, rites of degradation followed by exaltation. Thus Job's 'glory' is stripped away, possibly reflecting the taking away of royal garments, and his crown is removed from his head. Like an ancient Near Eastern king, Job stands degraded and humiliated before God. But unlike a king who may expect rites of exaltation to follow by which he is installed once again as ruler, Job can expect only continued scorn and humiliation from God. The language of Psalm 8 may be echoed once again. In v. 6 of the Psalm, God crowns humanity with glory and honor (כבוד והדר תעטרהו) in an image reflecting the ritual of exaltation of the king who is installed as ruler during the New Year. By contrast Job is portrayed as a degraded king, whose symbols of rule have been stripped away. Once again, Job is no exalted king ruling over creation. Rather his royal glory is removed, and his capital city is besieged by a vicious army awaiting the final assault. The mythic world of wisdom's and Job's construction awaits its inevitable collapse.

4. Bildad: The Sovereignty of God and the Folly of Revolt (Job 25; 26.1–14)

Introduction. The metaphors of creation appear now and again in the speeches of the third cycle (21–27), especially in the legal process of indictment and the rendering of an edict by God. Eliphaz finally accuses Job directly of legally defined crimes, making clear in no uncertain terms what he considers to be Job's guilt (22.5-11). And if

---

1. See Frankfort, *Kingship and the Gods*, 215-333. For a social-anthropological description of the rites of passage, including rituals of degradation and exaltation, see Victor Turner, *The Ritual Process* (Ithaca, NY: Cornell, 1969). For an examination of the ritual of coronation and the issuance of a 'royal testament', see my article, 'Liminality and the Social Setting of Wisdom Instructions', *ZAW* 93 (1981), 114-26.

one could locate the divine dwelling and approach God, Job believes he could obtain a judgment of innocence from the Almighty (23.3-7). But it is Bildad who uses creation language in the most elaborate and graphic way in this last preserved, though partially displaced speech of the friends:

Strophe I (25.2-6)

2. Dominion and terror are his, he who establishes peace in his heights.
3. Is there any number to his troops? Upon whom does his light not shine?
4. How then may a man be righteous before God? And how may one born of woman be pure?
5. Behold he commands the moon, and does it not shine; even the stars are not pure in his eyes.
6. How much less then the human creature who is a maggot, And the son of humanity who is a worm.

Strophe II (26.5-10)

5. The Rephaim writhe below, the waters and their denizens.
6. Sheol is naked before him, and Abaddon has no covering.
7. He is the one who stretches Zaphon over the abyss, and hangs the earth over nothingness.
8. He gathers the water in his thick clouds, and the cloud beneath them is not split open.
9. He encloses[1] the appearance of (his) throne, he spreads his cloud over it.
10. He has inscribed a circle over the face of the waters, at the boundary of light and darkness.

Strophe III (26.11-14)

11. The pillars of heaven tremble, stunned by his rebuke.
12. By his strength he has quieted the sea, and by his perception he smote Rahab.
13. By his wind he ensnared Sea[2] in a net,[3] his hand pierced the fleeing serpent.

---

1. פרשׁז is a rare Pilel form of פרשׂ, possibly meaning 'to envelop'.
2. Reading שׂם ים ('place Sea') for MT's שׁמים ('heavens').
3. שׁפרה occurs only here and is often understood to mean 'fairness, clearness' of the sky (*BDB*, 1051). However, Marduk ensnares Tiamat in a 'net' (*saparu*), and then dispatches her with an arrow which 'cut through her insides, splitting the heart' (*ANET*, 67). With this slight change, the bicolon reads smoothly and also reflects the same action of slaying the chaos monster. See N.H. Tur-Sinai, *The Book of Job* (Jerusalem: Kiryath Sepher, 1957), 383; and Pope, *Job*, 185-86.

14. Behold these are only the traces of his power, and how small a whisper
    we hear of him. And the thunder of his strength who could
    perceive?

The Metaphors of Combat and Rebellion. The controlling theme of
Bildad's speech is the unchallenged and universal dominion of God
whose terrible power put down a rebellion in heaven, made the rulers
of the underworld tremble in submission, and defeated the forces of
chaos. While this awesome God is concealed in mystery, his all-seeing
light penetrates even to the darkest regions of his empire, enabling
him to see and know all that happens. How foolish then it is for Job, a
wretchedly sinful and weak mortal, to dare to revolt against God and
his unlimited power and omniscience. Following an initial disputation
contrasting the power, dominion, and purity of God with the sinful-
ness and weakness of humanity (25.1-6), the poem presents a doxology
possessing two movements: God's control over the underworld (26.5-
9) and the defeat and containment of the fearsome powers of chaos.
While the dominating metaphor is that of conflict, the language and
images become distorted, resulting in a theological conceptualization
that legitimates divine tyranny and deprecates human creatures and
their function in the world. For the use of divine power was not to
create a world in which life could flourish, but a blatant display of
force intended to intimidate all the powers of heaven and earth into
frightened submission.

The opening bicolon of the initial strophe contains the theme for the
entire speech: 'dominion and fear are his'. Bildad limits 'dominion'
(משל) over creation exclusively to God. Unlike one major trajectory
which speaks of the creation of humanity to rule over creation, functioning as the surrogate of God (P = Gen. 1.26-28; Ps. 8), God alone
exercises the prerogatives of kingship. Divine sovereignty is not
delegated to humanity in general or even to chosen kings (Ps. 89.20-
38).[1] 'Fear' (פחד) connotes not the typical wisdom expression of the
confession and praise of God who creates and sustains life ('the fear of
God', יראת אלהים), but rather 'terror' or 'dread' before the awe-
someness of divine power (Exod. 15.16; Isa. 2.10, 19, 21). Unlike P
which makes humanity the surrogates of divine presence and power on

---

1. Psalm 89 places the dynasty of David within the order of creation and speaks of
his reign controlling even the powers of chaos: 'I will place his hand on the sea and
his right hands on the rivers' (v. 26).

the earth before whom all other creatures 'fear' (Gen. 9.1-7), for
Bildad only the terrible power of God evokes universal dread.

Dominion and fear result from the establishing of 'peace' (שלום) in
the heights, probably an allusion to a theomachy in which God made
himself the unquestioned ruler of the gods.[1] The *Enuma elish*
provides the clearest example of gods warring for power in heaven, a
struggle precipitated by the 'noise' of the younger gods.[2] When Tiamat
was dispatched and the rebel gods bowed to the sovereignty of
Marduk, peace in the heavens was established, Marduk's city and
temple were constructed, and the world was created.[3] By contrast a
continuing struggle for power is evidenced by the Baal Cycle in which
Yam, Mot, and Bal vie seasonally for rulership over the earth at the
expense of El, who once wrested rule from his father, but now finds
his power limited to the issuing of decrees legitimating the rule of one
god over another.[4] Isaiah 14 incorporates the myth of Day Star who
attempted to ascend to the heights and rule as El Elyon, but was
defeated and cast down into the darkness of Sheol. For Bildad God has
indeed established 'peace', but it is not the condition of harmony and
well-being which sustains and enhances existence. Rather the 'peace' of
which Bildad speaks is the suppression of any and all resistance to a
divine tyrant who has established a martial law enforced by an
unlimited number of celestial troops.

Added to the images of divine rule in the first strophe is Bildad's
reference to God's 'light' (אור) which 'rises' (קום) over all which
exists. In the creation story in P, 'light' is the first of God's creations
which limits the power of darkness and makes life possible. The 'great
light' is the sun which 'rules' the day and the 'lesser light' is the moon
made to rule the night. They along with the stars of heaven shine upon
the earth and separate light from darkness. In Egypt the rising of the
sun each day signals a new creation and ordering of life following the
defeat of Apophis and the successful voyage through the cosmic ocean

---

1. Fohrer, *Hiob*, 375; Gordis, *Job*, 276; Pope, *Job*, 181 (cf. Isa. 1.12-20;
24.21ff.; 34.4).

2. This 'noise' has been variously interpreted as loud dancing and playing and as
rebellious actions designed to overthrow Apsu and Tiamat.

3. *ANET*, 60-72.

4. *ANET*, 129-42.

(cf. Ps. 104.19-23).[1] Thus God is the sun god who 'rises' and shines divine light over all beings. Yet for Bildad the all-encompassing light points to God's knowledge of everything which occurs in his cosmic empire, a terrifying thought for those seeking to challenge divine rule.

Slavery and the Corruption of Human Nature. The second part of this initial strophe contrasts the unlimited sovereignty of God with the corruption and weakness of human beings. The rhetorical question ('How shall a human creature be righteous before God, and how shall one born of woman be pure?') has frequently occurred in the speeches of the friends in expressing their anthropology. For the friends, humanity is no exalted creature, raised to a position just below the gods in the order of creation (Ps. 8). Indeed 25.6 reflects in a negative fashion the language of Ps. 8.5 with the same parallelism of אנוש and בן אדם. Neither is humanity the special creature, formed and fashioned in the womb, given birth by God, and nurtured by providence. Rather humans are creatures corrupt by nature, made of dust and clay (4.19) from the infernal regions in which there is only death and decay. עפר is associated with death (7.21; 17.16, 20.11; 21.26) and humiliation (16.15; 30.19; 40.13) in the poetry of Job. The image of corruption is given its most repugnant expression in Bildad's metaphor of humans as 'maggots' and 'worms', creatures which devour the dead (Job 7.5; 17.14; 21.26; 24.20; Isa. 14.11). If even the brilliant light of the moon and stars is not clean and pure in God's eyes, then how could corrupt and weak humans hope to be declared innocent by this all powerful God?

The Combat Metaphor. The second strophe moves from theomachy in the heavens to the establishment of divine sovereignty over the underworld. In the Old Testament Sheol is associated with chaos and therefore is a sphere in which death, darkness, and disorder prevail. In early conceptions it represented a region not merely hostile to God but also absent of divine knowledge, presence and rule. By contrast, Bildad's description of Sheol points to its terrified submission to the sovereign rule of God. Thus the Rephaim[2] and other inhabitants of the

---

1. Shamash is the Babylonian sun god who descends into the nether world bringing light, food, and drink to the dead before rising the following morning. For an Ugaritic parallel, see *CTA* 6.
2. The Rephaim in this context are probably either a group of dead aristocratic heroes or the entire citizenry of the underworld. L'Heureux (*Rank Among the*

underworld, in this case imagined as a watery abyss,[1] quake in fear before God's awesome might. Stripped of all emblems of status and power, Sheol and Abaddon,[2] personified as both the spheres and lords[3] of death, stand naked[4] before God's power and all-seeing eye. Symbolic of God's mastery of the underworld and its inhabitants as well as chaos itself is the depiction of God's erecting of the sacred canopy over the abyss (בלימה תהו),[5] spreading (נטה)[6] Zaphon[7] like a tent and hanging the earth (like a vessel?) from its top.[8] The clouds

Canaanite Gods, 201-27), opting for the latter, traces the mythic origins and development of the term from Canaan into the final stages of the Old Testament, from the divine *rapi'uma* who celebrated the *marzeah* (a sacred banquet) with El *rapi'u*, El the 'hale one', to their earthly counterparts who were an aristocratic group of warrior-charioteers celebrating the *marzeah* with El *rapi'u* their patron, to an aristocracy among the dead (Isa. 14.9; RS 34.126), to the final democratization of the term to include all the dead (Isa. 26.14; Prov. 2.18; 21.16; and Ps. 88.11).

1. Old Testament conceptions included both a wet (Gen. 1.2) and a dry (Gen. 2.4b-6) chaos, as well as an underworld which was primarily either dust or water (see Tromp, *Primitive Conceptions of Death and the Netherworld in the Old Testament*, 85ff.).

2. Abaddon, 'place of destruction', is a sapiential synonym for Sheol, not a compartment within the underworld (Prov. 15.11; 27.20; Job 28.22; 31.12. See Tromp, *Primitive Conceptions of Death and the Netherworld in the Old Testament*, 80).

3. Like Mot, Sheol is sometimes personified as a king of the underworld (see 'King of Terrors' in Job 18.14).

4. When Inanna/Ishtar descends into the nether world, she is stripped naked, an act demonstrating her impotence and complete lack of status in the world of the dead ('Inanna's Descent to the Nether World', 11.120ff., *ANET*, 55).

5. תהו is the formlessness of primeval chaos in Gen. 1.2 (cf. Jer. 4.23), while the compound בלי-מה, occurring only here, parallels תהו, and conveys the image of 'nothingness' or the 'abyss'.

6. נטה is frequently used in the idiom, 'pitching a tent' (Gen. 12.8; 26.25; 35.21). 'Pitching a tent' becomes a common metaphor for creating ('spreading out') the heavens (cf. Jer. 10.12). Since Zaphon is the object of the verb, not 'heavens', the image may be that of extending a tent pole (cf. the extending of a rod in Josh. 8.18).

7. Zaphon is the sacred mountain in Canaanite mythology where Baal dwells, has his throne, enages in combat with Mot, and builds his palace. Unlike *hursanu*, El's mountain where the divine council meets and issues decrees ordering the world, Baal's mountain is the scene of combat, deciding life and death for the inhabitants of the earth (R.J. Clifford, *The Cosmic Mountain in Canaan and the Old Testament* [HSM 4; Cambridge, MA: Harvard, 1972], 97). In Hebrew adaptation of the mythology, Zaphon becomes the mount of assembly, the dwelling place of El, and the seat of the divine throne (Isa. 14.13-14). Mt Zion appropriates this mythical imagery as well (cf. Psalm 48).

serve as the canopy which restricts the cosmic waters, but is not torn[1] by the force of their flow and weight. And under this sacred canopy God places the throne and hides it from view by enclosing it within a sacred cloud.[2] Sitting under the canopy, located at the inscribed boundary[3] between light and darkness, God issues divine decrees before which even the powers of death fearfully submit.[4] This imagery reflects Tablet I of the *Enuma elish* where Ea casts his spell on Apsu, the primordial fresh waters, removes his crown, slays him, and erects over his body a sacred hut in which he determines destinies and engenders Marduk. Similarly Lord Marduk, following his victory over Tiamat, has the gods construct the sacred city Babylon and the temple Esagila which become the center of the cosmos, uniting heaven and earth and keeping the cosmos secure.[5] And it is from Mt. Zaphon

8. Efforts to see the images in v. 7 as suggesting *creatio ex nihilo* or the earth as a sphere placed in space are misguided. תלה suggests an object which hangs from something else, e.g. a tree limb (2 Sam. 18.10).

1. צרר conveys the image of 'restricting, containing' (cf. 2 Sam. 20.3). בקע refers to the 'cleaving open' or 'dividing' of the waters of sea or chaos in Exod. 14.16; Ps. 78.13; and Hab. 3.9 and to the 'bursting open' of the waters of the great deep at the beginning of the flood (Gen. 7.11).

2. See Ps. 29.10 where Yahweh is 'enthroned on the flood'. The 'Tent of Meeting' (אהל מועד) is the place of divine revelation where the Lord appears in a sacred cloud and issues his decrees (Exod. 33.7-10; Num. 12.4).

3. חג refers to the horizon which serves as the line of demarcation between heaven and earth and the unmovable boundary between the light above the earth and the darkness below the earth. It may also refer to the space located beneath the dome of heaven, separating the heavens and the earth from the waters of chaos which surround and threaten to engulf creation (Luis I. Stadelmann, *The Hebrew Conception of the World* [AB 39; Rome: PBI, 1970], 41ff.). In Job 26, the 'circle' is inscribed (חקק), evoking the image of the issuing of a divine decree which sustains the cosmos.

4. El's sacred tent where he issued his edicts was also located at the *axis mundi*, at 'the Sources of the Two Floods, In the midst of the headwaters of the Two Oceans' (II AB iv-v, 11.21-22; *ANET*, 133). The 'Two Floods' and 'Two Oceans' are the upper and lower waters of chaos which are above and below the earth (cf. Gen. 7.11; 8.2). It is here that El's mountain is located, with its base in the underworld and its height reaching into the heavens (cf. McCurley, *Ancient Myths and Biblical Faith*, 133-35).

5. Unlike Baal who must share his dominion with Mot, Bildad's doxology indicates God has defeated and continues to rule over Sheol. Other texts alluding to the defeat of Death by God are Hos. 13.14 and Isa. 25.8. God's control over death (cf. Job 11.7-9; Ps. 139.8; Prov. 15.11; Amos 9.2) is not consistently asserted in the Old Testament. Several texts suggest Sheol remains outside God's domain: Pss. 6.5; 30.10; 88.11-13; 115.16-17; and Isa. 38.18-19.

with its peaks reaching high into the clouds, located at the boundary between light and darkness and creation and chaos, that God, enveloped in the sacred cloud filling and surrounding the tent, issues decrees which determine the fates of people, nations, and cosmic powers. Bildad asks if Job dares to challenge the supremacy and rule of such an awesome God before whom even the powers of death, including Lord Mot, bow the knee. And how foolish it is for Job to think that he could hide in Sheol, protected from the wrath of God.

The third and final strophe continues the metaphor by referring to God's primordial victory over the powers of chaos. The initial act of the Divine Warrior was the uttering of the 'rebuke' (גערה),[1] a disassembling word intended to assert authority and to stun the opponent by paralyzing him with fear. Indeed even the 'pillars of heaven', the mountains which support the roof of the cosmos, quake in fear at the terrible sound of God's voice.[2] Immobilized by this command, the raging waters of Prince Yam were 'stilled' (גרע).[3] Yet it is not simply by brute strength that chaos (Rahab) was defeated, but also by a warrior's cunning (תבונה). And in an image appropriate for a storm god doing battle, God used the 'wind' (רוח) to place Yam in a net, containing the destructive power of his proud waves. Finally with his hand God 'pierced' (חלל) the 'fleeing serpent' (נחש בריח).[4] Like Marduk's defeat of Tiamat and Baal's vanquishing of Yam, the victory over chaos established God as the ruler of the earth.[5] Bildad's implication is clear: does Job foolishly intend to continue his assault on

1. The 'rebuke' of chaos (mythical and historical) is found in Pss. 9.5; 18.16 = (2 Sam. 22.16); 76.6; 104.5-9; Isa. 17.13; 50.2; and Nah. 1.4. And in Zech. 3.1-2 the Lord 'rebukes' Satan for opposing his anointed one, Joshua the high priest (cf. McCurley, *Ancient Myths and Biblical Faith*, 46-51). The 'rebuke' is issued against any power which seeks to oppose the authority of divine rule and its chosen symbols of expression (the nation, Jerusalem, the Davidic king, and the high priest).

2. See 2 Sam. 22.8 = Ps. 18.8; Isa. 13.13; and Joel 2.10 which speak of God's shaking the heavens or foundations of the earth. 'Pillars of heaven' is an expression occurring only here, leading Fohrer to suggest an Egyptian origin (*Hiob*, 385, n. 11). Elsewhere the Old Testament speaks of the 'pillars of the earth' (Job 9.5; Ps. 75.4).

3. The Qal form of the verb occurs only three times, each occasion in reference to Yahweh's action against the sea: Jer. 31.35; Isa. 51.15, and here in Job 26.12.

4. Cf. Isa. 27.1 and *ANET*, 137.

5. Marduk's slaying of Tiamat followed the same pattern: ensnaring the monster in a net, using the wind to keep open her mouth, and piercing her entrails with a well-aimed arrow through her open jaws.

heaven, seeing that his formidable foe is the unrivalled conquerer of chaos?

5. *Job: The Oath of Innocence and the Revolt of the Hero*
(Job 29–31)

Introduction. Job's assault against creation has deconstructed all traditional metaphors: artistry, word, procreation, and combat. In their place he has posited the metaphor of a tyrant who has become a corrupt judge and vicious warrior, turning against creation. Yet to this point, his portrayal of humanity as a degraded slave has prevented him from taking the final step of legal indictment leading to wholesale revolt. In chs. 29–31, however, Job changes his anthropological metaphor to ruler. This new metaphor already has been opposed by Eliphaz in ch. 15, whose arguments are supported by the other opponents (cf. especially Job 25.1-6; 26.5-14). Only the hubris-filled Primal Man has dared to revolt against God, and the result was his fall to destruction. Nevertheless, in the transition from dialogue to theophany, Job discards his slave metaphor for the one of ruler. Job is the man who would be king over God's creation. Now the mythic patterns of cosmology represented by the *Enuma elish* and of anthropology as portrayed in *Atra-hasis* intersect at the point of conflict. Having experienced creation as slavery, Job revolts against the God of heaven and earth.

The speech between the dialogues of Job and the three friends is actually an extended complaint addressed to God (chs. 29-30), coupled with a series of 'oaths of innocence' (ch. 31) designed to clear Job of any and all charges.[1] Thus the movement is away from responding to the arguments of the friends to the direct challenge of God. The decision to revolt against the creator is formally taken. But before that occurs in ch. 31, Job provides a narrative summary leading to his decision. It is a summary focusing on the metaphors of ruler and slave. In ch. 3, the movement is from past, to future, to present, emphasizing the angst and suffering of present being. However, in

---

1. Parallels have been drawn with the 'negative confession' in the Egyptian Book of the Dead. The Babylonian *Shurpu* texts, 'oaths of purity' in the Code of Hammurabi, the 'entrance liturgies' in the Psalter (Pss. 15; 24), and the attestation of innocence in Old Testament laments (see Fohrer, 'The Righteous Man in Job 31', *Old Testament Ethics* [ed. J.L. Crenshaw and John Willis; New York: Ktav, 1974], 1-22).

chs. 29–31 there is the movement from past, to present, to future, as consciousness attends to haunting memory, expresses the pain of present existence, and anticipates new life in self-rule.

Chapter 29 presents a description of Job's former days, before the onslaught of disaster, when his relationship with God was strong and good, and he was a highly respected leader of his community. An aristocrat, Job even portrays himself in royal terms. This idyllic description of bygone days contrasts dramatically with Job's present existence in which he is a social outcast, rejected by rabble, racked with pain, and hounded by a malevolent God bringing him to a sure and certain end. Finding his penitential appeals and threat of legal petition for judicial redress have thus far been cast aside by God, he turns to his final recourse: a series of self-imprecations by which he may prove he is legally innocent of serious crimes and sins.[1] Yet the list of these 'oaths of innocence' also has a second equally important function: to force God into the open, i.e. to appear and defend divine integrity in the governance of creation. For if Job is indeed innocent, God by implication must either be guilty or forced to respond to the indictment of misgoverning creation. And deafening silence as a response would only underscore divine culpability.

Job's specific use of creation theology occurs in two places: first, in the defense of his dealings with household slaves (31.13-15), and second, in the assertion of just treatment of land, workers, and owners (31.38-40). These belong to a series of self-imprecations occurring within the formal context of a 'declaration of innocence'. The declaration consists of some twelve sins or crimes[2] placed within the formal structure of oaths consisting of one or more protases (condition), introduced by אם or אם לא ('if' or 'if not'), and an apodosis (result). The protasis presents in a conditional clause the crime or sin, while the apodosis contains the punishment to be experienced, if guilty.[3] Four

---

1. Beginning with the third cycle Eliphaz has accused Job of specific crimes or sins which justify the terrible suffering he is experiencing (22.2-20).

2. Catalogues of ten and twelve were common for Old Testament laws and curses. Series of twelve laws are found in Exod. 23.10-19; 34.10-26; and Lev. 18.6-18, while a series of twelve curses is found in Deut. 27.15-26 (See Fohrer, 'The Righteous Man in Job 31', 9). This imitation of a common number of series of laws underscores the legal character of the oaths and draws on the ordering power of law to establish justice.

3. See Sheldon H. Blank, 'The Curse, Blasphemy, the Spell, and the Oath', *HUCA* 23 (1950/51), 73-95; Delbert Hillers, *Treaty-Curses and the Old Testament*

topics follow this oath pattern (vv. 7-8, 9-12, 16-23, and 38-40), while the others contain the protasis, but either leave out the apodosis (vv. 24-25, 33-34, common in Old Testament oaths since it was implied),[1] or shape it into a declaration (vv. 26-28, 29-30, 31-32), an imperative (vv. 5-6), or a rhetorical question (vv. 1-2, 13-15). In most cases the punishment is designed to fit the crime. Thus in vv. 9-10

> *Protasis:* If my heart has desired another woman, and I have lain in wait at the door of my neighbor,
>
> *Apodosis:* then let my wife grind for another, and let others bow down upon her.

Occasionally combined with an ordeal,[2] this type of conditional self-imprecation (normally called the אלה) was used in sanctuary courts to determine by divine judgment a person's guilt or innocence, including the suspected thief (Exod. 22.6-12) or adulterer (Num. 5.5-28). The referral to divine justice in assessing guilt or innocence was especially undertaken when suspicions were not confirmed by eyewitnesses (1 Kgs 8.31-32).[3] The integrity of the process depended on societal belief in the power inherent in the curse and ordeal and in the justice of God to vindicate the innocent and punish the guilty.

Also included in the chapter is Job's written and legal signature appended to the written series of oaths, a wish that someone would 'hear' the case,[4] and a direct appeal to God, his 'legal adversary' (איש ריב),[5] to present the 'indictment' (ספר)[6] specifying the crimes of which

---

1. In the Old Testament the apodosis was customarily omitted in its entirety, since the self-imprecation was so laden with dreaded, destructive power. This defiance of convention produces the desired dramatic effect by one so thoroughly convinced of his own integrity (see Blank, 'The Curse, Blasphemy, the Spell, and the Oath', 92).

2. See Richard Press, 'Das Ordal im alten Israel', *ZAW* 51 (1933) 121-40; and G.R. Driver, 'Ordeal by Oath at Nuzi', *Iraq* 7 (1940) 132-38.

3. Another example comes from Elephantine. See Paul Volz, 'Ein Beitrag aus den Papyri von Elephantine zu Hiob Kap. 31', *ZAW* 32 (1912) 126-27.

4. Dick argues that the appeal for one to 'hear' (שמע) the case is for an unspecified, yet impartial arbiter who would preside over the civil process ('The Legal Metaphor in Job', *CBQ* 41 [1979] 37-50).

5. See Judg. 12.12.

6. Habel suggests the ספר may well have been a 'deed of renunciation' which would have formally exonerated Job (*Job*, 439). In this case Job would be asserting he has proved his innocence by means of the 'declaration of innocence'.

he has been accused (vv. 35-37). The appeal becomes a direct challenge to God to appear in public view and bring charges. Let the creator respond to this indictment. Were that to happen, Job boasts he would carry such a document on his shoulder and wear it as a crown, for public display. The action may simply indicate Job's confidence he could easily refute any flimsy evidence arrayed against him, and therefore be vindicated. However, Fohrer has suggested that the wearing of the indictment is a type of ordeal designed to demonstrate publicly the power of the curses have no effect.[1] There is however, a more convincing explanation.

Metaphors of Word and Birth. As in ch. 3, Job combines the metaphors of curse (in the literary form) and birth to speak, in this case, of his proper treatment of slaves. The disassembling character of the language is contained in the implicit use of self-imprecation to condemn God.

Treatment of Slaves (31.13-15)

13. If I have despised the justice of my slave and maidservant, when they contended with me,
14. Then what should I do when God rises up, and when he examines me, how shall I answer him?
15. Did not he who made me in the womb also make him,[2] did not the same one fashion us[3] both in the womb?

This fifth topic of self-imprecations in Job 31 centers on the legal treatment of slaves. Old Testament lawcodes include a variety of laws designed to protect the life, insure proper treatment, and in certain cases allow for the release of slaves.[4] These texts presuppose that slaves who were denied their rights could take their owners to court and receive fair judgments for their grievances.[5] Job denies he has disregarded the rights of slaves, either in his own treatment of them or as judge in hearing their cases even if brought against him. That Job

1. 'The Righteous Man in Job 31', *Essays in Old Testament Ethics*, 3-4.
2. אֹתִי is the subject of the verb 'made', and not a modifier of 'womb' as the LXX has it.
3. Reading 'us (נוּ-) for MT's 'him' (וֹ).
4. See Roland de Vaux, *Ancient Israel* 1, 80ff. For example see Exod. 20.10; 21.1-11, 20ff., 26ff., Lev. 25.39-55; Deut. 5.14ff.; 12.18; 15.12-18; 16.11; 23.16ff.; and Jer. 34.8-22.
5. Dhorme, *Job*, 455-56.

functioned as a judge in those days preceding his misfortune is attested elsewhere (e.g. 29.7-12). Underlying the civil protection of slave rights were two related theological affirmations: first, the righteousness of God underlay social justice; and second, the common origins of all humans, regardless of social class. For Israel all law was understood as promulgated by God. Social justice was therefore rooted in the righteousness of God. Thus Job states that his guilt would negate any proper response to divine interrogation when God 'arose'[1] to protect the rights of oppressed slaves. What makes this imprecation ironic is that Job, the slave of God, is denied the very justice he is required by law to practice (cf. Job 7.1-2). At the center of Job's repeated complaint is his continued mistreatment at God's hands and the refusal by God to hear his case.

The second theological undergirding of the ordinances protecting the rights of slaves to legally defined justice is the sapiential teaching that common origins require all humans be given goods necessary for life and treated with dignity.[2] In shaping this understanding the sages drew on the tradition depicting God as both the artisan shaping the fetus and the Lord of fertility who causes conception and provides nourishment in the womb. The theological affirmation of the common origins of all humans, including slave and free, and the divine care exerted in shaping and caring for the fetus, found legal conceptualization in the enactment of laws designed to protect the lives and existence of slaves. Justice permeating creation requires all have the rightful claim to fairness, dignity and the necessities of life. It is the same theological tradition used by Job in ch. 10 in the vain effort to influence God to save him from his desperate situation. Now God's own laws condemn their divine author.

The Curse of the Land. The second reference to creation theology in the 'declaration of innocence' occurs rather significantly at the very end:

---

1. 'To rise up' in a legal context means either a witness standing to testify against the accused (Deut. 19.15-16; Mic. 6.1) or a judge standing to give the verdict (Ps. 74.22).

2. Prov. 17.5; 22.2, and 'The instruction of Amenemopet', xxvi 12: 'God desires respect for the poor more than the honoring of the exalted' (*ANET*, 424). Cf. Mal. 2.10.

Exploitation of Land and Farmers (31.38-40)

38. If my land has cried out against me, and its furrows have wept together,
39. If I have eaten of its yield without payment, and I have extinguished the life of its owners,[1]
40. Let thorns grow in the place of wheat, and stink weeds instead of barley.

Central to this oath is the denial of pollution of the land (אדמה; cf. P's charge against humanity leading to the Flood). The first protasis (v. 38) personifies the tilled soil, protesting to the heavens wrong has been committed, presumably against it, though the crime is not specified.[2] Agricultural laws protecting the soil included the sabbath and jubilee year (Exod. 23.10-11; Lev. 25.1-22), the prohibition of mixing seeds (Lev. 19.19; Deut. 22.9), forbidding harvesting the entire crop with none left for the poor (Lev. 19.9-10; 23.22), and not eating fruit of newly-planted trees for the first three years (Lev. 19.23-25). Indeed the law of familial land ownership was designed to keep plots of land within the generations of the family (Lev. 25.23-28). The intent of agricultural laws was to protect the soil, provide for the needs of the poor, maintain land ownership within the family, and ensure offerings were made to the sanctuary. It may be that Job is affirming he has carefully observed specific agricultural laws. However, the declaration may be even more general. Social crimes and religious sins were thought to affect the land adversely, resulting in famine (Deut. 28.22; Amos 4.6). In P's primeval narrative, the earth was polluted by violence (חמס, 'murder'), leading to the onslaught of the flood.[3] The protest of the personified soil has two parallels: in Gen. 4.10 murdered Abel's blood cries out (זעק) for vengeance 'from the land' (אדמה), and in 16.18 Job beseeches the earth not to hide his murder by God, but to let his cry (זעקה) continue to be heard.

The second protasis (v. 39) is more specific. Here Job denies he has either eaten produce from the soil 'without payment' or 'extinguished the life of its owners'. The first bicolon may simply refer to robbery, though it more likely means the withholding of wages to day laborers.

1. On the basis of Ugaritic evidence, Pope (*Job*, 230) argues בעלים should be understood as 'workers' (פעלים).
2. The mythological background for this personification is the earth-mother goddess (cf. Job 1.21).
3. Deut. 19.10, 13; 21.1-9 are laws and rituals based on the common notion that the shedding of innocent blood polluted the land.

Lawcodes required the prompt payment of the day laborer at the end
of the workday, before night begins, lest he cry out in protest to God
(Lev. 19.13; Deut. 24.14-15). The prophets often decried the violation of this law (Jer. 22.13; Mal. 3.5), indicating these workers were
often victimized by unprincipled landowners. The second bicolon
refers to actions leading to the death of those who own the land. One
narrative example of this crime occurs in 1 Kgs 21. Jezebel and Ahab
stole Naboth's vineyard by hiring false witnesses to testify he had
committed the capital crime of blasphemy. Tried and declared guilty,
Naboth was executed and Ahab had his coveted vineyard.

The apodosis contains the punishment of the curse: thorns and weeds
would grow in place of wheat and barley. The language strongly
echoes that of Gen. 3.17-18 and 4.12, the curse placed on the soil.
Included in God's curse of the land due to Adam's and Eve's sin was
the growing of 'thorns and thistles', while the punishment of the curse
for murdering Abel resulted in the land's not producing its yield for
Cain. In each case, including that of Job, the curse is sterility of the
land. It could be that both protases and the apodosis are to be read as a
unit, indicating that murder and larceny polluted the land, leading to
its protestation to God to take vengeance against the criminal. Thus the
curse would cause the soil to produce only useless thorns and weeds
for the thief and killer. In this case, we would have strong parallels
with J's narrative of the murder of Abel and the curse of Cain and P's
more sweeping pronouncement that violence polluted the earth and led
to the flood.

In any case, we have here an excellent example of the conventional
sapiential understanding of the entwinement of creation and society.
Righteous actions and attitudes led to well-being for society, including
the reaping of nature's gifts, while sinful and criminal deeds which
violated and exploited creation led to social harm. Underlying both
was the just order permeating all reality, an order established and
maintained by a righteous God. The major theological grounding for
Job's 'declaration of innocence' is the metaphor of word, specifically
in the form of the divine judge who issues just laws maintaining the
harmony and well-being of society. Instead of limiting freedom,
Israelite laws were designed to enhance life by regulating social
interaction and behavior and establishing harmony between nature,
humanity, and God. Individual laws gave concrete form to the underlying, righteous order that permeated nature since the time of
creation. Hence adultery would result in 'fire' burning the root of

Job's crops (v. 11),[1] while withholding wages of farm workers or the killing of land owners to take their fields pollutes the soil, allowing only the yield of thorns and weeds (v. 40). On a social level, illicit desire would result either in others eating the yield of Job's land or his crops being pulled out by the roots. Finally, it is important to recognize the fact that Job's legal formulation of innocence serves as an implicit indictment of God who has perverted the righteous order of creation. For Job even God must be made subject to law, for it is rooted in the very fabric of creation itself.

The Metaphor of Ruler. Twice in this concluding soliloquy Job describes himself in the images of a king, first in ch. 29 when he speaks as though he were an honored ruler and again in 31.35-37 when he dares to approach the creator of heaven and earth 'like a prince'. Chapter 29 is a portrayal of Job's past in royal terms, contrasting it with the present in which he has undergone degradation and rejection, much in the fashion of a psalmist in a lament who contrasts his former days of well-being with his present distress.

Strophe I (29.2-6)

2. Oh, that I might return to the months that are past, the days that God protected me.
3. When his light shone over my head, and I would walk by its light through the darkness.
4. When I was in my autumn days, and the council of God was over my tent.
5. When Shaddai was with me, and my children were about me.
6. When my steps were washed with curds,[2] and the rock poured out for me streams of oil.

Strophe II (vv. 7-13)

7. When I went to the gate of the city, in the square I set my judgment seat.
8. The youths saw me and hid themselves, and old men arose and stood.
9. Princes refrained from speaking, and placed their hand on their mouth.
10. The voice of the nobles grew quiet, and their tongue cleaved to the roof of their mouth.
11. When the ear heard, it called me 'blessed', and the eye that saw approved what I said.

---

1. תבואה often means crop yields (Exod. 23.10; Lev. 19.25, etc.).
2. Reading with a few MSS בחאמה for L's בחמה.

12. For I would deliver the poor man who would cry out, and the fatherless who had no one to help him.
13. The blessing of the one about to perish came upon me, and the heart of the widow I made sing for joy.

Strophe III (vv. 14-20)

14. I wore righteousness, and it clothed me, my justice was like a robe and crown.
15. I was eyes to the blind, and feet to the lame.
16. I was father to the needy, and I searched out the case of one I did not know.
17. I broke the fangs of the wicked, and I cast forth the prey from their teeth.
18. And I said, 'I shall expire in my nest, and like the sand I shall multiply my days'.
19. My roots spread out to the waters, and the dew lodged on my branches.
20. My glory remained ever new, and my bow was renewed in my hand.

Strophe IV (vv. 21-25)

21. People listened to me and waited, they kept silence for my counsel.
22. After I spoke they would not speak again, and my word dripped like dew upon them.
23. They waited for me as for the rain, and they opened mouths as for the spring rain.
24. I smiled at them when they lacked confidence, and they did not reject the light of my countenance.
25. I chose their path, and I sat as their head, I dwelt like a king among his troops, even as one who comforted mourners.

Through imaginative remembering Job enters into his past, describing his former existence in royal images. Instead of limiting these only to Job,[1] one should view them more as a metaphorical description of those who, in the fashion of Genesis 1 and Psalm 8, were commissioned by God to go forth into the world and rule over creation. Through exaltation and wisdom's gift, humans were sovereigns over the earth. Indeed the Israelite royal tradition provided the images for this self-description which includes laudative self-praise bordering on self-idolatry.

The pair, light and darkness, reminding once again of creation, opens the initial strophe, only in this case the motif connotes provi-

---

1. Albertz, 'Der sozialgeschichtliche Hintergrund des Hiobbuches'.

dential[1] guidance and blessing of the royal Job. God's lamp provided Job light as he walked through the threatening shadows of darkness, fearing no evil, an image used in the royal tradition by the king who sings a thanksgiving psalm for divine help and protection in the struggle with enemies (Ps. 18.29 = 2 Sam. 22.29). Night had not yet surrounded Job with its opaque cloud. Divine presence and counsel (עצה), which come from the divine judge in guiding and directing a wise and successful existence, hovered over the royal tent. Classical images of well-being characterized Job's life: children and the abundance of curds and oil.

Job continues his royal portrait in the second strophe as he describes the adulation and praise of great and small who marvelled at his judgments. Job is a king who came to the city's gate to sit in judgment (cf. 2 Sam. 18.24; 19.19; Ps. 72; Amos 5.12, 15). Young and old, princes and nobles reacted in astonishment and awed silence as they saw Job take his seat and heard him issue wise and life-giving edicts. The imagery reconstructs that of the wise king, particularly Solomon, whose famous wisdom at court brought 'awe' to those who observed him in judgment (1 Kgs 3.28). And like an Israelite king, Job's decrees delivered the poor (עני), the orphan (יתום), the widow (אלמנה), and the one sentenced to death (אבד).[2] Those who tasted of his justice called him 'blessed' (cf. Ps. 17).

In Strophe III Job turns to a more general depiction of his reign. Job is dressed in the royal robe (מעיל)[3] and crown (צניף)[4] of justice and righteousness (משפט, צדקה), two terms describing the beneficent order of society established by wise rule. The poor and oppressed victims of society, those who were to come under the protection of law and royal oversight, benefitted from Job's righteous and gracious rule. By contrast, the wicked—the perverts of society and creation who preyed especially on the weak of society—are described in the typical guise of ferocious and devouring beasts who were destroyed by his righteous acts (cf. Ps. 72.14). Consequently, in those days Job took his ease in the comfort of secure assurance that he would live well and long (Ps. 72.17). And the mythical, royal image of the well-watered tree

1. שמר ('guard, keep, watch') in v. 2 expresses providential care (cf. Gen. 28.15, 20; Josh. 24.17; Ps. 91.11).
2. Isa. 1.17, 23; 10.2; and Jer. 22.3.
3. The term refers to the robe worn by those of rank (1 Sam. 18.4; 24.5, 12; Job 1.20; 2.12; and 9.3, 5).
4. The word refers to the royal turban in Isa. 62.3.

(Isa. 11.1; Ps. 1) returns (cf. v. 14) to suggest a long and full life was anticipated by this royal Job. And this unites with the figures of royal glory and the sprouting, living bow to convey vital and continuing power and wise judgment.[1]

The final strophe contains another element of royal rule: the forming and giving of wise counsel (עצה), a plan for a course of action leading to successful outcome. A necessary feature of royal rule, Isaiah speaks of the ideal king as one who bears the honorific title of 'wonderful counselor' (9.7). Like a 'king among his troops', Job would sit in council and provide life-giving insight to those who sought and needed his wisdom. People would come and sit in the 'light of Job's countenance', an image used of the blessing of divine favor. Indeed the language of this chapter borders on self-idolatry as Job describes himself in terms rarely used of kings and often reserved for God.

Of course we may take this rather exalted self-praise simply as social description and argue that Job was a Near Eastern king dethroned by some unknown catastrophe. But it is wise to see the language in its full metaphorical range as it describes the nature and function of Job and others who saw themselves in the 'divine image', that is as sovereigns commissioned by God to master and rule over creation. Sages especially use royal language to speak of their tasks and mission in the world (cf. Qoh. 1.12–4.3). It is this powerful metaphor in the sapiential and priestly traditions that the book of Job seeks to deconstruct. But the character Job has not completely abandoned it as false. Though the royal metaphor has seemed to shatter in the literary world of his experience, he returns to it in his challenge hurled in the face of God in 31.35-37.

> 35. Oh, that I had someone to listen.[2] Behold, here is my signature, let Shaddai answer me, let my adversary write a document.
> 36. Surely I would wear it on my shoulder, I would fasten it to me like a crown.
> 37. I would provide him an accounting of my steps, like a prince I would approach him.

In this climactic section of the concluding speech, Job taunts the ruler of the divine council to hear his case and either write down the

---

1. Cf. the glorious bow of Aqhat (*ANET*, 151).
2. The first לֹ is omitted in a few Heb. mss.

indictment[1] or admit the judgment of exoneration.[2] Whether indictment or attestation of innocence, Job would then approach in court his divine adversary, not as a meek and lowly slave, but as the royal hero ready to sit upon the divine throne. More is at stake here than the braggart's tongue. The book of Job moves on a mythic level. The metaphors and therefore the language of faith have been subverted. A new mythos waits to be born, engendered by the metaphor of human king. And now the Primal Man, flushed by the ambition of coveted royalty, steps forth to claim his throne. A human ruler voicing the anguish and pride of all humanity is set to abandon God and the folly of religion for mortal rule. The tale of Job is a redescription of the mythic drama of the fall. Job is the man who would be god.

Mythic Patterns and the Metaphorical Process. Job and the implied audience have arrived at the point of mimesis. With the oath of innocence, Job has convinced his audience of his integrity, confirming the narrative description of the Prologue. And now Job has constructed a new and compelling mythos. He integrates a cosmology in which God is the corrupt judge and malicious warrior destroying his own creation with royal anthropology inspired by the dream of human rule. With the deposing of God from the throne of heaven and earth, Job as Primal Man would gain the rule over all creation. Now the metaphorical tradition constructed by Job approaches transforming vision.

6. *The Metaphorical Process: Transformation and Restabilization*

Once again the two mythic patterns of creation featuring battle and slavery are integrated in Job's speeches. The final step to outright rebellion is contemplated and finally taken. Job has now moved beyond the point where he has sought reconciliation with the friends and the reparation of the breach with the Divine Warrior. Both God and friends have violated trust and become his enemies. The wistful hope for resurrection is abandoned. There is no redeemer who can enter Sheol and deliver him from death. Humanity is born to corruption in the tomb, and any hope for a redeemer is false illusion. The movement

1. Fohrer, 'The Righteous Man in Job 31'.
2. Habel, *Job*, 438-39.

toward mimesis has occurred, and the transformation of vision is begun. There is something inherently true about the metaphor of battle, though not in the sense of God's struggle against chaos. Drawing a devastating implication from this metaphor, Job depicts God as the one who destroys both the creature and creation. And the metaphor of slavery has already obtained the level of certainty for Job and the audience. Life is oppressive drudgery imposed by the sentence of a heartless judge. Creation is experienced, not as 'good' (Gen. 1.1–2.4a), but as a monstrous evil and a prison of no escape, save through death. Outright revolt is the only hope, and the last obstacle to that action, the disputation of the friends, no longer convinces, for Job has nothing more to lose.

Sensing the direction of Job's protest, Eliphaz reminds Job of the fate of the Primal Man who dared to challenge God. Eliphaz characterizes Job's words as rebellion against the divine judge, and with the earlier allusions to the Primal Man tradition and the theme of revolt against the gods, he warns Job of the ultimate fate of all rebels. Furthermore, Eliphaz seeks to convince Job that he is but a mere mortal, corrupt to the core. All thoughts of revolt should cease, if Job wishes to escape the terrible fate of those who defy divine rule and mastery over creation and history.

In his disputation, Bildad draws from the cosmological pattern of creation, depicting the terrible power of God in subduing rebel gods in heaven, overcoming the challenge of Mot, building his canopy over death's domain, and conquering the chaos monsters. Like Baal, God has defeated Mot and Yam, and has erected his tent signifying present rule. From here God in the fashion of the Canaanite El issues edicts which order the world. Yet these examples of God's power framed in the strophes of doxology are for Bildad only a mere hint at the great and majestic might of God. The doxology expresses Bildad's own theology: God possesses unchallenged supremacy and power over all reality, divine edicts order the world, and both deity and decrees are hidden in unfathomable mystery. No one can hope to challenge or even understand the terrible workings of God, for humans are allowed only brief glimpses and whispers of information about divine nature and activity in the world. Like the gods in heaven, the powers of death, and the forces of chaos, mortals can only bow the knee before the awesome ruler of heaven and earth. Rebellion by Job would be sheer folly.

With the Oath of Innocence, however, Job ignores the warnings of his human opponents and begins the formal contestation of rule over the cosmos. Restabilizing mythic metaphors, Job draws particularly on the myth of the Primal King. Since God has abused divine privilege in the misrule of heaven and earth, it is time for humanity, incorporated within the metaphor of the primal king, to assault the divine throne, remove the divine ruler, and take charge of the cosmos. In the emerging vision of Job, the world is to be ruled by human kings, guided by wisdom and expressing their own humaneness in their policies and actions. The assault on divine rule has now reached its climax. The contest with the Creator of Heaven and Earth, taking the form of trial and disputation within the divine assembly, is to begin.

Chapter 8

FALL AND JUDGMENT:
THE SPEECHES OF GOD AND THE NARRATIVE TALE

1. *The Speeches from the Whirlwind: Introduction*

Previous Interpretations. The series of self-imprecations in ch. 31 is not only a clear affirmation of innocence in the face of the friends' accusations, but also a challenge to God to appear in court to contest or affirm Job's integrity. Ironically, cursing is used once more, this time not to hurl the created order back into the dark oblivion of night (ch. 3), but, more conventionally, to confirm the moral integrity of Job. Let God either present his own indictment or pronounce Job free of guilt. Further, Job's promethean challenge is designed not only to substantiate his own integrity but also to indict God for malevolent misrule of the cosmos. Job's self-imprecations draw on the power of curse to indict and drive God from the throne.

While the 'Speeches from the Whirlwind' (38–42.6) provide the climax of the poetic book, no consensus of their interpretation has emerged. However, the general tendency has been to emphasize either the theophanic event itself or the content of what Yahweh says as the key to solving the enigma of interpretation. Many scholars, seeking a conceptual formulation of justice, have argued that the content of the speeches is irrelevant to the significant issues of justice, suffering, and integrity raised by Job in the Dialogues. Thus, Yahweh's descriptions and praise of divine wisdom and power, as well as creation, all the while contrasting the impotence and ignorance of the mortal opponent, appear to ignore the crucial points under contention. However, it is the event of Yahweh's appearance that gives existential meaning to the theophany.[1] God has turned the divine countenance toward Job, demonstrating in this most unusual encounter compassion and care for

1. H.-P. Müller, *Hiob und seine Freunde* (Theologische Stüdien 105; Zürich, EVZ, 1970), 42; Murphy, *Wisdom Literature*, p. 44.

the human creature in torment.[1] Either that, or in the context of human suffering Job's primal encounter with the *mysterium tremendum* negates the theory of retribution and makes insignificant all prior experience with its questions. Disputation turns to praise in the experience of awed fascination with the Holy whose mystery is beyond human comprehension.[2] And it may be that the very appearance of God vindicates Job, removing all questions about his integrity (13.16).

Other interpreters have chosen the more risky path of attempting to find the meaning of the book in the content of the divine speeches. However, very little agreement has been reached on any one position. The major interpretations include the following:

1. Although there is chaos in the world, God acts with freedom to sustain justice in creation and history.[3]
2. God's actions in the world are paradoxical: he nurtures but limits Yam, checks the power of death by the recurring cycle of birth, and feeds the offspring of eagles with the dead flesh of other creatures. In a world of paradoxes, Job's speeches rooted in retribution make no sense and thus are dismissed. Paradox is overcome by community with God.[4]
3. Reality is amoral, while God transcends human standards of justice. Retribution as a vehicle for the operation of God and creation is rejected. Piety is either unrewarded or does not exist.[5]

---

1. Fohrer, *Hiob*, 534; Andre Lacocque, 'Job or the Impotence of Religion and Philosophy', *Semeia* 19 (1981), 33-52; R.A.F. MacKenzie, 'The Purpose of the Yahweh Speeches in the Book of Job', *Bib* 40 (1959), 435-45; Von Rad, *Wisdom in Israel*, 221-26.

2. Millar Burrows, 'The Voice from the Whirlwind', *JBL* 47 (1928) 117-32; Crenshaw, *Old Testament Wisdom*, 110-25; Johannes Hempel, 'Das theologische Problem des Hiob', *Apoxysmata* (BZAW 8; Berlin: Töpelmann, 1961), 114-73.

3. Michael Fox, 'Job 38 and God's Rhetoric', *Semeia* 19 (1981) 53-61; Gordis, *Job*, 560; Othmar Keel, *Jahwes Entgegnung an Ijob* (FRLANT 121; Göttingen: Vandenhoeck & Ruprecht, 1978), 156-57; Veronika Kubina, *Die Gottesreden im Buche Hiob* (Freiburger Theologische Studien 115; Freiburg: Herder, 1979), 143-58. Gordis elaborates that God admits in the second speech that the world is not perfect, and that evil and suffering still exist. Yet the beauty and harmony of nature point to a similar pattern of a moral order issuing from God. In spite of imperfection, the world is basically good (*Job*, 566).

4. Fohrer, *Hiob*, 500.

5. Crenshaw, *Old Testament Wisdom*, 110-25; Lacocque, 'Job or the Impotence of Religion and Philosophy', 33-52.

4. While God's darker side has created evil, he acts to constrain its destructive effects. However, God is limited in power and unable to eradicate evil from the earth.[1]

5. God's wisdom and justice transcend human comprehension. Efforts to impugn divine justice are sheer folly.[2]

6. God's sovereignty as Creator and Lord of history is upheld, leading to the rejection of false questioning and the proper response of confession and praise.[3]

7. The blustery attack by God reveals that he is a capricious, chaotic, and even jealous tyrant whose abuse of power leads to Job's proper renunciation.[4]

8. Creation is nihilistic, possessing no meaning in and of itself. Yet in coming as savior, God offers a new creation.[5]

Equally diverse are interpretations of the responses of Job to the 'Voice from the Whirlwind'. The majority position understands Job to have repented of his attack because of something God has said,[6] though the assessments of the reason for this recanting are varied. Generally speaking, Job is thought to recognize that he has spoken in rashness and ignorance about God and creation. Recognizing and confessing his own impotence and ignorance in the face of divine power, wisdom, and providential care, and now understanding retribution is a bankrupt dogma, Job repents of his blasphemous pride in daring to question God's rule. Job's transformation is described in terms of humility, faith, trust, serenity, and thankfulness issuing in praise.[7] Others have

---

1. Athalya Brenner, 'God's Answer to Job', *VT* 3 (1981), 129-37.

2. Dhorme, *Job*, 645-46; Rowley, *Job*, 325-26.

3. Horst Dietrich Preuss, 'Jahwes Antwort an Hiob und die sogenannte Hiobliteratur des alten Vorderen Orients', *Beiträge zur Alttestamentlichen Theologie* (ed. Herbert Donner et al.; Festschrift Walther Zimmerli; Göttingen: Vandenhoeck & Ruprecht, 1977), 338-43; Margaret Crook, *The Cruel God* (Boston: Beacon, 1959), 153-56; Terrien, 'Job', 1183-84.

4. David Robertson, 'The Book of Job: A Literary Study', *Soundings* 56 (1973), 446-69; James Williams, '"You have not spoken Truth of Me." Mystery and Irony in Job', *ZAW* 83 (1971), 231-55.

5. Masao Sekine, 'Schöpfung und Erlösung im Buche Hiob', *Von Ugarit nach Qumran* (2nd edn; BZAW 77; Berlin: Töpelmann, 1961), 213-23.

6. Pope, *Job*, 348; Rowley, *Job*, 341; Norman Snaith, *The Book of Job* (SBT 11; Naperville, IL: Allenson, 1968), 39-43.

7. E.g. Fohrer, *Hiob*, 532-34; Kubina, *Die Gottesreden im Buche Hiob*, 152. For Fohrer, the poetry reaches how one should respond to suffering, and that is in patient trust that comes from communion with God.

suggested Job repented because of his encounter with Yahweh. Robert Polzin has argued 'God's power-play tells Job nothing that he does not already know. It is the impact of his appearance before Job that produces the change rather than anything God says.'[1] Thus Job is said to repent of his hubris, death wish, or bad faith, because he has now experienced the loving concern of God and communion with the Holy.[2] Job's transformation is characterized as serenity, trust, and disinterested piety. A third position denies Job repents. In the divine speeches, Yahweh is revealed as the imposter god who has abused divine power and knowledge in bringing havoc to creation. These speeches are ironic in the sense that they accomplish just what Job had desired: they show Yahweh to be a malevolent, foolish ruler of the universe. Job then is the dissembler whose repentance is 'tongue-in-cheek'. While Job goes through with the pretense of submission, he is all the while smiling to himself for having exposed the true nature of God.[3] A variation of this last position sees Job directly and unequivocally rejecting God as a cosmic tyrant who deserves only contempt, not praise.[4]

Part of the difficulty in reaching any general consensus is the failure to take seriously the metaphorical language present in the Yahweh speeches and the mythological traditions from which it derives. And while metaphor suggests and connotes rather than concretely defines, the images present in the speeches give important clues to interpretation. It is the evocative imagery and experience of theophanic event, coupled with the metaphorical content of the speeches, that present a new linguistic vision of creation, divine rule, and human existence. On a mythic level Job experiences the fall. In terms of the metaphorical model, the character and the implied audience, now fully identified with Job, experience once again metaphorical shock and disorientation. Their task, which is also that of the heroic Job, is to come to a new reconstruction of faith and the articulation of compelling vision.

The Question of Literary Integrity. The complete elimination of the Yahweh speeches as a subsequent addition to the poetic dialogues is no

---

1. *Biblical Structuralism* (Semeia Supplements; Philadelphia: Fortress/Scholars Press, 1979), 105.

2. Crook, *The Cruel God*, 156; Von Rad, *Wisdom in Israel*, 221-26.

3. Robertson, 'The Book of Job', 446-49; Williams, ' "You have not spoken Truth of Me" ', 231-55.

4. John Biggs Curtis, 'On Job's Response to Yahweh', *JBL* 98 (1979), 495-511.

longer a serious position. However, it is still common to reconstruct the two God speeches and the two responses by Job into one speech followed by a single response.[1] Most commonly excised are the sections concerning the ostrich (39.13-18), Behemoth (40.15-24), and Leviathan (40.15–41.26). Contrary to the dominating interrogative style of the other parts of the speeches, these sections are primarily descriptive in form. Further, the unusual length of the Leviathan speech (34 verses) brings it under suspicion, while the content of the second speech is thought to add very little to the debate. Job's responses are generally trimmed to those of chs. 40.3-5 and 42.2, 3b, and 5-6, thereby eliminating the prose introduction to the second speech (42.1) and vv. 3a and 4 as repetitious glosses from Yahweh's initial speech (38.2, 3b).

These efforts are not convincing for the following reasons.[2] First, removal of the ostrich passage disregards the literary pairing of animals according to common traits. The ostrich is yoked with the horse due to their great speed and irrational disregard for life. Further, while questions dominate the style of the first speech and description the second, both speeches exhibit an alternation of questions and description. Thus both the Behemoth and Leviathan sections are stylistically consistent with the first speech and are essential to understanding the book. The Leviathan passage also provides an important inclusion for the dialogues (cf. 3.8).[3] As will be argued, the effort to depose God as ruler of the universe is met with the challenge for Job to ascend to the throne and rule, a position which requires he subdue the powerful and fearsome monster of the deep. The second speech does advance the thought: the first speaks of the origins of creation and providence, while the second describes the maintenance of creation by means of the battle with chaos, an engagement Job would have to undertake to become unchallenged ruler of the cosmos. Likewise the two responses of Job should be retained as they presently exist. In terms of content there is thematic movement from silence

1. For example, see Preuss, 'Jahwes Antwort an Hiob und die sogenannte Hiobliteratur des alten Vorderen Orients', 336-37; Rowley, *Job*, 254ff.; and Westermann, *The Structure of the Book of Job*, 122, 125.

2. For a detailed analysis supporting the integrity of the present structure of two speeches and two responses, see Veronika Kubina, *Die Gottesreden im Buche Hiob*, 115-23.

3. See Keel's defense of the inclusion of the Behemoth and Leviathan sections (*Jahwes Entgegnung an Ijob*, 38ff.).

(40.3-5) to doxology (42.1-6). And the quotation of statements made by Yahweh is not an uncommon procedure in both the Old Testament as a whole and the book of Job in particular.[1]

While the first speech has a more developed structure, the basic outline is the same: an introduction consisting of Yahweh's challenge to Job, a three-part main section with rhetorical questions, ironic imperatives, and descriptive praise, and an inclusio at the end. The first speech deals with creation and providence, while the second focuses on ruling the cosmos in the face of the threats posed by chaos.

Literary Form. Assessments of the literary form of the divine speeches have placed them in the categories of hymn, onomasticon and disputation.[2] Westermann argued that the speeches are divine self-praise, featuring Yahweh first as 'Lord of Creation' and then as 'Lord of History'. In keeping with the structure of the lament, Westermann saw these hymns serving as Yahweh's 'Oracle of Salvation', moving Job from lament to thanksgiving.[3] Drawing on Egyptian analogies, von Rad traced the formal characteristics of the speeches to onomastica which are set in the context of creation mythology.[4] These lists order reality by naming and relating existing phenomena. Even God's questioning of Job, like a schoolteacher interrogating a student, is paralleled by the Papyrus Anastasi I in which the official Hori issues ironic questions to his scribal colleague Amenemope. Hans Richter classified the speeches as legal disputation, containing God's judgment of Job.[5] Instead of issuing the usual apodictic judgment, however, God chooses to argue with Job.

Murphy has correctly pointed to the mixture of forms in these speeches, but in keeping with the preceding argument, has noted the

---

1. For a detailed discussion of the questions of literary integrity, see Gordis, *Job*, 556-63, 567.

2. For a critical summary, see Keel, *Jahwes Entgegnung an Ijob*, 24-34; and Kubina, *Die Gottesreden im Buche Hiob*, 124-42.

3. *The Structure of the Book of Job* (Philadelphia: Fortress, 1977). Westermann recognizes that God's answer to Job is a disputation speech, but is transformed into hymnic praise by frequent descriptions of God and creation.

4. Gerhard von Rad, 'Job XXXVIII and Ancient Egyptian Wisdom', *The Problem of the Hexateuch and Other Essays* (New York: McGraw–Hill, 1966), 281-91.

5. Hans Richter, *Studien zu Hiob*. See also Kubina, *Die Gottesreden im Buche Hiob*, 141.

dominance of the disputation.[1] Thus God comes first to contest Job's accusation of divine misrule and then to render judgment. The first transpires in the two speeches, and the second in the first part of the epilogue (42.7-9). This position is consistent with the disputative nature of the dialogues between Job and the three friends, Job's continued efforts to have his day in court, and one of the major metaphors for creation and providence: the ordering of the world by divine decree. Yet the language of the speeches points to the specific type of theophanic judgment detailed in hymnic images having their origins in combat myths of creation and world maintenance. Those who challenge Yahweh's rule include Behemoth, Leviathan, the wicked, and now Job. The Divine Warrior comes as the storm god to defeat his enemies and render judgment resulting in the repelling of the threats of chaos against his rule. In keeping with the imagery of theophanic judgment, God comes in the 'whirlwind' (סערה—38.1, 40.6). This storm with mighty winds most often occurs in the context of theophanic judgment and the destruction of chaos in its various incarnations.[2] God's raging tempest is the mighty force which carries away the wicked (Isa. 40.24; 41.16). Theopanic judgment, depicted in Yahweh's coming in the whirlwind, serves as the controlling image for the two speeches. Drawing on the metaphorical language of myths of origins and maintenance which include the battle with chaos, the Yahweh speeches portray both the nature and operation of creation and the character of divine rule. Consistent with theophanic judgment structured by mythic pattern, Yahweh has come to engage chaos in battle, reassert divine sovereignty, and issue judgment leading to the ordering of the world. The means by which all of these are accomplished is language which re-establishes a new and daring structure of faith in which meaning is possible and reality is ordered.

---

1. Murphy, *Wisdom Literature, 44; cf.* Fohrer, *Hiob,* 496-98; Müller, *Hiob und seine Freunde,* 38ff. Keel agrees the speeches are a *Streitrede,* though this is not a precise *Gattung* with a specific *Sitz im Leben.* Rather the *Streitrede* is more of a literary work which draws from many specific life situations. Consistent then with this form is the combination of imperatives, questions, and praise to convince the opponent of the correctness of one's position (*Jahwes Entgegnung an Ijob,* 27-33).

2. For this meaning of the noun and its related forms (סער, סערה, שׂערה, and שׂער), see Job 9.17; Pss. 50.3; 58.10; Isa. 29.6; 40.24; Jer. 23.19; 25.32; Hos. 13.3; Amos 1.14; Nah. 1.3; and Zech. 7.14.

2. The First Speech of God and Job's Response
(Job 38.1–40.5)

Restabilization of Metaphors of Cosmology. The introduction to Yahweh's answer to Job includes both the controlling image for the speeches ('whirlwind') and two of the dominant forms which structure the literary texture of the speeches: rhetorical question (v. 2) and imperative (v. 3).

> Then Yahweh answered Job out of the whirlwind and said:
> Who is this who darkens counsel with words lacking in knowledge?
> Gird up your loins like a warrior,[1]
>> I will question you and you reveal to me (38.1-3).

With the image of whirlwind Yahweh is depicted in the guise of the storm god coming to do battle with chaos.[2] The initial question in v. 2 provides the basis for all others in the two speeches: 'Who is this who darkens (מחשיך) counsel (עצה) with words lacking in knowledge?' This rhetorical question does not merely seek the identity of the one who has dared to challenge divine rule, but more importantly expresses contempt for the opponent. מי זה ('Who is this?') is often used by one who scoffs at the status and power of a challenger. For example, in responding to the command of Moses to allow the Israelites to go into the wilderness to celebrate a festival, Pharaoh contemptuously responds: 'Who is Yahweh that I should obey his voice and release Israel? I do not know Yahweh, and moreover I will not allow Israel to go' (Exod. 5.2; cf. Judg. 9.28, 38; 1 Sam. 17.26; 25.10; Isa. 28.9; and Job 26.4). 'Counsel' is a common wisdom term, referring to a well-conceived plan that results in a success. In v. 2, it refers to Yahweh's plan in creating and ruling the world (cf. Job 12.13; Prov. 8.14; Isa. 5.19; and 46.10). Used in this sense the term would underscore Yahweh's providence, i.e. design of creating and sustaining life and well-being for the created order. Moreover, the question serves to accuse Job as the one who 'darkens this plan with knowledge-less words'. Job's language is destroying God's life-sustaining plan by returning creation to the darkness of chaos (cf. ch. 3). And the 'knowledgeless words' do not simply point to ignorance, but more

---

1. One Hebrew MS reads גיבור ('warrior') for גבר ('male').

2. Preuss, 'Jahwes Antwort an Hiob und die sogenannte Hiobliteratur des alten Vorderen Orients', 338. Cf. Marduk coming to do battle with Tiamat (*ANET*, 66-67) and Baal as the battler of Yam (*ANET* 129-31). Key theophanic texts in the Old Testament include Judg. 5; Hab. 3; and Ps. 18.7-16.

importantly to foolish, chaotic language that subverts the orders of creation and society. It is the language of curse, indictment, and disputation which deconstructs both the articulation of the meaning of creation faith, and its power to shape and sustain the structures of life. Job's words are not sagacious language which orders and sustains life, but rather subversive speech that destabilizes both the meaning system that gives understanding and direction to existence and the very structures of life contained in Yahweh's counsel. Job has attempted to deconstruct the metaphor of creation by word with his own linguistic assault, thereby returning the world to the darkness of night.

In v. 3 Yahweh issues his own challenge to Job to engage him in debate, but it is expressed in the metaphor of battle: 'Gird up your loins like a warrior'. גבר is either to be changed to גבור ('warrior', Judg. 6.12; 11.1; 1 Sam. 9.1; 16.18; and 2 Chron. 13.3)[1] or to be understood in the sense of a male who may be counted in the military census (Exod. 12.37; Judg. 5.30). A warrior 'girds up his loins' by placing around his waist a belt for weapons in preparation for impending battle (Ps. 45.4; Isa. 5.27; 8.9; and Jer. 1.17).[2] The metaphor is more than literary enhancement, for it evokes the image of preparing for mortal combat. The challenge to do battle has its place in mythological texts involving the theme of *Chaoskampf*, and, often in the language of taunt, is a prelude to struggle.

The opening component of the main section of Yahweh's speech combines rhetorical questions with hymnic descriptions pertaining to God's creation and rule of the cosmos (38.4-18).

Strophe I: The Earth (38.4-7)

4. Where were you when I founded the earth? Tell me, if you have insight.
5. Who established its measurements? Surely you know! Or who stretched out the measuring line upon it?
6. Upon what were the earth's pillars sunk, or who laid its cornerstone,
7. When the morning stars cried in exultation, and all the Sons of the gods shouted in praise?

---

1. Budde, *Hiob*, 241; and Tur-Sinai, *Job*, 521.
2. Pope, *Job*, 291; and Fohrer, *Hiob*, 500. On the basis of a Nuzi parallel Gordon understands the idiom to refer to a wrestling ordeal in which opponents at law struggle with belts that are linked together ('Belt-wrestling in the Bible World', [*HUCA* 23 {1950–51}, 131-36]; also Tur-Sinai, *Job*, 442). This would fit the metaphor of the patriarch Jacob struggling with God in Gen. 36.22.

Strophe II: Sea (38.8-11)

8. Who shut in Yam with doors, when he burst forth, issuing from the womb,
9. When I made a cloud his garment, and a dark cloud his swaddling band,
10. When I restrained him with my statute, and I set up a bolt and doors,
11. And I said, 'Thus far you may come, but no farther, and here must your arrogant waves be stayed?'[1]

Strophe III: The Heavens (38.12-15)

12. Have you in your lifetime[2] commanded Morning, or have you made the Dawn[3] know his place,
13. In order to seize the corners of the earth and shake out the wicked,
14. When it[4] changes like clay pressed by a seal, or like a garment which is dyed?[5]
15. Their[6] light is withheld from the wicked, whose uplifted arm is broken.

Strophe IV: The Underworld (38.16-18)

16. Have you entered into the sources of the sea, and have you walked in the recesses of the Deep?
17. Have Death's gates been revealed unto you, and have you seen the gates of the Netherworld?

These four strophes reflect the four parts of the cosmos: earth, sea, heaven and Sheol. The rhetorical questions which reverberate throughout these strophes have obvious answers: Yahweh, not Job, has the knowledge and power to rule the cosmos. Their function is not to obtain information from Job or even to test his knowledge, but rather by contrasting divine knowledge and power with human ignorance and impotence they seek to humble Job into submission and to elicit from him the first beginnings of a new articulation of faith.[7] In each case the

---

1. שׁית ('place, put') may parallel Ugaritic *yst ym*—'he (Baal) scattered ('drank?') Yam' (CTA 2 iv 27). The context is Baal's 'cutting down' and 'annihilating' Prince Yam (Pope, *Job*, 294).

2. Read the interrogative ה with many Heb. MSS and edns.

3. Reading the *Qere* (ידעת השׁחר) for the *Kethib* (ידעתה שׁחר).

4. That is, the earth's color changes as the light of morning appears and intensifies.

5. Reading הצבע ('to be dyed') for MT's יתיצבו ('to set or station oneself, take one's stand').

6. The light of Morning and Dawn.

7. Kubina (*Die Gottesreden im Buche Hiob*, 131-42) has pointed to the similarity of the form and function of these questions to those found in Deutero-Isaiah. Second

attempt is made to gain from Job a doxology praising God for originating and ordering a world in which chaos and evil are given limits and boundaries that prohibit but do not eradicate their destructive powers.

In speaking of the origins and operation of the cosmos, the poet uses the three common metaphors found in traditional wisdom literature to speak of creation: artistry, birth and word. In Job 38.4-7 Yahweh is the divine architect (cf. Woman Wisdom in Prov. 9.1-6) who established a foundation (יסד) for the earth,[1] built it according to precise measurements (מדד), and stretched out a line to mark its length and width (cf. 2 Kings 21.13; Isa. 34.11; 44.13; Jer. 31.39; Zech. 1.16).[2] Further, God sets pedestals for the earth's pillars (Exod. 26.19; Song 5.15) and a cornerstone (Ps. 118.22; Isa. 28.16; Jer. 51.26) to ensure enduring stability. The precision and stability of the earth convey a majestic order, an elegant aesthesis that evokes praise by the divine council.[3] Praise,[4] not reproach and indictment, is the proper response of gods and humans to the work of the creator.[5] The artistry metaphor evokes these images of order and beauty which sustain life and inspire the response of praise and thanksgiving. Far from ignoring Job's accusations of God's returning the world to chaos, the first strophe asserts the stability and beauty of the earth as due to the divine craftsman's originating activity.

The second strophe moves from the earth to the sea, and from the metaphor of artistry to those of fertility, combat, and word. The fertility metaphor resides in the theogonic depiction of the birth of

---

Isaiah's questions are placed in the context of trial speeches to point to Yahweh as the true God over against false gods and idols (see 40.12-26).

1. Cf. Marduk's building activity in the *Enuma elish* (*ANET*, 67), where the Esharra (the palace of the gods) is built over the cosmic abyss, even as the earth is constructed over Apsu.

2. See Pss. 24.2; 78.69; 89.12; 102.6; 104.5; Prov. 3.19; Isa. 48.13; 51.13, 16; Zech. 12.1.

3. The 'sons of God(s)' is an expression for the divine council in Gen. 6.2, 4; Job 1.6; 2.1; and Pss. 29.1; 89.7.

4. רנן refers to joyous praise (Isa. 12.6; 24.14; and Jer. 31.7), while רוע is the 'cultic shout' of praise (Pss. 47.2; 66.4; 81.2).

5. See Ps. 148. Ezra 3.10-12 speaks of the festive praise of the priestly orders and the people in response to the completion of the laying of the temple's new foundations (cf. Zech. 4.7, the praise of Marduk following creation and the completion of his city and temple [*ANET*, 68-72], and the festivities of the gods following the completion of Baal's temple [*ANET*, 134]). The construction of a temple is often understood as a cosmogony.

Yam, the god of chaos. Here Yahweh is either Yam's father,[1] mother,[2] or more probably the midwife,[3] who takes the newly-born Sea and wraps him in swaddling clothes.[4] With parental care, Yahweh nurtures Sea from birth (cf. Job 10.10-12; Ps. 139.13-16). What is particularly stunning is the use of the language of the tradition of individual creation (cf. Job 10; Jer. 1) to speak of God's nurturing of chaos. Indeed references to the creation of humans is almost absent from the Yahweh speeches. The single example is Yahweh's statement to Job: 'I created Behemoth even as I made you' (40.15). Yet the metaphor shifts to conflict when Yahweh, much like Marduk, shuts Yam in prison with doors[5] strengthened by a crossbar. Then in the metaphor of word Yahweh issues an edict (חֹק)[6] which establishes the boundaries for Yam's domain, keeping the destructive forces of his proud waves[7] from flooding creation, when the waters burst forth from the womb. The metaphor indicates that God has established an order at creation which gives chaos its own place to exist, but denies the power and opportunity to overwhelm the earth. The world exists by the restraining power of divine decree.

In 38.12-13 Yahweh describes the daily appearance of Morning and Dawn who come in response to divine command and eliminate the wicked from the earth, much like shaking the corners[8] of a carpet to

1. See Canaanite mythology where El is the father of Yam.

2. Yahweh gives birth to Israel in Deut. 32.18 and Isa. 46.3 and to the mountains in Ps. 90.2.

3. See Pss. 22.9-11 and 71.6 where Yahweh assists at the birth of the psalmist.

4. See *CTA* 12 i 18-19 which refers to the swaddling bands of the bovine monsters who kill Baal, and Ezek. 16.4 which mentions Yahweh's wrapping of Israel at birth.

5. 'Doors' can also refer to the aperture of the womb (Job 3.10) and the openings of heaven through which the rain comes (Ps. 78.23). Cf. the window in Baal's palace through which the threatening rains may come (*ANET*, 135). Yahweh is the one who 'opens' or 'shuts' the womb in the fertility metaphor (Gen. 29.3; 30.22; 49.25).

6. Cf. Ps. 104.9; Prov. 8.29; and Jer. 5.22. The constraining of chaos by bars and guards is a motif originating in the *Enuma elish* (*ANET*, 67), and is found elsewhere in Job 7.12; 9.13; and 26.12.

7. Yam's arrogance points to his desire to challenge Yahweh's sovereignty and overflow the created order (Ps. 46.4). The bursting forth of the waters if metaphorically used of pharaoh as the chaos monster in Ezek. 32.2.

8. כְּנַף ('skirt, ends of a garment, corners of a carpet') figuratively refers to the 'ends' or 'corners' of the earth in Isa. 11.12; 24.16; and Job 37.3.

remove its dust.[1] Morning and Dawn function like Shamash who uses his light to discover and judge evil during his daily course across the heavens. Thus their light slowly changes the radiant colors of the earth, ends the period of darkness in which evil is perpetrated, denies to the wicked life-giving rays, and destroys their defiant power.[2] Here the poet entwines the aesthetics of early morning light with the morality of bringing the wicked to justice and limiting, if not ending, their reign. Once again by means of the power of divine word the perverters of justice (רשע) are limited to the time of darkness, that temporal vestige of primeval chaos. And while they may 'lift their arm' in defiance of divine rule, that hubris is broken by God's power. Thus each day is a new creation in which the powers of darkness and evil are once again limited, in this case by the divine word, and orders for life are renewed.

The final strophe speaks of the mystery of the cosmic ocean and the underworld. Job has neither descended to the sources of the Abyss nor stood at the gates of the city of Mot.[3] El's tent was located on his sacred mountain which stood at the 'Sources of the Two Floods, in the midst of the headwaters of the Two Oceans'.[4] In Canaanite mythology this is the 'Center of the Earth', located at the entrances to heaven and the underworld. Not only do the regions of the cosmic ocean and Sheol stand as an impenetrable mystery to all living mortals, Job has not approached these regions over which Yahweh has stretched the sacred canopy, rules in sovereignty, and issues divine oracles that maintain the order of creation. Further, both the deep and the underworld are spheres in the cosmos ruled by God. They are an integral, though subjugated, part of the dominion of God.

The second portion of the main section of Yahweh's initial speech comprises six strophes of questions and hymnic descriptions about meteorological phenomena: light and darkness, the variety of moisture, and the constellations.

1. By contrast in 3.4 Job had attempted to command day to return to the darkness of chaos.

2. In Israel and Mesopotamia, the night was the time of demonic attack (see Fohrer, *Hiob*, 504).

3. The underworld is often depicted as a city with gates in the ancient world. See Pss. 9.14; 107.18; Isa. 38.10; and the seven gates through which Ishtar passes in entering the netherworld ('Ishtar's Descent', *ANET*, 107).

4. *ANET*, 133.

Strophe I: Light and Darkness (38.19-21)

19. Where is the path to the dwelling of light, and as for darkness, where is its place,
20. That you may take to its border, and perceive the pathways to its house?
21. You know, for you were born then, and the number of your days are many!

Strophe II: Snow, Hail, Light, East Wind (38.22-24)

22. Have you entered the reservoirs of the snow, and have you seen the storehouses of the hail,
23. Which I have reserved for a time of trouble, for the day of battle and war?
24. What is the manner by which light is distributed, or the east wind travels over the earth?

Strophe III: Rain (38.25-27)

25. Who has cleft a channel for the flood, and a path for the thunderbolt,
26. To bring rain upon the earth when there was no human, upon the desert when there was no person upon it?
27. To satisfy the desolate land, and to make the grass sprout forth?

Strophe IV: Rain, Dew, Hoarfrost, Ice (38: 28-30)

28. Does the rain have a father, or who fathered the dewdrops?
29. From whose womb did the ice come forth, and who gave birth to the hoarfrost of heaven?
30. The waters become hard like stone, and the face of the deep is frozen.

Strophe V: Constellations (38.31-33)

31. Can you bind the bonds[1] of the Pleiades, or loose the cords of Orion?
32. Can you bring forth the Mazzaroth[2] in its season, and can you guide the Bear and her cubs?
33. Do you know the statutes of heaven, or can you establish heaven's rule on the earth?

---

1. Reading מעגדות ('bonds'—Prov. 6: 21, Job 31: 36)) for מעדנות (Pope, *Job*, 300, and Tur-Sinai, *Job*, 531).

2. Perhaps a variation of Mazzalot, thus referring to the southern constellations (2 Kgs. 23: 5). See Pope, *Job*, 301.

Strophe VI: Clouds (38.34-38)

34. Can you lift your voice to the clouds, so that the flood of waters will obey[1] you?
35. Can you send forth lightnings so that they may go, and will they say to you, 'here we are?'
36. Who placed wisdom in the ibis,[2] or who gave insight to the cock ?
37. Who counts the clouds by wisdom, and who can tilt the waterskins of heaven,
38. When dust compacts into a mass, and clods cleave together?

The four metaphors of creation also shape the language of these strophes: crafting, fertility, word and conflict. The crafting metaphor is used to characterize God's construction of an irrigation canal for the flow of rain and a highway for thunder to travel (v. 25) in order to bring water to a wasteland uninhabited by humans (vv. 26-27). Tsevat has used this verse as the linchpin for his argument that Yahweh's speeches deny there is either a moral order operating in creation or that God rewards the good and punishes the wicked.[3] Pointing to the biblical concept that rain is the instrument for blessing for the righteous, Tsevat contends that Yahweh's sending the rain on a desert where no person dwells, therefore wasting it from a human perspective, is proof that there is no just order permeating creation. Therefore Tsevat understands the speeches as positing a God who transcends all standards of good and evil. For Tsevat, God is neither good nor evil; rather God is God.

This well-constructed argument does not finally convince. While it becomes clear in the theophany that neither God nor the world operates according to a simplistic Deuteronomic theory of retribution in which the righteous are rewarded and the wicked punished, the metaphors indicate that God has created and continues to sustain a reality in which both chaos as a threat to life and the wicked, the perverters of order, are limited in their destructive actions. Far from suggesting that reality is amoral, the strophe under discussion refers to God's originating act of creation: watering the primordial desert before the creation of humans (Gen. 2.4b-7). In J and elsewhere,

1. Following the LXX (ὑπακούσεταί σου) to read 'obey' (תענך) for MT's תכסך ('will cover you').
2. For מחוח ('ibis') and שכוי ('cock'), see Gordis, *Job*, 453.
3. M. Tsevat, 'The Meaning of the Book of Job', *HUCA* 37 (1966), 73-106.

wilderness, like the sea, is seen as chaos (e.g. Isa. 51.42-43). Indeed the poet strongly echoes the language of Gen. 2.5b:

> and before the plants of the field had sprouted (יצמח), because the Lord God had not yet made it rain upon the earth (לא המטיר יהוה אלהים על הארץ), and there was no human to work the soil (ואדם אין).

In Job, God 'brings rain upon the earth *when* there was no human, upon the desert *when* there was no person upon it' (המטיר על ארץ לא איש, מדבר לא אדם בו). God's 'construction' of canals and highways for the storm[1] has watered the earth, making it inhabitable by all creatures, including humans. This negative introduction, 'when there was no. . .' is a standard feature of many cosmogonic myths, including the mythic introduction to the theogony of Woman Wisdom in Prov. 8.22-26. In this way the poet follows J in making God responsible for the fertility of the soil, not the slave labor of humans as in *Atra-hasis*.

The fertility metaphor is used in 38.28-30 to indicate that God is both the father and the mother of moisture.[2] In originating moisture, God continues to provide the sustenance necessary for the ongoing cycle of life. And the imagery associated with the storm-cloud deity continues to correlate with the tradition of theophanic judgment. While these types of moisture make life possible, the formation of ice demonstrates God's power over chaos. God freezes over the Deep, even as ice forms over water. This is hardly an image of blatant, uncontrolled power, but rather intimates God's limitation of the threats of chaos against all life.

In 38.34-38 Yahweh's thunderous voice controls the waters of the clouds that cover the earth, while divine wisdom is given to the ibis and cock who predict the approaching storm.[3] God's wisdom, decree and power tilt the waterskins of the heavens and regulate storm clouds which bring life to creation. Indeed divine ordinances (חקות) govern the operation of the heavens, a divine order which Job is not able to establish upon the earth. This may suggest a perfection of order in heaven that is not true of earth where chaos and the wicked continue to have their presence felt.

---

1. שטף refers to the mighty waters of the flood in Ps. 32.6; Nah. 1.8; Dan. 9.26.

2. As the storm-god, Baal is the father of Pidrya, the daughter of dew.

3. See Gordis, *Job*, 453. Gordis notes that the ibis was associated with the god of wisdom, Thoth, in Egypt, and was thought to forecast rain and proclaim the coming of dawn.

Most important, however, is the initial occurrence of the battle metaphor in 38.22-24 and 31-33. In the first instance Yahweh speaks of storing snow and hail for use during 'a time of trouble' and 'the day of battle and war'. In acting in human history, God's fighting through nature, particularly using meteorological phenomena like rain and wind as weapons, is common in theophanic hymns (Judg. 5.20-21; Pss. 18.3-4; 29.1ff.; Isa. 30.30; Amos 5.8-9; 9.6).[1] However, the text may also refer to creation and the maintenance of order against the threat of chaos. In the primordial battle preceding creation, Marduk comes as the storm god to fight against Tiamat and is well armed with winds and lightning. Baal, of course, used the roar of thunder, wind and lightning bolts to defeat his opponents in maintaining the order of creation. The second text (vv. 31-33) speaks of Yahweh's defeat and binding of the Pleiades and Orion, perhaps reflecting a myth of the rebellion of Titans against divine rule (cf. 25.2-3; 9.9). This second echo of theomachy stresses the resulting peaceful and regulated rule of the heavenly world, due to Yahweh's fearsome power. Does Job possess the ability to bind the Titans or even unleash them to join him in his assault against the heavens?

The Destabilization of the Metaphor of Ruler. In the fourth part of Yahweh's opening speech (38.39–39.30), the subject moves from the origins and rule of creation to the providential care and feeding of animals.[2]

Strophe I: Lion and Raven (38.39-41)

39. Can you hunt prey for the lion, (or) can you satisfy the appetite of young lions?
40. When they crouch in the dens, and lie in wait in the thicket?
41. Who provides the raven its prey, when its offspring cry out ot God, and wander about without food?

Strophe II: Ibix and Hind (39.1-4)

1. Do you know the time when mountain goats are born, do you observe the travail of hinds?
2. Can you number the months they must fulfill, do you know the time when they bring forth?

---

1. Also see Isa. 28.17; 30.30; Ezek. 13.13; and Sir. 39.29.
2. See Pss. 104; 145.9; and 'A Hymn to Amon-Re', *ANET*, 365-67.

3. When they crouch down to give birth to their young, when they bring forth their offspring?
4. Their young ones grow strong, they grow up in the open, they go forth and do not return to them.

Strophe III: Wild Ass and Wild Ox (39.5-12)

5. Who sends forth the wild ass to freedom, and who looses the bonds of the onager,
6. Whose home I have made the steppe, and whose habitat is the salt plain?
7. He laughs at the noise of the city, and shouts of the driver he does not hear.
8. He ranges over the mountains as his pasture, and he searches after all that is green.
9. Is the wild ox willing to serve you, or to spend the night at your feeding trough?
10. Can you bind him in the furrow with ropes, or will he harrow the valleys behind you?
11. Can you trust him when his strength increases, or can you leave your produce to him?
12. Do you trust him to return, and gather your seed to your threshing floor?

Strophe IV: Ostrich and Horse (39.13-25)

13. The wing of the ostrich flaps joyously; is it a kindly pinion and plumage?
14. For she leaves her eggs on the ground, and lets them be warmed on the soil.
15. For she forgets that a foot may crush them, or a wild beast may trample them.
16. Her offspring are treatly roughly without her; while her labor may be in vain, she remains without fear.
17. Because God has made her forget wisdom, and has not imparted insight to her!
18. When she flaps proudly, she scoffs at the horse and its rider.
19. Did you give the horse its strength, did you clothe his neck with a quivering mane?
20. Do you make him leap[1] like a locust? His snorting is majestic and dreadful.
21. He paws[2] in the valley and rejoices in his strength, he goes out to meet the weapons.

1. Changing the ה to an interrogative ה. רעש ('leap') is often used to refer to the 'quaking, shaking' of the earth in Yahweh's theophanic actions, and in these contexts intimates a return to chaos (cf. Hag. 2.6, 7, 21; Isa. 29.6; Jer. 10.10).
2. Reading the singular verb חפר ('paws'; LXX, S and V) instead of the MT's plural.

22. He laughs at fear and is not dismayed, he does not retreat from the sword.
23. The quiver rattles upon him, the flashing lance and javelin.
24. He stamps the ground and shakes with excitement, not able to believe that the trumpet sounds.
25. At the trumpets blast he says, 'Aha', and sniffs out the battle from afar, the shouts of officers and the cry of war.

Strophe V: Hawk and Vulture (39.26-30)

26. Does the hawk soar by means of your wisdom, when he spreads his wings toward the south?
27. Does the vulture[1] mount up at your command, and make his nest on high?
28. He makes his home on the rock, upon the pointed crag and towering cliff.
29. He searches for food from there, his eyes gazing from afar.
30. His brood drink blood, for where the slain are, there he is.

The poet groups together five pairs of animals, characterizing each one by common features: the ravenous appetites of lions and ravens, the reproduction of mountain goats and hinds, the freedom of the wild ass and wild ox, the speed and irrational courage of the ostrich and horse, and the wisdom that preserves the hawk and vulture. Yet even more important is Yahweh's providential care for these creatures, enabling them to survive in the world: the young offspring of lions and ravens are fed,[2] mountain goats and hinds are given the instinct to reproduce, the wild ass and wild ox are freed from human servitude,[3] the irrational ostrich and the horse are given speech, while the hawk and vulture are endowed with wisdom. Yet what is particularly striking about the selection of these specific creatures is the fact that, with the exception of the horse, they are wild animals which live in areas uninhabited by human beings: the wilderness, thick forests, abandoned cities and fields, the steppes, salt land, mountains, and rocky cliffs. In addition, save for the horse they are successful in resisting efforts at domestication, and many are harmful to human life.

---

1. נשר is the name for both eagle and vulture, though the latter is more probable in this conext (see Gordis, *Job*, 463).

2. See Pss. 18.7; 22.25; 28.2; and 31.23.

3. This motif of freedom from the taskmaster, especially in 39.5, echoes the language of 3.18-19, Job's longing for death where the captive 'does not hear the voice of the taskmaster' and 'the slave is free from the master'. Unlike these wild creatures, humans enjoy freedom only in the silence of the grave.

While the wild ass and wild ox devour the produce of humans, vultures feast on the flesh of human corpses.[1] Even the horse charges fearlessly into battle bringing death and destruction, a description corresponding to the mainly negative depiction of this animal in the Old Testament.[2] And most significantly they are creatures who know no fear of humanity. Once again P's covenant theology, this time in the words of Gen. 9.1-17 where animals stand in 'fear' of the human kings, is destabilized and falls into fragments.

One other feature characterizes these creatures. Most of these wild animals are hunted by ancient Near Eastern kings, while the horse is ridden in pursuit of the prey. Royal hunts were ritual acts by which the order of the kingdom was established and maintained. By killing these animal embodiments of chaos, order was restored and life was secured. Humanity is in a struggle with these creatures for the control of the earth.[3] Yet it is not about the hunt that Yahweh speaks, but providential care, not for humans but for the wild. Yahweh nurtures and sustains an alien world hostile to human life, indeed flourishes in regions uninhabited by people (see Isa. 13.9-22; 32.12-14; 34.8-15; Jer. 50.39-40). Thus God repudiates the arguments of both the friends who contended the wild beasts were punished and destroyed by a retributive order that protected the righteous (4.10-11) and Job who pointed to God's oppression of creatures as evidence of divine misrule (12.7-10). Yahweh is the true 'Lord of the Creatures' who provides for the sustenance of animals. The anthropological tradition grounded in the metaphor of humanity as king is deconstructed and left in pieces. In its place, Yahweh sets forth in no uncertain terms the radical sovereignty of God and the providential sustenance of animal life that may even be hostile to human existence. Yam is the darling of Yahweh who is nurtured, though constrained, from birth. The creatures of the wild are nourished and sustained from the rhythm of birth, to the provisions for food, to the gift of freedom from human dominion. Reality is not anthropocentric. Humans are not commissioned as in P

---

1. חללים most probably refers to corpses of those slain in battle (Num. 31.8, 19; and 1 Sam. 23.8, 18).

2. See the passages listed by Keel, *Jahwes Entgegnung an Ijob*, 70, including Exod. 23.6, 12, 20, and 23.

3. Keel, *Jahwes Entgegnung an Ijob*, 65, 71ff.

to go forth into the world and bring it under subjection. Neither do the wild animals fear and submit to human reign.[1]

The first speech ends with a resumption of challenge to Job. He has dared to revolt against God (ריב). Let this mortal contender (מכיח) answer these questions, admitting his own weakness and ignorance while acknowledging the strength, wisdom, and justice of God. Uttering such an admission, Job would thereby confess he is incapable of ruling the comsos.

> And Yahweh answered Job and said,
> > Will he who presents a case against Shaddai also instruct him?
> Can the one who reproves God answer? (40.1-2).

The First Reponse of Job and the Metaphorical Process: Absurdity and Destabilization. Job's response to Yahweh's challenge formulated in an overwhelming cadence of questions is silence, though the meaning and implications of not speaking are unclear. The general tendency has been to understand this as the first step towards repentance. Seen in this way, Job's silence is tacit admission of his ignorance and impotence and a recognition of the wrongfulness of his attack on God. However, neither the language of the response nor the reaction in Yahweh's second speech suggests Job is on the verge of confessing his sins.

> Then Job answered the Lord.
> Since I am despised (by you), how shall I answer you?
> > I place my hand on my mouth.
> Seeing I have spoken once, I will not answer,
> > I will not continue a second time (40.3-5).

קלתי is often taken to mean 'self-abasement'. The RSV translates the initial line: 'Behold, I am of small account'. This translation makes Job confess his own lack of significance in a posture of humble submission, admitting his own ignorance in being unable to answer these impossible questions. However, an alternative interpretation is much more likely. First of all, the Hebrew particle הן normally introduces a fact upon which a conclusion or action is based and thus should be translated: 'since' or 'seeing that is so'. The fact which leads to Job's action, or in this case his silence, is embodied in the word קלתי. In each use of the Qal form the verb clearly means 'to be held in contempt' by

---

1. Note the description of the horse in 39.22 ('He laughs at fear and is not dismayed') and the ostrich in 39.16 ('She is without fear').

another person or group (Gen. 16.4, 5; 2 Sam. 1.23; Jer. 4.13; Hab. 1.8; Nah. 1.4). It does not indicate personal remorse, repentance, or self-deprecation. Thus the fact introduced by הן that leads to silence is God's contempt for Job and his challenge to divine sovereignty. At this point, Job's mood appears to be that of complaint, not contrite repentance. Second, many of the questions asked by Yahweh in this first speech are not impossible to answer. Rather they are rhetorical questions with obvious answers. 'Where were you when I laid the foundation of the earth?' The answer would have been: 'I was not yet born.' 'Who determined the earth's measurements?' The answer would have been the acknowledgement that God did. The questions are designed to begin to evoke from Job the hymnic confession that God originated and continues to rule a creation that is both wondrously beautiful in its appearance and supportive of life, although there is a limited place for chaos. Yahweh has provided a new language of praise for creation and providential rule which Job should emulate.

Yet Job does not respond with this new expression of faith, for two reasons. First his own experience of chaos is so powerfully real, so destructive in its force, that he has been robbed of the power to praise. It is not merely that he cannot praise, but also that he will not praise. He has become inarticulate. Like the narrative's depiction of the three friends who are struck dumb by what has happened (2.13), Job is speechless. Second, Job cannot speak a new language of faith, because he does not know how. He has not yet shaped a new discourse of meaning that gives form to theological language. His own attack on God had presupposed that justice was a retributive order in which righteous deeds are rewarded, and wicked ones punished. Since the moral order had ceased to operate, it must be that God has become perverse, attacking creation and its life-enhancing order. With the disputation interfacing rhetorical questions and elegant praise, Yahweh has now dismissed both the accusation and the basis on which it rests, by arguing there is justice in the world, but it has a new and significantly different construction. While chaos is constrained, it is not eliminated. And what is often seen as chaotic and destructive to life from a misguided anthropocentrism, say the lion or the vulture, are under the providential care of God. The wild and untamed world is nurtured and sustained by God, even if its wildness may adversely affect human life. By contrast, Job the human creature, certainly no king in God's creation, is held in divine contempt. Job cannot answer then with a doxology of praise. His own efforts to destabilize the language of creation faith by incantation, lament, and indictment had resulted, at least for him, in a new though perverse meaning system to explain the nature of God and his own humanity. Now that this sytem of deconstruction has itself disintegrated, Job has become dumb and cannot speak. Thus it is correct to translate מה אשׁיבך: 'How shall I answer you?' Placing his hand upon his mouth,[1] Job cannot speak. Job cannot respond in doxology, but only in silence.[2]

3. The Second Speech of God and Job's Response (40.6–42.6)

The Deconstruction of the Metaphor of Ruler. Yahweh's second speech is also a disputation comprised of rhetorical questions, imperatives and descriptive praise, designed not merely to humble Job, but to re-establish a structure of meaning by which dumb lips may become articulate. However, there is both a formal shift from a predominance of questions to an emphasis on imperatives and descriptive praise and a thematic shift from Yahweh's own creation and rule of the cosmos to the extending of challenge to Job to ascend the throne and rule as the head of the divine council. If Job cannot or will not construct his own language of faithful discourse, if he attempts to continue to indict God for misrule within a discredited system of retribution, then let him assume God's throne and reorder the world. Questions eliciting praise are now replaced with imperatives nuanced by taunt. If a hubris-filled Job wishes to join the mighty heroes of mythic tragedy, let him experience their ignoble fall in his own.

Strophe I: Challenge to Rule (40.8-14)

8. Will you negate my justice, will you pronounce my guilty that you might be declared innocent?
9. Do you have an arm like EL, and can you thunder with a voice like this?
10. Deck yourself with greatness and exaltation, clothe yourself with majesty and splendor.
11. Scatter forth your fury, look upon every arrogent one and humble him.

---

1. See B. Couroyer, '"Mettre sa main sur sa bouche"', *RB* 67 (1960), 197-209.
2. Silence is often the response to theophany, not only induced by fear and feelings of insignificance before the Holy, but also because the worshipper comes to recognize the inadequacy of all speech and understanding about God. In the presence of the Other, all attempts at God language falter (cf. Gen. 32.31; Exod. 3.6; Isa. 6.5).

12. Look upon every proud person and subdue him, and tread down the wicked in their place.
13. Hide them in the grave together, bind their faces in the darkness.
14. Then I will also praise you, because your right hand will have brought you victory.

The initial rhetorical question responds to the charge of divine misrule of the cosmos, a charge based on the mistaken belief that the condemnation (הרשיע) of God would necessitate Job's own exoneration (צדק). This question neither explicitly nor implicitly accuses Job of wrong. Rather it denies that the innocence of Job depends upon the guilt of God. משפט ('justice') in this context of royal language refers to the just rule of the cosmos by God, a rule which both undergirds the ordinances of creation and provides for the necessary needs of living creatures to exist. Job's assault on divine governance is more than simply denying God's justice. It is the attempt 'to annul' (פרר) the righteous rule of God which sustains creation. This verb describes the splitting of the chaos dragon in half, the first act in constituting creation.[1] In a reversal of meaning, Yahweh is asking Job if he thinks his own destructive assault is the first necessary step in reordering a new reality.

The parallel questions (v. 9) contrast the power of God with the implied weakness of Job. Some interpreters have mistakenly seen this interrogation as arrogant boasting and cruel taunting designed to humiliate Job for his mortal limitations. Yet the issue is divine justice, not the massive strength of God which Job has often acknowledged. Is this pretentious, mean-spirited rhetoric on God's part, or a blatant, boastful rhetorical display of power? Perhaps neither. The images conveying power (זרוע—'strong arm',[2] and קול—'thunder')[3] are those of the storm god who comes in theophanic judgment to do battle with the forces of chaos.[4] Fear-inspiring power is a major component of the theophanic tradition, but it is shaped by the context of justice: the

---

1. The *pô'êl* form is used in Ps. 74.13 to speak of God's 'splitting' or 'rending assunder' the chaos monster (cf. Isa. 24.19).

2. See Exod. 15.16; Ps. 89.11, 14, 22; and Isa. 52.9-10. Both זרוע (Exod. 6.6; Deut. 4.34; 9.29) and ימין ('right hand' in 40.14; cf. Exod. 15.16, 12; and Ps. 20.7) are symbols of Yahweh's power in creation and history to deliver and save.

3. Ps. 18.14 = 2 Sam. 22.14 and Ps. 29.3, 5, 7, 9. קול plus רעם are often combined in contexts of judgment: Isa. 30.30ff.; Amos 1.2; and Joel 4.16.

4. See Weiser, *Hiob*, 258.

defeat of chaos leads to the re-establishment of the reign of God over the earth. Creation is renewed, and the structures of life are continued. And it is in this same context that God refers to the power necessary to conquer an awesome enemy. If the divine king is to abdicate his throne and yield to another's rule of the cosmos, then the pretender must possess the power necessary to contend with chaos and maintain the order of creation. It is one thing to assert how the creation should operate. It is another actually to establish the rule.

In vv. 10-14, the language changes from question to imperative, as Yahweh taunts[1] Job to dress in the royal vestments of 'greatness', 'exaltation', 'majesty', and 'splendor', terms describing the glory of divine sovereignty expressed in creation and history (Pss. 21.6; 45.4; 104.1; 111.3).[2] In the mythic pattern, enthronement and/or other ritual moments (temple building, festivals) follow the defeat of the chaos monster. And the first action of the newly-installed king is to sentence the wicked to destruction. As enthroned ruler, Job must perform the primary task of kings: establish justice by conquering the 'proud' (גאה) and 'wicked' (רשעים), those who arrogantly oppose the sovereignty of a ruler and subvert decrees designed to effectuate social harmony.[3] 'Humbling' (שפל), 'subduing' (כנע), and 'treading' (הדך) on the backs of enemies are typical images often captured in the pose of victorious ancient Near Eastern gods and kings standing with one foot placed on the neck or back of a defeated foe. These same images are used to depict the defeat of God's foes in theophanic judgment.[4] If Job can 'pour out his wrath'[5] to bring the arrogant wicked into the 'dust' of Sheol, then Yahweh will 'praise' him (אודה), a technical term in the Psalter for worship which acknowledges and glorifies divine rule (see Pss. 18.50; 30.13; 35.18; 43.4; 44.9; 54.8; 99.3). Yahweh would not become inarticulate, as has Job, in responding to these marvelous deeds. Praising deities for the defeat of enemies who challenge both their own rule and that of their human surrogates is an important

---

1. Cf. the taunt of the fallen King of Tyre in Ezekiel 28.

2. גאון (Exod. 15.7; Isa. 2.10, 19, 21; 24.14), גבה (Qoh. 5.7), הוד, and הדר (Pss. 96.6; 111.3; and 104.1). The latter two are a frequent example of hendiadys, meaning 'majestic splendor'.

3. See Ps. 72 for the duty of kings to establish justice. In the concluding line of the second speech, it is Leviathan who is the ruler of the 'sons of pride' (Job 41.28).

4. E.g. Isa. 13.11.

5. 'Outbursts of divine fury' refers to God's wrath in theophanic judgment (Isa. 13.9, 13; Hab. 3.8).

theme in mythic literature detailing the origins and rule of creation. Indeed the divine ruler sits enthroned on the responsive praises of creation (cf. Ps. 22.4), an image pointing to the power of creative event and authentic theological language to structure a meaning system in which faith is made possible. While it is not explicitly stated that God humbles the proud and wicked, it is nonetheless implied. Yet justice is not a static principle inherent in the structure of creation, but rather a dynamic force which must be continually established and agressively maintained by means of victory (חושע) over evil (v . 14).

The Metaphor of Struggle and the Battle with Chaos. Yahweh does give voice to praise in the third section of the speech, but in a shocking, even absurd twist, it is Behemoth followed by Leviathan, not Job or humankind, whom Yahweh extols.[1] It is not merely the disassembling of conventional wisdom and priestly theology that is intended here, but the movement to the reorientation to reality through a new language of meaning. In the new language of transformed faith, Job must learn to extol an existence in which chaos is a real and threatening force. Mythically formulated, Yahweh is the warrior who praises the might and prowess of the enemy shortly before the battle begins. If Job wishes to sit on the throne of El, he must defeat this terrifying foe.

Strophe II: Behemoth's Power (40.15-19)

15. Behold now,[2] Behemoth, whom I made as I made you, he eats grass like an ox.
16. Behold, his strength is in his loins, and his rigor is in the muscles of his belly.
17. He stiffens his tail like a cedar, the sinews of his thighs are knit together.
18. His bones are bronze tubes, his limbs are like iron bars.
19. He is the first of the works of God, let the one who created him bring near his sword.

Strophe III: Behemoth's Domain (40.20-24)

20. For the mountains bring him their tribute, where every beast of the field cavorts.

1. This pair of beasts continues the coupling of animals in the first speech. This literary technique should discourage efforts to regard Behemoth and Leviathan as a single beast.
2. והנה־נא signals the move from direct address to hymnic description.

21. Under the lotus plants he lies, in the covert of reeds and swamp.
22. The lotus trees cover him with shade, the willows of the brook surround him.
23. If the river swells with turbulence, he is not alarmed, he is confident though Jordan burst forth against his mouth.
24. One takes him by his eyes, and pierces his nose with lures.

Written without the definite article, Behemoth (בהמות) is a personal name probably derived from the 'plural of intensity or majesty' for 'beast'. Thus the name means 'great beast'. However, the specific identity of this creature is far from certain. The common identifications may be broken down into three categories: a large animal (hippopotamus[1] or water buffalo),[2] a mythological beast similar to Leviathan or the 'bull of heaven' in the Gilgamesh Epic, or an animal with mythic features who ritually symbolizes chaos.[3] Several clues are provided in Yahweh's praise of Behemoth. The first strophe (vv. 15-19) describes a beast who is herbivorous, yet extremely powerful. Yet his creation by God is underscored twice: at the beginning in v. 15, and as an inclusion in v. 19. Whatever Behemoth represents, he is a creature God has made, no matter how strong and fearsome he may be. Behemoth is also the 'first of God's works' (ראשית דרכי אל).[4] Echoing the opening word of the P creation narrative (בראשית, Gen. 1.1) and especially the description of Woman Wisdom in Prov. 8.22 (ראשית דרכו, 'his first work'), the expression connotes both temporal primacy and chief status among God's creatures.[5] Neither Wisdom nor Primal Man may boast of primacy in God's creation. Rather it is Behemoth who holds that august position.

The second strophe continues the image of royal status for Behemoth, who receives tribute from the mountains and presides over

1. Fohrer, *Hiob*, 523; Gordis, *Job*, 571.
2. B. Couroyer, 'Qui est Behemoth?', *RB* 82 (1975), 418-43.
3. Keel sees both Behemoth and Leviathan as creatures (hippopotomus and crocodile respectively) who symbolize mythical chaos (*Jahwes Entgegnung an Ijob*, 127ff.).
4. דרך is subject to several interpretations, including cosmic 'design' (Habel, *Job*, 566; cf. Job 26.14), divine actions of salvation from creation to the present (Weiser, *Hiob*, 260), and 'powers' (cf. Ugaritic *drkt*). However, the language is too close to that of Prov. 8.22 to be merely coincidental. And the parallel couplet of Prov. 8.22 strongly indicates 'created work' (פעל). Only in Job it is Behemoth, not Wisdom, who is the first thing created by God.
5. Primogeniture was an important social principle in Israel, though it was occasionally ignored in divine election (cf. e.g. Gen. 49.3ff.).

a domain in which the other wild beasts cavort. The mountains may represent all nature yielding to the suzerainty of Behemoth. Yet they are also both the most majestic feature of creation with peaks rising up into the realm of the gods and the massive pillars which secure the stability of the created order. In the theophanic tradition the mountains quake in submissive terror before the approach of the Divine Warrior. And now Yahweh speaks of the mountains bringing tribute to the mighty Behemoth. Other wild beasts cavort about in his kingdom, an image paralleled by Leviathan's sporting in the sea as Yahweh's tame pet (Ps. 104.26) and conveying subjection to the sovereignty of a greater power. The physical character of Behemoth's domain includes marsh and swampland, streams and rivers. Even the mythic image of the great rush of the swollen waters of the Jordan poses no threat to this beast. Behemoth is a mighty creature, the 'king of the beasts' who fears no natural power, and is at home in marshes and streams.

Yet the double occurrence of the battle metaphor suggests more than an extraordinary creature is the subject of hymnic praise, and it is this metaphor which provides the key to the identity of the beast and the meaning of this section of the second speech.[1] In v. 19 Yahweh exclaims that only the creator dares to bring his sword against mighty Behemoth,[2] the primordial and chief of all God's creatures, to do battle. And in the concluding line (v. 24), Yahweh speaks of one luring the creature with a snare, taking him by the eyes, and piercing his nostrils. In the *Enuma elish* a well-armed Marduk ensnares Tiamat with a net, keeps her mouth extended with the Evil Wind, and penetrates her entrails with a well-aimed arrow, while Kothar wa-Khasis fashions for Baal two magically empowered maces to defeat Prince Yam. The defeat of these gods of chaos leads either to creation in the first instance, or recreation in the second. True, Behemoth is a creature, not a god, in spite of his extraordinary strength and primal position in the animal kingdom.[3] Even so the mythological texts speak

1. See Kubina who demonstrates that many characteristics of Behemoth and Leviathan cannot be identified with the ordinary hippotamus and crocodile (*Die Gottesreden im Buche Hiob*, 44). This does not eliminate in my own judgment, the two animals as symbols for mythical chaos, since animals are often the symbolic vehicles for gods (e.g. Baal as the 'bull').

2. The sword is mentioned frequently as a divine weapon (cf. Judg. 7.20; Isa. 34.6; Jer. 1.12; 47.6).

3. It is possible that Isa. 30.6ff. identifies Behemoth with Rahab, the chaos monster.

of monstrous animals who incorporated the powers of chaos in doing battle with gods of creation and order. In the *Enuma elish* the goddess Hubur fashions monsters and dragons, gives them the power of gods, and sends them forth to join with Tiamat and the rebel gods against the Divine Assembly. Among these awesome creatures are the Viper, the Dragon, the *Sphinx*, the Great-Lion, the Mad-Dog, the Scorpion-Man, lion-demons, the Dragon-Fly, and the Centaur, all 'bearing weapons that spare not, fearless in battle'.[1] In CTA 12, El hatches a devious plot to destroy Baal. He commands young goddesses to go to the wilderness and give birth to a hoard of bovine creatures ('Eaters' and 'Devourers') with 'horns like bulls and humps like buffaloes' who attack Baal in the marshes and undo him. The result is seven years of famine, before his renewal ends the drought.[2] And in the Baal Cycle, Anat boasts of having slain a series of fearful chaos monsters, all enemies of Baal including 'El's *Bullock* 'Atak'.[3]

Another possible parallel comes from the 'Epic of Gilgamesh' in which the 'Bull of Heaven' was sent by Anu as punishment to kill Gilgamesh for his outrageous refusal to become Ishtar's consort. Scorned, Ishtar demands vengeance from Anu, but the head of the Assembly is reluctant, since the unleashing of this mighty Bull would result in seven years of famine for Uruk. Thus the beast incorporates chaos in the form of drought. Ishtar overcomes Anu's hesitancy by indicating she has provided stored grain to offset the effects of resulting famine. Killed by Gilgamesh and Enkidu, the power of the beast is praised, especially the great size of his horns:

> The artisans admire the thickness of his horns:
> Each is cast from thirty minas of lapis;
> The coating on each is two fingers (thick);
> Six measures of oil, the capacity of the two,
> He (Gilgamesh) offered as ointment to his god, Lugalbanda.
> He brought (them) and hung them in his princely bed chamber.[4]

Perhaps the best parallel for the identity and meaning of Behemoth comes from the mythological and ritual character of the red hip-

---

1. *ANET*, 64.
2. This odd myth may reflect the hunting ritual of kings whose killing of wild bulls ritually secured order for the kingdom.
3. *ANET*, 137.
4. *ANET*, 85. Glyptic art often depicts bull-faced humans struggling with heroes (E. Porada and B. Buchanan, *Corpus of Ancient Near Eastern Seals* [1948], pls. ix-x, nos. 53, 56, 57, 60, pp. xxii-xxvi).

popotamus in Egyptian religion.[1] Beginning as early as the First Dynasty and continuing into the New Kingdom, the motif of the royal hunt of the red hippopotamus is found in texts, grave scenes, and seals. The scenes, well represented in Theban graves from the New Kingdom, and especially the temple of Horus in Edfu, portray an Egyptian King, gigantic in size and armed with a net and harpoon, doing battle with a red hippopotamus. By harpooning the nose the nasal passages are destroyed, and the beast, unable to submerge (cf. Job 40.24), is killed. These grave scenes reenact the mythological struggle between Seth and Horus. Osiris, the father of Horus, is killed by Seth, the god of chaos. When Horus comes to contest the throne of Egypt, Seth takes the form of a red hippopotamus[2] and is harpooned by Horus. With the victorious Horus assuming the throne of Egypt, well-being is guaranteed for the kingdom. The myth was enacted at the time of enthronement. The ritual defeat of the red hippopotamus, symbolizing the historical and mythological forces of chaos threatening the rule of the new king, ensured order and prosperity during his reign.

While the presumed linguistic relation between the word Behemoth and the Egyptian term for hippopotamus has been shown to be false,[3] this Egyptian parallel best explains the meaning of this part of Yahweh's speech. As the Divine Warrior, Yahweh has come to do battle with the mighty creature Behemoth, who symbolizes the powers of chaos (mythical, natural, and historical) resisting divine rule. If Job truly wishes to dethrone Yahweh and rule over the divine council, then he must do battle with this awesome creature, defeating him as an Egyptian king would fight and kill the hippopotamus. This section parallels the previous one in 40.8-14 in which Job is challenged to ascend the divine throne and establish order by defeating the wicked. Finally, God is both the one who does battle with this creature of

---

1. Hans Bonnet, 'Nilpferd', *Reallexikon der Ägyptischen Religionsgeschichte* (Berlin: de Gruyter, 1952), 528-30; G.J. Botterweck, 'בהמה *behemah*', *TDOT* II (1975), 6-20; Keel, *Jahwes Entgegnung an Ijob*, 127ff.; E. Ruprecht, 'Das Nilpferd im Hiobbuch', *VT* 21 (1971), 209-31; and T. Säve-Söderbergh, *On Egyptian Representations of Hippopotamus Hunting as a Religious Motive* (Horae Soederblomianae 3; Uppsala: Gleerup, 1953). Ruprecht's arguments are followed by Kubina, *Die Gottesreden im Buche Hiob*, 69ff., though she insists on two monsters, one representing chaos in the form of wilderness and the other the sea.

2. Seth also is known to take the form of a crocodile (Hans Bonnet, 'Krokodil', *Reallexikon der Ägyptischen Religionsgeschichte*, 392-94).

3. Pope, *Job*, 318; Ruprecht, 'Das Nilpferd', 217-18.

chaos, and the one who is his creator. It may be that this implies divine culpability for the origins of evil, thus paralleling the strongly monotheistic affirmation in Isa. 45.7 that Yahweh 'creates evil'. Seen in this way chaos would be a part of the design of God's creation. In any case Behemoth is a creature whom Yahweh has made and who, in the theopoeic realm of myth and ritual, symbolizes the power of chaos. If Yahweh can defeat such an awesome creature, how much more easily can he deal with the feeble challenge of the mortal Job.

What is particularly disassembling about this section is its *praise* of a mighty creature symbolizing the forces of chaos. In the Old Testament praise not directed towards God was considered idolatrous. Although there is precedent for this in the mythic and heroic traditions of the ancient Near East, the praise of chaos certainly dismisses the Deuteronomic theory of retribution central to the cosmology and ethics of Job's opponents. And the charge of Job that God had perverted the moral world is also shattered by this most unusual hymnic description of the monster. One of the functions of the Behemoth section is not to assert that God wreaks havoc in creation, but that the powers of darkness are mighty and fierce and must be intimidated and confronted to keep the world from entering the realm of oblivion. God praises the mighty enemy to be faced in battle.[1] God limits, but does not eliminate, chaos from reality. In this hymnic praise of Behemoth, then, there is a parallel to the praise of the ten animals who inhabit a world hostile to human existence, almost as stunning to Job, the friends, and conventional faith as this hymn to Behemoth. Indeed Behemoth, not Job as Primal Man, is Lord of the Creatures. He is king in God's creation. Yet the shock of the absurd which destabilizes meaning systems may lead to mimesis. Can Job see this as a new revelation which would allow him to begin to restructure his own language of faith to praise the God who either provides a place for chaos in the world, or is not powerful to remove it from reality? This becomes the fundamental question of the book.

The final section of Yahweh's second speech includes hymnic praise of Leviathan, the monster of the Deep, and the challenge to Job to engage him in combat.

---

1. Cf. the praise of Yam at the beginning of his battle with Baal (*ANET*, 131): 'Yam is firm, he is not bowed; His joints bend not, nor breaks his frame.'

Strophe IV: Fighting Leviathan (40.25-32)

25. Can[1] you draw out Leviathan with a hook, and press down his tongue with a cord?
26. Can you place a rope in his nose, or pierce his jaw with a hook?
27. Will he multiply his supplications to you, or speak to you soft words?
28. Will he cut a covenant with you, will you take him as a servant forever?
29. Will you make sport with him as though he were afraid, or bind him for your girls?
30. Will partners barter for him, will they divide him up among merchants?
31. Can you fill his skin with spears, and his head with a fishing harpon?
32. Lay your hand upon him and think of the battle, you will not do so again!

Strophe V: Opposing Yahweh (41.1-3)

1. Behold one's hope is shown to be false, is one not overwhelmed at the mere sight of him?
2. There is no one so fierce that he should awaken him, and who is he who would dare to stand before me?[2]
3. Who has confronted me that I should make him payment? All under the heavens is mine.

Strophe VI: Leviathan's Frame (41.4-9)

4. I will not keep silent about his limbs, or his strength and the grace of his proportions.
5. Who can strip his outer garment, who can penetrate his double coat of mail?[3]
6. Who dares to open the doors of his face? Terror surrounds his teeth.
7. His back consists of rows of shield, shut up tightly like a seal.
8. They are so close to each other, no air comes between them.
9. They join one to another, each clasps the other and cannot be separated.

Strophe VII: Breath of Fire (41.10-13)

10. His sneezings[4] flash forth light, and his eyes are like the eyelids of the dawn.
11. Torches go forth from his mouth, they escape like sparks of fire.

---

1. Following one Heb. MS which has the interrogative ה.
2. Many Heb. MSS read 'him' for 'me', but the following verse indicates L's reading ('me') is correct.
3. רסן normally means 'halter' (Job 30.11; Isa. 30.28), but it is better taken to mean 'armor' or 'mail' in this context, following the LXX's θώρακος.
4. עטישׁה, occuring only here, appears from the context to point to the exhaling of breath in the fashion of a 'fire-breathing dragon'.

12. Smoke comes forth from his nostrils, as from a boiling pot set upon dry rushes.
13. His breath ignites coals, and a flame burns from his mouth.

Strophe VIII: Intimidation of Gods (41.14-17)

14. Strength resides in his neck, and terror dances before his eyes.
15. His heart is hard as a rock, as hard as a lower millstone.
17. At his rising[1] gods stand back in fear, at his crashings they are awestruck.

Strophe IX: Repelling Weapons (41.18-21)

18. Though the sword may reach him, it has no avail, neither does the spear, the dart and the lance.
19. He considers iron as straw, and bronze as rotting wood.
20. An arrow cannot put him to flight, slingstones become as stubble to him.
21. Clubs are accounted as straw, and he laughs at the casting of javelins.

Strophe X: Home in the Deep (41.22-24)

22. His underparts are sharpened potsherds, he spreads out like a threshing sledge on the mire.
23. He makes the deep boil like a cooking pot, he makes the sea like an ointment pan.
24. He leaves a shining wake behind him, one would think the Deep has a hoary head.

Strophe XI: The Rule of Leviathan (41.25-26)

25. No one upon the earth can rule over him, a creature[2] without fear.
26. He beholds everyone who is haughty, he is king over all the proud beasts.

The most extensive section of this speech is devoted to Leviathan, the monster of the Deep, who represents in the biblical tradition the mythological and historical forces of pre-existent chaos.[3] Dominating both the hymnic characterization of Leviathan and the rhetorical questions is the metaphor of combat. If Job is to replace Yahweh as the head of the divine council, then he must fight against Leviathan in order to become king. Yet the rhetorical questions in the first strophe

---

1. Reading מאשתו with many Heb. MSS for L's משאתו.
2. A number of Heb. MSS have העשיו ('the one made, creature') for L's העשו.
3. I.e. against the argument that Leviathan is a creature, e.g. a crocodile (Fohrer, *Hiob*, 528).

(40.25-32) underscore the inability of the mortal Job to defeat Leviathan in battle. Job cannot take hooks and ropes and capture his awesome opponent, making him beg for his life[1] before forcing him to enter a covenant[2] to be his slave forever.[3] Unlike Yahweh who makes the dreaded monster into a pet (cf. Ps. 104.26), Job cannot play with Leviathan as he would a caged bird or place him on a leash to entertain little girls. Neither can he take the carcass of the freshly-killed monster, and deliver it to merchants to butcher and sell for food.[4] Nor can Job imitate Egyptian kings who harpoon the red hippopotamus that symbolizes Seth and the powers of darkness. Indeed the impotence of Job in standing before Leviathan is made clear in the concluding line: 'Lay your hand upon him and think of the battle, you will not do so again!' By contrast these questions imply that only Yahweh as Divine Warrior has the power to defeat Leviathan.

The fifth strophe turns to the motif of challenging Yahweh to combat. If mortals are terrified at the thought of 'arousing'[5] Leviathan, how much more should they be in daring to stand before the dragon slayer himself. 'To stand before one' often means 'to confront with hostile intent' (see 2 Sam. 22.6, 19 [= Ps. 18.6, 19]; Job 30.7; and Ps. 17.13), and this is the clear meaning in this context. No one, god or mortal, has defeated Yahweh and received tribute. To receive tribute from an enemy brought into submission is an important motif of rule in the Baal Cycle. When the divine assembly yields to Yam's demand for Baal, the gods headed by El cowardly proclaim that the

---

1. See Asherah's intrusion to save her son's life, when Baal stands ready to dispatch the defeated Yam (*ANET*, 131).

2. The reference covenant is one of two strong allusions in this extended section to Gen. 9.1-17 which establishes the sovereignty of humans over the animals and limits the power of the flood by the intimidating symbol of the divine warrior—the drawn bow in the clouds (cf. Job 41.25-26). However, the allusions are not to support P's theology of covenant following the flood, but to repudiate this theology. Leviathan is no ordinary creature, ruled over by humans. Only the threat of the divine warrior keeps the monster in check.

3. Yam's messengers demanded and received from the divine assembly the decision that Baal be given to him as 'slave forever' (*ANET*, 130). Later a defeated Baal sends this message to Mot: 'Be gracious, O Godly Mot; thy slave I, thy bondman for ever' (*ANET*, 138).

4. Psalm 74 speaks of devouring the carcass of Leviathan (v. 14), a theme picked up in later apocalyptic literature (*IV Ezra* 6.49-52 and Bar. 24.4).

5. This same verb (עור) is used in Job 3.8 to speak of incantation priests 'stirring up' Leviathan to destroy creation.

Son of Dagon is to be Sea's tribute.[1] And after Baal's palace is
constructed, signaling his rule over the earth, he announces he will not
send tribute to his nemesis Mot.[2] Yet Yahweh neither shares dominion
with other gods nor has ever yielded to the power of an opponent. By
winning kingship through the defeat of all challengers, including
Leviathan, Yahweh has dominion over all that 'is under heaven'
(41.3). Such a proclamation is made when victorious gods come to
their thrones and inaugurate their rule.[3]

Strophes VI-X hymnically detail the terrible features of Leviathan's
great power,[4] yet graceful build.[5] His frame is likened unto a
warrior's armor, with an impenetrable hide of mail and rows of
shields covering his back.[6] He breathes torches of fire and boiling pots
of oil like those used to incinerate the defenses and flesh of an
opposing army. Weapons of war, whether spears or darts, arrows or
slingstones, clubs or javelins, are of no avail against a monster whose
rising forth from the deep causes even the gods to cower in fear.[7] At
home in the deep, Leviathan makes the primeval ocean boil and foam
from his thrashing about.

The dominion motif recurs at the end of the speech, thereby
emphasizing its strategic importance in the overall theme. Yet clear
interpretation is hindered by a textual problem. In 41.25 the Len-

---

1. *ANET*, 130.

2. *ANET*, 135.

3. Cf. Pss. 47.10 and 95.3-5.

4. נבורות may express a plural of intensity ('mighty power'), but the plural is often
used to refer to the 'mighty deeds' of God: Deut. 3.24; Pss. 20.7; 71.16; 106.2;
145.4, 12; and 150.2. This rather shocking use of hymnic language, normally
expressive of praise of God's great, salvific deeds, tends to disintegrate the structure
of conventional piety, calling on a radical reformulation of the language and structure
of faith.

5. Beauty as well as power is a significant feature of Leviathan's appearance.
While the descriptions of Leviathan in art and language normally picture a terrifying,
horribly ugly monster, Yahweh uncharacteristically glories in the beauty of this divine
being.

6. See the battle dress of Goliath in 1 Sam. 17.5.

7. See the fear of the gods at the threatening approach of Tiamat (Tab. II,
11.84ff., *ANET*, 63-64) and the destructive results of the primeval flood in 'The
Gilgamesh Epic' (Tab. XI, 11.110ff., *ANET*, 94), as well as the cowering of the
divine assembly before the fearsome presence of Yam's messengers (*ANET*, 130).
ANEP, 671, contains a depiction of a god bowing before a monster with seven heads
and shooting flames.

ingrad codex reads הָעֹשׂוֹ, a corruption.[1] However, if the massoretic pointing is changed to הָעֹשׂוֹ the reading would parallel 40.19, 'the one who made him'.[2] Then the subject for v. 26 would be Yahweh, not Leviathan. Thus unlike the other gods and mortals, only Yahweh would stand before Leviathan without fear.[3] If this translation is followed, Yahweh, like Marduk and Baal, is the conqueror of chaos who stands fearlessly before the engagement of battle. And due to his defeat and continuing intimidation of Leviathan, Yahweh is king over the earth, including the 'sons of pride' (שׁחץ), an expression probably referring to the noble and mighty beasts (see 28.8), even those in the first speech who are uncontrolled by humans. Yahweh, not Leviathan or humanity, is 'Lord of the Creatures'.[4] How ludicrous and futile it is for Job to rouse up Leviathan to attempt to defeat Yahweh, much less for Job to think his own feeble efforts would prevail. However, the more likely alternative is to take הָעֹשׂוֹ as הֶעָשׂוּי ('the creature') who is king over the creatures, one so powerful and fearsome that no human could possibly rule over him. In a total deconstruction of the language of covenant in the P narrative (Gen. 9.2) which speaks of the creatures in fear (חת) of humanity chosen to rule over creation, Leviathan is a 'creature without fear' (חת).[5] He, not humanity, is the 'Lord of the Creatures'. He is king over the 'sons of pride', i.e. the wicked who oppose divine rule. This would parallel, then, the same imagery used of Behemoth as King of the Beasts. As mythic creature, Leviathan represents the power of chaos. He, not Job the Primal Man, is king of God's creation.

Thus Yahweh has come as the Divine Warrior to contend with those who oppose divine rule, Job and the ever threatening monsters of chaos. Victory over these opponents, either through actual combat or more likely the intimidating power of presence and language, would win kingship once again for Yahweh who would ascend the throne as

1. *GKC* (no. 75 v) indicates the Qal passive participle has the unusual form עשׂו in Job 41.25.

2. A number of Hebrew MSS add a *yod* at the end (העשׂוי), thus translating 'the creature'.

3. יצב is often used to indicate 'standing without fear' before an enemy: Exod. 14.13; Num. 22.22; and Jer. 46.4.

4. See the the list of references to pieces of glyptic art depicting the theme of the 'Lord of the animals' in Keel, *Jahwes Entgegnung an Ijob*, 86-87.

5. These are only two occurrences of חת ('fear'), indicating an unquestionable reference to this significant text dealing with humanity as the surrogate of divine sovereignty. Time and again the poet has devastated Priestly creation theology.

ruler of the cosmos, that most contested realm in mythological thought. Yet even in the defeat of chaos, the forces of darkness are not forever vanquished; rather they are only restrained. They continue to dwell in regions of wilderness and sea, ever biding their time till they rise up again to challenge the creator of heaven and earth. Yahweh has created an order that sustains life, but it is is maintained only by continual struggle.

The Second Response of Job and The Metaphorical Process: Mimesis. Yahweh's first speech was directed toward the origins and providential governance of creation. The objective of the disputation was to evoke from Job a proper doxology in which he praised God for creating and maintaining the structures of life for all creatures. In a legal setting a doxology could be either a confession of guilt and affirmation of the justness of the verdict rendered or thanksgiving for a judgment of innocence and deliverance. Or in appealing to the divine judge the doxology could be a statement of confidence that justice would be obtained when the decision was made. Since God delivered a disputation in the two speeches, and not a legal decision, a doxology from Job would be not a confession, but rather a statement of confidence in impending divine judgment. Job's initial response, however, was not praise but silence. He cannot and will not utter a new language of faith. There was neither confidence in divine justice nor the generation of a new language. The second speech does lead to Job's attempts at doxology, though some have questioned whether this is authentic praise or a cynical imitation, say in the fashion of 9.5-12 and 12.13-25. Much hinges on the oft-debated translation and interpretation of 42.6.

1. Then Job answered the Lord:
2. I[1] know that you are capable of all things, and that no plan you propose will be impossible for you.
3. 'Who is this who conceals counsel without knowledge?' Therefore I have acknowledged I do not understand, there are divine acts too wonderful for me which I do not know.
4. 'Listen now, and I will speak, I will question you and you inform me.'
5. I have heard you with my own ears, even now my eye beholds you.
6. I reject[2] and am comforted over dust and ashes (42.1-6).[3]

1. Following Q and the versions which have ידעתי ('I') for K's ידעת ('you').
2. On the basis of the LXX (cf. the Qumran Targum), some scholars (e.g. Terrien, 'Job', 1191) read מסס ('to melt, be poured out') for MT מאס ('to despise, reject,

Job's response is generally interpreted as contrite repentance in which he regrets having attacked the justice of God.[1] Yet there is the matter of Job's own integrity. Job has attacked God with powerful language for abusing creation, an attack that has some justification in light of the Prologue. In the Prologue God has killed Job's children, stripped him of all that he possesses, and subjected him to intense suffering. All this occurs 'without cause', i.e. without justification. With a pronounced suspicion about the motivation of Job's righteous piety aroused by the satan's innuendoes, God issues the catastrophic edicts that devastate the servant's very life. Has Job finally abandoned his relentless pursuit of self-vindication? Or is he so intimidated by the fury of threatening power that he buckles the knee before the divine despot? Or is the narrative unrelated to the poetry?

There is also a form-critical consideration. A doxology of confession normally would follow judgment, not precede it. For a writer who often abandons precedent, indeed makes departure an integral feature of deconstruction, a poetic drama unrelated to the narrative could replace judgment with disputation and have doxology follow an implicit condemnation in the divine speeches. This would be a common feature of a most uncommon text. However, as argued earlier, the Prologue provides a necessary context for the poetry, identifying both Job and the three friends and explaining the reason behind the startling lament and series of imprecations contained in ch. 3. It is more likely the poet has taken the older narrative and used it to provide the introduction and conclusion for his own novel work. Read together, the reworking of the old story provides, as we shall see, a new and very different meaning for the tale. Perhaps the best interpretation, then, regards the response of Job as doxology, not one that follows judgment, but rather precedes it. The judgment comes in the first episode of the concluding narrative (42.7-9). Since we are not allowed into the 'black box' of Job's inner thoughts and motives, we

protest'). However, מאס ('to reject') is retained as a transitive verb, having the hendiadys עפר ואפר ('dust and ashes') for a direct object.

3. The lack of agreement regarding the proper rendering of v. 6 is reflected in the early translations. The Qumran Targum translates this last verse: 'Therefore I am poured out and dissolved, and I am become dust and ashes.' The LXX translates: 'Therefore, I hold myself in contempt, and I am melted and consider myself dust and ashes'. The Targum tanslates the second bicolon: 'I am comforted over my children who are dust and ashes'.

1. N. Snaith, *The Book of Job*, 39-43.

are permitted to assess only the content of the response. If the praise is insincere or evoked by frightened intimidation, it would have to be demonstrated by the language.

It seems clear from the content and structure of the response that Job ends the dialogues in the desire to praise.[1] He begins with an affirmation of divine sovereignty: 'I know you are capable of all things, and that no plan you propose will be impossible for you' (42.2). With the prose shortened to adapt to poetic constraints, the second bicolon of this verse quoted Gen. 11.6—'And now no scheme which they propose will be impossible for them'.

Job 42.2b   לא יבצר ממך מזמה
Gen. 11.6   ועתה יבצר מהם כל אשר יזמו לעשות

To abbreviate, the poet has substituted the noun מזמה for the noun clause of Gen. 11.6b. The Niphal of בצר occurs only in these two texts, and in both instances the form is the masculine singular imperfect, preceded by לא. Besides wording, the two sentences are identifical in syntax: the negative לא plus the Niphal, third person, masculine, singular, imperfect verb יבצר followed by מן and an attached object pronoun, and concluding with the subject (noun or clause). Quoting and echoing biblical texts is a common device of the poet: Gen. 4.10-11 (Job 16.18), Ps. 8 (Job 7.17-18); and Jer. 20.14-18 (Job 3).

Even more revealing, however, is the recognition that Gen. 11.1-9 is the concluding episode in J's primeval narrative, and tells of humans, filled with hubris, attempting to reject the sovereignty of Yahweh and the divine council by scaling the heavens and gaining the power to issue edicts determining their own destiny. For J only Yahweh and the divine council may legitimately establish cities, civilizations, and religions. Yahweh recognizes that the building of the city and the tower ascending into the heavens is only the beginning of human efforts at self-rule. Thus judgment is rendered: their languages are multiplied, their ability or will to understand[2] each other is lost, and they are scattered to various regions. Yahweh's judgment limiting human titanism is the dominant theme which shapes the primeval

---

1. Kubina, *Die Gottesreden im Buche Hiob*, 152; Dale Patrick, 'Job's Address of God', *ZAW* 91 (1979), 268-82; Westermann, *The Structure of the Book of Job*, 105-29.

2. See Walter Brueggemann, *Genesis* (Atlanta: John Knox, 1982), 97ff.

narrative in J, beginning with the Fall and concluding with the Tower of Babel episode. For the Joban poet, this quotation of the basis for divine judgment against human attempts at self-rule in the primeval narrative of J brings into full view the issue of divine sovereignty. Only now it is Job, the former disputant of divine sovereignty, who praises the royal power which enables Yahweh to act according to divine caprice.[1] מזמה ('purpose, proposal, scheme') is an ethically neutral term, referring to both righteous purposes (Jer. 23.20; 30.24; 51.11) and evil schemes (Job 21.27; Pss. 10.2, 4; 21.12). Thus, there is no obvious, unequivocal avowal of divine justice in this initial line of Job's response. But it seems this is the case in the poet's quoting from a judgment scene and the typical rendering of judgment in theophanic scenes. The echo of a classic judgment scene in which Yahweh limits the efforts of humans to wrest away divine sovereignty emphasizes that he alone is the unquestionable head of the divine council. Job now begins to praise Yahweh as the divine judge who has both the position and the power to issue decrees governing the fate of human beings. God can defeat both Leviathan and any mortal challenger.

On two occasions in his brief response, Job quotes words of God occurring at the beginning of the two speeches from the whirlwind:

(38.2)	Who is this who darkens counsel by words without knowledge?
(42.3)	Who is this who conceals counsel without knowledge?
(38.3b = 40.7b)	I will question you, and you declare to me.
(42.4b)	I will question you, and you declare to me.

The first quotation is from Yahweh's introduction to the initial speech, while the second repeats a sentence from the introductions of both divine speeches. If the argument that Yahweh has come as Divine Warrior to defeat chaos and render judgment is correct, Job once again quotes words from a judgment context, only in this case it is his own. The first instance is God's accusing question meant to show contempt for the mortal who has dared to question divine justice and to indicate that his verbal assault threatens to destroy the life-enhancing design of creation. The quotation is followed by Job's acknowledgement (הגדתי)[2] that in the first response he did not

---

1. Dhorme, *Job*, 645.
2. נגד means to 'acknowledge, confess' in Ps. 38.19; Isa. 3.9; and 48.6.

understand, i.e. that he could not reconstruct a new language of faith to replace the hermeneutic shattered by the first Yahweh speech. Thus he could only remain silent. Now in the second response, Job admits that he does not know about the 'wondrous things' (נפלאות) Yahweh does in creation and history. He cannot easily articulate a new system of faith. 'Wondrous things' refer to divine actions in history and creation which are redemptive and life-sustaining. The praise of God for these great acts is a typical feature of doxologies (cf. Job 5.9; 9.10). Job admits to having characterized divine actions as destructive and chaotic. With the revelation of Yahweh having deconstructed, at least in part, that formulation of accusing distrust, Job wishes to praise, to discover a language of faith that would begin to recreate the world. For a sage, speech informed by knowledge and understanding shapes and creates a beneficent reality, whereas uninformed language distorts and destroys. Job's knowledgeless rhetoric, charged with accusations, is now replaced with at least the renewal of will to praise God's life-giving actions. But he does not know how. He must be taught a new language.

The second quotation is from the challenge Yahweh issued to Job to answer questions about creation and divine rule. As argued above, the questions are not simply limited to the purpose of demonstrating Job's lack of knowledge, though they do that very well. More importantly many of the questions have answers provided by the tradition of faith: Yahweh is the creator who understands and nurtures what has been made. Job may not possess the power and knowledge to originate and maintain life against the threats of chaos, but Yahweh does. Job's first-hand experience of 'hearing and seeing' Yahweh in the theophany, an idiom emphasizing both the content ('hearing') of the speeches and the event ('seeing') of theophany, leads from indictment, to silence, to the beginnings of reconstruction; and from accusatory lament, to dumbness, to the will to utter hymnic praise. Now he will ask Yahweh for instruction in faith, for the creation of a new hermeneutic which will reorganize the fragments of collapsed meaning. And metaphor, especially that of conflict, will provide the organizing principle. What Job now rejects, at least, is penitential incantations and angry indictment attempting to destabilize the order of creation and the providence of God. Yet what is not rejected is the process of engaging in lament, indictment, and assault which have led him and the implied audience to this point. On the basis of the revelation Job has experi-

enced, he abandons his lament ('I reject [מאס][1] but am comforted over
[נחם על][2] dust and ashes [אפר ועפר]'),[3] and begins the attempt to utter
what his prior experience and dumbness have not allowed.[4] He may
not yet have completely reconstructed that language of faith in which
meaning is found, but he has the components of a new grammar in
which speech may find structure. These components are question,
command, disputation, imperative and praise. And in openness he
awaits the fuller understanding that will come from God's instruction.
This transformation of will unites with confident expectation that the
impending judgment will be a fair and just one. The time for lament
and accusation is at an end, due to Yahweh's revelatory reconstruction

1. מאס is an active, not reflexive, form, and therefore cannot mean 'I despise
myself'. Without a direct object the verb means 'to protest' (Job 7.16; 34.33; and
36.5). With a direct object, as is the case here ('dust and ashes'), the verb means to
'despise' (Amos 5.21; Job 19.18; Prov. 15.32) or 'reject' (Hos. 4.6; 9.17; 1
Sam. 15.23, 26; Jer. 7.29). Kuyper incorrectly argues the direct object must be
supplied, and that is his former arguments attacking God ('The Repentance of Job',
VT 9 [1959], 91-94). The direct object is 'dust and ashes'.
2. The Niphal of נחם followed by the preposition על means 'comforted over' (2
Sam. 13.39; Jer. 16.17; Ezek. 14.22; 32.31), 'have compassion for' (Ps. 90.13),
and 'repent of', but only when followed by the term 'evil' (Jer. 8.6; 18.18; Joel
2.13; Jon. 4.2). Job is not 'repenting in' dust and ashes, but rather is 'comforted' by
the theophany, i.e. he realizes the time for mourning and accusation is at an end. In
the Prologue Job's friends had come 'to comfort him' over the loss of family and
possessions and the agony of his affliction, that is to help him move beyond grief to
praise. But where they had failed, Yahweh succeeds.
3. In Job עפר may mean 'dust' sprinkled upon the head in a lament ritual (Job
2.12), 'mortality/death/the grave' (Job 4.19; 7.5, 21; 10.9), the 'earth' (Job 8.19;
30.6), or 'soil' (Job 22.24; 39.14), while אפר may mean 'ash-heap' (Job 2.8) or
indicate 'worthlessness' (Job 13.12). There are two other occasions in the Bible
when the expression is an example of hendiadys, expressing the idea of
'worthlessness'. In Job 30.19 Job complains that Yahweh has swept him into the
mire, as one cleaning a house would sweep worthless dust and ashes into the street,
while Abraham uses the expression as rhetorical self-abasement in the context of his
challenging and bringing into judgment the justice of God (Gen. 18.27). Questioning
the justice of the decision to destroy Sodom and Gomorrah without seeming to
discriminate between the good and the wicked, Abraham actually brings God into
judgment ('Yahweh stands before him'). Then recognizing the threatening danger of
daring to judge God, Abraham conditions his questioning by admitting that he is but
'dust and ashes', that is, a worthless mortal. Thus Job is either leaving behind the
lament ritual designed to question God and to obtain a hearing from the head of the
divine council, or recognizes he is not a contemptible creature, without worth, or in
the words of Bildad, a 'worm' (25.6). In the context of Job, the former interpretation
seems the more likely.
4. Dale Patrick, 'The Translation of Job LXII 6', *VT* (1976), 369-71.

of theological language, and Job seeks a new hermeneutic, while expecting justice to be done in the final judgment.[1]

4. *The Final Judgment (Job 42)*

The Exoneration of Job and the Redemption of God. With Job's initial efforts to praise God for 'wondrous deeds', and his confidence in imminent vindication by divine judgment, the poetry comes to an end. However, the conclusion of the old narrative (42.7-17) is used by the poet as the proper ending to his new formulation of the story. In following the mythic pattern represented by *Atra-hasis*, the prose ending is necessary, since it contains the verdict of Yahweh and narrates the restoration of Job. Redemption is the final and climatic end of the mythic pattern which internally organizes the stages of dramatic enactment.

The Epilogue contains two narrative sequences: the judgment of Job and the friends (42.7-9), and the restoration of Job (42.10-17). The first scene in the original narrative most probably vindicated Job's heroic refusal to curse or even question God in spite of the likely counsel of the friends to do so. At least this was the advice of the wife. Job's pious acceptance of divine sovereignty at the end of each test has proven his religious and ethical motives are pure and selfless. He does 'fear God for naught' and responds in praise. Job does not worship Yahweh because it pays. Since the middle section of the narrative is replaced with the poetic dialogues, this reconstruction remains hypothetical. But it makes good sense of the fragmented story separated from the poetry. The poet's reworking of the narrative provides a reading that deconstructs the original meaning, but then rebuilds it with a radically different understanding. In 38.1–42.6 Yahweh has come in theophanic judgment to defeat, at least through intimidating presence and language if not actual combat, those who have challenged his rule. And he does so by the language of question, disputation, praise, and command. His discourse results in Job's feeble, though significant, first utterances of doxology and the discontinuance of his indictment of God for divine malfeasance.

---

1. Habel (*Job*, 578) correctly argues the second portion of the response (vv. 4-6) is Job's retraction of his lawsuit: 'therefore I retract and repent of dust and ashes (v. 6)'. Job has already lamented. What occurs is not lament, but doxology which is the next stage after lament is concluded.

Yet through the issuing of divine edict, Yahweh renders judgment, announcing in very surprising terms that Job, not the friends, has spoken 'rightly' about God. In this judgment, Job's integrity is clearly affirmed, and the false charges brought against him by the friends are dismissed. Yet even more striking is the statement that what Job has said about *God* is judged to be correct, while the friends who had defined and then unquestionably affirmed divine justice in retributive categories had spoken 'incorrectly' about God. Indeed it is language about God, not Job's integrity, that is the significant and important basis for judgment. This fact itself moves the direction of the meaning of the book away from the moral theory of retribution. In finding for Job over against the friends, what God does is vindicate Job's stringent questioning of divine justice and deconstruction of the friends' false theology of retribution and unquestionable sovereignty. And also 'correctly' spoken about God is Job's recognition that both of his former constructions of faith, the one of the Prologue in which the sovereignty of God could not allow the possibility of challenge and the one of accusatory indictments and laments in the dialogues which demanded God act according to the Deuteronomic theory of retribution or give up the throne, are incapable of functioning as proper faith language. What is correct is the willingness to begin again the efforts to rebuild the language of faith made inarticulate by anger, pride and inauthentic speech.

But also important is the *act* of judgment which not only vindicates Job, but also rescues divine integrity. According to the theology of the Prologue, Yahweh had greatly wronged the servant. Due to unfounded suspicions raised by 'the satan', God had stripped Job of all honor, killed his children, and afflicted him with great physical suffering. God's sentencing Job to this fate was grossly unjust and brought the universe to the brink of oblivion. These foul deeds even raise questions about Yahweh's power. Has God become weak and corrupt like El, struggling to maintain the right of divine edict at all costs? With this new verdict, Job's integrity is not only affirmed, but the soiled righteousness of God has been rescued. Indeed the actions of the Prologue had threatened to negate even the possibility of new faith language. The God who claims to sustain creation and limit the destructive effects of chaos cannot grind righteous men and women into the dust 'without cause'. Indeed it is the integrity of God, more than Job's, that is rescued by the final judgment. Like Abraham Job has rightly questioned divine justice, deconstructed the inadequate, naïve language of faith formulated by the friends, and moved to re-establish a discourse that makes faith articulate. In this new reading forged by the poet, the demonic God of the prose story has been redeemed. The structure of its meaning has been disassembled and reconstituted into a new and vital shape. Now through the issuance of divine decree, the integrity of Yahweh is regained, the world is ordered, and creation is sustained.

The Metaphorical Process: Transformation and Restabilization. The ending of the story returns to its beginning, thereby completing the mythic pattern concluding in judgment and redemption. After Job's intercession, God restores him to honor among his community, doubles his former wealth, blesses him with seven sons and three daughters whose beauty became legendary, and grants him coveted longevity. With this 'happy ending' Job disappears into his timeless future. Yet the world of the narrative remains, in which the character Job lives between the 'once upon a time' and the 'happily ever after'. Job as character exists in the crises and tensions of the dialogue, eternally moving from despair and angry pathos toward that new creation of justice, faith language, and the redemption of God. For the restoration is actually divine restitution: Job's family, friends, and acquaintances 'showed him sympathy and comforted (נחם) him on account of all the evil Yahweh had brought upon him' (42.11). Job's struggle for justice results in the righteousness of God. Like another patriarch whose narrative journey is captured by the metaphor of conflict, Job has wrestled with God and won. And as Yahweh had contended earlier, it is justice alone that liberates the world from the oblivion of darkness.

PART III

THE RETURN TO NAÏVETÉ AND CONCLUDING SUMMARY

Chapter 9

THE RETURN TO FIRST NAÏVETÉ:
THE SEARCH FOR WISDOM AND THE SPEECHES OF ELIHU

Two insertions in Job represent early efforts to articulate the language of faith required by the theophanic revelation. Disputation, question, praise, and imperative are to comprise the grammar, while the metaphors of creation and anthropology and their mythic patterns should reconstruct the vision of the new hermeneutic. The origins of creation, divine sovereignty, and the place and function of humanity in the world are to provide the content of the new confession.

1. The Wonder of Creation and Human Piety: The Wisdom Hymn
(Job 28)

Introduction. Job 28 is a wisdom hymn consisting of four strophes: vv. 1-6, vv. 7-12, vv. 13-20, and vv. 21-28.[1] Its theme is captured in the refrain: 'Where shall wisdom be found, and where is the place of insight?' (vv. 12, 20).

Strophe I (vv. 1-6)

1. For there is a mine for silver, and a place where gold is refined.
2. Iron is taken from the earth, and copper is melted for ore.
3. Humanity puts an end to darkness, and searches every hidden recess for ore in dark and gloomy places.
4. They open shafts where there are no inhabitants, places untrod by the foot of humans, bereft of the presence of people who wander about.
5. The earth—from it comes bread, but below it is transformed by fire.

---

1. Its wisdom character is seen in its content and formal structure which expands a riddle found in the refrain in vv. 12 and 20 and answered in v. 23 (Westermann, *The Structure of the Book of Job*, 136). For an analysis of the expansion of wisdom sayings in the structure of wisdom poems and psalms, see my *Wisdom and Cult*, 261-343.

6. It is a place for lapis lazuli embedded in its stones, while its particles of dust contain gold.

Strophe II (vv. 7-12)

7. That path is unknown by the bird of prey, and unseen by the falcon's eye.
8. The proud beasts have not trodden it, nor has the lion passed over it.
9. Humans put their hands to the flint, they overturn mountains at their base.
10. They cut channels in the rocks, and everything precious their eyes have seen.
11. They probe the sources of rivers, and each secret they bring to light.
12. But where shall wisdom be found, and where is the place of insight?

Strophe III (vv. 13-20)

13. Humans do not know her value,[1] and she cannot be found in the land of the living.
14. The Abyss says, 'She is not in me', and Yam says, 'She is not with me.'
15. Gold cannot be given for it, nor can silver be weighed out for her price.
16. She cannot be valued in the Gold of Ophir, in precious onyx or lapis lazuli.
17. Gold and glass do not equal her value, nor can vessels of fine gold be exchanged for her.
18. Corals and crystal need not be mentioned, Wisdom's price is above that of pearls.
19. Topaz from Ethiopia does not equal her value, she cannot be valued in pure gold.
20. Yet from where does Wisdom come, and where is the place of insight?

Strophe IV (vv. 21-28)

21. She is hidden from the eyes of all living, and concealed from the birds of heaven.
22. Abaddon and Death say: 'We have heard a rumor of her.'
23. God perceives her way, and knows her place.
24. For he looks to the ends of the earth, he observes all things under the heavens.
25. When he allotted weight to the wind, and meted out water by measure.
26. When he made an ordinance for the rain, and a way for the thunderbolt.
27. Then he saw her and described her, he established her, and searched her out.

---

1. 'Value' is the suggested translation for ערך (cf. 2 Kgs 23.35; Ps. 55.14). The LXX reads 'her way' (ὀδὸν αὐτῆς = דרכה).

28. Then he said to Adam, 'Behold the fear of the Lord[1] is wisdom, and to turn from evil is insight'.

Metaphor and Creation. The language of this hymn is shaped by the crafting and word metaphors for creation. In the final strophe (vv. 21-28), the role of divine providence is briefly mentioned as God is praised for having the capacity to observe all things throughout the creation.[2] Unlike Yahweh in the Prologue who is dependent on the satan for information about the inhabited world, God in this hymn has an all-seeing eye. Indeed it is this omniscience that enables the ruler of the world to see and know the path to Wisdom's door. Unlike humans who search in vain for Wisdom, the richest of all gifts, God knows her place. For the sages, Wisdom is valued above all else, for she possesses and bestows the treasures of knowledge and rule (Prov. 8.12-21). She holds in her hands life, wealth and honor (Prov. 3.15-18).

And Wisdom is the mediator between God and the world, revealing both the creator and the order of creation. Through Wisdom one comes to a knowledge of the world and God, experiences the beneficence of life, and exists in harmony with order in nature and society. The sources for these descriptions of Wisdom are ultimately mythological, for she is personified as a goddess of insight and life in much the fashion of Maat or Isis in Egypt.[3]

For the traditional sages Wisdom is not only accessible to humans, but indeed goes in search of them, even to the highways and cities where they may be found (Prov. 1.20-21; 8.1-3). And as a goddess initiating her cult, she sends out her maidens to invite the unlearned to her banquet (Prov. 9.1-6). This personification of Wisdom as a goddess is continued here in Job 28, yet now she no longer seeks humans as her lovers, but hides in secret from their desire. Only God knows where she resides.

Indeed God has known her intimately since the beginnings of the world. As the final strophe continues, the Creator is praised as the

1. Many Heb. MSS have יהוה ('the LORD') for L's אדוני (Adonay).
2. 'The ends of the earth' is a common expression for all creation (Deut. 28.49; Ps. 19.5, 7; Prov. 17.24; Isa. 5.26; 42.10; 43.6; 49.6).
3. See W.F. Albright, 'The Goddess of Life and Wisdom', *AJSLL* 36 (1919/20), 258-94; Christa Bauer-Kayatz, *Studien zu Proverbien 1–9* (WMANT 22; Neukirchen: Neukirchener Verlag, 1966); and Helmer Ringgren, *Word and Wisdom* (Lund: Hakan Ohlssons Boktryckeri, 1947). B. Lang gives an overview of identifications of Woman Wisdom in *Frau Weisheit*. He draws the conclusion that she is portrayed in Proverbs primarily as a teacher.

architect who gave the wind its weight and the waters their measure, two primal elements of nature which constitute the substance and power of a large portion of reality. And as divine judge, God decreed the destiny for rain and lightning, elements which along with water and wind evoke especially the imagery of cosmology. Thus the cosmos is an ordered and elegant structure, not threatened by the attacks of chaos. It was at this time of beginnings that God, much like Ptah, 'envisioned' (ראה) Wisdom in his mind and spoke (literally, 'described, narrated') her into existence. God then 'established' her (כון), a hiphil verb which in creation texts refers to the securing of the world (Jer. 10.12), the cosmic mountains (Ps. 65.7) and the Heavens (Prov. 8.27). Following this direction, the reference would be to God's anchoring of wisdom in the cosmos, say in the manner of Maat in Egyptian mythology forming the stable basis for the created order. However, the verb is also used to speak of the establishing of a king on the throne (2 Sam. 5.12; 1 Kgs 2.24), an image in line with the regal position of Woman Wisdom in Proverbs 8. Cosmological wisdom reigns as Queen on her throne dispensing her gifts to those who find her. And finally God 'searched her out (הקר)', a verb pointing to the act of thorough examination of a subject (Job 5.27; Prov. 25.2) or human being (Ps. 139.1), leading to knowledge of even the most secret thoughts and desires. Only God knows Woman Wisdom intimately.

Finally, as judge in primordial times, God issues the command to the Primal Man (*'adam*), giving him and all humans the directive for life:

Behold the fear of the Lord is wisdom, and to turn from evil is insight.

Normally this concluding verse is regarded as either a later pious addition,[1] or a total abandonment of the futile quest for wisdom. A better interpretation, however, is to see piety and ethics as the means to acquire wisdom and its gifts. Since Yahweh originated and knows wisdom, it may come to mortals not through human quest, but through divine gift. As is often heard in the tradition, the 'fear of the Lord' is the 'beginning', but also the 'first' and 'best' (ראשׁית) of wisdom (Prov. 1.7). The 'fear of the Lord' points to the humble acknowledgment of the sovereignty of God as creator and ruler of creation. 'Turning from evil' is an expression for ethics, an apt phrase for

1. Fohrer, *Hiob*, 392; Pope, *Job*, 206.

avoiding actions that pervert the righteous order of creation and lead to ruin for individual, community and world. Indeed Job 28 is a hymnic incorporation of the central tenet of sapiential faith: 'the fear of God is the beginning of wisdom'.

The Human Task in the World. While the words 'ruler' and 'slave' are not present in Job 28, it is clear that this poet's anthropology is derived from the interaction of these metaphors, not in terms of origins and nature, but in regard to humanity's being in the world. The first three strophes point to the futility of the humanity, in the guise of the Primal Man, to discover wisdom. In their lustful search for the hidden treasures of the earth, humans sink deep shafts into the earth, while their efforts to exploit its resources lead to the leveling of mountains and the damming of streams. Even the dark recesses of the underworld and the distant deserts where no human dwells are regions of chaos unprotected from human desire for treasure. What is particularly striking about the language in vv. 9-11 is its echoing of literary images of theophanic destruction of the earth (9.5-10) and divine actions against chaos. Thus humans 'overturn' (הפך) mountains, even as El does in his destructive rage against creation (9.5). They create channels for water by 'cleaving' (בקע) rocks in half even as the creator–redeemer split Yam in half in primeval times and at the Red Sea (Exod. 14.16; Neh. 9.11; Pss. 74.15; 78.13). Mortals also 'bring forth earth's hidden things', even as God 'uncovers the deeps from the darkness and brings to light deep darkness' (12.22). And humans dam up the rivers, blocking their flow, perhaps in imitation of the restraining of chaos and its waters by Marduk and Yahweh. Entering the sources of the waters humans even approach the forbidden and secret watery world of El.[1] But in their lust for treasure, humans seek to obtain divine wisdom, the greatest wealth of all, but to no avail. Similar to another depiction of hubris leading to fall the king of Tyre corrupted his wisdom in the pursuit of wealth, becoming so proud that he attempted to take the throne of El (Ezekiel 28). Yet for Job 28 that which is most valuable of all, Wisdom and her gifts of life and well-being, remain hidden from all human grasping. Far more valuable than jewels or gold, humans would give all and risk everything to possess her. What this poem presents in hymnic form is the mythic quest

---

1. Pope, *Job*, 203. Cf. *CTA* 4 iv, 20-24. Pope translates v. 11a: 'The sources of the rivers he probes.'

of the hero for the wisdom of the gods, a theme in more familiar guise in Genesis 3 and Ezekiel 28.

What then are humans to do? Are they condemned to repeat forever the folly of their grasping for what is unattainable? Is the world an unfathomable mystery which defies human understanding? For the poet of Job 28 God gives definition to life in teaching Adam, the Primal Man, the first and all of human creatures: 'the fear of the Lord is wisdom, and to turn from evil is insight'. Gift, not grasping, is the way to wisdom. Yet the accepting of the gift of wisdom, which not only comes by means of but is piety and ethics, requires the renunciation of human hubris and efforts at self-deification and rule. Woman Wisdom comes only to the one who acknowledges the rule of God. Read in this way, Job returns to the posture of the Prologue, 'fearing God and turning from evil' (1.1).[1] Job becomes the unquestioning, obedient 'slave' of God.

The Return to First Naïveté. The new hermeneutic set forth in Job 28 does use some of the grammar of faith: question and praise. And the language of the hymn incorporates form, metaphors, and content from the other sections of the book, including the theophanic speeches. However, what is missing brings into serious question the validity of this expression for the new structure of belief. Conflict in either the metaphor of battle with the monster or the disputation is absent. As the Yahweh speeches demonstrate, even hymns may include the metaphor of conflict (Behemoth and Leviathan). The intensity of struggle and the authentic questioning of radical faith are not present. Regardless of its redactional positioning in the book of Job, the hermeneutic of Job 28 leads to no revelation, produces no theophanic vision, and structures no alluring mythic world into which humans may enter. It attempts to return to a simpler, precritical faith yet unchallenged by the crisis of holocaust. While elegantly crafted, it still represents the naïve stance of Job in the Prologue and of the friends in the Dialogues: wisdom is unquestioning piety and obedience to divine commands.

---

1. Cf. Job 1.8; 2.3; Prov. 3.7; 14.16; 16.16.

2. *The Sovereignty of God and Human Slavery:*
The Speeches of Elihu (Job 32–37)

Introduction. The second effort to structure a new hermeneutic that would engage the imagination and provide a new myth for living in the world is contained in the four disputations of Elihu, placed in chapters 32–37. Opened by a brief narrative introduction in 32.1-5, the Elihu intrusion consists of four lengthy disputations: 32.6–33.33; 34.1-37, 35.1-16, and 36.1–37.24.[1] The narrative setting explains Elihu's unexpected interruption as due to Job's self-justification and the friends' inability to answer Job's charges and questions. Indeed the friends had even declared God was guilty.[2] Creation language figures prominently in the first, second, and especially fourth disputations. The first two draw on the anthropological tradition, while the cosmological tradition is at the center of the last speech.

The Metaphors of Word and Artistry. In the midst of attempting to justify his right to speak, Elihu broaches the topic of authority. While admitting he is young and not equal in age to Job and the friends, Elihu argues against the tradition's affirmation that wisdom is a characteristic of those advanced in age. Instead he submits in 32.8:

> But it is the spirit (רוח) in a person, the breath (נשמה) of the Almighty that makes him understand.

In formulating a rather unique theory of inspiration, Elihu draws on the tradition of the creation of humanity that presents God as the artisan who shapes the clay into human form and breathes into the nostrils the 'breath' (נשמה) of life (Gen. 2.7; 7.22; and Job 27.3; 33.4; 34.14). The parallel term, 'spirit' (רוח), also includes among its meanings the 'animating breath' of God (Gen. 6.17; 7.15, 22; Isa. 42.5; Zech. 12.1; Ezek. 37.5, 6, 8, 10, 14; Qoh. 3.19). Yet it is this vital principle of life originating with God and existing in all humans that Elihu considers the source of inspiration.[3] He takes this general 'vital principle', this 'breath of Shaddai', and makes it a prophetic charisma

---

1. Murphy, *Wisdom Literature*, 40-42.

2. In a rare example of *tiqqune sopherim* ('corrections of the scribes') a copyist changed 'they declared God guilty' to 'they declared Job guilty'. The present book does not contain such a startling declaration, though speculation based on silence might suggest that some such conclusion was reached in the now disturbed end of the third cycle.

3. See Habel, *Job*, 450-51.

(cf. Num. 11.26-30).[1] Eliphaz had claimed a type of prophetic vision in attempting to legitimate his own teaching in Job 4.12-17, a claim continued by Ben Sirah. The implication is that all humans, possessing the breath of God, are inspired.

Thus, Elihu rejects the traditional affirmation that the ideal sage, whose head is hoary and back is bent, is the source of wisdom, not the young person who has yet to experience life fully and to study and learn. Wisdom is neither the special prerogative of the sages nor gained through study, but rather is the universal possession of humans in whom the spirit of God dwells. Elihu even sees the inability of Job and the friends to find a solution to the problem of divine justice and the suffering of the innocent as evidence of the failure of traditional wisdom in the schools. Elihu's anthropology becomes both a radical rejection of sapiential tradition, and a claim that all humans possess the innate power to create mythic worlds through words. Wisdom, spirit, and words create and maintain the world. Using then this innate power, Elihu can no longer restrain himself, but must speak creative words of truth fashioning a new mythical reality.

In Job 32.21-22 Elihu combines this argument of inspiration with the recognition of responsibility to his 'creator' to speak words of truth uncorrupted by flattery:

> Let me not show respect of persons, or attempt to flatter any person.
> For if I knew how to flatter, my creator would destroy me.

Flattery and deference to persons because of social status are two breaches of sapiential ethics which are grounded in creation theology.[2] Flattery is one type of improper, deceptive, even chaotic language which destroys the order of 'righteousness' permeating both creation and social constructions of reality. Showing deference, especially to the wealthy and powerful, not only violates Israelite law, but also the sapiential formulation of the anthropological tradition.

Yet Elihu adds one further motivation to his self-directed admonition: the doctrine of retribution. In a word-play on the Hebrew word 'lift up' (נשא), Elihu will not 'show respect to persons' (literally, 'lift up a person's face'), lest the creator destroy him (literally, 'lift him up'). As God shapes and breathes into a person a vital spirit which is the source of inspiration and authentic language, so the creator

---

1. Robert Wilson, *Prophecy and Society in Ancient Israel* (Philadelphia: Fortress 1980), 135ff.
2. Prov. 2.16ff.; 7.21; and 22.2.

destroys those who mis-speak: in this case, those who distort truth and order with words of flattery.

A third instance of creation theology in this initial speech which draws on the anthropological tradition occurs in 33.4-6.

> 4. The spirit of God has made me, and the breath of Shaddai has given me life.
>
> 5. If you are able, answer me, set before me your reasoned argument.
>
> 6. Behold, my mouth is like your own before God, I too was formed from the clay.[1]

This text continues the populist case for authentic wisdom. Elihu uses the creation of humanity tradition to emphasize that both Job and he are mortals, animated by the same breath of God, which is the true source of inspiration. Unlike God, whose presence so intimidates that human lips become frozen, and words cannot be uttered, Elihu confesses he is a mere mortal who will speak words of truth to which Job should respond, if he can.

Elihu concludes his case for universal inspiration in 33.12-33 when he uses the argument of Eliphaz that God warns people of the destructive results of sin. In dreams and visions of the night, common prophetic imagery for inspiration, God warns the wicked of their misdeeds in order to keep them from death. Properly warned, they may seek out a heavenly mediator from the divine council who will intercede on their behalf when petition is made. In this fashion the sinner may gain divine forgiveness and redemption. Yet the strong populist claim for inspiration does not depend entirely on charismatic experiences and the indwelling of the divine spirit. In line with conventional wisdom, God also instructs through nature, if people will only listen and learn (34.10-11).

In the second speech, Elihu responds to Job's attack on divine justice. And in his defense of God, the metaphor of word (breath) once again comes into play (34.14-15). This text makes use of the common theme of God's breath which animates all creation. In supporting the complete and radical sovereignty of God, Elihu emphasizes

----

1. Among others, Pope (*Job*, 248), Dhorme (*Job*, 448-89) and Gordis (*Job*, 372) point to the use of the Mesopotamian creation of humanity tradition at this point, specifically the image of 'formed' (קרץ=Akkad. *iktaris*) from clay ('Gilgamesh', *ANET*, 74). Also see *CTA* 16 v, 29 where *qrs* means to 'create' from clay; and the 'The Instruction of Amenemopet', XXV, II. 3-4. (*ANET*, 424): 'For man is clay and straw, And the god is his builder.'

not only that all life is due to divine gift, but that creation hangs precariously by the thread of divine pleasure. Should God withdraw his animating spirit for any reason, all life would end, and humans would return to dust. Here Elihu alludes several classical creation texts.[1]

Ps. 104.29bc
Should you gather their breath,
   they will expire,
and to their dust they shall return

חסף רוחם יגועון
ואל עפרם ישבון

Exod. 7.21 (P)
And all flesh expired. . .

ויגוע כל בשר

Gen. 3.19 (J)[2]
. . . to dust you shall return

אל עפר תשוב

Job 34.14b-15
Should he gather to himself his
   spirit, and his breath
all flesh will expire together,
and humanity will return unto
   dust

רוחו תשמרו אליו יאסף
יגוע כל בשר יחד

ואדם על־עפר ישוב

And yet the context for Psalm 104 and even J's fall narrative is very different from P's flood narrative and Elihu's portrayal. Psalm 104 tells of God's gift of life and gracious, providential care for all creation. Along with birth, death is a part of the natural cycle. Even in Genesis 3 the Yahwist incorporates the promise of victory over evil (3.15) in the midst of tragic alienation and the judgment of death. And grace is extended to the primordial pair by allowing them to live long lives and procreate.

However, P's flood narrative depicts the destruction of humanity as due to collective sin, and the salvation of Noah is due to human merit, not divine grace as in the J document. Elihu, following the priestly narration of the flood, describes the radical sovereignty of God who acts according to the theory of divine retribution, making life dependent on moral behavior. Grace and providential care in Psalm 104 are

---

1. The mythic theme of the divine judgment to end all life may be at the basis of Elihu's use of this metaphor. See the flood narrative in Genesis 6–9 and especially Gen. 7.21-23.
2. See Qoh. 12.7.

replaced by retributive justice which puts all life in a most precarious and threatened position. Elihu's understanding of justice is the same retributive theory of the friends. Gracious and sustaining providence presented in the metaphor of the breath of God has been corrupted by a theology of retributive terror.[1]

The Attempt to Reclaim the Royal Metaphor. Elihu returns to his populist tradition and defends divine rule by asserting that God shows no deference to the powerful and wealthy (34.17-20).

> 17. Shall one who hates justice govern, or would you condemn one who is just and mighty?
> 18. Who says[2] to a king, 'Worthless one', and to princes, 'Guilty'.
> 19. Who does not show deference to princes, and does not favor nobles over the poor, because they are the work of his hands.
> 20. In a moment they die, at midnight, people are convulsed and they pass away, the mighty[3] are taken away, but not by a human hand.

Once again Elihu draws on the anthropological tradition of the craftsman God to emphasize that both rich and poor, powerful and weak, are the work of God's hands. Even kings and princes are 'worthless' and 'wicked' sinners whose lives are ended suddenly, without appeal. And in an echo of the tenth plague (Exod. 12.4-5), Elihu exemplifies how the sovereign God may end human lives, great and small, 'at midnight'. The same dark view of human nature, articulated by the friends, is reasserted by Elihu (see 34.21-30). No one is worthy in the sight of a righteous God. How dare Job expect his day in court and attempt to bring God to trial. God destroys the mighty without any judicial enquiry (34.24), and who is to say that he cannot. Even the cries of the oppressed are not heard by God, since they have their origins in the deceitful pride common to human nature.

The royal imagery used by Elihu does appear to reflect social categories. Kings are especially those who experience the wrath of a righteous God. And the social character of the Elihu speeches reflects a type of populist wisdom which has strong parallels with the anti-monarchial tendencies of the Deuteronomic school. Kings are

---

1. Job uses similar language in 12.10 ('In his hand is the life of every living creature, and the breath of humanity'), but in order to indict God's misrule, not to legitimate divine justice.

2. Reading the one Heb. MS, LXX, S and V: 'the one who says'.

3. Following one Heb. MS which reads the plural for 'mighty' over against L's singular.

responsible for the difficulties of the people, oppress the poor and righteous, and turn away from God. Therefore they are the sure and certain victims of divine wrath. Yet the question is why this bitter tirade against kings is addressed to Job. It seems clear that the poet responsible for the Elihu speeches regards Job as a royal figure, at least on a mythic level, and therefore is deserving of his misfortune. Job fits the mythic pattern of the wicked king who has been deposed and brought to utter ruin by a righteous God. The Elihu speeches recognize that in the poetic dialogues Job takes on the aura of the Primal Man who seeks the throne of God.

Elihu has attempted to construct a populist metaphor of the 'common person' in whom the revelatory spirit of God dwells.[1] The poor and weak are as much the creation of God as the great and powerful. And yet even the victims of royal oppression who cry out to God are corrupted by pride and evil. They are not delivered because of their own perversion. Elihu does not fashion the dark view of the friends who regarded humans as possessing a corrupt nature. Nevertheless, for Elihu even the weak and poor, and much more the powerful rulers, are prone to evil deeds. In a poem (36.5-12) praising God's retributive justice, Elihu uses the metaphors of king and slave to describe the righteous.

5. Behold God is powerful, but does not despise, he is powerful and mighty in heart.
6. He does not sustain the life of the wicked, but justice he gives to the opressed.
7. He does not withdraw his eyes from the righteous, but enthrones them with kings,
8. And if they are imprisoned in fetters,
   Captured by cords of affliction,
9. Then he will reveal to them their work, and their transgressions, that they have become arrogant.
10. He opens their ear to discipline, and tells them they should turn from evil.

---

1. A populist wisdom tradition developed at approximately the same time in Egypt and is represented by the Papyrus Insinger (P.A.A. Boeser, *Transkription und Übersetzung des Papyrus Insinger* [Oudheidkundige Medeelingen 3; Uit 'Srijksmuseum van Oudheden Te Leiden, 1922]; cf. Aksel Volten, *Das Demotische Weisheitsbuch* [Kopenhagen: Einar Munksgaard, 1941]); and Onchsheshonq (S.R.K. Glanville, *Catalogue of Demotic Papyri in the British Museum* II. 'The Instructions of "Onchsheshonqy"', London: The British Museum, 1955).

11. If they are obedient and subservient, they will complete their days in well-being, and their years in delight.
12. And if they are not obedient, they will perish by the sword, and they will expire without knowledge.

Using the imagery of the enthronement of human kings (cf. 1 Kgs 1.32-40; Job 40.10-14; Pss. 2 and 110; cf. Ps. 8 and Gen. 1), Elihu describes God's exaltation (גבה) of the oppressed righteous to sit on royal thrones forever.[1] And as kings they will enjoy the 'well-being' (טוב)[2] and 'delightful things' (נעימים)[3] of life. Yet by contrast, the imagery of imprisonment and slavery is used to describe those who are chained by sin, specifically the sin of hubris (יתגבר).[4] Once again the myth of the fall is formulated. Elihu draws on the tradition in which kings and lower gods, filled with hubris, attempt to assault the throne of God, and fall to their destruction (Isa. 14, Ezek. 28). Even so, for Elihu there is hope for rebels, including Job, if they listen to divine instruction, repent, and submit as slaves to serve (עבד) the divine sovereign. They then will join with the righteous and experience well-being and prosperity. This poem retells the myth of the fall, offering the hope of redemption only through submission as obedient slaves to divine sovereignty. Exaltation to kingship entails total, unquestioning submission to the divine Lord. The alternative is imprisonment and death. This formulation of the royal metaphor reflects the Mesopotamian royal tradition in which kings are the slaves of God. And for Elihu, even exaltation of the righteous to the thrones of kings does not entail ruling as surrogates over divine creation. Instead God is the mighty sovereign to whom all creation must and does submit.

The Language of Doxology. Following an exhortation to praise God, Elihu offers to Job a doxology that he should sing, not as one who expects to be declared righteous, but as one who is guilty and hopes for the mercy of the court.

---

1. See von Rad, 'Royal Ritual in Judah', *The Problem of the Hexateuch and Other Essays* (New York: McGraw–Hill, 1966), 222-31.
2. See Ps. 34.13, a wisdom psalm; and Qoh. 2.3.
3. 'Delightful things' may refer to wealth (Prov. 24.4), beauty (Song of Songs 1.16), amicable relations between brothers (Ps. 133.1), and spiritual joy (Ps. 16.6, 11). In this context the term probably designates prosperity.
4. See Job 15.25.

Exhortation (36.22-25)

22. Behold God is exalted in his power, who is the teacher like him?
23. Who appoints for him his way, who will say to him you have acted wickedly?
24. Remember to extol his creative action, about which all humans have sung.
25. All humans have gazed upon it, humankind has observed it from afar.

Strophe I (36.26-33)

26. Behold, God is great, and we do not know him, the number of his years are unsearchable.
27. For he draws up the drops of water, they distill his mist as rain.
28. The clouds pour down, they shower upon humanity in abundance.
29. Can anyone understand the spreading of clouds, the devastating noise of his pavilion?
30. Behold he scatters his lightning about him, and he covers the roots of the sea.
31. Because by them he judges the people, he gives food in abundance.
32. He covers his hands with lightning, and commands it to strike.
33. Its crashing announces concerning him, and the storm is his jealous anger.[1]

Strophe II (37.1-13)

1. My heart trembles at this, and leaps from its place.
2. Listen intently to the shaking of his voice, for rumbling goes forth from his mouth.
3. He releases it under all the heavens, and his lightning unto the corners of the earth.
4. After it his voice roars, he thunders with his majestic voice. He does not restrain them, when his voice is heard.
5. God thunders wondrously with his voice, he does great things we cannot know.
6. He says to the snow fall to the earth, and to the shower and the rain[2] be strong.[3]
7. By power he seals up every person, so that all people whom he has made may know it.
8. The wild beast goes into its lair, and dwells in its dens.
9. From the chamber comes the whirlwind, and cold from scattering winds.

---

1. Changing מקנה ('cattle') to קנאה ('anger'), and עולה ('going up, ascending') as עלעולה ('storm'). See Gordis (*Job*, 422-424) for a full discussion.
2. Reading 'rain shower' and 'shower of rains' as a dittography for 'the shower and the rain'.
3. Reading עזו ('his strength') as עזז ('be strong').

10. Ice is given by the breath of God, and the expanse of waters becomes solid.
11. He loads the thick cloud with moisture, the cloud scatters his lightning.
12. It turns round and round at his direction, to do all which he commands them, on the face of the inhabited world.
13. Whether for the rod, or for his creation, or for love, he makes it happen.

Elihu's fashioning of the hermeneutic of faith and praise selectively draws features from the Yahweh speeches, especially the first one. What is presented is a storm theophany in which the imagery of rain, thunder, and lightning describe the terrifying judgments of El before whom humans and wild creatures cringe in fear. And God sends the rain to sustain human life. Unlike Yahweh in the theophany who sent rain on the wilderness when there was no Adam, God in this hymn uses rain as a means of retribution: the rains 'shower upon humanity (אדם) in abundance'. Yet what is missing in this hymn of praise are two features fundamental to the Yahweh speeches: the conflict metaphor and revelatory word. Due to Elihu's insistence on the radical sovereignty of God there is no possibility that chaos looms in the background to challenge divine rule. Unlike theophanic texts, God has not come to defeat the new mythic or historic threats against divine rule and the order of creation. Further, there is no revelation, no intelligible voice from the whirlwind. Yahweh's voice (קול) is only the deafening roar of crashing thunder (cf. Psalm 29). God pronounces judgment in a cloud of total secrecy. In language very much like that of Qoh. 9.1, God's commands direct the cosmos, whether for discipline, for the creation, or for love, one may not know. Using the image of a gigantic hand (יד) which encloses humanity in its grip, Elihu emphasizes all people are sealed in mystery by divine power. Job's insistence on a trial in which he may confront his creator is sheer folly. But is there anything actually new in this doxology? It has surely been sung by the friends. Even Bildad had spoken of theomachy and the battle against chaos in the beginning (25.1-6; 26.5-14).

Strophe III (37.14-24)

14. Give ear to this, O Job, stand and consider the wonderful works of God.
15. Do you know how God has ordered them, and causes the lightning of his cloud to shine?
16. Do you know the swayings of the clouds, the wonderful deeds of one perfect in knowledge?
17. You whose garments are hot, when the earth is silent from the south.

18. Can you spread out the clouds like him, we cannot draw up our case because of darkness.
19. Make me know what we shall say to him, we cannot draw up our case because of darkness.
20. Shall it be told to him that I should speak, has a person ever wished to be swallowed up?
21. And now people cannot see the light, it is bright in the clouds, when the wind has passed and cleared them away.
22. From the north the golden hue approaches, around God is terrible majesty.
23. Shaddai, we can not find him, he is great in strength, justice and great righteousness he will not violate.
24. Therefore people fear him, he does not regard all those who are wise in heart.

Elihu concludes with a series of questions concerning the rule of God, questions which have mainly been taken from the speeches of Yahweh. Yet the intent of these questions for Elihu is significantly different from that of the Voice of the Whirlwind. In the Yahweh speeches the questions were designed not to evoke subdued silence or even repentance, but to elicit the confession that God rules the cosmos in justice. And the Yahweh questions were designed to shock Job out of a distorted anthropocentrism wherein divine actions are only properly just when used to aid human life and rule over creation. Yahweh is the 'Lord of the Creatures', including those beasts which are harmful to humanity. The intent of Yahweh's questions was not merely to oppose an inauthentic faith rooted in retribution, but also to enable Job to begin to address God anew, to recreate a language of faith in which humanity may speak to God. But Elihu's questions are designed to contrast the magnificent power and wisdom of God with the weakness and ignorance of the mortal Job. Properly humiliated, Job should respond to God not in language, but in silence. Enshrouded in chaotic darkness and terrified of the awesome God, Elihu's own lips are sealed. He dare not speak to God. His new hermeneutic which he initially boasted would take shape through divine inspiration now collapses.

3. *The Metaphorical Process: Dead Metaphors and Sterile Faith*

Neither the Wisdom Hymn (ch. 28) nor the Elihu intrusion (32–37) succeeds in fashioning a new construction that brings together the components of grammar (disputation, question, imperative, and praise) in a compelling vision. Job 28 selects the cosmological metaphor of the craftsman God who created the world in beauty and order, yet has purposefully hidden the key to its understanding, Woman Wisdom, from human view. The anthropological metaphor that dominates the poem is the hubris-filled king: humanity assumes divine characteristics in the attempts to find Woman Wisdom, the key to understanding and self-rule. Humans search for wisdom in the earth, Sheol, and the heavens. Yet these titanic efforts are to no avail, for Wisdom remains beyond human reach and is known only to God. The contrasting and legitimized human metaphor is that of slave, present in the concluding revelation of God to humanity in v. 28: piety and morality defined in terms of human actions are true 'wisdom'.

The mythic pattern, grounded in the metaphor of the proud king, is that of Eliphaz in Job 15 (cf. Gen. 3 and Ezek. 28): hubris leads to the search for divine wisdom, but results in failure. The only proper recourse is humble submission before the divine artist who has created an elegant and ordered world in which life is possible. Job 28 is a poetic redescription of the myth of the Fall. Yet, as the poet of the dialogues has demonstrated, this is a construction which fragments in the crisis of holocaust. The metaphorical process is one that leads to mimesis and transformation of vision, by turning from the royal metaphor of earlier wisdom, to that of the slave who abandons the efforts to master life and to rule as divinely appointed sovereigns over the earth. It marks the turn in wisdom circles from an optimistic view of human being in the world to one of pessimistic limits ascribed to human nature and function. The sage is one who bows the knee before the sovereign Lord of creation.

Elihu also presents metaphors of humanity and creation in his four lengthy speeches. He attempts to reclaim the royal metaphor by speaking of humanity as specially crafted by God to have the divine spirit which provides inspired knowledge. And he grants the possibility of the exaltation of the oppressed to rule as kings in God's world. Yet this is no optimistic tradition of earlier wisdom recast by a later hand. For Elihu also speaks of the corruption of human nature and the wrathful threat of divine destruction which looms ever large and ominous. Indeed, he draws on the mythic pattern of hubris-filled kings who rebelled against God and met sure destruction. Their end holds out a warning to all who would question the rule of God. Elihu's metaphor of kingship in reality turns out to be a recasting of the slave metaphor, in the tradition of the king who is slave to God.

While Elihu depicts God as artist in shaping humanity, what dominates his God-talk is the metaphor of powerful judge. Central is the image of the sovereign Lord whose decrees determine human destinies and govern the operations of creation. The breath of God, a variant of the word metaphor, animates human beings and all life. And it is only by the will of God alone that life continues. Should God desire to withdraw the divine, life-giving spirit, all flesh would turn to dust. God demands and receives unquestioned obedience, else his wrath comes forth to destroy the obstinate. The dogmatic character of Elihu's theology produces not live engagement, but sterile faith.

Chapter 10

WISDOM IN REVOLT: CONCLUDING SUMMARY

1. *Metaphors of Cosmology and Anthropology in Job*

Introduction. Creation theology in the ancient Near East was expressed by root metaphors which were central to the two major thematic traditions: cosmology (origins and maintenance of creation) and anthropology (human origins and divine providence). The metaphors for divine action were procreation, artistry, word and battle. In addition two metaphors conveyed the understanding of human nature and humanity's function in the world: ruler and slave. These root metaphors resided at the core of the mythic traditions which became their most common narrative expressions.

The Metaphor of Struggle. The dominant metaphor for the cosmological creation tradition in the ancient Near East was the primordial battle between the creator and the dragon. Following the defeat of chaos and its hosts, reality was brought into existence by the victorious creator. However, the threat to the ongoing order of life continued as the powers of chaos had to be subdued, both daily during the sun's nocturnal journey, and annually, especially at the time of transition to the new year. Reality, therefore, was not static, achieved once-for-all during a primeval occasion, when distant struggle shaped a changeless future. Rather, creation is a process of continuous struggle with the ominous forces of the dragon who bides its time in darkened regions waiting to dethrone the ruler of heaven and devour the good earth. In mythic form, the metaphor structures a continuous conflict between life and death in which the gods of life have the better of the struggle. Life and cosmos endure, but ever under the threat of extinction.

The metaphor of battle dominates the God-talk of Job, appearing in the hero's speeches in a reversal of meaning that poses the Divine Warrior running amok in his own creation, bringing devastation to the very structures of life he had fought so valiantly to originate and sustain. Now El Gibbor comes in visions of the night and in theophanic judgment, not to subdue the mighty dragon, but to torment and then annihilate the faithful servant. Every living creature has suffered the humiliation and agony of the brutal, heavy-handed God who oppresses and victimizes without cause. Yet it is Job who feels especially singled out, for unknown reasons, to suffer the deadliest of the Warrior's thrusts. This is the uncommon use of a most common metaphor that subverts the mythic narrative, and disassembles the structure of faith which it had erected. Fragmented, Job seeks a new mythic paradigm to restructure meaning and provide orientation to life. He finds the paradigm in the mythic and epic literature of the struggle of the Primal Man. Job, sure of his own integrity and equally convinced of the tyranny of divine sovereignty, seeks to replace the God of Heaven with human rule.

The friends of Job rarely use the imagery of the battle metaphor. Its one significant occurrence is Bildad's praise of the Warrior's past defeat of the dragon and her allies who had bowed the knee in submission to a greater, more deadly power (25.1.6; 26.5-14). Yet, for Bildad, struggle is past and conflict is locked within the primordial moment of a victory long since won. Now, no power dares challenge God's authority, for all reality, including Sea, the monsters of the Deep, and the dreaded Lords of the Underworld, submit to heaven's rule. Even Titans, long ago subdued, dare contemplate no present challenge to this fearful power. Unrivalled, God rules in retributive justice, bringing punishment and a certain end to those who violate the norms of moral justice. Human revolts are sheer folly and only meet with destruction. Indeed, another metaphor dominates the friends' theological language, that of word, particularly expressed in the formulation of edicts by the judge of the divine council. God is the divine judge whose decrees, rooted in and legitimated by unrivaled power, determine fate. Considered by the friends to be unquestionably just, God rewards virtuous actions and punishes those who violate heaven's commands.

Not surprisingly the conflict metaphor dominates the images of creation in the 'Speeches from the Whirlwind'. But here we find the language couched in mythic formulation. In primordial time, God did restrict, through divine edict, the bounds of Prince Yam's kingdom, allowing him to reign only in the waters of the cosmic sea. Yet chaos ever finds new modes of present incarnation, in both nature and the historical embodiments of peoples and persons who distort justice and life and must be limited in their rule. Even at the moment of theophany, the Divine Warrior has come in judgment once again to confront his eternal rivals, Behemoth, the 'Mighty Creature', and Leviathan, the dragon of the Deep. Like a heroic warrior of romantic epic, in the prelude to deadly battle, Yahweh praises the enchanting beauty and fearsome power of these two mythical beasts who must again be subdued to ensure the ongoing of the good creation.

While mostly avoiding the subject of the origins of evil, outside the one intriguing admission that Behemoth is a creature who may be truly challenged in battle only by the creator, Yahweh admits that there are hostile and chaotic forces in reality which ever appear to challenge divine rule. Through continuing acts of creation, including sustaining edict and violent battle, the integrity of the structures of life is upheld. Reality countenances no simplistic theory of retribution which must logically gear to a static order uninterrupted by intrusions from another world of disarray. In the world of God's own making, reality includes struggle, pain, agony, even death, though the ongoing-ness of life is gained through continual acts of divine creation. God is not removed from the world of tragic moment, but is incarnate in its most intense expression.

If mythic acts are in any fashion imitative, then struggle with chaos becomes the paradigm for human existence in the world. Even in the God–human relationship, 'wrestling' with the creator, especially over issues of justice, must continue. Actions that are divine must be questioned and brought into judgment. Unlike the friends' contention, humanity's role is not that of passive recipient of divinely allotted destiny, but that of questioning, challenging and sparring with a God whose silence or even overt behavior may distort the ground of life. And even in the intensity of agony, Job does not end his indictment of God and quest for justice, for struggle would have ceased, human participation in divine creativity would have ended, and the universe would have collapsed. Justice is no static, ideal norm transcending creaturely life, but a process enabling human and divine encounter and shaping authentic participation the world. Justice is created through intense struggle, only to be subverted once again, requiring ever new and repeated reconstruction. And it is this dynamic that reconstitutes creation.

The Slave of God. In the mythic tradition and its epic, sapiential and liturgical reformulations, two metaphors expressed the nature and function of the human creature: king (ruler) and slave. The king metaphor emphasized the essential goodness of humankind and the freedom to go forth into the world to master creation and to rule responsibly and well as the vice-regent of deity. As king humanity actively participated in the beneficent ordering and sustaining of nature and society. The slave metaphor eradicated significant human freedom, placed severe restrictions on the human capacity to create and shape the world, and constructed an unbridgeable chasm between the divine sovereign and the human creature. This metaphor portrayed human nature as weak and sinful.

Much of the narrative energy for the book of Job derives from the opposing of these two fundamentally different portrayals of being human in the world. While conventional wisdom came to democratize the royal tradition and to speak of the sages in royal guise, the Prologue opens with the radically different depiction of Job as the 'slave' of Yahweh, subject to brutal treatment, all in the virtuous name of proving loyalty. 'Does Job *serve* God for naught?' Certainly human nature is bent towards evil, and stripped of divine favor Job's inner and truest self would clearly emerge. At least this is the satan's contention. And Yahweh as divine master has no imposed restraints in his treatment of human mortals. Thus Job becomes the innocent victim of divine suspicion and caprice. And perhaps unbelievably so, Job holds true to the portrayal of loyal slave who accepts without complaint the hand of the Master turned cruel.

Following the seven-day interval of silence, residing between pious response and open lament, Job again speaks, this time words of curse and not blessing. Yet in his lament, designed to return the world to darkness, Job too uses the metaphor of slave for victims who seek the only liberation available to them from the torture and oppression of their lives, the sweet release of death. And in his disputations with the friends (chs. 3–27), Job continues to build the images of the slave metaphor, using it to describe the drudgery and oppression of all human life, tormented by the unrelenting God. Job admits to being one who is sinful, yet he does not buy into the argument of the friends that humanity possesses a corrupt nature. He also fails to understand why he has become the object of divine fury. Even his laments receive no acknowledged response. And the metaphor of humanity as ruler, poetically captured in Psalm 8, deconstructs in the face of Job's own experience.

The friends share the slave metaphor with Job, only they give it an even more depressing cast to incorporate it within their own dogmatic theory of retributive justice. Humanity is perverse by nature, deserving of any and all punishment from a righteous God. It is only by the radical grace of the sovereign God that humanity is spared from total annihilation. Job's and humanity's suffering is deserved punishment for sinful deeds resulting from a corrupt nature. The only action a slave can take, contend the friends, is to beg for mercy from the mighty Judge.

The alternative metaphor, humanity as ruler, is initially subverted by Job's experience and words. And its negative depiction in the mythic tradition of the revolt of the Primal Man is taken up by Eliphaz in ch. 15, designed as a warning expressed to Job to cease his angry outburst against the justice of God. Otherwise, Job would re-experience the fall of Adam and his later incarnations. However, in the transitional chs. 29–31, the metaphor changes from slave to king, as Job envisions himself in the role of a just and god-like Primal Man whose own judgment and dispensations of justice contrast dramatically with those of the corrupt God. Now Job becomes the man who would be god, desiring to approach the divine throne as a prince demanding both an audience and a written indictment of crimes.

The Yahweh speeches shatter Job's emerging vision of Primal Man, as the Divine Warrior comes in theophanic judgment to reassert his rightful sovereignty over the earth. And in a series of stunning revelations, Job's and Wisdom's anthropocentrism shatters. First, the list of animals in the second part (Job 38.39–39.30) of the first speech is comprised primarily of creatures mysterious to human beings and often inimical to their way of life. Indeed, Yahweh acts to sustain and nurture these animals. God, not Job in the guise of Primal Man, is the 'Lord of the Creatures'. Second, Yahweh invites the man who would be king to ascend the divine throne and rule over the earth. Yet Job is to be aware that he must eradicate the wicked from their sovereign domains, the task of any king, including the ruler of heaven and earth. Third, as would-be king over the earth, Job must face the contesting of his rule by the monsters of chaos, Behemoth, the 'Mighty Creature', and Leviathan, fearful dragon of the sea. These two beasts from mythological lore know no human conqueror. They alone are the kings of the beasts, not human creatures. Only the Divine Warrior may 'bring near his sword' to do them battle. As in the aeons that have passed, only victory secures the right to heaven's throne. And fourth, throughout the expanse of these two lengthy speeches from the whirlwind, no mention of humanity is made, save the one incidental remark that Behemoth is a creature like Job, fashioned by the hand of God.

The Epilogue deals with judgment as Job's theology is affirmed and that of the friends is spurned. And to the point of human metaphor, Eliphaz and the other two are condemned for not having 'correctly spoken' about God, as has God's 'servant Job'. In this refashioning of the meaning of the narrative story, Job as slave re-emerges as the proper metaphor for humanity, but renewed with a different content. Now humanity, like Job, is a slave who has learned to struggle with divine caprice. Even a divine master may not transcend the bounds of righteous rule. Indeed Job is the slave who has struggled with God and has won. In the victory there is redemption, not only for the mortal Job, but also for the capricious Judge who had brought against Job such unjustified evil. And in God's own self-condemnation, creation is sustained and the orders of life continued.

2. *Mythic Patterns in Job*

The Battle with Chaos. Cosmological myths of origins and maintenance are numerous and varied in ancient Near Eastern literature. Myths are many things, but we have followed the argument that they are extended metaphors. Central, root metaphors provide the images, vision and pattern for mythic texts. Thus the conflict metaphor dominates the *Enuma elish*, the major cultural myth of Babylonia, dealing with the origins and ongoing maintenance of the world. Its pattern includes the features of battle, victory over chaos, kingship, judgment, and creation. Though the components vary in their order, these same features comprise the literary pattern of the Baal Cycle, the major Ugaritic maintenance myth. In the Babylonian form of the story, Marduk defeats Tiamat and her forces, becomes king of the gods, issues decrees as the head of the divine council, and creates and orders the world. While defeated, Tiamat ever waits to challenge Marduk once again for supremacy over reality. Thus the performance of the myth in the *akitu* festival leads to the securing of the order of society and creation for the coming year.

This literary pattern of the combat myth provides the narrative world for the book of Job and its characters. God is the Divine Warrior whose primordial victory over chaos won the position of king of the gods and ruler of the divine council. The decrees of the divine judge continue to order the world brought into existence in primeval times. Yet chaos is a real and potent force, threatening creation and challenging divine rule. Thus Yahweh is the mighty warrior who must continue to engage the dragon in battle in order to reassert divine sovereignty and recreate the structures of life necessary for the ongoing of creation.

In the Prologue, Yahweh is the head of the divine council which convenes on the day of the New Year to determine the fates of people and nations for the coming year. God's edicts incorporate the decision of the supreme council of the gods. And in two cases edicts are issued which determine the destiny of Job: first the loss of family and wealth, and second the affliction of unspeakable suffering. In no instance is Yahweh's position as supreme judge or the integrity and justice of the divine edicts questioned by Job. It is true that Job's wife prompts him to 'curse God and die', though this seems to be less of a direct challenge to Yahweh's authority and more a counsel to escape the hideous lot which has been determined for him. Certainly, the wife begins the movement towards rebellion, but her counsel is rebuffed by Job as foolish talk.

The emergence of the first suggestion of battle between God and the dragon occurs in ch. 3 as Job calls upon the magicians, skilled in power-laden language and ritual, to summon sleeping Leviathan and Prince Yam from the primordial Deep to devour the creation God has made. This bold affront is Job's attempt to renew the conflict between the creator and the powers of darkness, in the hope that chaos would prevail and return the world to nothingness. Yet as the drama continues into the dialogues, Job complains God has recast him in the mythic role of the dragon. Now El Gibbor has begun to direct his full fury against this weakened mortal who has offered no previous threat to divine rule. And in the Joban dialogues, the hero speaks of the primeval judgment which has predestined all humanity to the onerous lot of lowly slave. Even the friends use the slave metaphor to describe the corruption of human nature and to legitimate all punishment of human creatures as proper and just.

The theophanic speeches operate within this mythic pattern, as the creator comes once again to do battle with age-old rivals, the 'mighty

Creature' and Leviathan, and the weak, audacious Job who had presumptuously attempted to initiate legal proceedings to oust God from the throne of heaven and earth. Yet divine fury against Job is transformed into instruction about the nature of creation and even mockery of Job's obvious weakness. If Job is indeed to ascend the divine throne, he must win his place as ruler of the divine council by doing battle not merely with the wicked of the earth, but also the primeval monsters, Behemoth and Leviathan, before whom even gods tremble in fear. Kingship is not grasped, it is won through victory over chaos, a thought that silences even a formerly loquacious Job.

Finally, in the Epilogue the judgment scene returns, bringing the drama to full closure. In Yahweh's ordering of creation through the utterance of divine decree, the world is recreated and Job is restored. A new creation, rooted in the justice of divine decree, emerges. The structures of life are continued by redeeming the justice of God.

The Revolt Against the Gods. Another mythic pattern, grounded in the metaphor of humanity as slave, and expressed most compellingly in *Atra-hasis*, shapes the internal structure of the book of Job. The salient features of this pattern include the decree of slavery for humanity, the experience of slavery and toil, the revolt of humans against the gods, fall, and concluding judgment leading to reprieve. In *Atra-hasis*, following the revolt of the lower gods due to their lot of onerous toil, humanity is created and destined by divine decree to experience eternal slavery. However, having tasted of drudgery long enough, the 'noise' (revolt?) of the humans comes to disturb the gods. Enlil decides to eradicate the entire lot by a series of plagues, diverted by the philanthropic Ea. Finally, a new judgment is rendered and humans— though their purpose in existence remains that of slaves to the gods— gain the gifts of civilization to become a well-ordered society.

The structure of Job proceeds in similar fashion. In the Prologue Job, already the slave of Yahweh, is sentenced to endure the devastating loss of status, wealth, and children. Then in the second edict, he is afflicted with fearsome sores covering his body. While the narrative suggests that Job remains the faithful slave, blessing not cursing the name of his Master, the narrator's omission of affirming that Job did not sin in his heart, a judgment present in Job's response to the first ordeal, may intimate that the hero had begun to waver. In any case, ch. 3 and the following dialogues of Job depict an angry man, no longer content to praise, but now intent on destructive curses. The curses designed to extinguish all life are transformed into an anguished defense of personal integrity and righteous indictment of the creator who had turned to destroy not only Job, but all creatures. Wavering between the desire for justice and the fear of awesome power, Job having experienced creation as oppressive slavery, finally engages in full-scale revolt against the creator of heaven and earth (chs. 29–31). Job's fall is experienced in the theophany (38.1–42.6), not in being destroyed by an angry God, but subdued by the One who maintains the order of creation only at the expense of continual struggle. Job's pretentious desire for rulership over creation quickly dissipates in the face of dreaded Leviathan. Thus in the Epilogue judgment is rendered, not to condemn Job for his angry attack, but to affirm his 'correct' God-language. God had acted capriciously and destructively in the Prologue, and Job's contention, pressed in words, had been the proper speech. By contrast, the friends' defense of divine honor, by an appeal to a simplistic theory of retribution, was roundly condemned. And it was only the intercession of Job that led to the redemption of the friends.

What unites these two major mythic patterns, the first contexting the narrative world of Job and the second providing the internal pattern, is the feature of conflict. When humans experience creation as oppressive, they rebel against heaven's rule. Revolt intersects with the divine struggle against the chaos monster to unite the two mythic structures brought into play by the poet.

A second anthropological pattern appears in the speeches of the friends and finally emerges as the redescription of Job and proud humanity: the one of hubris, revolt and fall. This mythic structure is best known in Genesis 3, though other texts, including Ezekiel 28, reactualize it in different forms. Thus Eliphaz in Job 15 uses the myth of the Primal Man who revolted against the rule of heaven to warn Job of the dire consequences of the course of action he had chosen to pursue. In the crucial transition chapters (29–31), located between the cessation of dialogical disputation and the beginnings of theophanic revelation, Job moves from the metaphor and pattern of the slave tradition to that of the royal Primal Man whose hubris leads to the challenge of the creator for sovereignty over the earth. And it is in response to this challenge that the Divine Warrior appears and intimidates the would-be challenger into recognizing his own impotence and folly. Indeed the royal metaphor that Job had assumed for himself is negated in the judgment contained in the Epilogue, for Eliphaz is condemned for not having spoken correctly as had God's 'slave Job'.

3. *The Metaphorical Process and the Narrative Quest for Faith*

With its central metaphor of conflict, the book of Job is a narrative journey of a character whose life is a quest for the knowledge of God and the why of human existence. In this quest for the articulation of meaning, Job moves through a series of collapsing and emerging worlds, ending with another deconstruction of mythic reality, but also the promising beginnings of new creation. In this dramatic rendering of Job's journey, the story becomes the verbalization of the metaphor of struggle. Through Job's experience, there is movement, both for the character and the implied audience, from absurdity and the shock of disorientation, to the collapse of all meaning, to the second shock of mimesis, to new transformation. Along the way, as well as at the beginning, the tensive relation between metaphorical construction and the objects it seeks to depict continues to provide creative energy for the vitality of the tradition. And also along the way, as well as at the end, ambiguity is ever present in the company of true metaphor.

Absurdity and Destabilization. The narrative opens with the absurd. Yahweh, head of the divine council, appears as a capricious judge whose suspicions about his servant are aroused by the one whose task it is to present an evil report. Ironically the narrator had described to the implied audience the scrupulous piety and unquestionable integrity of the one 'who feared God and turned away from evil'. Two edicts by the unjust judge devastate not only the innocent victim, but also the meaning world of a wisdom audience whose fundamental tenets were the justice of God and the royal status of the wise and righteous creature. God as capricious judge, threatened by the consumption of his own unfounded suspicion, and Job as a humiliated, groveling slave who accepts all from the master's hand, fragment the meaning world of a wisdom audience. And yet, by entering into the narrative world of Job, the audience along with the main character begin to experience that unsettling disorientation that comes from the questioning of the meaning structure that provided direction and an interpretative frame for human experience.

Deconstruction of Metaphors of Creation Faith. With the opening of the dialogues in ch. 3, the character Job engages in a wholesale assault on all meaning structures, hoping with their collapse the world would return to primordial beginnings, 'when there was no. . .' One by one, metaphors of creation—word, artistry, fertility and battle—begin to collapse from the sheer weight of Job's linguistic assault on meaning. And also disassembled is the tradition of humanity as king, commissioned by God to go forth into the world to rule over the good creation. Now humans, like Job, are contemptuous slaves whose life of toil and drudgery expects no release, save the common end that awaits all life in the darkness of the underworld. Job's efforts to return meaning to chaos, and to collapse the world construction of conventional wisdom, are grounded in the center of his own disconfirming experiences.

The Defense of Creation Metaphor. Job's friends attempt to counter his disputative assault on meaning by the use of the stock metaphors of God as righteous judge maintaining the creation with retributive justice and of humanity as slave, corrupt to the very core. However, what disconfirms their depiction of God is the opening Prologue in which a capricious God sentences the perfectly obedient slave to the catastrophes of devastating loss. For the implied audience, their doxologies of praise shatter before the shocking narrative world of Job 1–2. Even the depiction of humanity as corrupt slave offers little solace to a wisdom audience whose tradition had exalted the place and role of the righteous sage in the world, a place and role grounded in the freedom to choose the good and in the very goodness of creation and life itself. The efforts of the friends to sustain traditional, stock metaphors fail to convince.

The Move Toward Mimesis. Job's linguistic assault on meaning does not end in a blind, destructive rage attempting to return the world to chaos. Rather, he begins to refashion his own mythos, beginning with a transformed metaphor, God as Mighty Warrior. Choosing the metaphor of the battler of chaos from the mythic tradition, Job moves to depict God as the Warrior who has irrationally turned against his own creation. As destructive tyrant, the ground for his rule over creation is now removed. God has become identified with the chaotic forces he had formerly controlled. As such, he must be removed from heaven's throne. Recognizing his own impotence and limited wisdom,

Job attempts to bring Yahweh into the arena of a cosmic court in which he would be condemned for violating the norms of justice and be removed.

In the significant transition from disputation to theophany (chs. 29–31), Job achieves mimesis for himself and his audience. God has become the corrupt judge who destroys even his most faithful creatures. In a series of self-imprecations, Job legally proves his own innocence and then challenges God to appear with his flimsy indictment. In such a legal setting, Job is convinced he could easily disprove God's charges and submit his own weighty counter-indictment. And Job renounces the metaphor of slave for the one of king as he moves into full-scale revolt. Now Job desires to replace divine rule with that of the Primal Man.

Collapse and Reconstruction of Creation Faith. But before the transformation constructed by the emerging new vision occurs, the Divine Warrior comes in theophany to defeat his opponents, render judgment, and recreate the world. And in the revelation from the storm, Job's emerging mythos is destabilized, ironically by the vision of language. One by one, Yahweh poetically rehabilitates the metaphors that Job had attempted to deconstruct: word, artistry, fertility, and especially combat. But unlike the friends, this renewal of metaphor is accomplished not by literalizing meaning or by dogmatic assertion, but by reconfirming, renewing, and reshaping their images. Thus, the divine word which limited Yam's sphere in the beginning directs the morning and dawn to shake the wicked from their place. And as architect Yahweh has constructed and maintains a world of elegance and order, before which even the gods respond in praise and exultation.

Yet traditional metaphorical meaning is not always simply restated. In the representation of the images, new intimations also tend to shock a conventional wisdom audience and bring them into disarray. This is especially noticed in the birth metaphor. As loving parent, God sustains Yam and even creatures of the wild, aiding in the birth of their offspring and providing wisdom and sustenance necessary for their survival. These animals, often inimical to human life, are sustained by divine providence. And the images of the birth tradition, normally associated with the care of the human creature, are transferred to creatures often dangerous to human life. Certainly, this imagery collapses the anthropocentrism of wisdom and its emerging, new formulation in the speeches of Job.

But it is especially the battle metaphor that is revitalized in the speeches of God. Yahweh has come to engage his two opponents: Behemoth and Leviathan, the two 'Lords of the Creatures' who rule over the chaotic forces continuing in the world. Before such an awesome Warrior, Job has no chance. Yet he is offered the throne, if he can defeat the wicked, and their mythical incarnations. Of course, Job is wise enough to make no such futile attempt. Thus, while Yahweh struggles to subdue chaos, its power is not eliminated from the earth. Chaos continues to lurk in darkened regions, biding its chance to defeat the creator and return the world to nothingness.

Mimesis, Transformation, and Restabilization. With the collapse of his newly emerging mythos of the Primal Man, Job is once again reduced to 'dust and ashes'. And in his second response, he attempts to reformulate the language of faith, the metaphors and grammar for which are provided in the speeches of God. Disputation, imperative, question and praise comprise the structure of the divine speeches and emerge in an initial fashion in Job's final speech. Of course, the poet of Job has constructed a new mythos in the divine speeches, and the character Job and the implied audience are on their way once more to the reconstruction of the language of faith. Job's world once again has collapsed, but he and his audience stand at new beginning.

Finally, what enables silent tongues to speak is the last judgment in which the Divine Warrior, now sitting on the throne of king, issues his world-creating decree. Eliphaz and the friends, not Job, are condemned for erroneous God-talk, while the language of the defiant, accusing, struggling Job is declared as right and true. For it is the struggle for justice, initiated by the caprice of an unjust judge, that is the proper way of being human in the world. And in the restoration of Job, there is the redemption of God.

Tension and Ambiguity. The metaphorical journey of Joban faith is not without tension and ambiguity, from its inception, to its conclusion, to its new beginning. God is not parent, or artist, or judge, any more than warrior. Tension between tenor and vehicle, and God and the images of faith, remains and must endure to continue to attract the imagination and allow not only heroic characters but also the implied audience to enter into the narrative world of human journey and experience both collapse and new beginning. Many of Job's questions, and those of the implied audience, are ignored. Indeed the God of the whirlwind comes not with answers, but with questions. While the quest for meaning continues in the effort to speak correctly about, but also to, God, clarity of vision eventually eludes. And with each new construction there follows eventually the disconfirming experience which leads again to collapse. But with the disassembling of old vision, there is the compelling dream of new beginning.

SELECT BIBLIOGRAPHY

Albertz, Rainer, 'Der sozialgeschichtliche Hintergrund des Hiobbuches und der "Babylonischen Theodizee"'. *Die Botschaft und die Boten*, ed Jörg Jeremias and Lothar Perlitt. FS Hans Walter Wolff. Neukirchen: Neukirchener Verlag, 1981, 349-72.

—*Weltschöpfung und Menschenschöpfung*. Calwer Theologische Monographien. Reihe A: Biblewissenschaft, 3. Stuttgart: Calwer, 1974.

Albright, W.F. 'Anath and the Dragon'. *BASOR* 84 (1941), 14-16.

—'The Goddess of Life and Wisdom', *AJSL* 36 (1919/20) 258-94.

Alonso-Schökel, Luis. 'Sapiential and Covenant Themes in Genesis 2–3'. *Studies in Ancient Israelite Wisdom*, ed. James L. Crenshaw. New York: Ktav, 1976, 468-80.

Alt, Albrecht. 'Zur Vorgeschichte des Buches Hiob'. *ZAW* 14 (1937), 265-68.

Anderson, B.W. *Creation Versus Chaos*. New York: Association, 1967.

Anderson, B.W. (ed.). *Creation in the Old Testament*. Issues in Religion and Theology 6. Philadelphia: Fortress, 1984.

Barbour, Ian. *Myths, Models and Paradigms*. New York: Harper and Row, 1974.

Barr, James. 'The Book of Job and its Modern Interpreters'. *BJRL* 54 (1971–72), 28-46.

Barta, W. 'Das Gespräch des Ipuwer mit dem Schöpfergott'. *Studien zur altägyptischen Kultur* 1 (1974), 19-33.

Baumgartner, Walter. *Israelitische und Altorientalische Weisheit*. Tübingen: Mohr (Paul Siebeck), 1933.

—'The Wisdom Literature'. *The Old Testament and Modern Study*, ed. H.H. Rowley. Oxford: Clarendon, 1951, 210-37.

Barton, John. 'Understanding Old Testament Ethics'. *JSOT* 9 (1978), 44-64.

Bernhardt, K.H. *Das Problem der altorientalischen Königsideologie im Alten Testament*. VTS 8. Leiden: Brill, 1961.

Becker, Joachim. *Gottesfurcht im Alten Testament*. AB 25. Rome: Pontifical Biblical Institute, 1965.

Bic, M. 'Le juste et l'impie dans le livre de Job'. *VTS* 15 (1966), 33-43.

Blank, S.H. 'Curse'. *HUCA* 23 (1950–51), 73-95.

—'Men Against God'. *JBL* 72 (1953), 1-14.

Boecker, H.J. *Redeformen des israelitischen Rechtslebens*. WMANT 14. Neukirchen, 1964.

Boer, P.A.H. De. 'Haalde Job Bakzeil? (Job xlii 6)'. *NTT* 31 (1977), 181-94.

—'The Counsellor'. *SVT* 3 (1955) 42-71.

Bonnet, Hans. 'Krokodil'. *Reallexikon der Aegyptischen Religionsgeschichte*. Berlin: de Gruyter, 1952, 392-94.

—'Nilpferd'. *Reallexikon der Aegyptischen Religionsgeschichte*. Berlin: de Gruyter, 1952, 528-30.

Brandon, S.I. *Creation Legends of the Ancient Near East*. London: Hodder & Stoughton, 1963.

Braslavy, J. 'The End of Pharaoh—the Great Crocodile in the Light of the Worship of the Crocodile in Egypt'. *Beth Mikra* 53 (1973), 143-49.

Brenner, A. 'God's Answer to Job'. *VT* 31 (1981), 129-37.

Brueggemann, Walter. *In Man We Trust*. Atlanta: John Knox, 1972.

—'Scripture and an Ecumenical Life-Style'. *Interpretation* 24 (1970), 3-19.

Budde, K. *Das Buch Hiob*. 2nd ed. Göttinger Handkommentar zum Alten Testament 2. Göttingen: Vandenhoeck & Ruprecht, 1913.

Buren, E.D. van. 'The Dragon in Ancient Mesopotamia'. *Orientalia* 15 (1946), 1-45.

Burrows, Millar. 'The Voice from the Whirlwind'. *JBL* 47 (1928), 117-32.

Caird, G.B. *The Language and Imagery of the Bible*. Philadelphia: Westminster, 1980.

Cassuto, U. *The Goddess Anath*. Jerusalem: Magnes, 1951.

Cazelles, Henri. 'Bible, Sagesse, Science'. *RSR* 48 (1960), 40-54.

—'Les debuts de la sagesse en Israel'. *SPOA*, 27-40.

Childs, Brevard, *Myth and Reality in the Old Testament*. 2nd edn *SBT* 27; Naperville: Alenson, IL, 1962.

Clifford, R.J. *The Cosmic Mountain in Canaan and the Old Testament*. *HSM* 4; Cambridge, MA: Harvard University Press, 1972.

Clines, D. 'Job 5.1-8: A New Exegesis', *Bib* 62 (1981), 185-94.

Conrad, D. 'Der Gott Reschef', *ZAW* 83 (1971), 157-83.

Couroyer, B. 'La "glaive" de Behemoth, Job XL 14-20'. *RB* 84 (1977), 59-75.

—'Qui est Behemoth?'. *RB* 82 (1975), 418-43.

Cox, D. 'Reason in Revolt: The Poetic Dialogues in the Book of Job'. *Studi Biblici Franciscani* 24 (1974), 317-28.

—*The Triumph of Impotence, Job and the Tradition of the Absurd*. Rome: Universita Gregoriana, 1978.

Crenshaw, James L. 'Impossible Questions, Sayings, and Tasks'. *Semeia* 17 (1980), 19-34.

—'In Search of Divine Presence'. *REx* 74 (1977), 353-69.

—*Old Testament Wisdom*. Atlanta: John Knox, 1981.

—'Popular Questioning of the Justice of God in Ancient Israel'. *ZAW* 82 (1970), 380-95.

—'Prolegomenon'. *Studies in Ancient Israelite Wisdom*. New York: Ktav, 1976, 1-45.

—'Wisdom'. *Old Testament Form Criticism*, ed. John H. Hayes. San Antonio, TX: Trinity University Press, 1974, 225-64.

Crook, M.B. *The Cruel God*. Boston: Beacon, 1959.

Cross, Frank M. 'The Council of Yahweh in Second Isaiah'. *JNES* 12 (1953), 274-77.

Crüsemann, F. 'Hiob und Kohelet'. *Werden und Wirken des Alten Testaments*. FS Claus Westermann, ed. Rainer Albertz *et al.* Göttingen: Vandenhoeck & Ruprecht, 1980, 373-93.

Curtis, J.B. 'On Job's Witness in Heaven'. *JBL* 102 (1983), 549-62.

Dennefeld, Louis. 'Les discours d'Elihou'. *RB* 48 (1939), 163-80.

Dhorme, E. *A Commentary on the Book of Job*. London: Nelson, 1967.

—'The Legal Metaphor in Job 31'. *CBQ* 41 (1979), 37-50.

Doll, Peter. *Menschenschöpfung und Weltschöpfung in der alttestamentlichen Weisheit*. Dissertation Heidelberg, 1980.

Driver, S.R. and G.B. Gray. *The Book of Job* 1 and 2. ICC 14. Edinburgh: T. & T. Clark, 1921.

Dünner, Alfred. *Die Gerechtigkeit nach dem Alten Testament*. Schriften zur Rechtslehre und Politik 42, ed. Ernst von Hippel. Bonn: H. Bouvier, 1963.

—*Die Wertung des Göttlichen Wortes im Alten Testament und in Antiken Orient*. MVAG 42. Leipzig: Hinrichs, 1938.

Dürr, Lorenz. *Das Erziehungswesen im Alten Testament und im Alten Orient*. MVAG 36. Leipzig: J.C. Hinrichs, 1932.

Eichrodt, Walther. '"In the Beginning". A Contribution to the Interpretation of the First Word of the Bible'. *Creation in the Old Testament*, ed. B.W. Anderson. Issues in Religion and Theology 6. Philadelphia: Fortress, 1984, 65-73.

Eliade, Mircea. *Cosmos and History. The Myth of the Eternal Return*. New York: Harper & Row, 1954.

—*The Sacred and the Profane*. New York: Harcourt, Brace, and World, 1959.

Emerton, J.A. 'Wisdom'. *Tradition and Interpretation*, ed. G.W. Anderson. Oxford; Clarendon, 1979, 214-37.

Engnell, I. ' "Knowledge" and "Life" in the Creation Story'. *SVT* 3 (1955), 103-19.

Eyre, C. 'Crocodiles and the Judgment of the Dead. Some Mythological Allusions in Egyptian Literature'. *Studien zur altägyptische Kultur* 4 (1976), 103-14.

Fensham, F. Charles. 'Widow, Orphan, and the Poor in Ancient Near Eastern Legal and Wisdom Literature'. *JNES* 21 (1962), 129-39.

Ferre, Frederick. 'Metaphors, Models and Religion'. *Soundings* 51 (1968), 327-45.

Fichtner, Johannes. *Die altorientalische Weisheit in ihr israelitisch-jüdischen Ausprägung*. BZAW 62. Giessen: Töpelmann, 1933.

Finkelstein, Chanan. 'The Book of Job and the Wisdom of the Ancient Near East'. *Beth Mikra* 51 (1972), 428-38.

Fishbane, M. 'Jer. 4 and Job 3: A Recovered Use of the Creation Pattern'. *VT* 211 (1971), 151-67.

Fisher, Loren R. 'Creation at Ugarit and in the Old Testament'. *VT* 15 (1965), 313-24.

Fohrer, Georg. *Das Buch Hiob*. KAT 16. Gütersloh: Gerd Mohn, 1963.

—'Dialog und Kommunikation im Buche Hiob'. *La Sagesse de l'Ancien Testament*, ed. M. Gilbert. BETHL 51. Leuven: Leuven University Press, 1979, 219-30.

—*Studien zum Buche Hiob*. 2nd edn. Gütersloh: Gerd Mohn, 1982.

—'The Righteous Man in Job 31'. *Essays in Old Testament Ethics*, ed. James L. Crenshaw and John T. Willis. New York: Ktav, 1974, 1-22.

Fontaine, Carole R. *Traditional Sayings in the Old Testament*. Sheffield: Almond, 1982.

Foster, Benjamin R. 'Wisdom and the Gods in Ancient Mesopotamia'. *Or* NS 13 (1974), 344-54.

Freedman, D.N. 'Job 38 and God's Rhetoric'. *Semeia* 19 (1981), 53-61.

—'The Structure of Job 3'. *Bib* 49 (1968), 503-508.

Gadd, C.J. *Ideas of Divine Rule in the Ancient Near East*. London: Oxford University Press, 1948.

Gammie, John. 'Behemoth and Leviathan: On the Didactic and Theological Significance of Job 40.15–41.26'. *Israelite Wisdom*, ed. John G. Gammie, *et al.* FS Samuel Terrien. Missoula, MT: Scholars Press, 1978, 217-31.

—and Leo G. Perdue (ed). *The Sage in Israel and the Ancient Near East*. Winona Lake: Eisenbrauns, 1990.

Gaspar, Joseph. *Social Ideas in the Wisdom Literature of the Old Testament*. The Catholic University of America Studies in Sacred Theology. 2nd Series 8. Washington: Catholic University Press, 1947.

Gemser, B. 'The *rîb*–or Controversy–Pattern in Hebrew Mentality'. *VTS* 3 (1955), 120-37.

—'The Spiritual Structure of Biblical Aphoristic Wisdom'. *Adhuc Loquitur*. Pretoria Oriental Series 7. Leiden: Brill, 1968, 138-49.

Gerstenberger, Erhard. 'Covenant and Commandment'. *JBL* 84 (1965), 38-51.

Gese, Harmut. *Die Religionen Altsyriens, Altarabiens und der Mandäer*. Die Religionen der Menschheit 10. Stuttgart: W. Kohlhammer, 1970.

—*Lehre und Wirklichkeit in der alten Weisheit*. Tübingen: Mohr (Paul Siebeck), 1958.

Gevirtz, Stanley. 'West-Semitic Curses and the Problem of the Origin of Hebrew Law'. *VT* 11 (1961), 137-58.

Ginsberg, H.L. 'Job the Patient and Job the Impatient'. *Conservative Judaism* 21 (1967), 12-28.

Gordis, Robert. *The Book of Job*. New York: Jewish Theological Seminary of America, 1978.

—'The Lord Out of the Whirlwind. The Climax and Meaning of Job'. *Judaism* 13 (1964), 48-63.

—'Virtual Quotations in Job, Sumer and Qumran'. *VT* 31 (1981), 410-27.

—'Wisdom and Job'. *Old Testament Issues*, ed. Samuel Sandmel. New York: Harper and Row, 1968, 216-38.

Gordon, C.H. 'Leviathan. Symbol of Evil'. *Biblical Motifs*, ed. A. Altmann. Cambridge, MA: Harvard University Press, 1966, 1-9.

Gowan, Donald E. *When Man Becomes God*. Pittsburgh Theological Monograph Series 6. Pittsburgh: Pickwick, 1975.

Gray, John. 'The Book of Job in the Context of Near Eastern Literature. *ZAW* 82 (1970), 251-69.

—*The Legacy of Canaan*. *SVT* 5. Leiden: Brill, 1965.

Guglielmo, A. de. 'Job 12.7-9 and the knowablity of God'. *CBQ* 6 (1944), 476-82.

Guillaume, A. *Studies in the Book of Job*. Leiden. Brill, 1968.

Habel, Norman. 'He Who Stretches Out the Heavens'. *CBQ* 34 (1972), 417-30.

—*Job*. Old Testament Library. Philadelphia: Westminster, 1985.

—'Naked I Came. . . Humanness in the Book of Job'. *Die Botschaft und die Boten*, ed. Jörg Jeremias and Lothar Perlitt. Neukirchen: Neukirchener Verlag, 1981, 373-92.

—'Only the Jackal is My Friend: On Friends and Redeemers in Job'. *Interp*. 31 (1977), 227-36.

Hempel, Johannes. *Das Ethos des Alten Testaments*. 2nd edn. Berlin: Töpelmann, 1964.

—'Das theologische Problem des Hiob'. *Apoxysmata*. BZAW 81. Berlin: Töpelmann, 1964, 114-74.

Hermisson, Hans-Jürgen. 'Observations on the Creation Theology in Wisdom'. *Israelite Wisdom*, ed. John G. Gammie *et al*. Missoula: Scholars Press, 1978, 43-47.

Herrmann, Siegfried. 'Die Naturlehre des Schöpfungsberichtes'. *ThLZ* 86 (1961), 413-24.

—*Time and History*. Nashville: Abingdon, 1981.

Hillers, D.H. *Treaty Curses and the Old Testament Prophets*. Biblica et Orientalia 16. Rome: Pontifical Biblical Institute, 1964.

Hölscher, G. *Das Buch Hiob*. 2nd edn. HAT 17. Tübingen: Mohr (Paul Siebeck), 1952.

Horst, Friedrich. 'Naturrecht und Altes Testament'. *Gottes Recht*. Theologische Bücherie 12. München: Chr. Kaiser, 1961, 235-59.

Horst, F. *Hiob*. BKAT 16. Neukirchen: Neukirchener Verlag, 1969.

Irwin, William A. 'Job's Redeemer'. *JBL* 81 (1962), 217-29.

Janzen, J. Gerald. *Job*. Interpretation. Atlanta: John Knox, 1985.

Jepsen, A. *Das Buch Hiob und seine Deutung*. Arbeiten zur Theologie 14. Stuttgart: Calwer, 1963.

Jeremias, J. *Theophanie*. WMANT 10. Neukirchen: Neukirchener Verlag, 1965.

Johnson, A.R. 'The Primary Meaning of G'l'. *SVT* 1 (1953), 67-77.

Kaiser, O. *Die mythische Bedeutung des Meeres in Aegypten, Ugarit und Israel*. BZAW 78. Berlin: Töpelmann, 1959.

Kaiser, O. and E. Lohse. *Tod und Leben*. Stuttgart: Kohlhammer, 1977.

Kanatz, Christa Bauer. *Einführung in die alttestamentliche Weisheit*. Biblische Studien 55. Neukirchen: Neukirchener Verlag, 1969.

Keel, O. *Jahwes Entgegnung an Ijob*. FRLANT 121. Göttingen: Vandenhoeck & Ruprecht, 1978.

—*The Symbolism of the Biblical World*. New York: Seabury, 1978.

Kluger, Rivkah S. *Satan in the Old Testament*. Evanston, IL: Northwestern University Press, 1967.

Knierim, Rolf. 'Cosmos and History in Israel's Theology'. *Werden und Wirken des Alten Testaments*, ed. R. Albertz, *et al*. Göttingen: Vandenhoeck & Ruprecht, 1980, 59-123.

Koch, Klaus. 'Gibt es ein Vergeltungsdogma im Alten Testament?' *ZThK* 52 (1955), 1-42.

Köhler, L. *Der Hebräische Mensch*. Tübingen, 1953.

Kovacs, Brian. 'Is there a Class-Ethic in Proverbs?' *Essays in Old Testament Ethics*, ed. James L. Crenshaw and John T. Tillis. New York: Ktav, 1974, 171-90.

Kubina, Veronika. *Die Gottesreden im Buche Hiob.* Freiburger Theologische Studien 115. Freiburg: Herder, 1979.

Lacocque, Andre. 'Job or the Impotence of Religion and Philosophy'. *Semeia* 19 (1981), 33-52.

Landes, George M. 'Creation and Liberation'. *Creation in the Old Testament*, ed. B.W. Anderson. Issues in Religion and Theology 6. Philadelphia: Fortress , 1984, 135-51.

Lang, Bernhard. *Die weisheitliche Lehrrede.* Stuttgarter Bibelstudien 54. Stuttgart: KBW, 1971.

—*Frau Weisheit.* Düsseldorf: Patmos, 1975.

Laurin, R. 'The Theological Structure of Job'. *ZAW* 84 (1972), 86-89.

Leveque, J. *Job et son dieu.* 2 Vols. Paris: Librairie Lecoffre, 1970.

Loretz, Oswald. *Schöpfung und Mythos. Mensch und Welt nach den Anfangskapiteln der Genesis.* Stuttgarter Bibelstudien 32. Stuttgart: Katholisches Bibelwerk, 1968.

Maag, V. *Hiob: Wandlung und Verarbeitung des Problems in Novelle, Dialogdichtung und Spätfassungen.* Göttingen: Vandenhoeck & Ruprecht, 1982.

McCarthy, Dennis J. '"Creation" Motifs in Ancient Hebrew Poetry', *CBQ* 29 (1967), 393-406.

McCurley, Foster, *Ancient Myths and Biblical Faith.* Philadelphia: Fortress, 1983.

McFague, Sallie. *Metaphorical Theology. Models of God in Religious Language.* Philadelphia: Fortress, 1982.

McKane, William. *Prophets and Wise Men. SBT* 44. Naperville, IL: Allenson, 1965.

Mackenzie, R.A.F. 'The Purpose of the Yahweh Speeches in the Book of Job'. *Bib* 40 (1959), 435-45.

May, H.G. 'Prometheus and Job: the Problem of the God of Power and the Man of Worth'. *AThR* 34 (1952), 240-46.

Mendenhall, George. 'The Shady Side of Wisdom: The Date and Purpose of Genesis 3'. *A Light Unto My Path.* FS Jacob M. Myers. Gettysburg Theological Studies 4. Philadelphia: Temple University Press, 1974, 319-34.

Mesnard, R. 'Les constellations du livre de Job'. *Revue belge de philosophie et d'histoire* 30 (1952), 1-11.

Mettinger, T.N.D. *Solomonic State Officials.* Coniectanea Biblica. Old Testament Series 5. Lund: Gleerups, 1971.

Moore, B.D. 'The Integrity of Job'. *CBQ* 45 (1983), 17-31.

Mowinckel, Sigmund. 'Hiob's *gō' ēl* und Zeuge im Himmel'. *Vom Alten Testament*, ed. Karl Budde. FS Karl Marti. Giessen: Töpelmann, 1925, 207-12.

Müller, H.-P. 'Die weisheitliche Lehrerzählung im Alten Testament und seiner Umwelt'. *WO* 9 (1977), 77-98.

—*Hiob und seine Freunde.* Theologische Stüdien 105. Zürich: EVZ-Verlag, 1970.

—'Welt als "Wiederholung"'. *Werden und Wirken des Alten Testaments*, ed. Rainer Albertz *et al.* FS Claus Westermann. Göttingen: Vandenhoeck & Ruprecht, 1980, 355-72.

Mullen, E. Theodore. *The Assembly of the Gods.* HSS 24. Missoula: Scholars Press, 1980.

Murphy, Roland. *Introduction to the Wisdom Literature of the Old Testament.* Collegeville, MN: Liturgical Press, 1965.

—*Wisdom Literature.* FOTL 13. Grand Rapids: Eerdmans, 1981.

Notter, Viktor. *Biblischer Schöfungsbericht und ägyptische Schöpfungsmythen.* Stuttgartner Bibelstudien 68. Stuttgart: KBW, 1974.

Patrick, Dale. 'Job's Address of God'. *ZAW* 91 (1979), 268-82.

—'The Translation of Job XLII 6'. *VT* 26 (1976), 369-71.

Perdue, Leo. G. *The Collapse of History. Creation, Narrativity and the Reconstruction of Theological Language*. Overtures to Biblical Theology. Minneapolis: Augsburg–Fortress, forthcoming.

—*Wisdom and Cult*. SBLDS 30. Missoula: Scholars Press, 1977.

—and John G. Gammie (ed.). *Paraenesis: Act and Form. Semeia* 50 (1990).

Plath, Siegfried. *Furcht Gottes*. Arbeiten zur Theologie 2. Stuttgart: Calwer, 1962.

Pope, Marvin. *Job*. AB 15. Garden City: Doubleday, 1965.

Porteous, Norman W. 'Royal Wisdom'. *SVT* 3 (1955), 247-61.

Preuss, H.D. 'Jahwes Antwort an Hiob und die sogenannte Hiobliteratur des alten Vorderen Orients'. *Beiträge zur alttestamentlichen Theologie*, ed. Herbert Donner *et al*. FS W. Zimmerli. Göttingen: Vandenhoeck & Ruprecht, 1977, 323-45.

Pritchard, James B. (ed.). *The Ancient Near East in Pictures*. 3rd edn. Princeton: Princeton University Press, 1968.

Rad, Gerhard von. 'Das Theologische Problem des alttestamentlichen Schöpfungsglaubens'. *Werden und Wesen des Alten Testaments*, ed. Johannes Hempel. BZAW 66. Berlin: Töpelmann, 1936, 138-47.

—*Old Testament Theology* 1. New York: Harper & Row, 1962.

—*Wisdom in Israel*. Nashville: Abingdon, 1972.

Ricoeur, Paul. 'The Metaphorical Process'. *Semeia* 4 (1975), 75-106.

Richter, H. 'Die Naturweisheit des Alten Testament im Buche Hiob'. *ZAW* 70 (1958), 1-19.

—'Erwägungen zum Hiobproblem'. *EvTh* 18 (1958), 302-24.

—*Studien zu Hiob*. Berlin: Evangelische Verlagsanstalt, 1955.

Robertson, David. *The Old Testament and the Literary Critic*. Philadelphia: Fortress, 1977.

Rowley, H.H. *Job*. The Century Bible. Don Mills, Ontario: Nelson, 1970.

Ruprecht, E. 'Das Nilpferd im Hiobbuch. Beobachtungen zu der sogenannten zweiten Gottesrede'. *VT* 21 (1971), 209-31.

Rylaarsdam, J. Coert. *Revelation in Jewish Wisdom Literature*. Chicago: University of Chicago Press, 1946.

—'Leiden und Gerechtigkeit bei Hiob'. *ZThK* 73 (1976), 424-45.

Säve-Söderbergh, T. *On Egyptian Representations of Hippopotomus Hunting as a Religious Motive*. Horae Soderblomianae 3. Lund: Gleerup, 1953.

Schmid, H.H. 'Creation, Righteousness, and Salvation'. *Creation in the Old Testament*, ed. B.W. Anderson. Issues in Religion & Theology 6. Philadelphia: Fortress, 1984, 102-17.

—*Gerechtigkeit als Weltordnung*. BHT 40. Tübingen: Mohr (Paul Siebeck), 1968.

—*Wesen und Geschichte der Weisheit*. BZAW 101. Berlin: de Gruyter, 1966.

Schmidt, P. 'Sinnfrage und Glaubenskrise. Ansätze zu einer kritischen Theologie der Schöpfung im Buche Hiob'. *Geist und Leben* 45 (1972), 348-61.

Schottroff, *Der altisraelitische Fluchspruch*. WMANT 30. Neukirchen: Neukirchener Verlag, 1969.

Scott, R.B.Y. *The Way of Wisdom*. New York: Macmillan, 1971.

Seele, K.C. 'Horus on the Crocodiles'. *JNES* 6 (1947), 43-52.

Sekine, Masao. 'Schöpfung und Erlösung im Buche Hiob'. *Von Ugarit nach Qumran*. BZAW 77. Berlin: Töpelmann, 1961, 213-23.

Seybold, K. *Das Gebet des Kranken im Alten Testament*. BWANT 99. Stuttgart: Kohlhammer, 1973.

—'Der Turmbau zu Babel . . .' *VT* 26 (1976), 453-79.

Shapiro, David S. 'The Book of Job and the Trial of Abraham'. *Tradition* 4 (1962), 210-20.

Shea, W.H. 'Adam in Ancient Mesopotamian Traditions'. *Andrews University Semitic Studies* 15 (1977), 27-41.

Skehan, P.W. 'Job's Final Plea (Job 29–31) and the Lord's Reply'. *Bib* 45 (1964), 51-62.

Smith, Morton. *Palestinian Parties and Politics that Shaped the Old Testament*. New York: Columbia University Press, 1971.

Snaith, Norman. *The Book of Job*. SBT 11. Naperville, IL: Allenson, 1968.

Stadelmann, Luis I. *The Hebrew Conception of the World*. AB 39. Rome: Pontifical Biblical Institute, 1970.

Steck, Odil Hannes. *Der Schöpfungsbericht der Priesterschrift*. Göttingen: Vandenhoeck & Ruprecht, 1975.

Terrien, S. 'The Book of Job'. *The Interpreter's Bible* 3, ed. G.A. Buttrick. Nashville: Abingdon, 1955, 877-1198.

—'The Jahve Speeches and Job's Responses'. *REx* 68 (1971), 497-509.

Tromp, Nicholas J. *Primitive Conceptions of Death and the Nether World in the Old Testament*. Biblica et Orientalia 21. Rome: Pontifical Biblical Institute, 1969.

Tsevat, Matitiahu. 'The Meaning of the Book of Job'. *HUCA* 37 (1966), 73-106.

Tur-Sinai, N.H. *The Book of Job*. Jerusalem: Kiryath Sepher, 1957.

Vaux, Roland de. *Ancient Israel* 1 & 2. New York: McGraw-Hill, 1965.

Wakemann, Mary K. *God's Battle with the Monster*. Leiden: Brill, 1973.

Weiser, Artur. *Das Buch Hiob*. 7th edn. ATD 14. Göttingen: Vandenhoeck & Ruprecht, 1980.

Westermann, Claus. *Genesis 1-11: a Commentary*. Minneapolis: Augsburg, 1984.

Whedbee, J.W. 'The Comedy of Job'. *Semeia* 7 (1970), 182-200.

Wheelwright, Phillip. *Metaphor and Reality*. Bloomington, IN: Indiana University Press, 1962.

Wilde, A. de. *Das Buch Hiob*. Oudtestamentische Studiën 22. Leiden: Brill, 1981.

Widengren, Geo. 'Early Hebrew Myths and Their Interpretation'. *Myth, Ritual, and Kingship*, ed. S.H. Hooke. Oxford: Clarendon, 1958, 149-203.

Williams, James G. 'Deciphering the Unspoken: The Theophany of Job'. *HUCA* 49 (1978), 59-72.

—' "You have not spoken Truth of Me". Mystery and Irony in Job'. *ZAW* 83 (1971), 231-55.

Williams, R.J. 'Theodicy in the Ancient Near East', *CJTh* 2 (1956), 14-26.

Wolf, Hans Walter. *Anthropology of the Old Testament*. Philadelphia: Fortress, 1974.

Zimmerli, Walther. 'The Place and Limit of the Wisdom in the Framework of the Old Testament Theology'. *SJTh* 17 (1964), 146-58.

INDEXES

INDEX OF BIBLICAL REFERENCES

OLD TESTAMENT

INDEX OF AUTHORS